Bert van Dam

PIC™ Microcontrollers

PIC™ Microcontrollers

Bert van Dam

Elektor International Media BV
Postbus 11
6114 ZG Susteren

British Library Cataloguing in Publication Data
A catalogue record for this book is available from the British Library

ISBN 978-0-905705-70-5
NUR 980

Translation: Bert van Dam
Prepress production: Autronic, Blaricum
Design cover: D-Vision, Oss
First published in the United Kingdom 2007
Second edition November 2008
Printed in the Netherlands by Wilco, Amersfoort
© Elektor International Media BV 2007

069016/UK

Content

Introduction

This book covers a series of exciting and fun projects such as a silent alarm, a people sensor, radar, a night buzzer, a clock, a VU meter, an RGB fader, a serial network, and a poetry box.

You can use it as projects book and build more than 50 projects for your own use. The clear explanations, schematics, and pictures of each project on a breadboard make this a fun activity.

You can also use it as a study guide. The technical background information in each project explains why the project is set up the way it is, including the use of datasheets. This way you'll learn a lot about the project and the microcontroller being used, and you can expand the project to suit your own needs. For this reason most of the projects use the same microcontroller, the PIC^{TM} 16F877.

In Chapter 13, three other microcontrollers are discussed, the 12F675, 16F628 and 16F876A. Also explained is how to migrate programs from one microcontroller to another.

Apart from that the book can be used as a reference guide. The explanation of the JAL programming language and all of the expansion libraries used in the book is unique and nowhere else to be found. Using the index, you can easily locate projects that serve as examples for the main commands. Even after you've built all the projects in this book it will still be a valuable reference guide to keep next to your PC.

At this point I would like to thank Stef Mientki and Wouter van Ooijen for their help with the technical editing of this book, and also for their support many years ago when I first got my feet wet in the exciting world of microcontrollers. For the English version I would like to thank Mike Kerna and Kyle York for their help with the final editing.

Bert van Dam

1 What is a PIC^{TM} microcontroller?

PIC^{TM} is a trademark of the Microchip Corporation.[1] It's not quite clear whether this is just a name or an abbreviation. On the Internet names like Peripheral Interface Controller or Programmable Integrated Controller are occasionally used, but on the website of the manufacturer PIC^{TM} is used as if it is a normal name which just happens to be spelled in capitals.

A PIC^{TM} is actually a complete mini computer on a chip. As opposed to a computer, such as a PC (which is an abbreviation and stands for Personal Computer), a PIC^{TM} is not designed to work with people but with machines.[2] This means there is no simple way to connect it to a keyboard or a terminal. There are however many ways to connect it to machines or parts of them, such as switches, LEDs, variable resistors, temperature sensors, infrared sensors, or even other PIC^{TM} microcontrollers.

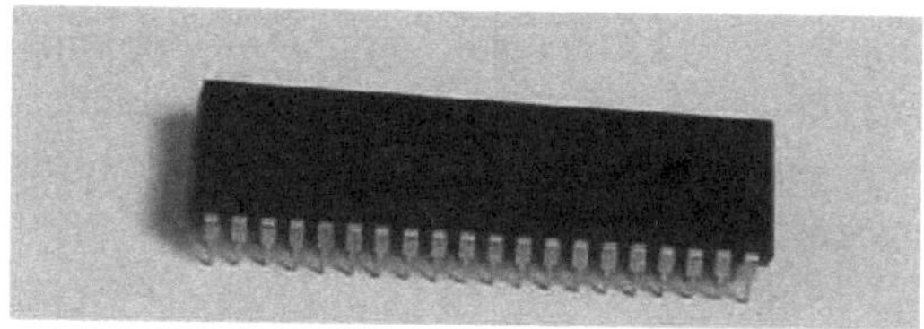

Figure 1. PIC^{TM} microcontroller (16F877)

Because they can be programmed PIC^{TM} microcontrollers can be used in many different ways. You can find PIC^{TM} microcontrollers in VCRs, remote control units, vending machines…they control motors and heaters, decipher remote control signals, measure temperatures, and much more. It is this reason of being found inside machines that microcontrollers are often called "embedded systems".

You can even design and build applications like these embedded systems yourself. With a few simple parts and the instructions in this book you can build some very interesting projects. Each project comes with a clear and complete explanation of both the software and hardware. Perhaps even more important is that for each project the technical

---

[1] Officially, PIC™ is a trademark or registered trademark of Microchip Technology Inc.

[2] There is another important but very technical difference. In a PC both program and data occupy the same memory. This is called the von Neumann architecture. The advantage is that there is a flexible relationship between the available memory for the program and the data. In a PIC™ separate memory is used for the program and the data, the so called Harvard architecture. The advantage is that program and memory can be accessed at the same time, which significantly improves the processing speed.

1 What is a PICTM microcontroller?

background is explained in detail. This allows you to understand how and why these projects work, so that you can easily adapt them to your own needs and ideas.

The book starts very simply with a tutorial project and step-by-step instructions. As you go along the projects increase in difficulty and only the new concepts are explained. By the end of the book you will no longer be a beginner!

Chapter 14 contains a complete and unique overview of all of the commands of the JAL programming language and the expansion libraries used. You won't find this anywhere else! You can use it as reference guide, but also to find fun and useful commands and options.

All of the software used in the book is explained and shown. To avoid having to type in the programs yourself, they are included along with the other software needed in a complete package, which you can download for free at http://www.boekinfo.tk.

To get started quickly, a hardware kit is also available. It contains all of the parts needed for the first few projects. The kit is designed for your convenience, but of course you can also obtain and use your own parts. More information on ordering and international shipping can be found at http://www.boekinfo.tk.

All of the projects in this book are built on a breadboard. This allows you to easily build and expand them before you design a printed circuit board. It is more fun to see the projects in this book as a starting point for something that suits your own needs rather than finished projects.

Okay, enough talk… let's get started with our first PIC^{TM} microcontroller project!

2 What you will need

This chapter covers all of the materials needed to start with this fascinating hobby. And there are many different options to choose from. Other choices may work just as well as the ones chosen here. What's important is that the selected materials work together perfectly. The Wisp628 programmer, Xwisp2, JALedit IDE, JAL v2 and the 16F877_bert library are just such a combination; a perfect fit, giving you many hours of fun.

Of course you also need this book - preferably your own copy - so you can make notes and even write in the book. Your own experiences and notes about the parts that you use will make this book even more valuable. Writing in a new book for the first time may not be easy, but it gets easier in time.

A lot of the software (at least the most important software) can be downloaded from the website http://www.boekinfo.tk in the section "download packet". You'll also find information on a hardware kit that you can buy, links to suppliers, and lots of other information.

2.1 Necessary items

Breadboard

Unless you're the type that goes for the soldering iron immediately it is a wise idea to use a breadboard. This will allow you to build and modify projects quickly, making it ideal for prototyping.

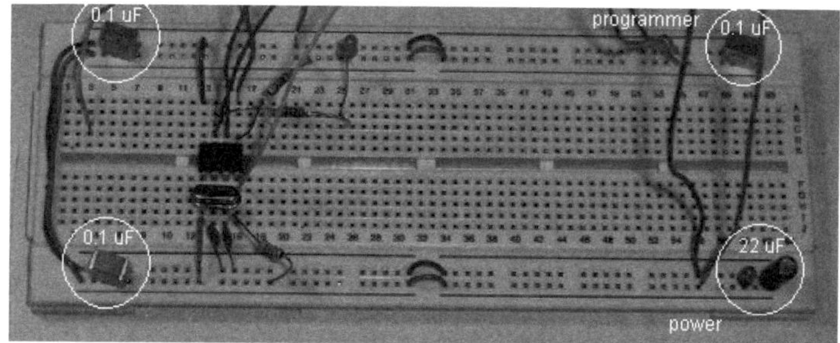

Figure 2. Breadboard with decoupling capacitors.

To prevent power issues, decoupling capacitors of 0.1 uF are inserted on the power strips at the corners. In one of the corners a stabilizing capacitor of 22 uF is used, as well as a small LED (reverse mounted), which serves as a limited safety diode against an accidental reversed power connection.

2 What you will need

Depending on what you want to build you will need electronic parts. If possible try to get parts that fit into a breadboard. Some parts may have wires that are too thick. Don't force them into the breadboard, but solder small wires to them instead.

Many suppliers sell small bags of mixed parts (resistors, LEDs, capacitors). This may be a good way to start your parts collection.

Long breadboards such as the one in Figure 2 have a power rail that is split into two parts. They are not necessarily internally connected. The top and bottom rails are almost never internally connected. So, before you start a project it's best to prepare the breadboard by connecting all the power rails and inserting the parts described. You wouldn't be the first to wonder why a project doesn't work only to find out later that part of the power rail you used was not connected to the power source.

Power source (UA7805)

All PIC™ microcontrollers use 5 volts, and that has to be rather accurate, especially during programming. Use a good stabilized power source with a UA7805 (or similar[3]) active stabilizer, connected according to the schematic below.

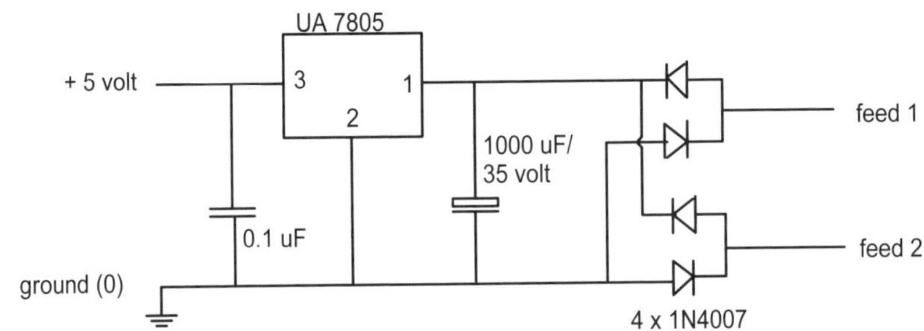

Figure 3. Stabilized 5V power supply.

A transformer is connected to feed 1 and feed 2. This may very well be a wallwart power supply, as long as the voltage is high enough. Preferably 9 to 24 volts if the transformer is alternating current (AC), or 9 to 32 volts if the transformer is direct current (DC).

It doesn't make any difference how you connect a DC transformer, since the current is still rectified by the four diodes. Of course the transformer needs to have sufficient capacity.

---

[3] For example the LM7805 manufactured by Fairchild Semiconductor. This power regulator can handle 1 Amp max, while the UA7805 manufactured by Texas Instruments can handle 1.5 Amp.

How much "sufficient" is depends on your project. Several hundred milliamps is usually enough. If you use more power it is advisable to equip the UA7805 with a heat sink to provide cooling.

Programmer (Wisp628)

Once you have written a program it needs to be transferred into the PIC™. This is the task of a programmer. Some programmers can program a PIC™ while it is still in the circuit on the breadboard. This is called "in-circuit programming". Trust me, you really, really, REALLY want this feature. It gets annoying very quickly when you have to wriggle the PIC™ off the breadboard each time you forgot a comma in your program.

We'll be using the Wisp628, an intelligent programmer than can handle a wide array of different PIC™ microcontrollers. The intelligence of this programmer is, by the way, contained in its own PIC™; so you can make your own updated version of the program software if needed. Also important is that this programmer has a pass-through feature. Without touching as much as a single wire you can communicate from your PC directly with the PIC™. This makes it ideal for debugging your software.

Figure 4. The Wisp628 in-circuit programmer.

PIC™ (16F877)

Which PIC™ to choose is a difficult question. There are dozens of different types, each with different options and cost. For the majority of the projects in this book the 16F877 is used.

This 16F877 is loaded with possibilities and features, and has many pins. This is an advantage because it means fewer combined pins are used, which is always a difficulty for starting programmers. Besides, it's a popular microcontroller, which means a lot of information (and thus help) is available on the Web. A disadvantage is that this PIC™ is relatively expensive, US$ 7 to US$ 11.

2 What you will need

Figure 5. The 16F877 with 40 pins.

At this point the specifications probably don't mean too much yet:

Item	Specification
Program memory	8192 words (14 bit)
RAM size	368 bytes
EEPROM size	256 byte
I/O pins	33
Analog inputs	8 (10 bit each)
USART	Yes (c6/c7)
Speed	5 mips
Cost	US$ 7 to 11
I2C	yes (c3/c4)

When you order this microcontroller you will need to know which package you want. This doesn't refer to the box the microcontroller is shipped to you in, but to the external connections of the chip. For instance, whether the PIC™ should have long pins that fit into a breadboard or printed circuit board, or small pins for surface mounting. The package shown in Figure 5 is called PDIP (or Plastic DIP), and this is what we'll be using.

Programming language (JAL)

Many different languages for programming PIC™ microcontrollers exist on the market. The most commonly used language is arguably assembler (ASM) - a very powerful but extremely cumbersome language. Even the simplest program in assembler contains a long list of commands...definitely not suitable for beginners.

This book uses JAL (Just Another Language), a Pascal-like high-level language. It is the only advanced language that is completely free, and has a large international and very active user base. JAL is configurable and expandable using libraries, and can even be combined with assembler. This allows you to incorporate ASM snippets[4] found on the Internet.

This is an example of a JAL program that flashes an LED connected to pin 23 (c4):

```
-- JAL 2.0.4
include 16F877_bert

-- define variables
var bit flag

-- define direction of the signal of this pin
pin_c4_direction = output

forever loop

   -- change pin 23 status
   flag = ! flag
   pin_c4 = flag

   -- wait 100 milliseconds
   delay_100ms(1)

end loop
```

The address of the JAL usergroup is listed on the website, www.boekinfo.tk.

---

[4] Small pieces of program that do something "convenient" and are exchanged between users.

2 What you will need

Library (16F877_bert)

Libraries contain additional functionality that can be added to JAL. You can, for example, make serial connections, read an analog signal, and much more.

In this book, the standard library 16F877_bert[5] is used. It is basically a combination of the most used libraries off the Internet,[6] that all fit together perfectly, and is included as part of the download package. By using this standard library a lot of additional functionality is made available:

Functionality (with the standard library)	16F877
Serial communication - hardware	✓
Serial communication - software	✓
Pulse Width Modulation (PWM)	✓
A/D conversion	✓
Program memory	✓
EEPROM memory	✓
ASCII	✓
Delay	✓
Registers and variables	✓
Random numbers	✓

Because part of the library functionality is automatically loaded, a few of the pins are assigned by default. If you want to use these pins for another purpose you will need to modify the standard library. This will rarely be necessary.

---

[5] A silly name for a library. When I made the first one many years ago I called it _bert to distinquish it from the libraries I got off the Internet. The library became much more popular than I imagined, and since they are so well know I can't get rid of the name anymore!

[6] Mainly written by JAL expert Stef Mientki.

This is the default configuration:

16F877 pins	Function
13 and 14	crystal
16	PWM(2)
17	PWM(1)
25	RS232 hardware TX
26	RS232 hardware RX
39	RS232 software RX
40	RS232 software TX
2 to 5 and 7 to 10	analog in (adaptable)
other pins	digital in/out

The analog pins 2 to 10 can be switched to digital using a command from the library (see section 14.2).

Editor (JALedit)

You can use JAL from the command line, but an editor is much more convenient. The recommended editor is JALedit. This freeware editor has a number of unique advantages:

- JAL commands are color coded
- Overview of variables, constants, and procedures used in a program
- Block comment add or remove
- One click compile and download
- Built in ASCII table, calculator, and terminal
- Source export to html (for publication on a website)
- Automatic backup
- Compiler output in a separate window
- Load multiple files at the same time
- Jump to offending program line on error

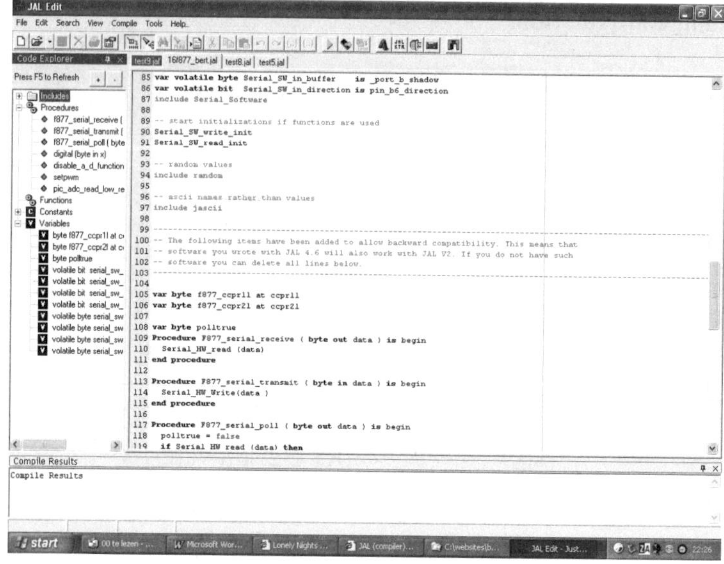

Figure 6. JALedit.

This beautiful editor is part of the download package.

Terminal software (MICterm)

A serial connection to the PC is used in many projects to display data. It also can be a convenient tool for debugging.

You could use a standard terminal program, but a much easier way is to use something written especially for microcontrollers: MICterm. This freeware program has a number of unique features:

- Switches the programmer automatically to pass-through[7]
- Data can be shown raw, in hex or in ASCII.
- Data can be displayed in any combination of numbers, binary, on a dial or in a graph (with average).
- Separate window for send and receive
- Optionally send files to, or receive files from, the PIC™

---

[7] For Wisp628 only.

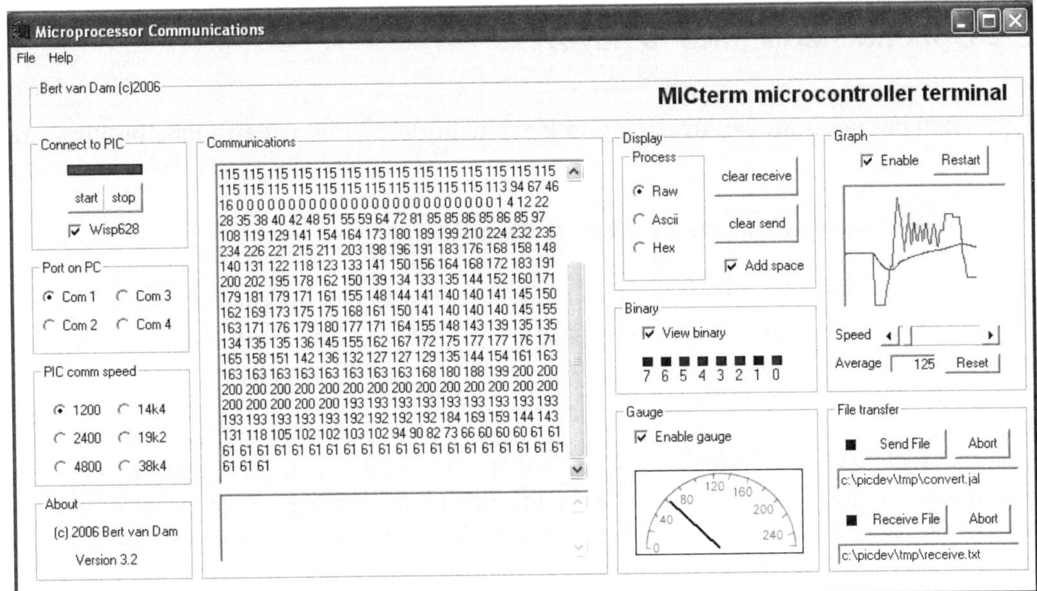

Figure 7. MICterm.

MICterm is part of the download package.

2.2 Optional items (nice to have)

The following items are not necessary to work with PIC[TM] microcontrollers, but they are very convenient.

Development software on the PC (Visual Basic)

Since the PIC[TM] can communicate with the PC it's fun to write special software for this. It is not necessary, since you can do all the projects in this book with the supplied software in the download package.

If you own Visual Basic, for example, you could write beautiful applications for your projects such as a voltmeter, several graphs on one page, and visualization of measurements. Many PC applications in the download package have been written in Visual Basic, and in many cases the source code is included. You can of course use another language if you want.

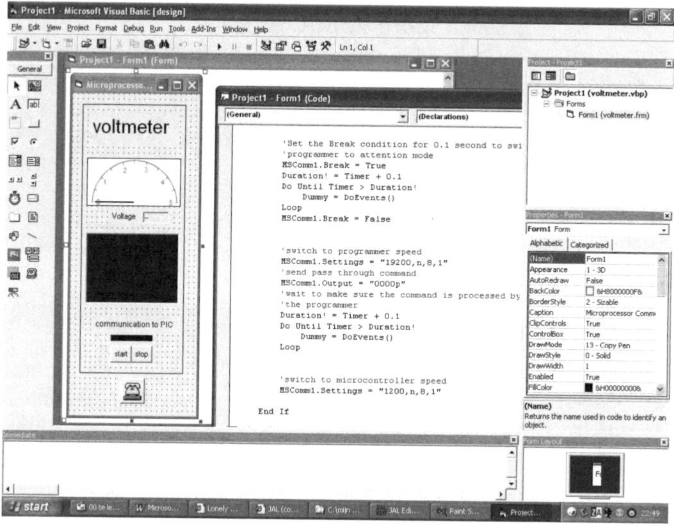

Figure 8. Visual Basic.

Visual Basic[8] is commercial software, so it's not part of the free download[9].

---

[8] Visual Basic is supplied by Microsoft. See http://www.microsoft.com
[9] For free PC development software try http://www.thefreecountry.com.

Oscilloscope (Software)

For power spikes and ripples, and projects with inexplicable behavior, sometimes it's very convenient to have a simple oscilloscope.

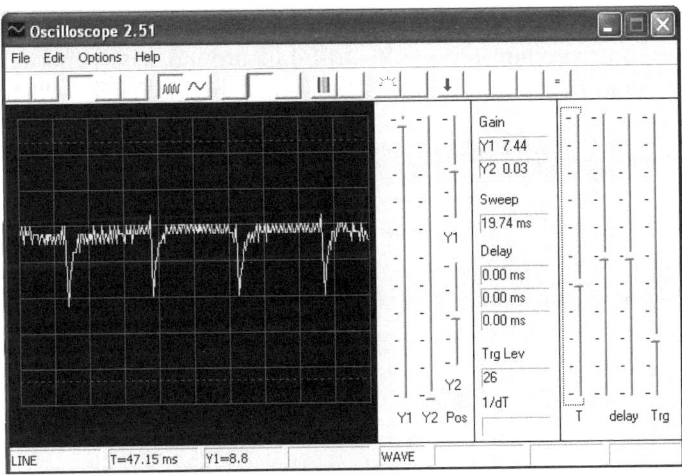

Figure 9. Software Oscilloscope.

The software oscilloscope uses the soundcard of a PC to convert the signals. One of its limitations is that you need to make a small interface to protect the soundcard.

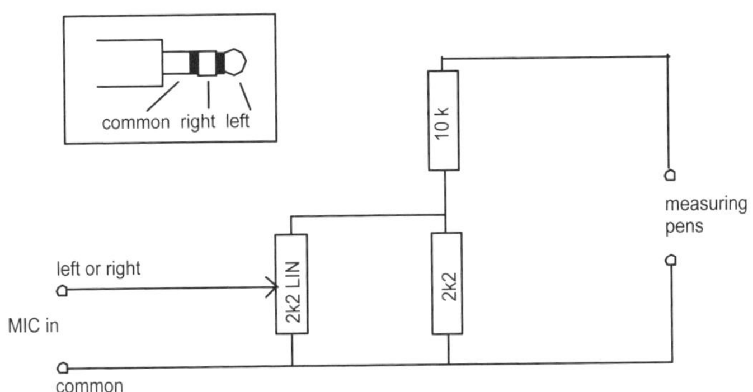

Figure 10. Interface for mic or line input of a soundcard on a PC.

2 What you will need

The interface in Figure 10 is used to reduce the maximum voltage on the microphone, or line input of the soundcard, from 5 volts to 0.9 volts. The maximum frequency is also limited, but the price is right (the program is freeware).

Resistor and capacitor codes

Resistors and capacitors usually have a (color) code to indicate their value. This value can be found in tables, but you didn't buy a PC to fiddle around with paper tables. Two small programs can do the job for you:

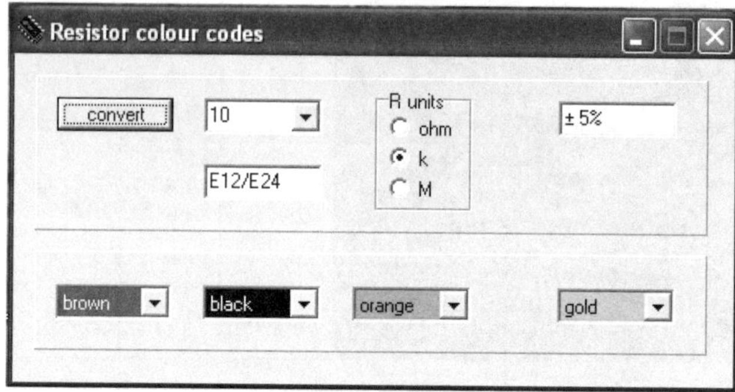

Figure 11. Resistor color-coding.

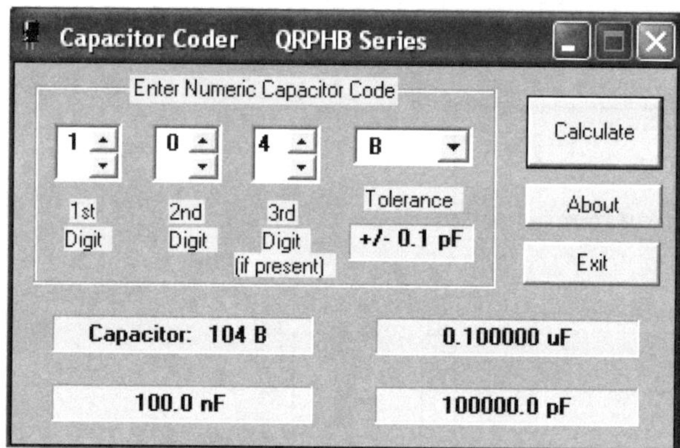

Figure 12. Capacitor coding.

Programmer dongle

For some PIC™ microcontrollers the pin that is used to switch the PIC™ to programming mode can also be used for other purposes. If that is the case, the power must be brought to ground during the switchover to programming mode. This is the case with the tiny 12F675. In these situations you need a special dongle. For the 16F877 the dongle is <u>not</u> <u>needed</u>.

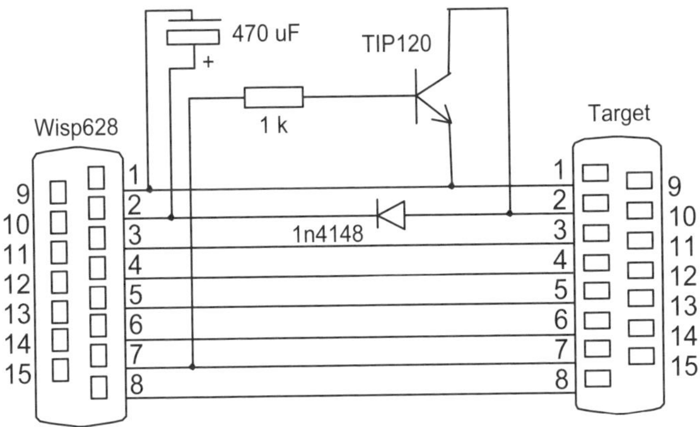

Figure 13.The schematic of the dongle.

Figure 14. The finished dongle.

2 What you will need

Frequency counter (Software)

When you are working with interrupts or sound a frequency counter can be very convenient. The frequency counter uses the soundcard of the PC, and requires the same interface as the software oscilloscope.

Figure 15. Software frequency counter.

3 Tutorial project

Now that all of the materials have been acquired it's finally time to get started! The purpose of this tutorial project is to build a flashing light. In preparation it may be convenient to read Chapters 1 and 2, but if you'd like to move right along that's no problem.

In this tutorial it is assumed that you have downloaded and properly installed the free software package from the website http://www.boekinfo.tk. The package contains the JAL programming language and the libraries, so you cannot continue without installing these first.

The package also contains an editor (JALedit) specifically designed for use with JAL. You can use your own editor (and if you don't have Windows on your PC you may even have to), but you'll need to follow the instructions that came with it. You might miss certain features such as syntax color-coding, single click compile and download, library view, and the procedure/function overview.

It is also assumed that you use the recommended programmer Wisp628. You can use any other programmer (that can program a 16F877), however you must also follow the instructions that came with it. And, again, you might not be able to use all of the functionality assumed in the book, such as in-circuit programming and RS232 pass-through.

3.1 The hardware

First of all, a PIC™ must be selected. Normally that would be the smallest and cheapest PIC™ that just meets all of the demands. For this project, however, we will select an easy PIC™, which can be used to build most of the projects in the book (even the most complicated ones): the 16F877 from Microchip. It is an easy to use PIC™ with many features, but with a price of US$ 7 to US$ 11.

The 16F877 has 40 pins. What these pins can do is listed in its datasheet.[10] Don't let the word "datasheet" fool you; it's more like a book of over 200 pages!

---

[10] You can download the datasheet for free from Microchip at http://www.microchip.com. The datasheet name will resemble 16F87X, since similar chips are often combined into a single document.

3 Tutorial project

In the datasheet you'll find the following drawing of the configuration:

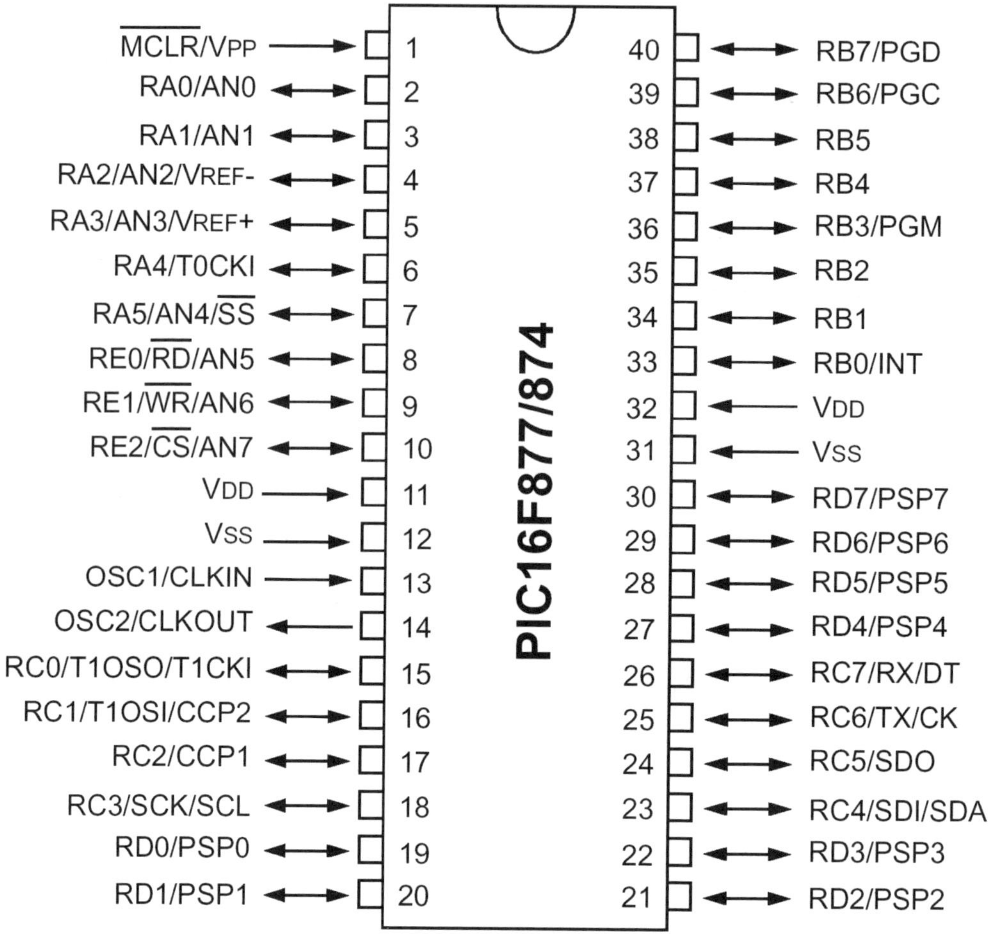

Figure 16. Pin layout for 16F877.

Shockingly complex, but perhaps adding a few words will simplify matters a bit.

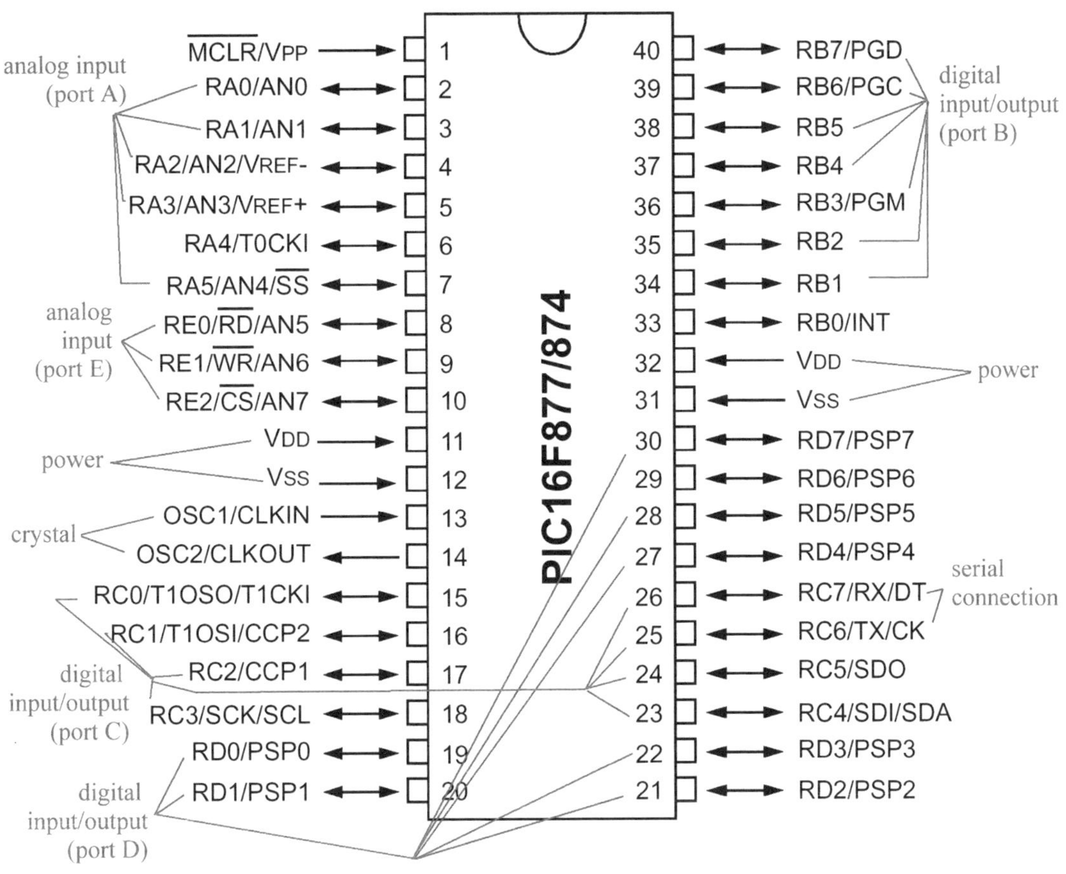

Figure 17. Pin layout for 16F877 with explanation.

3 Tutorial project

What this all means:

- Analog input means that these pins can accept an analog signal anywhere between 0 and 5 volts (for example, 3.56 volts).

- Digital in-/output means that these pins can process a digital signal…either 0 or 5V, but nothing in between. Since they are also outputs the pins can be made 0 or 5V by the PIC™ itself.[11]

- Power is obvious (Vss = 0V or ground, Vdd = +5V). Beware that <u>all</u> power pins must be connected!

- Crystal is where the crystal (with a few capacitors) must be connected. The crystal takes care of a very stable (electrical) vibration, which is used to accurately control the speed of the PIC™. This is called the (external) clock. All PIC™ microcontrollers can do without a crystal, but the speed will be lower and may be not accurate enough for communications with another PIC™ or a PC.

- Serial connection means that with these pins a serial (also called RS232) connection to another PIC™ or a PC can be made.

- I2C is a network protocol that can be used to connect multiple PIC™ microcontrollers together, or to connect peripheral devices to a PIC™.

A lot of pins have multiple abbreviations listed next to them. This means that they have multiple uses. Some of these uses will be addressed in this book. For the time being it's enough to remember which pins are analog and which are digital.

Now that we know what the pins are for the hardware can be built. If you purchased the hardware kit you can start immediately. Otherwise, you'll have to shop for parts. On the website http://www.boekinfo.tk you'll find an overview of the parts needed for each project. Since this is a tutorial project the parts for this project are listed here as well.

---

[11] The actual value of a digital signal is a bit more complex. For example, 4.8 volts is still regarded as "on" and 0.5 volts is still regarded as "off".

For this project you need the following parts:

Part	Type and number
PIC™	16F877
resistors	2 x 330 ohm (orange-orange-brown)[12] 1 x 10 k ohm (brown-black-orange) 1 x 33 k ohm (orange-orange-orange)
LED	2 pieces
capacitors	2 x 20 pF (code 20) 5 x 100 nF (code 104)
crystal	1 x 20 MHz
miscellaneous	breadboard programmer wire (22 gauge or 0.5 mm^2 Cu) stabilized 5V power supply

Pins 1, 11, 12, 31, and 32 must always be connected, regardless of the project you are making. When a crystal is being used, pins 13 and 14 must also always be connected.

The only thing we need to choose for this project is where to connect the LEDs. And since we can choose any pins of ports B, C or D, we'll just pick two at random: 22 (d3) and 23 (c4).

The components on pin 1 are mandatory for programming the PIC™. In older circuits you may find just a 33k resistor on this pin. This appears to work fine, but the manufacturer now recommends the setup used in this book. The crystal is also required and is connected with two capacitors to pin 13 and 14.

---

[12] In resistor and capacitor values you often find letters. These have the following meaning: k=1,000; m=1/1,000; u=1/1,000,000; p=1/1,000,000,000. The location of the letter is also important. For example, 22k means a resistor of 22,000 ohms, but 2k2 means a resistor of 2,200 ohms. Sometimes the letter R is used for a decimal point: 4R7 would indicate 4.7 ohms.

3 Tutorial project

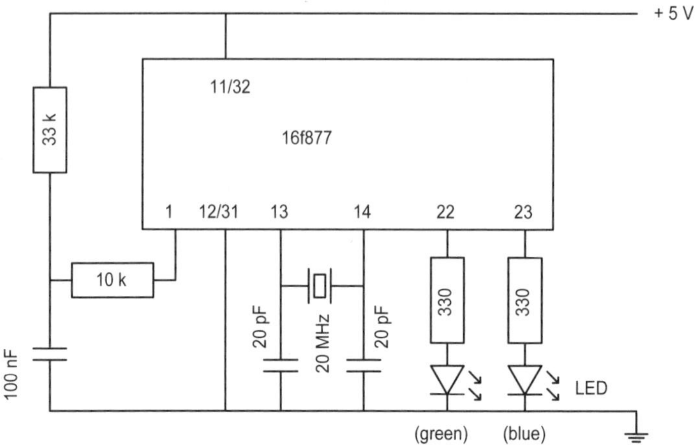

Figure 18. Schematic of the tutorial project.

In this example the LEDs are blue[13] and green. But the color is not important. The resistor in series with each LED, however, is very important. It limits the current through the LED. Without this resistor the PIC™ or the LED would break down - and it's usually the most expensive component that breaks first.

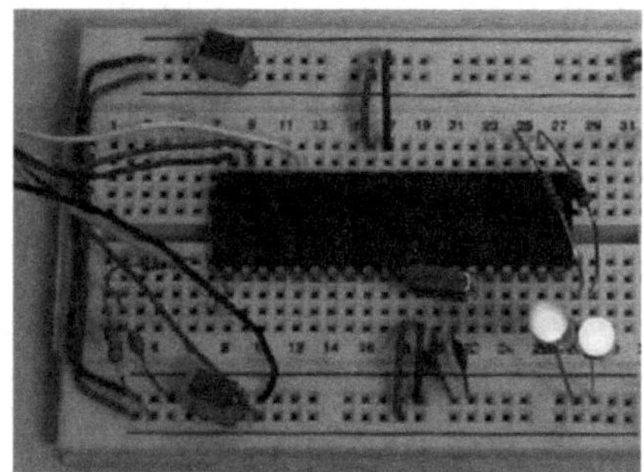

Figure 19. Hardware tutorial project.

Place all of the components on the breadboard. Be certain that all wires are actually inserted into the holes, and that all 40 pins of the 16F877 are in the holes as well and not bent underneath the PIC™. On one end of the PIC™ you'll see what looks like a half moon; this is where pins 1 and 40 are located. Often, there is also a small circle to indicate pin 1. Follow the schematic exactly, and use the picture in Figure 19 to verify

---

[13] Blue LEDs are very expensive. You'll find one in the hardware kit, because of the RGB fader project in section 13.1.5. If you didn't purchase the hardware kit you can replace the blue LEDs in this and other projects with red ones (except, of course, in the RGB fader).

that you understand the schematic correctly. On the left hand side you can see the wires that connect the top and bottom power rail, and the long wires from the programmer. These are never in the schematic, but you need to connect them anyway.

On the top right hand side of the breadboard are the wires from the 5V power supply. The power supply must be sufficiently stabilized (for example, with a UA7805). On each of the four corners of the breadboard is a 0.1 uF (which is the same as 100 nF) capacitor. (Note that in the picture only two corners can be seen.) These take care of power ripples.

The long wires leaving the picture on the left are from the programmer. If you use the Wisp628 in-circuit programmer the connections must be made as follows:

Color	Connection
yellow	pin 1
blue	pin 40
green	pin 39
white	pin 36
red	+5 V
black	ground

A number of parts, such as LEDs, have a positive and negative side.[14] If you look carefully inside the LED you'll see that one of the pins appears to be wider. This is the negative side and needs to be connected to the lower voltage. (Usually this wire is also shorter than the other side.) In the schematic, the symbol of an LED looks like an arrow. An easy rule to remember is that the arrow always points to the negative side.

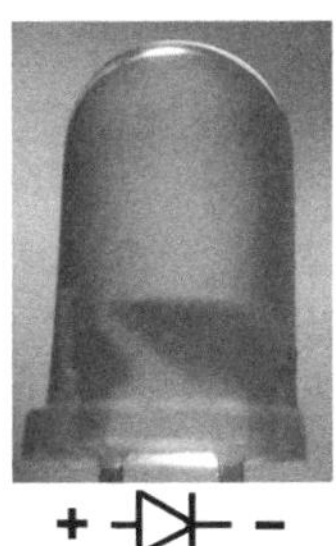

Figure 20. The positive and negative sides of a LED.

---

[14] The actual name for the positive side is the anode, and the negative side is the cathode.

3 Tutorial project

Check all parts and connections twice before turning on the power. Then switch the power off again.

3.2 The software

The program is written using an editor: JALedit. Of course any other editor could be used, but this one has special features that make is very well suited for use with JAL. Once the editor has started up you'll see an empty page; this is where you'll enter the program.

```
File  Edit  Search  View  Compile  Tools  Help

Code Explorer          4 ×   test9.jal

Press F5 to Refresh    +  -    1 |--Jal V2
                               2 include 16f877_bert
 Includes                      3 include conversion_bert
   Procedures                  4
   Functions                   5 -- definities
   Constants                   6 pin_c4_direction = Output
   Variables                   7 pin_d3_direction = Output
                               8
                               9 forever loop
                              10
                              11      -- LEDs in stand 1
                              12      pin_d3 = high
                              13      pin_c4 = low
                              14      delay_1s(1)
                              15
                              16      -- LEDs omgewisseld
                              17      pin_d3 = low
                              18      pin_c4 = high
                              19      delay_1s(1)
                              20
                              21 end loop
                              22
```

Figure 21. JALedit with tutorial program.

A program consists of a series of commands. These commands tell the 16F877 what it needs to do. The commands are processed starting at the top of the page and going down (some commands will cause it to jump to different parts). The JAL programming language is not very particular about how you space the commands over the page. But you need to be able to understand it yourself, so we'll make a few rules for ourselves:

1. Each line will have only one command.
2. Short comments will be used to explain what the program does.
3. At loops and conditional commands we indent.

The meaning of rule three will become clear later. To make the program easier to read JALedit will color-code everything you enter. This has no impact on the functionality of the program.

The very first step in the program is to load a library. A library contains additional commands, which usually cannot be part of the JAL language itself because they may differ for each type of microcontroller. As a programmer you don't want to know about this stuff so it's hidden away in a library. The only thing you need to do is use the library that goes with the microcontroller. Since we are witing a program for the 16F877, the 16F877_bert library is loaded. The commands contained in this library are explained in Chapter 14, but as you read through the book you will encounter most of them, with a clear explanation.

Loading the library is done with the following command. It is a good idea, by the way, to wait before entering the program until all parts have been discussed, because this doesn't necessarily take place in the right order. At the end of this section you'll find the complete program.

```
-- JAL 2.0.4
include 16F877_bert
```

The standard JAL commands are recognized by the editor and color-coded. Variables and commands from a library are in blue. The first line starts with two hyphens to indicate a comment only meant for the user (you); the microcontroller will do nothing with it. The second line starts with *include* and then the name of the library. Everything that this library contains is inserted at this point (without you ever seeing it).

Since the digital pins on the 16F877 can be either input or output we need to define the directions of the pins that we intend to use. For this program we want them both to be outputs, because we want to switch LEDs on and off with these pins.

```
pin_c4_direction = output
pin_d3_direction = output
```

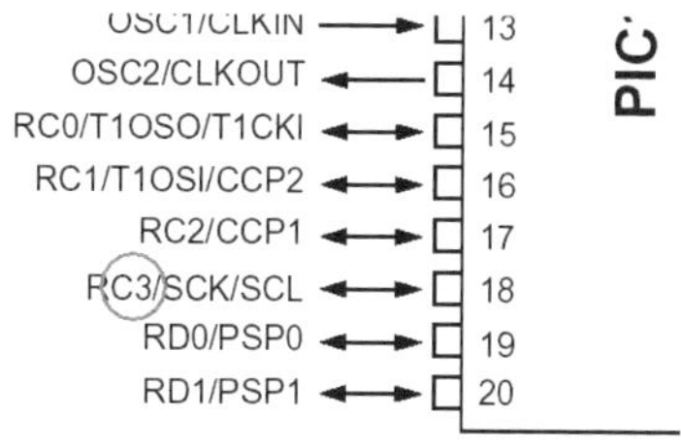

Figure 22. This is where you'll find the pin names.

3 Tutorial project

The pin names can be found in Figure 22. A good idea would be to look for this figure in the datasheet of the 16F877 (on the website of Microchip: http://www.microchip.com) and print it out. You can keep it handy when building projects (this is what I do).

You must indicate the direction of a pin for every pin you use. This can easily be forgotten.

Lighting an LED is done by applying power to the pin that the LED is connected to.[15] This is done by making the pin high. We turn the power off by making the pin low.

```
pin_d3 = high
pin_c4 = low
```

After these commands are executed the LED on pin d3 is on, and the LED on pin c4 is off. Since we want to make the LEDs flash, the next step has to be the reverse.

```
pin_d3 = low
pin_c4 = high
```

In between a pause must be inserted. Otherwise, the flashing will be too fast to see. The pause we'll use is a one second delay:

```
delay_1s(1)
```

The number between the parenthesis specifies how many times the program should wait one second. Had we used, for example, delay_1s(3) then the program would wait 3 x 1 = 3 seconds.

---

[15] Because the other side of the LED is connected to the ground.

With the commands used so far the LEDs will only flash once, but a real flashing light doesn't stop. So our commands need to be repeated continuously, in fact, "forever":

```
forever loop
end loop
```

Here's what the entire program looks like:

```
-- JAL 2.0.4
include 16F877_bert

-- definitions
pin_c4_direction = output
pin_d3_direction = output

forever loop

        -- LEDs in starting state
        pin_d3 = high
        pin_c4 = low
        delay_1s(1)

        -- LEDs switched
        pin_d3 = low
        pin_c4 = high
        delay_1s(1)

end loop
```

You see that the loop, which is repeated forever, is indented. This makes it very clear where the loop starts and where it ends. Remember, this was the third rule we made about program entry: "At loops and conditional commands we indent."

Now is a good time to enter the program into the editor and save it. In the file menu select "Save as" and enter a good name for this program, such as "tutorial". Don't enter a file extension, it will be added automatically.

It may be a good idea to use a separate directory for each project that you build. This way everything that has to do with the project is neatly grouped together.

3.3 Compiling and downloading

The first check is to see if the program has been entered correctly. Click on the button with the green triangle (compile active JAL file), or press F9.

Figure23. Compiling the active JAL file.

You can open multiple files at the same time, but only one of them is the "active" file. For this file the tab at the top is blue. If you followed the instructions you only have one file open (the one you just entered) so this is automatically the active file.

A small window will briefly appear, and then in the "compile results" window at the bottom a message is displayed. Hopefully it starts with:

> jal 2.0.4 (compiled Aug 16 2006)[16]
> 0 errors, 0 warnings

Following these two lines are many others, but they're not important at this point. No errors, by the way, doesn't mean your program will do what you want, or even work. It simply means you haven't made any syntax errors. Let's assume, for example, that you accidentally entered *ouput* instead of *output* you would immediately get an error message like this:

> jal 2.0.4 (compiled Aug 16 2006)
> [Error] (tutorial.jal) [Line 6] "ouput" not defined
> 1 errors, 0 warnings

The compiler reports that the error has been made on line 6.

Assuming you have made no errors the program can be downloaded to the PIC™. The hardware discussed in the previous section needs to be completed and connected to the programmer and power supply. Switch on the power[17] and on the PC click on the button with the integrated circuit and the green arrow (compile + program), or press Ctrl-F9.

---

[16] If a more recent version of JAL is used this line will show a different number and date. This has no impact on the results.

Figure 24. Compile and Program.

The compile window appears again, but this time it is followed by a window with a black background. This second window belongs to the software of your programmer, in this case the Xwisp2 software.

```
C:\PICdev\xwisp2\xwisp2w.exe                                          _ □ ×
 xwisp2 version 1.9.1 for Windows (Sep 06 2006, Open Watcom C 1.50)
File C:\PICdev\Projecten\lopend\test8.hex loaded and is Intel Hex format conform
ing
Detected programmer: Wisp628, firmware version 1.09
Detected target: 16F877 revision 06 (ID=09A6)
Target erased
Transferring program to 16F877 via Wisp628
Transferring program memory...000100 : 1d03
```

Figure 25. Programmer software Xwisp2 in action.

You can observe the progress of the download in the black window. After downloading the program the PIC™, the program is automatically checked to confirm that downloading was successful. If everything is OK the LEDs will start flashing and the window will close.

3.4 Debugging

If everything went well you can skip this section and go straight to section 3.5. If it didn't go as planned look for your symptom in the table below and follow the instructions.

---

[17] Note: these instructions only apply if you use the recommended programmer, Wisp628. If you use another programmer you need to modify the settings of JALedit to suit that programmer. Wisp628 is an in-circuit programmer. If yours isn't, then the PIC must be removed from the breadboard (with the power switched off) and then follow the instructions that came with your programmer.

Symptom	**Remedy**
The window with the black background doesn't come up.	1. There are errors in the program. Check the window at the bottom (compile results) for error messages.
	2. You didn't install the downloaded software package correctly. Some software is missing or cannot be found, particularly the programmer software (xwisp2). Carefully read the instructions of the download package and follow them exactly.
	3. You have installed the software to a different location than instructed. Go to "environment options" in the "compile" menu, select the "programmer" tab and enter the correct location. Note that <u>spaces are not permitted</u> in directory or file names.
	4. You have connected the programmer to another comport than port 1. Go to "environment options" in the "compile" menu, select the "programmer" tab and add port x to the line that contains "go", where x is the comport number that you are using. So if you use com 4 this line would become "port 4 go %F"
The window with the black background shows a lot of complicated text and then disappears.	1. The programmer is not connected or not connected correctly. Switch off the power and connect the programmer correctly (all wires!).
	2. The power is off. Switch it on and retry. If you use a breadboard make sure the top and bottom power rails (and segmented rails) are connected.
	3. Another program is using the same serial port as the programmer, possibly a terminal program. Close the program and try again. You may need to restart the PC if the program doesn't release the port.
	4. Your power supply isn't stabile enough. Make sure you use a stabilized power supply where the voltage is maintained at the proper level with, for example, a UA7805. Make sure the voltage of the transformer used to feed the power supply is high enough. (See section 2.2 for the requirements.) Do not forget the 0.1 uF capacitors on the four corners of the breadboard.
	5. The voltage of the power supply is not 5V. Even though you can sometimes program at 4.7V, this usually doesn't work.

The program is downloaded but the LEDs aren't flashing.	1. The LEDs are connected backwards. Insert them in the opposite direction. 2. The LEDs are connected to the incorrect pins. Switch off the power and check all connections. 3. The LEDs do flash, but extremely fast. Check if both delay statements have been entered into the program.

The program and the hardware schematic contain no errors. If despite the instructions above the program still won't work check everything again and again. Perhaps it's best to call it a day and check again tomorrow. Sometimes a good night's sleeps does wonders.

If you're still convinced that you've done everything right then meet us in the JAL usergroup at Yahoo (see http://www.boekinfo.tk for the correct address and post your question). Note that this is an international group with users all over the world, so the mandatory language is English.

3.5 Done!

Congratulations. You've just made your first microcontroller program! In the upcoming chapters it is assumed that you will remember what you have learned in this tutorial project. In those projects you will just be shown a schematic and a breadboard photograph, and we will assume you've built it, including the power rail connectors, and the capacitors on the corners. We'll also assume that you can identity resistors and capacitors using the handy programs in the download package, so that you are capable of figuring out what the different value resistors look like.

The program itself will be shown and we will assume you've entered it into JALedit, connected the programmer, and downloaded the program into the PIC^{TM}. Use this tutorial as a reference if you forget how to do any of these steps.

3.6 Other results

Apart from compiling and downloading, a few additional files have appeared in the program directory on your PC with the extensions of .asm and .hex. It's not necessary to know what these are for, so if you want you can skip this section and continue with the projects in Chapter 4.

3 Tutorial project

The hex file

This is the file that is actually sent to the programmer to load into the PIC™. It contains the compiled program in hexcode[18]. Here is a fragment of it:

```
:10001000840AA00B07280800A0018313263084005F
:100020000330042083132B308400063004201E2864
:100030002708870008002808880008008312A30109
:100040008B014528AF01B0013C2883120313F23025
:10005000A0000A30A1002830A2000A128A11A20BC7
```

The asm (assembler) file

This is an extra file generated so that you can use your program with tools that were specifically designed to use assembler, such as the free editor/simulator offered by the manufacturer Microchip.[19]

If you look at this file you'll immediately understand why JAL is such a popular language. Each line of JAL code is shown with the assembler translation below it.

```
;  13     pin_d3 = high
                  datalo_clr v__port_d_shadow
                  bsf    v__port_d_shadow, 3
                  call   l__port_d_flush
;  14     pin_c4 = low
                  datalo_clr v__port_c_shadow 83
                  bcf    v__port_c_shadow, 4
                  call   l__port_c_flush
;  15     delay_1s(1)
                  movlw   1
                  call   l_delay_1s
```

---

[18] Read more about hex files in section 14.7.

[19] This program is called MPLAB® and can be downloaded for free from http://www.microchip.com. Search for MPLAB® EDI. There are paid versions as well, but the free version will do just fine.

Sharing your knowledge

If you have written an interesting program or discovered a useful trick you might want to post it on the Internet. That way other people can learn from your experience. And if you write your page in English you can get in touch with hobbyists from all over the world. As a result of my website I have friends in many different countries!

On the website http://www.boekinfo.tk you'll find a few of those links to JAL pages.

4 Switches

This chapter will cover projects that deal with a switch. It's not a very complicated topic, especially after having completed the tutorial in Chapter 3. But these projects are a good next step before the more difficult projects later on.

Project	Description
Timer	Also known as a monostable multivibrator (or a one-shot multivibrator). You press the push button once and the LED remains on for a fixed amount of time.
Two way switch	Use a push button to switch an LED on and off. Also known as a bistable multivibrator.
Dice	Electronic dice; an application for a debounced switch.
Secret doorbell	A doorbell that only rings when a secret code is entered on a keypad. Includes an explanation of how procedures and JAL libraries are made.

4.1 Timer

The timer illustrated in this project is also known as a monostable multivibrator; you press the push button once and the LED remains on for a fixed amount of time.

Technical background

A pin that is in use (meaning the microcontroller is "looking"at this pin) is never allowed to float - it must always be connected to either 5V or ground. This means you have two ways to connect a switch:

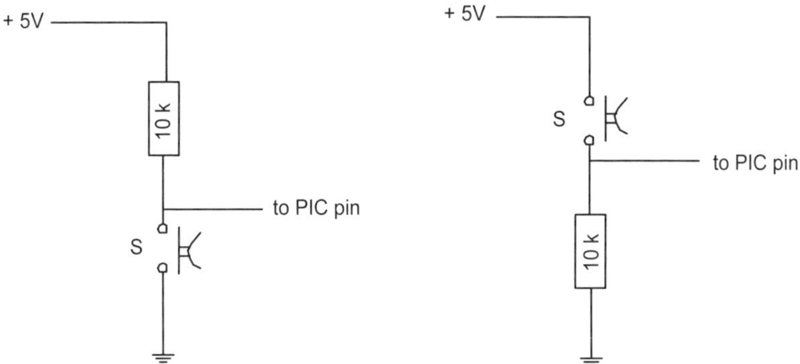

Figure 26. Connecting a switch.

In the situation on the left, the pin is normally at 5V. This is called "1", "true"or "high". As soon the switch is closed the voltage on the pin drops to zero. This is called "0", "false"or "low". At that point, a current of 0.5 mA will flow through the resistor.[20] It's not much current, but it gives us a reason to use a switch that is normally open and only closed when needed. With this setup a "low"signal is created when the switch is closed. This is called "active low".

The schematic on the right side of Figure 26 works the other way around. This is how to create a "high"signal. It doesn't matter which solution you select, but the one on the right (active high) seems a more natural way of thinking, since closing the switch applies power to the pin.

In theory, the switch can be connected to any pin of the 16F877 (except, of course, the power pins). The 16F877 has different types of pins (as you have already seen in the tutorial project). It's important to remember that ports A and E are analog inputs. These ports measure the voltage on their pins. You could connect a switch to them, but each time you wanted to know whether the switch is open or closed you would need to measure the voltage, or you would need to change the pins from analog to digital first. It is much easier just to use the regular digital pins, ports B, C[21] and D.

---

[20] Ohm's law is used to calculate this: V=I*R, voltage is current times resistance. In this case the voltage is 5V and the resistance is 10,000 ohms, so the current is 0.0005 Amps (0.5 mA).

[21] The 16F877_bert library assigns pins c6 and c7 to hardware serial (see section 11.1), so you can't use these.

4 Switches

If pin d1 (pin 20) is used with the schematic on the right (active high), the program can determine the position of the switch like this:

```
if pin_d1 == 1 then
    -- switch on
else
    -- switch off
end if
```

For the circuit on the left side, this would work the other way around.

For a computer "1"and "true"are the same thing, so a easier way to write this would be:

```
if pin_d1 then
    -- switch on
else
    -- switch off
end if
```

The switch will be used to switch on an LED using the PIC™. This LED needs a series resistor to limit the current. The LEDs I use need at least 4.8 mA, but others may need more. To cover all normal types I have chosen to supply a bit more current, at 15 mA. This means you need a 330 ohm[22] resistor. If power is scarce (perhaps because you are on battery power) you can use a 680 ohm resistor.

The software

The idea is that an LED will remain on even after the switch is released. The easiest way to do this is to use a delay statement (in section 14.2 you'll find an overview of the possible delay statements you can chose from). If you want the LED to stay on for three seconds you can use the one-second delay statement:

```
delay_1s(3)
```

This gives you get a delay of 3 times 1, or 3 seconds. The program looks like this:

---

[22] Ohm's law: $V=I*R$, voltage is current times resistance. In this case, the voltage is 5V and the resistance is 330 ohms, so the current is 0.015 Amps (15 mA). In reality, the voltage at the resistor is a bit lower, because both the LED and PIC have a small voltage drop.

```
    if pin_d1 then
        -- switch on
        pin_d2 = high
        delay_1s(3)
        pin_d2 = low
    end if
```

At the beginning of the program you need to define the direction of each pin used:

```
    pin_d1_direction = input
    pin_d2_direction = output
```

The switch is on pin d1, so that is an input[23]. The LED is on pin d2, so that is an output.

Here is the completed program:

```
    -- JAL 2.0.4
    include 16F877_bert

    -- define pins
    pin_d1_direction = input
    pin_d2_direction = output

    forever loop

        if pin_d1 then
            -- switch is on
            pin_d2 = high
            delay_1s(3)
            pin_d2 = low
        end if

    end loop
```

---

[23] Input means going *into* the microcontroller.

4 Switches

You may have noticed three special items in this program:

-- JAL 2.0.4	This is a comment line. The compiler will not do anything with it; it is meant for humans. It is a good idea to note the JAL version you used because not all versions are interchangeable.
include 16F877_bert	Before the program can be downloaded into the microcontroller the compiler needs to know which type it is. This information is in a separate file called a library. The standard library used in all projects in this book is called 16F877_bert. Apart from type dependant information it contains a whole range of additional command that you can use in your program. These command are described in section 14.2. So each program starts with this line.
English comments	Even in the non-English versions of this book English comments are used in the source code. This will facilitate exchanging programs and information with other users, since the primary language in international user groups is English.

It is rather inconvenient to have to remember what is connected to which pin. You can simplify matters considerably by naming the pins in your program, like this:

```
var bit switch is pin_d1
var bit led is pin_d2
```

This says that "switch"means the same as "pin_d1", and that "led" means the same as "pin_d2". You already know that, for the compiler, "on" means the same as "high"and "off" means the same as "low". So you could now write the program as:

```
if switch then
    -- switch is on
    led = on
    delay_1s(3)
    led = off
end if
```

Yes, that's much better. And you'll find that both techniques are used in the real world, and also in this book. For small, simple programs one usually doesn't take the trouble to define the pins, but in larger, more complex programs it is a great way to reduce errors.

So the "readable" version looks like this:

```
-- JAL 2.0.4
include 16F877_bert

var bit switch is pin_d1
var bit led is pin_d2

-- define pins
pin_d1_direction = input
pin_d2_direction = output

forever loop

    if switch then
        -- switch is on
        led = on
        delay_1s(3)
        led = off
    end if

end loop
```

4 Switches

The hardware

As discussed in the tutorial project a number of pins are required. This is the same for each project, so after this project it will no longer be mentioned.

Pin	Name	Description
1	MCLR/Vpp	Master Clear pin and programmer voltage input. This needs two resistors and a capacitor.[24]
11	V_{DD}	Power, +5V[25]
12	V_{SS}	Power, ground
13	OSC1/CLKIN	Crystal[26]
14	OSC2/CLKOUT	Crystal
31	V_{SS}	Power, ground
32	V_{DD}	Power, +5V

Apart from that, the switch and the LED need to be connected to the same pins that the program is expecting:

Pin	Description
20	switch
21	LED

---

[24] It can be done with just one 33k resistor to the positive supply. You may find this in older circuits. Nowadays, Microchip recommends using the two resistors and one capacitor combo.

[25] All power pins (11, 12, 31, 32) must be connected.

[26] A crystal is not mandatory, since the 16F877 can do without, but it'll be slower (at 4 MHz). In this book all projects use high speed and a crystal, and this information is recorded in the library.

The circuit looks like this:

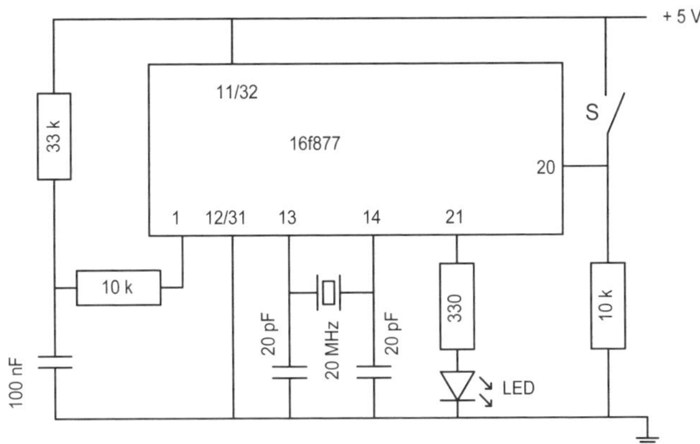

Figure 27. Timer.

You'll notice that the 16F877 is represented by a rectangle, and that only the pins in use have been drawn. This makes the schematic easier to read. Pins not drawn are not in use.

With each project a picture will be shown of the circuit on a breadboard. Sometimes it's convenient to see how the components are connected in real life. The pictures are made of actual working projects.

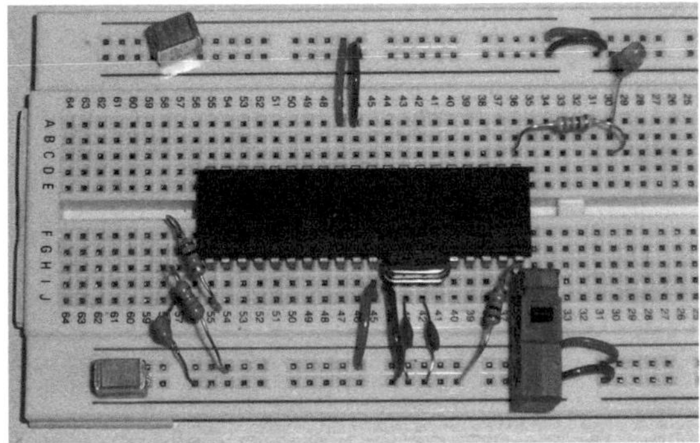

Figure 28. Timer.

4.2 Two-way switch

In this project a push button switch is used to turn an LED on and off. This two-way switch is also known as a bistable multivibrator .

Technical background

The plan is to press a button and turn an LED on if it happens to be off, or turn it off if it happens to be on. If this were a computer program the difficulty would be to know if the LED is currently on or off. Fortunately, this is a PIC™, so we can simply check the state of the pin, and then change it!

We will use the NOT (or Complement) operator[27] to do this. The NOT operator turns a 1 into a 0 and a 0 into a 1, and is written as an exclamation mark (!). To illustrate what an operator does we use a truth table:

Input	Output = ! Input
1	0
0	1

Since a digital pin can only be in one of two states (0 or 1), we can change its state like this:

```
pin_d2 = ! pin_d2
```

Or, when using names instead of pins:

```
led = ! led
```

So with this little piece of code the LED will turn on and off each time the switch is pressed:

```
if switch then
     led = ! led
end if
```

---

[27] See section 14.1 for a complete overview of all available operators.

This program will work, but you won't see it work the way we want it to. Before you even take your finger off the switch the LED turns on and off thousands of times, and it's anybody's guess which position it ends up in. So the program needs to wait for you to take your finger off the switch before doing anything. A small loop is used where the program will circle around until the switch is no longer pressed:

```
while switch loop
end loop
```

The only remaining problem is bouncing. When you press the switch the metal contacts inside approach and then glide over each other. During this time contact is made and lost, back and forth many times. You won't see any of this, but the microcontroller will. It will see this as a series of on/off switching. A short delay is enough to fix this. Here's what the entire code looks like:

```
if switch then
    led = ! led
    while switch loop
        delay_10ms(1)
    end loop
end if
```

Using *led = ! led* (or *pin_d2 = ! pin_d2*) involves a small risk. In order to make this work the program first needs to know what the current state of the pin is. Let's assume you make the pin high. On the pin is a large capacitor, which has to charge first before the pin is actually high (this loading capacitor "draws"the voltage down). If, at this moment, the microcontroller were to check the state of the pin it would find it low until the capacitor is charged. If the load is heavy enough the pin may never reach the high state!

Obviously the faster the pin changes state the more acute this problem becomes. With a visible switched LED it won't be much of a problem and we can safely using the elegant technique above. When the frequency is higher, however, or when a load is on the pin such as a capacitor or coil (like a loudspeaker), it's better to use an intermediate variable.

```
flag = ! flag
pin_d2 = flag
```

You are now "independent"of the real world.

4 Switches

Of course, you need to define the variable *flag* first:

        var bit flag

The software

When the project is switched on we must make sure the LED is turned off:

        led = off

The definitions can be copied from the program in section 4.1 (it's the same switch and LED on the same pins). So the complete program is:

```
-- JAL 2.0.4
include 16F877_bert

var bit switch is pin_d1
var bit led is pin_d2

-- define pins
pin_d1_direction = input
pin_d2_direction = output

led = off

forever loop

    if switch then
        led = ! led
        while switch loop
          delay_10ms(1)
        end loop
    end if

end loop
```

The hardware is identical to the project from section 4.1.

4.3 Dice

This project is a fun application of a debounced switch.

Technical background

To make an electronic die you need to generate random numbers. Strictly speaking this is impossible for any computer. All steps to get to the random number must be programmed and thus described, which means they are not random at all. What usually happens is that accidental counter positions or remains of prior calculations are used.

In the 16F877_bert library you will find a few of those "random" commands:

Command	Explanation
number = random_word	Chose a random number in the range 0 to 65,536.
number = random_byte	Chose a random number in the range 0 to 255.
number = dice	Chose a random number in the range 1 to 6 (specifically meant for dice)

Drawing a random number is now very simple:

    value = dice

Depending on the results, 1 to 6 LEDs need to be switched on. The simplest way is to use a series of *if...then* statements:

```
if value >= 1 then led1 = on else led1 = off end if[28]
if value >= 2 then led2 = on else led2 = off  end if
if value >= 3 then led3 = on else led3 = off  end if
if value >= 4 then led4 = on else led4 = off  end if
if value >= 5 then led5 = on else led5 = off  end if
if value >= 6 then led6 = on else led6 = off  end if
```

---

[28] Very experienced programmers might write: *led1 = value >= 1* which does exactly the same. It would be a bit advanced for this book however.

To make it interesting, we can simulate the effect of rolling dice by generating a random number several times, and then briefly show each result:

```
for 200 loop
        value = dice
        if value >= 1 then led1 = on else led1 = off end if
        if value >= 2 then led2 = on else led2 = off  end if
        if value >= 3 then led3 = on else led3 = off  end if
        if value >= 4 then led4 = on else led4 = off  end if
        if value >= 5 then led5 = on else led5 = off  end if
        if value >= 6 then led6 = on else led6 = off  end if
        delay_10ms(1)
    end loop
```

Each value is displayed for 10 ms, and then the final value will remain visible until the button is pressed again…thus rolling the dice again.

How to avoid bouncing of the switch contacts is discussed in the previous section:

```
-- switch is on
while switch loop
    delay_10ms(1)
end loop
```

The 6 LEDs can be connected to any of the digital pins with the exception of c6 and c7. The 16F877_bert library has these pins set up for a hardware serial connection (see Chapter 11).

The software

Our program is nearly complete; we just have to define the pins, name the switch and the LEDs, and load the standard library.

After adding those things the final program is:

```
-- JAL 2.0.4
include 16F877_bert
```

```
var bit switch is pin_d1
var bit led1 is pin_d2
var bit led2 is pin_d3
var bit led3 is pin_c4
var bit led4 is pin_c5
var bit led5 is pin_d4
var bit led6 is pin_d5

var byte value

-- define pins
pin_d1_direction = input
pin_d2_direction = output
pin_d3_direction = output
pin_c4_direction = output
pin_c5_direction = output
pin_d4_direction = output
pin_d5_direction = output

pin_d2 = 0
pin_d3 = 0
pin_c4 = 0
pin_c5 = 0
pin_d4 = 0
pin_d5 = 0

forever loop

if switch then
    -- switch is on
    while switch loop
        delay_10ms(1)
    end loop
    for 200 loop
        value = dice
        if value >= 1 then led1 = on else led1 = off end if
        if value >= 2 then led2 = on else led2 = off  end if
        if value >= 3 then led3 = on else led3 = off  end if
        if value >= 4 then led4 = on else led4 = off  end if
        if value >= 5 then led5 = on else led5 = off  end if
        if value >= 6 then led6 = on else led6 = off  end if
        delay_10ms(1)
```

        end loop
    end if

    end loop

The hardware

After adding the five LEDs we now have our 6 LED dice.

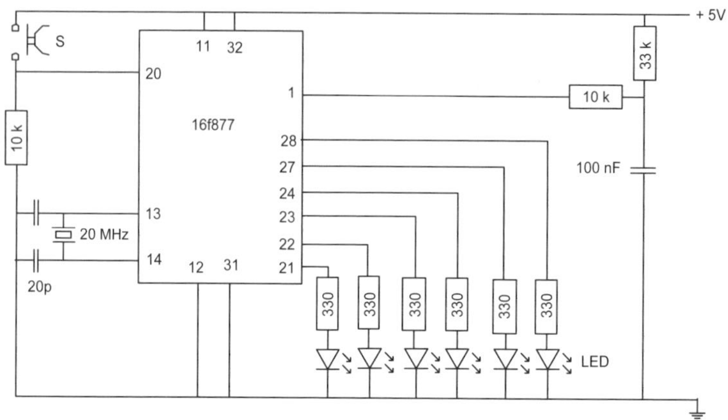

Figure 29. Electronic dice.

Which looks like this on the breadboard. A fun exercise would be to arrange the LEDs like the eyes on a die, and see what changes need to be made to the program to light the correct LEDs for each number.

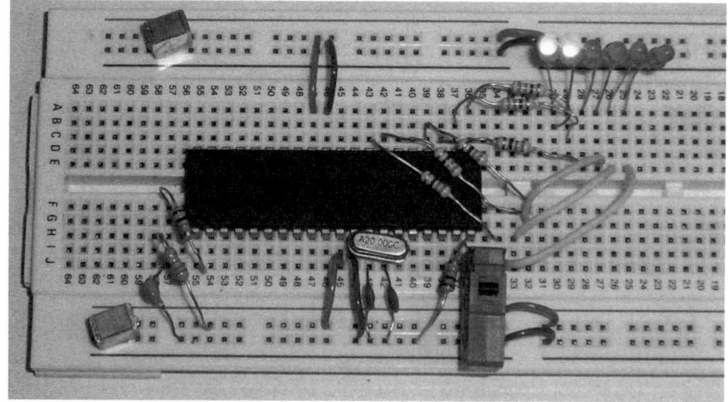

Figure 30. Electronic dice.

4.4 Secret doorbell

Here we have a doorbell that only rings when a secret code has been entered on a keypad. So now you get to choose who can ring your doorbell. In this project we will also explain how to design and build procedures and even create your own library.

Technical background

A keypad is simply a collection of push buttons. In this project, a 4x3 keypad (12 buttons) is used. These are numbered 0 to 9 and include the signs # and *. You might expect 24 connections for 12 push buttons, or maybe even 13 if they have one common lead, but when the buttons are arranged smartly only seven connections are required…as you can see in Figure 31.

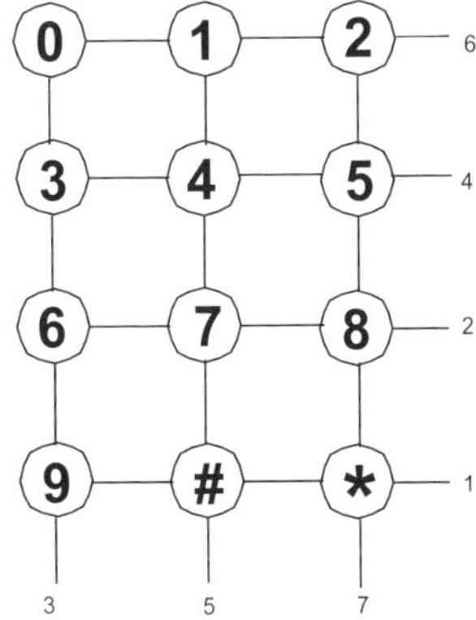

Figure 31. Key arrangement on the keypad.

With this keypad, when the number 0 is pressed, pins 3 and 6 are connected with each other. So the only thing the program needs to do is check if any pins are connected to each other. Here's how we do it…

The three rows are connected to pins of the microcontroller that are defined as inputs, and those pins are then connected through a resistor to ground. So the PIC^{TM} will see each of these rows as ground (low).

The columns are connected to microcontroller pins defined as outputs. All of these outputs are set to low.

Now, the PIC™ sets the keypad column connected to pin 3 to high. If none of the push buttons is pressed none of the inputs will show a signal. If, for example, the user presses "0", then the row connected to pin 6 will be high. This situation is shown in Figure 32.

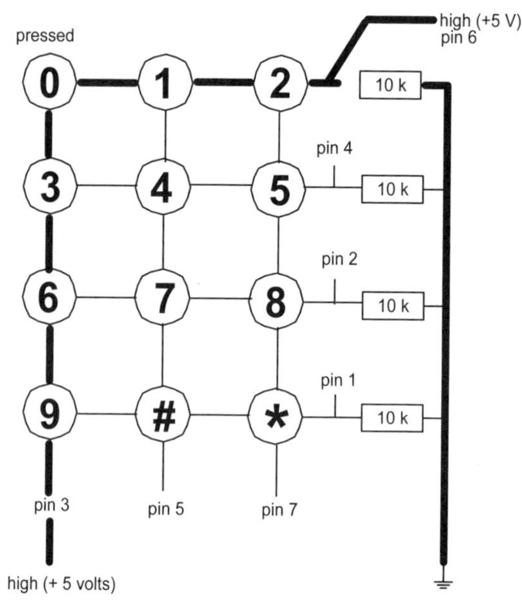

Figure 32. Push button 0 is pressed.

With a column connected to pin d0 and a row connected to pin c3, we could write our JAL code like this:

```
pin_d0 = high
if pin_c3 == high then
    key = 0
    debounce (3)
end if
pin_d0 = low
```

You see that the number of the key being pressed is stored in the variable *key*. If this variable is 0, it is unclear whether the "0" key has been pressed, or no key at all. So we set the variable to 255 at the beginning of the program. This is a good value for "nothing pressed", since there is no such key as "255".

```
--initialize key pressed
key = 255
```

Obviously, all rows need to be checked, not just pin c3. And once this is done the whole thing needs to be repeated for all columns.

I'm sure you noticed the command *debounce (3)* in the code fragment. This is the call to a procedure, which looks like this:

```
procedure debounce (byte in pinnr) is
   if pinnr == 0 then
      while pin_c0 == high loop
         delay_10ms(1)
      end loop
   end if
   if pinnr == 1 then
      while pin_c1 == high loop
         delay_10ms(1)
      end loop
   end if
   if pinnr == 2 then
      while pin_c2 == high loop
         delay_10ms(1)
      end loop
   end if
   if pinnr == 3 then
      while pin_c3 == high loop
         delay_10ms(1)
      end loop
   end if
end procedure
```

There are four loops, which you might recognize from section 4.2 as a way to eliminate switch bouncing. The procedure is called with a value of 3, which means that this part of the procedure is executed:

```
if pinnr == 3 then
   while pin_c3 == high loop
      delay_10ms(1)
   end loop
end if
```

Why use a separate procedure when it could be written into the main program? Well, in total 12 buttons need to be debounced, so each row is looked at three times. That would mean that this part of the program would have to be entered three times. It's possible, but it doesn't look very good. And if it turns out the debounce loop need to be changed we would have to do that 12 times. That's a recipe for mistakes. For that reason, it is better to use a procedure.

Making a procedure is very easy to do. You start with the outside:

```
procedure debounce is
end procedure
```

Now you need to figure out which data the procedure needs in order to function. In this case it's a number to indicate which pin to debounce. We'll call the variable *pinnr* for "pin number". And since there are only four possible pins a byte is large enough. The variable goes into the procedure like this:

```
procedure debounce (byte in pinnr) is
end procedure
```

No data needs to be returned (out), so we can start writing the body of the procedure. This is handled exactly the same way as regular programming. The code to debounce pin c3 would look like this:

```
if pinnr == 3 then
    while pin_c3 == high loop
       delay_10ms(1)
    end loop
end if
```

So we can add it to our procedure:

```
procedure debounce (byte in pinnr) is
  if pinnr == 3 then
     while pin_c3 == high loop
        delay_10ms(1)
     end loop
  end if
end procedure
```

Now all you need to do is add the debouncing routines for the other pins. We decide at this point that the other rows of the keypad are connected to pins c0, c1, and c2.

Before we were distracted by debouncing the pins it was clear that not just pin c3 needs to be looked at, but also the other rows. We also need to process all of the columns. Here's how it looks in JAL:

```
procedure read_keypad (byte out key) is
   --default settings
   pin_d0 = low
   pin_d1 = low
   pin_d2 = low

   --initialize key pressed
   key = 255

   pin_d0 = high
   if pin_c0 == high then
      key = 9
      debounce (0)
   end if
   if pin_c1 == high then
      key = 6
      debounce (1)
   end if
   if pin_c2 == high then
      key = 3
      debounce (2)
   end if
   if pin_c3 == high then
      key = 0
      debounce (3)
   end if
   pin_d0 = low

   pin_d1 = high
   if pin_c0 == high then
      key = 10
      debounce (0)
   end if
   if pin_c1 == high then
      key = 7
      debounce (1)
   end if
   if pin_c2 == high then
```

```
        key = 4
        debounce (2)
     end if
     if pin_c3 == high then
        key = 1
        debounce (3)
     end if
     pin_d1 = low

     pin_d2 = high
     if pin_c0 == high then
        key =11
        debounce (0)
     end if
     if pin_c1 == high then
        key = 8
        debounce (1)
     end if
     if pin_c2 == high then
        key = 5
        debounce (2)
     end if
     if pin_c3 == high then
        key = 2
        debounce (3)
     end if
     pin_d2 = low

  end procedure
```

You'll notice that I've used a procedure again. It seems that it's not needed or even useful. The reason for using it is simple: If you have a keypad you may want to use it in other projects. And in each project, you'll probably want to read and debounce the buttons. So rather than re-inventing the wheel multiple times we can put our newly found knowledge into a library, and in a library it has to be written as a procedure.

For a good library we need two important parts. First, a definition of the pins used. It's best to put this in the library; otherwise the next time you use it you won't remember which pin goes where.

```
-- define pins
pin_c0_direction = input    -- row 9 # *
pin_c1_direction = input    -- row 6 7 8
pin_c2_direction = input    -- row 3 4 5
pin_c3_direction = input    -- row 0 1 2

pin_d0_direction = output   -- column 0 3 6 9
pin_d1_direction = output   -- column 1 4 7 #
pin_d2_direction = output   -- column 2 5 8 *
```

It makes no difference which pins we use, as long as we use the same pins when building the hardware.[29]

The second important part is the section where you explain what the library does, give it a revision number and a date, and mention the copyrights.

```
-- ---------------------------------------------------------------------
-- <Title Library for use with a 4 x 3 keypad
-- <License
-- COPYRIGHT: This library and the ideas, software, models, pictures contained
-- herein are Copyright (c) 1995-2006 Bert van Dam, and are distributed under
-- the Free Software Foundation General Public License version 2.0. See the
-- FSF GPL page for more information.
-- It is explicitly forbidden to use any of the copyrighted materials for
-- commercial purposes including but not limited to books.
-- ---------------------------------------------------------------------
-- <Description
-- ---------------------------------------------------------------------
-- Library for use with a 4 x 3 keypad
--
-- <Version: 1.0  07 Oct 2006,  Bert van Dam
--   - original release JAL version 2.x
-- ---------------------------------------------------------------------
-- ---------------------------------------------------------------------
```

It is customary to keep ownership of the rights of the library, but release it for use by others. My libraries all have a limitation that they may not be used commercially. Everyone can use my work, but if you want to make money off of it you need to contact

---

[29] Another option is to put the definitions as remarks in the library. In that case you are supposed to copy the remarks to your main program and adapt them to your needs. This is more flexible for the user, so if you wish you can use that technique.

me. If you make changes to an existing library you should add your own name, date and revision number. The part about the rights cannot be changed, and the name(s) of the original authors must be left in the library.

So the completed library looks like this:

```
-- -----------------------------------------------------------------------------
-- <title Library for use with a 4 x 3 keypad
-- <License
-- COPYRIGHT: This library and the ideas, software, models, pictures contained
-- herein are Copyright (c) 1995-2006 Bert van Dam, and are distributed under
-- the Free Software Foundation General Public License version 2.0. See the
-- FSF GPL page for more information.
-- It is explicitly forbidden to use any of the copyrighted materials for
-- commercial purposes including but not limited to books.
-- -----------------------------------------------------------------------------

-- <Description
-- -----------------------------------------------------------------------------

-- Library for use with a 4 x 3 keypad
--
-- <Version: 1.0  07 oct 2006,  Bert van Dam
--   - original release JAL version 2.x

-- -----------------------------------------------------------------------------

-- -----------------------------------------------------------------------------


-- define pins
pin_c0_direction = input    -- row 9 # *
pin_c1_direction = input    -- row 6 7 8
pin_c2_direction = input    -- row 3 4 5
pin_c3_direction = input    -- row 0 1 2

pin_d0_direction = output   -- column 0 3 6 9
pin_d1_direction = output   -- column 1 4 7 #
pin_d2_direction = output   -- column 2 5 8 *

-- debounce the switches
procedure debounce (byte in pinnr) is
   if pinnr == 0 then
      while pin_c0 == high loop
         delay_10ms(1)
      end loop
   end if
```

```
   if pinnr == 1 then
     while pin_c1 == high loop
       delay_10ms(1)
     end loop
   end if
   if pinnr == 2 then
     while pin_c2 == high loop
       delay_10ms(1)
     end loop
   end if
   if pinnr == 3 then
     while pin_c3 == high loop
       delay_10ms(1)
     end loop
   end if
end procedure

-- determine key pressed
procedure read_keypad (byte out key) is
   --default settings
   pin_d0 = low
   pin_d1 = low
   pin_d2 = low

   --initialize key pressed
   key = 255

   pin_d0 = high
   if pin_c0 == high then
     key = 9
     debounce (0)
   end if
   if pin_c1 == high then
     key = 6
     debounce (1)
   end if
   if pin_c2 == high then
     key = 3
     debounce (2)
   end if
   if pin_c3 == high then
     key = 0
```

```
      debounce (3)
   end if
   pin_d0 = low

   pin_d1 = high
   if pin_c0 == high then
      key = 10
      debounce (0)
   end if
   if pin_c1 == high then
      key = 7
      debounce (1)
   end if
   if pin_c2 == high then
      key = 4
      debounce (2)
   end if
   if pin_c3 == high then
      key = 1
      debounce (3)
   end if
   pin_d1 = low

   pin_d2 = high
   if pin_c0 == high then
      key =11
      debounce (0)
   end if
   if pin_c1 == high then
      key = 8
      debounce (1)
   end if
   if pin_c2 == high then
      key = 5
      debounce (2)
   end if
   if pin_c3 == high then
      key = 2
      debounce (3)
   end if
   pin_d2 = low
```

```
end procedure
```

Please note that the button with the # has been assigned the number 10 and the * has been assigned the number 11.

Okay, now open a new file in JALedit, and enter the library. Select a good name so you'll be able to recognize the library in the future and know what it is for. We'll use the name *keypad4x3* (the .JAL extension is added automatically) and save the library in the same directory as the other libraries. If you downloaded the free software package this library is already in your library directory.

And now that you have seen how to create a procedure and a library, let's get back to the secret doorbell project!

The software

We now have all software components needed to reliably detect which button has been pressed. In this project we will assume a four-digit code, where all digits have to be in the correct order. First, we will define two arrays: one for the digits being entered on the keypad, and one for the secret code. For our secret code we will choose 5-5-7-8.

```
var byte doorbell[4]
var byte code[4]={5,5,7,8}
```

You have undoubtedly noticed that each variable in JAL has a name. In an array all variables have the same name. So we have to use an index with that name to indicate which variable in the array we want. For example, code[2] would have the value 7. (Notice that the array index starts at 0. So code[0] has the value 5.)

We won't give any visual or audio indication if a wrong button is pressed. This way the unwanted visitor doesn't know which keys are wrong, or even how many digits are in the secret code.

In fact, we'll put all entered numbers in a row and simply wait until the four correct digits appear in the correct order.

```
read_keypad (number)

-- see if the correct sequence has been entered
if number != 255 then
   correct = 0
   doorbell[0] = doorbell[1]
```

```
        if doorbell[0] == code[0] then correct = correct + 1  end if
        doorbell[1] = doorbell[2]
        if doorbell[1] == code[1] then correct = correct + 1  end if
        doorbell[2]= doorbell[3]
        if doorbell[2] == code[2] then correct = correct + 1  end if
        doorbell[3]= number
        if doorbell[3] == code[3] then correct = correct + 1  end if

    end if
```

The first step we take is to call the procedure *read_keypad* (in the library we just made) to see which key has been pressed. If the answer is 255 then no key was pressed, so nothing needs to be done. When a key is pressed the value is put into the *doorbell* array at the very end, and all previous numbers move one position to the left. At the same time we check if this number is the correct number for this position. If it is the variable *correct* is increased by one.

Let's suppose someone enters 3-6-7-5, and then enters an 8. At first the array looks like this:

doorbell[0]	doorbell[1]	doorbell[2]	doorbell[3]
3	6	7	5

Then the 8 is added, so everything shifts one position to the left to make room. The 3 at the far left "falls out of the array".

doorbell[0]	doorbell[1]	doorbell[2]	doorbell[3]
6	7	5	8

Comparing it with the correct sequence results in one correct answer:

code[0]	code[1]	code[2]	code[3]
5	5	7	**8**
wrong	wrong	wrong	correct

When all of the numbers are correct the bell will ring, or in this case the buzzer will buzz. The buzzer is connected to pin b5 and is switched on for 1 second.

```
-- if the code was correct then ring the bell
if correct == 4 then
   pin_b5 = high
   delay_1s(1)
   pin_b5 = low
   correct = 0
end if
```

Let's not forget to include our new library. The complete program looks like this:

```
-- JAL 2.0.6
include 16F877_bert
include keypad4x3

var byte doorbell[4]
var byte code[4]={5,5,7,8}
var byte number, correct
pin_b5_direction = output
pin_b5 = low

forever loop

 read_keypad (number)

 -- see if the correct sequence has been entered
 if number != 255 then
    correct = 0
    doorbell[0] = doorbell[1]
    if doorbell[0] == code[0] then correct = correct + 1  end if
    doorbell[1] = doorbell[2]
    if doorbell[1] == code[1] then correct = correct + 1  end if
    doorbell[2]= doorbell[3]
    if doorbell[2] == code[2] then correct = correct + 1  end if
    doorbell[3]= number
    if doorbell[3] == code[3] then correct = correct + 1  end if

 end if
```

> *-- if the code was correct then ring the bell*
> if correct == 4 then
>   pin_b5 = high
>   delay_1s(1)
>   pin_b5 = low
>   correct = 0
> end if
>
>   end loop

The hardware

In the schematic you will recognize the connections between the keypad and the PIC™ with the row of 10 k resistors to ground - just like the way other switches are connected. The buzzer contains a coil and can't be directly connected to a PIC, so a TC4427A MOSFET driver has been used. In sections 7.1 and 12.7 this device is discussed in detail. For the time being, we will take for granted that this adequately drives the buzzer.

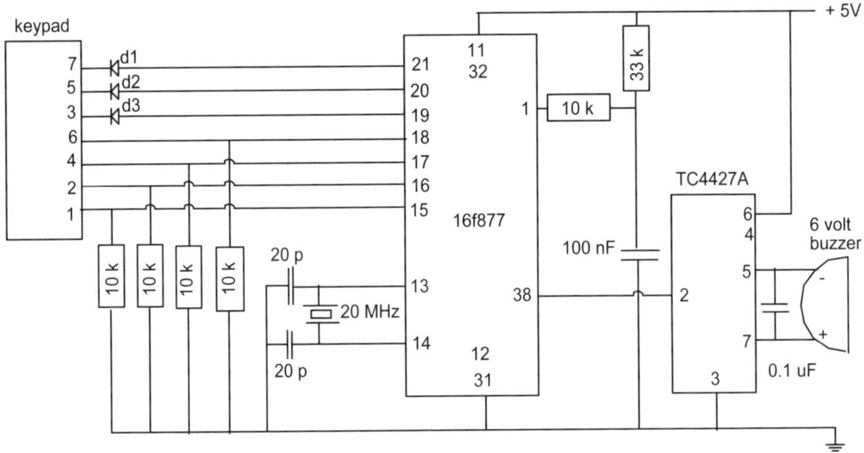

Figure 33. Schematic of the secret doorbell.

On the breadboard you can see the completed project. If you look closely you'll notice that the keypad has 10, not 7, connections. That's because it is an old telephone keypad with the keys rearranged. The green wires next to the connector correct for this by connecting wires 1 with 10, and 3 with 8 and 9.

If diodes d1, d2, and d3 are present in the keypad you do not need to add them. Otherwise, you can use 1N4007 diodes. These diodes ensure that you won't get a short circuit on the PIC pins if someone pushes two buttons at the same time.[30]

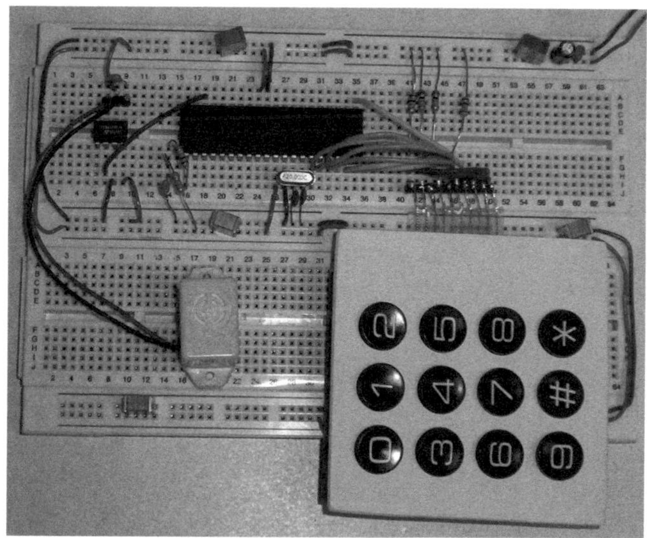

Figure 34. Secret doorbell with buzzer.

Option 1

Instead of a buzzer you could connect an electronic lock. In combination with a decent keypad you now have a code lock. Obviously the electronics should not be mounted in the same box as the keypad; otherwise it would be extremely easy for a burglar. And because there is no visual or audio indication of a wrong code the burglar has no idea which numbers are correct, or how long the code is. Nevertheless, this is still a toy and by no means burglar proof.

Option 2

If you have already read Chapter 5, and especially section 6.2, the thought might have hit you that by adding a few well-chosen resistors to the push buttons you only need one connection to the PIC™ instead of 7. This then becomes an analog input, where the voltage on the input indicates which key is pressed.

---

[30] You can also solve this without diodes by changing pins d0, d1, and d2 to inputs when they are not needed as outputs. In section 14.8 this very elegant, but seldom used, technique is discussed.

In theory this is correct, but in practice unfortunately not.[31] Each key of a keypad consists of a conductive pad that is held away from the contacts by a springy material. When you press the button the pad touches two metal contacts on the printed circuit board, thus connecting them. If you press lightly there is only a small amount of contact and thus a high resistance, but if you press firmly there is much more contact and thus a lower resistance. So the harder you press the lower the resistance, which means any meaningful measurement of this analog value is impossible.

---

[31] Someone once wrote that the difference between theory and practice is that in theory there is no difference, but in practice there is.

5 A/D conversion

Several pins of the 16F877 are capable of converting an analog signal to a digital one. In our case, an analog signal means any voltage between 0 and +5 volts. If you connect a voltage divider to one of these pins the values of the resistors will determine the voltage at the pin. So, indirectly, you are also measuring resistance.

Measuring a simple resistor is not very exciting. Electronic parts where the resistance is influenced by certain conditions, however, can be much more interesting. Such as, the turning of a knob (a variable resistor, or potmeter), the amount of light falling on a particular spot (an LDR[32]), or changes in temperature (an NTC thermistor[33]). In this chapter you'll find projects that use this analog-to-digital concept.

Project	Description
Variable speed flashing LED	Analog-to-digital conversion is used to control the speed of a flashing LED.
Dark activated switch	Switch an LED on automatically when it gets dark.
Voltmeter	Turn your PC into a graphing voltmeter.
Photometer with LCD display	A simple light-measuring device that displays the measured value on an LCD screen.
Sampling	Long-term temperature sampling for display on a PC.

---

[32] Light Dependent Resistor.
[33] Negative Temperature Coefficient resistor.

5 A/D conversion

5.1 Variable speed flashing LED

In this project the resistance[34] of a variable resistor is measured. Based on the result the speed of a flashing LED is adjusted.

Technical background

Most of the pins on port A and all of the pins on port E of the 16F877 are capable of analog-to-digital conversion. To enable this a few registers must first be set up. The standard library 16F877_bert takes care of this, but you may want other settings for your project. So we'll be taking a closer look at the inner workings of this library.

The most complicated task is to determine which pins are used for A/D ("a" for analog in the table), because it's not always apparent.

pin	A0	A1	A2	A3	A5	E0	E1	E2
	AN0	AN1	AN2	AN3	AN4	AN5	AN6	AN7
0 channels								
1 channel	a							
3 channels	a	a		a				
5 channels	a	a	a	a	a			
6 channels	a	a	a	a	a	a		
8 channels	a	a	a	a	a	a	a	a

Please note that pin a4 has no A/D converter and that a6, a7, and a8 do not exist (port A is only 6 bits wide). A/D converter (or "channel") AN0 is connected to pin a0. But, confusingly enough, AN4 is connected to pin a5, and AN7 is connected to pin e2. So take care when developing programs; mistakes are easily made.

Also note the strange configuration when three analog channels are selected. Against all expectations pin a2 is switched to digital and pin a3 is switched to analog.

In JAL we set the required number of channels like this:

```
const ADC_hardware_Nchan = 8
```

---

[34] In reality, we are not measuring the resistance, but the voltage, because the variable resistor is connected as a voltage divider. You might also say that we are measuring the rotation of the knob on the variable resistor. If this variable resistor was built into a robotic arm we could determine the arm's position.

The other settings are just as simple:

```
const ADC_hardware_NVref = 0
const ADC_hardware_Rsource = 10_000[35]
const ADC_hardware_high_resolution = true
```

We aren't using a reference voltage (everything will be measured against the +5V power), so NVref = 0. If you want to measure very small voltages you may consider using a reference voltage to make better use of the available resolution.

The maximum resistance that will be connected to the pins is 10k ohm[36], so Rsource = 10_000.

The resolution (accuracy) is set to 10 bits (high resolution).

Once these settings have been made a whole series of A/D related commands are available as part of the 16F877_bert library:

ADC_init	Initialize the A/D converter.
no_ADC = X	Set the number of A/D channels you want to use (see the table).
ADC_on	Switch A/D on (on the selected channels).
ADC_off	Switch A/D off (so all pins become digital).
ADC_read (ADC_chan)	Read the analog value on a channel[37] in a word.
ADC_read_bytes(ADC_chan, ADC_Hbyte, ADC_Lbyte)	Read the analog value on a channel[37] into two separate bytes.
ADC_read_low_res (ADC_chan)	Read the analog value on a channel[37] in one byte, so with low resolution (max value: 255).

---

[35] In JAL, underscores within numbers have no meaning and are only used for easier reading. So 10_000 is the same as 10000.

[36] The datasheet recommends this as the maximum value.

[37] Channel is the AN number in the table on the previous page.

5 A/D conversion

The software

After the variables and pin directions have been defined we can take a measurement in low resolution:

    resist = ADC_read_low_res(3)

We'll connect the variable resistor to pin a3 (A/D channel AN3). Note that *resist* has been defined as a byte, so it cannot hold a value higher than 255.

To get a flash frequency ranging between 30 and 157 ms *resist* will have to be adjusted. Division is without a remainder[38] (so 255/2 will equal 127).

    -- convert to a suitable range
    resist = (resist / 2) + 30

Now all we need to do is alternate the pin between high and low and wait a bit in between:

    -- and flash
    delay_1ms(resist)
    pin_d0 = low
    delay_1ms(resist)
    pin_d0 = high

Putting it all together gives us this:

    -- JAL 2.0.4
    include 16F877_bert

    -- define the pins
    pin_a3_direction = input
    pin_d0_direction = output

    -- general variable
    var byte resist

    forever loop

---

[38] See the explanation about operators in section 14.1.

```
        -- take a sample
         resist = ADC_read_low_res(3)

        -- convert to a suitable range
         resist = (resist / 2 ) + 30

        -- and flash
         delay_1ms(resist)
         pin_d0 = low
         delay_1ms(resist)
         pin_d0 = high

     end loop
```

The hardware

The 10k variable resistor is connected to pin a3. The value of 10k has been selected because in the settings section we entered that as the maximum resistance for the A/D converter[39]. On pin 19 (d0) an LED with a limiting resistor is connected.

Our circuit looks like this:

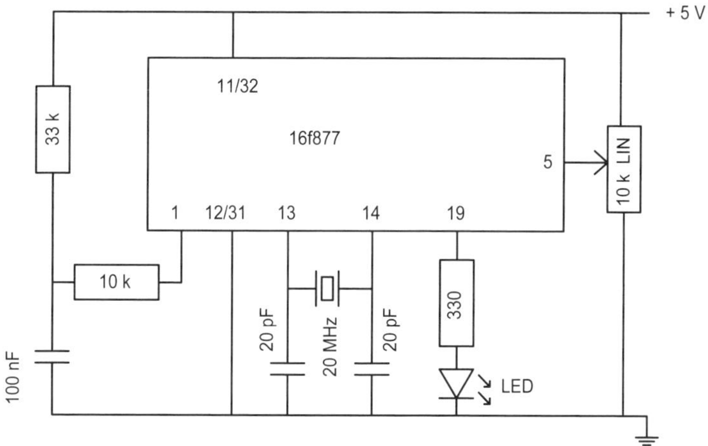

Figure 35. Variable speed flashing LED.

---

[39] This setting applies to the A/D converter, and thus to all A/D channels at the same time.

5 A/D conversion

Which looks like this on the breadboard:

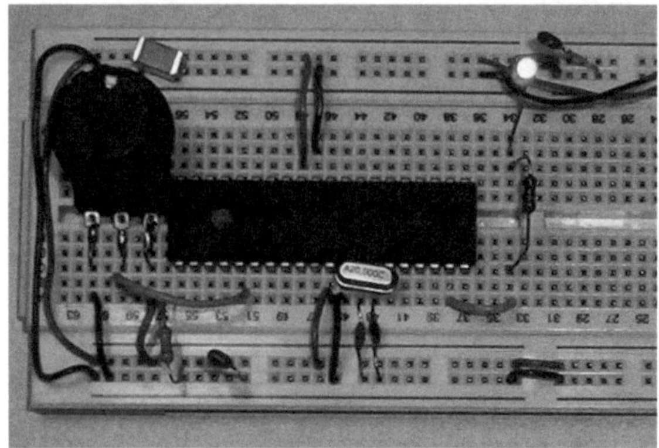

Figure 36. Variable speed flashing LED.

5.2 Dark activated switch

In this project an LED is switched on when it gets dark. In section 12.7 you can see how this technique can be used to switch on a house light, or even the street lights in case you find a small LED not impressive enough.

Technical background

The amount of light can be measured using an LDR[40]. This is a resistor whose value is dependent on the amount of light that hits it. The relationship between the resistance and the amount of light is not linear and is usually something like this:

R (in k ohm) = 500 / L (in Lux)

To get a feel for the meaning of Lux[41]:

direct sunlight	100,000 lux
cloudy day	10,000 lux
room with light bulb	350 lux
room with candle	50 lux

---

[40] LDR = Light Dependant Resistor.
[41] Lux = lumen/m^2, where a lumen is the amount of light from one candle.

Even "identical"LDRs can easily differ as much as 50%, so you'll need to calibrate it or use a variable resistor for fine adjustment. Keep in mind that the more light falling on the LDR the lower its resistance.

An LDR will normally consume about 50 to 80 mW of power, which at 5 volts equals a current of 10 to 16 mA. This means the LDR can be connected directly to the PIC™ without damage.

The software

The program will continually measure the resistance on pin a3.[42] If the measurement exceeds a certain threshold value the LED will switch on. Below the threshold value the LED will switch off.

```
-- JAL 2.0.4
include 16F877_bert

-- define the pins
pin_a3_direction = input
pin_d0_direction = output

-- general variable
var byte resist

forever loop

  -- take a sample
  resist = ADC_read_low_res(3)

  -- and switch
  if resist > 200 then
    pin_d0 = high
  else
    pin_d0 = low
  end if

end loop
```

---

[42] In reality, the voltage is measured and not the resistance.

5 A/D conversion

The hardware

The hardware is virtually identical to the previous project. Across the lower half of the variable resistor an LDR is connected. This way the variable resistor can be used to adjust the level of darkness at which the LED will switch on.

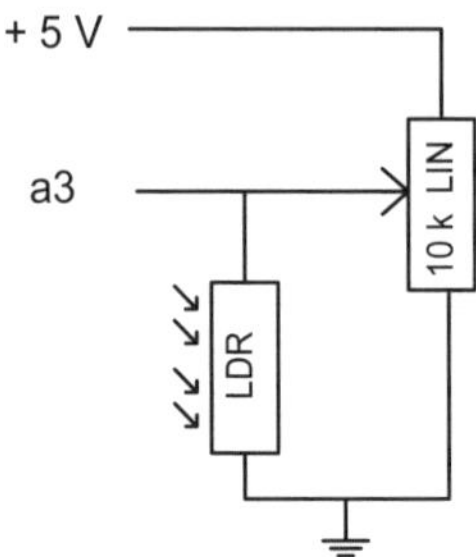

Figure 37. Connecting the LDR across the variable resistor.

5.3 Voltmeter

In this project the A/D converter is used to make a voltmeter.

Technical background

In the previous projects we didn't pay much attention to the actual measurements, but this time we'll have to take a closer look. We had mentioned that the resistance was being measured, but in actuality this is not quite true. The variable resistor was connected across the full power voltage with the center terminal connected to the PIC™. In this setup the center terminal carries a voltage that varies with the position of the dial. So, in fact, the variable resistor is used as a voltage divider.

The measurement takes place in 8 bits over a range of 5 volts. This means that the resolution is 5/255, or 0.01961 volts. This assumes, of course, that the power supply is indeed 5 volts and remains stable.

Please be aware that this voltage meter can only measure voltages between 0 and +5 V. If you want to go any higher you'll need to add a voltage divider, which is technically not very complicated. Figure 38 shows how you can apply this voltage divider to measure in the 0 to +10 V range. (This will, of course, cause the resolution will go down.)

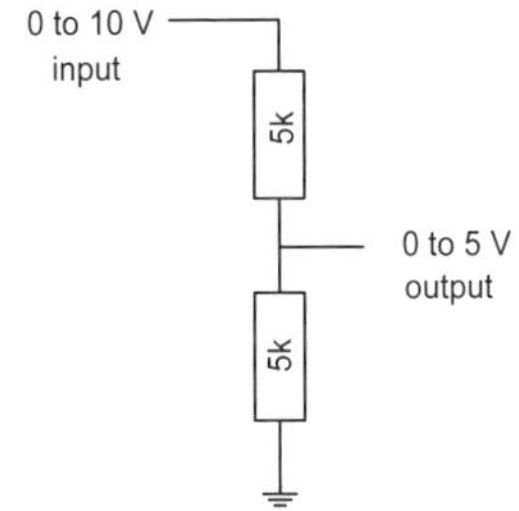

Figure 38. Voltage divider.

The software

The program continuously measures the voltage on AN3:

resist = ADC_read_low_res(3)

And sends that measurement to the PC:

serial_sw_write(resist)

The complete program looks like this:

```
-- JAL 2.0.4
include 16F877_bert

-- define the pins
pin_a3_direction = input
pin_d0_direction = output

-- general variable
var byte resist

forever loop

  -- take a sample
  resist = ADC_read_low_res(3)

  -- and switch
  serial_sw_write(resist)
  delay_100ms(1)
```

end loop

The PC can convert this value to our measured voltage simply by multiplying by the resolution (0.01961).

It is quite easy to add a small graph to show the actual measurement and the average value, as you can see in Figure 39. The red line is the actual measurement (as shown on the dial) and the purple line is the average. I have included the voltmeter software as part of the free download package.[43]

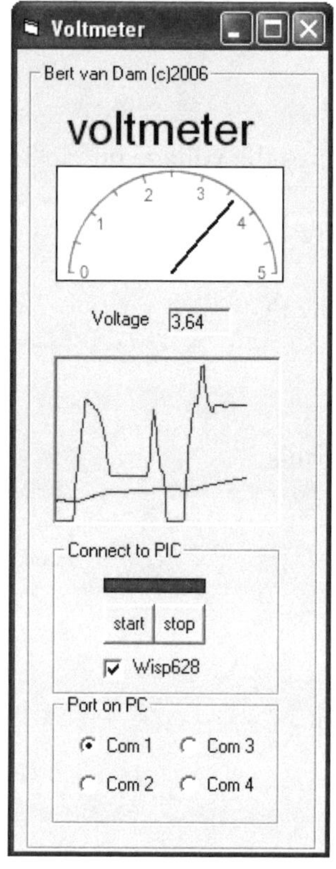

Figure 39. Voltmeter on the PC.

---

[43] Check out http://www.boekinfo.tk for a ready to run application, as well as source code for Visual Basic.

The hardware

The hardware is basically identical to project 5.1, except that the variable resistor is removed and replaced by a single wire to serve as the "measuring probe".If you want to measure parts that are connected to a different power supply you need to connect the ground wire with the ground of the voltmeter hardware.

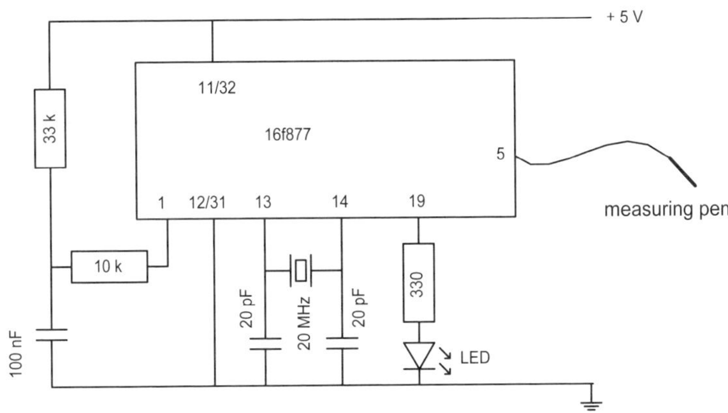

Figure 40. Voltmeter.

5.4 Photometer with LCD display

This project is a very simple photometer, which shows the amount of light measured on an LCD display.

Technical background

The basis for this project is the dark activated switch of project 5.2. In this case, however, the amount of light is measured continuously without switching anything. The measurement is shown on an LCD display as both a number and a bar graph.

The LCD screen is manufactured by Emerging Display Technologies Corporation[44] and has two lines of 16 characters each. Before you grab your soldering iron to start making

---

[44] Model number 162A0 (led types). The datasheet and other information can be found on the manufacturer's website at http://www.edtc.com. You'll probably find it more useful, however, to have the datasheet of the standard display, HiTachi hd47780, from http://www.hitachi-ds.com/en/download/brochures/.

connections you should know that the connections are on the topside of the display, and that pins 7, 8, 9 and 10 are normally not used.

The 16F877_bert library doesn't have any commands for LCD displays so we will have to load an additional library called lcd_44780[45]. The type code doesn't match the one on our display, but the 44780 is an industry standard; so most displays will be able to use this library.[46]

Library lcd_44780 adds a range of useful commands:

LCD_init	Prepare the LCD display for use (this command is automatically called when you load this library).
LCD_clear_line (line)	Clear line (note: the first line is number 0).
LCD_char_pos (character, position)	Print a character at the position indicated (note: the first position is 0).
LCD_char_line_pos (character, line, position)	Print a character at the position and line indicated.
LCD_num_pos (byte, position)	Print a number (0 to 255) at the position indicated.
LCD_num_line_pos (byte, line, position)	Print a number (0 to 255) at the position and line indicated.
LCD_num_pos_1dec (byte, position)	Print a number (0 to 255) at the position indicated with one decimal digit (so 255 will be printed as 25.5).
LCD_high_low_line_pos (hbyte, lbyte, line, position)	Print a number (0 to 65535) at the position and line indicated.
LCD_progress (byte, line)	Display a bar graph with length *byte* (maximum 16).

---

[45] Written by Stef Mientki and Bert van Dam.

[46] If you want to buy an LCD display make absolutely sure it is compatible with the 44780 standard. Otherwise, you will have to write your own library, and the support on the Internet will be minimal.

LCD_shift_right	Move the entire display (both lines) to the right.
LCD_shift_left	Move the entire display (both lines) to the left.
LCD_cursor_pos = position	Place the cursor at the position indicated.
LCD_cursor = off	Switch the cursor off ("on"turns it back on).
LCD_blink = on	Switch cursor blinking on (or "off").
LCD_display = off	Switch the entire display off (or "on").
LCD_custom (memory address)	Put a custom character in the LCD memory (use only addresses 0 to 7).
CharData[]	Array to define the custom character. Send to the LCD memory one character at a time.
LCD_clock_line_pos (byte, line, position)	Print a number (00 to 99) at the indicated position, uses a leading zero if less than 10.

In this project we will only use a few of these commands. Most of the others will be used in projects later in the book. Let's start by printing some text on the LCD display. We do this using our new command:

LCD_char_line_pos (character, line, position)

Note that both the line and the column numbers start at 0.

Line	Position															
0	0	1	2	3	4	5	6	7	8	9	10	11	12	13	14	15
1	0	1	2	3	4	5	6	7	8	9	10	11	12	13	14	15

The first character (at the upper left) is on line 0, position 0.[47] To print the word "Light" on the display the first command will be:

```
LCD_char_line_pos ("L", 0, 0)
```

This can be repeated for every letter, but it is easier to use an array. An array is a row of variables which all have the same name.

```
var byte Demo[5]={"L","i","g","h","t"}
```
[48]

This array is named *Demo*. So each letter[49] in the array is also named *Demo*, but referred to with a number to indicate its position in the array. *Demo[2]*, therefore, is the letter "g" (you can see that we start counting at 0).

We will use a small loop to get all 5 letters on the display:

```
counter = 0
for 5 loop
    LCD_char_line_pos(Demo[counter],0,counter)
    counter = counter + 1
end loop
```

Counter is used to keep track of the letter that needs to be printed. The cursor is an annoying flashing line that we will switch off:

```
LCD_cursor = off
```

The light is continuously measured like we have done before. Sending each measurement to the display is possible, however the constant rewriting may cause it to flicker. So we

---

[47] The highest position is 15. You can go higher, such as LCD_num_pos (byte, 18), but it will print outside the visible display and you won't see it. If you increase the position even further you will eventually end up on line 2. The column position at which this wraparound occurs depends on the display used. In this book we assume 40, but displays with 80 also exist.
[48] If you only use letters you can write them as one word: Demo[] = "Light"
[49] You can mix letters and numbers, a very nice feature of JAL.

will only write the measurement when it has changed. That is, the resistance is not equal to the previous resistance measured. In JAL, we write "not equal" as "!=":

```
if resist != history then
```

Now we need to print the measurement on the display. The word "Light" has 5 letters, and we also want a space after it. That means the measurement should be placed at position 6. You can count this out on the display shown on the previous page to see that it is correct. The command for this is:

```
LCD_num_line_pos(resist,0,6)
```

In the lcd_44780 library you'll find a convenient command to display a value as a bar. It is a bit crude because there are only 16 blocks, but still it's nice to quickly see an approximation of the amount of light measured. We divide the resistance by 16 and show the bar on the second line (because the word "Light" and the measurement are on the first line). The second line is line number 1, remember? So our next command is:

```
LCD_progress(resist / 16, 1)
```

The software

The rest of the program is not very complicated. At the start of the program both libraries are included:

```
include 16F877_bert
include lcd_44780
```

The next step is to declare the variables. The array is also declared and immediately filled. This is not mandatory; you could also declare the array first and fill it later.

As soon as a measurement has been displayed we need to remember it so it doesn't have to be displayed again:

```
history = resist
```

Putting it all together yields this program:

```
-- JAL 2.0.4
include 16F877_bert
include lcd_44780
```

5 A/D conversion

```
-- define variables
var byte resist, history, counter

-- set text
var byte Demo[5]={"L","i","g","h","t"}
counter = 0
for 5 loop
   LCD_char_line_pos(Demo[counter],0,counter)
   counter = counter + 1
end loop

-- make history unequal to resist for first measurement
history = resist + 1

-- switch the cursor off
LCD_cursor = off


forever loop

   -- convert analog on a4 to digital
   resist = ADC_read_low_res(4)

   -- check if the light intensity has changed
   if resist != history then

      -- display value (0 - 255)
      LCD_num_line_pos(resist,0,6)

      -- show bar on second line
      LCD_progress(resist / 16,1)

      -- remember the current value
      history = resist

   end if

end loop
```

The hardware

If you bought the LCD display used in this book you need to solder wires to it in order to connect it to the breadboard (or anything else for that matter). Notice that the connections are on the top of the display, and that connections 7, 8, 9 and 10 are not used.

Pin 3 of the LCD screen is used to control the brightness with a variable resistor. According to the datasheet the voltage on this pin is not allowed to drop below 1.5 volts. Using a 10k resistor between the variable resistor and the ground lead gives us a minimum possible voltage of 2.5 V, way above the recommended minimum. (I feel the optimum voltage is about 4.35 V.) If you switch on the project and you don't see anything (or only black blocks) try adjusting this variable resistor.

Pins 15 and 16 control the background lighting. According to the datasheet a 6 to 15 ohms resistor must be used. In the schematic, 10 ohms is used.

Please note that on the 16F877 pin b3 has been skipped. This is the programming pin and, if it is not strictly necessary for your project, it's much better to leave it unused.

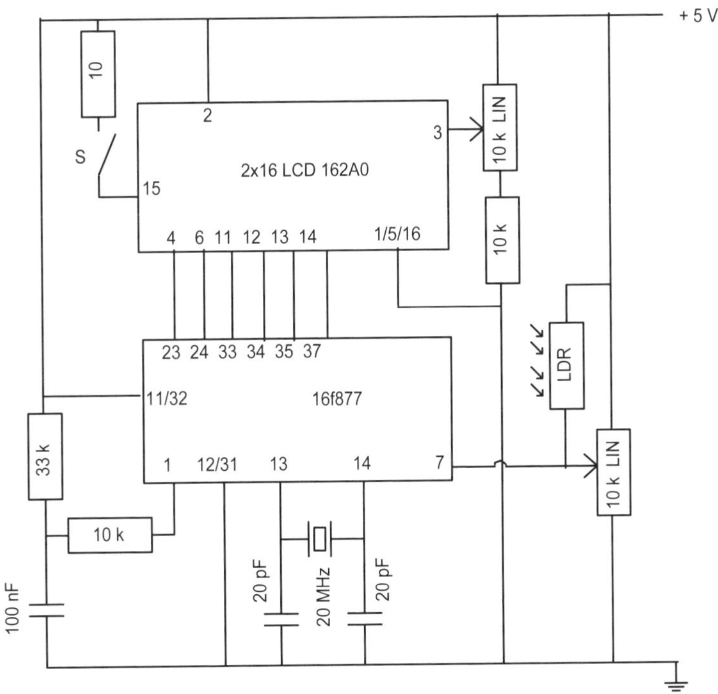

Figure 41. Photometer with LCD screen.

A few interesting observations:

- The LCD display is connected in 4-bit mode. That means 4 wires are used to send data from the 16F877 to the display. An 8-bit mode is also available, which will be faster, but you need much more pins on the 16F877. The library we use only supports 4-bit mode, since this is more commonly used.
- The "read/write select"pin (5) of the LCD display has been connected to ground, because no data are read from the display (in any of the projects in this book).

For both variable resistors I have used the trimpot versions, because once they are set correctly you never use them again. The variable resistor next to the LDR can be used to fine adjust the measurements to the quantity of light you want to measure.

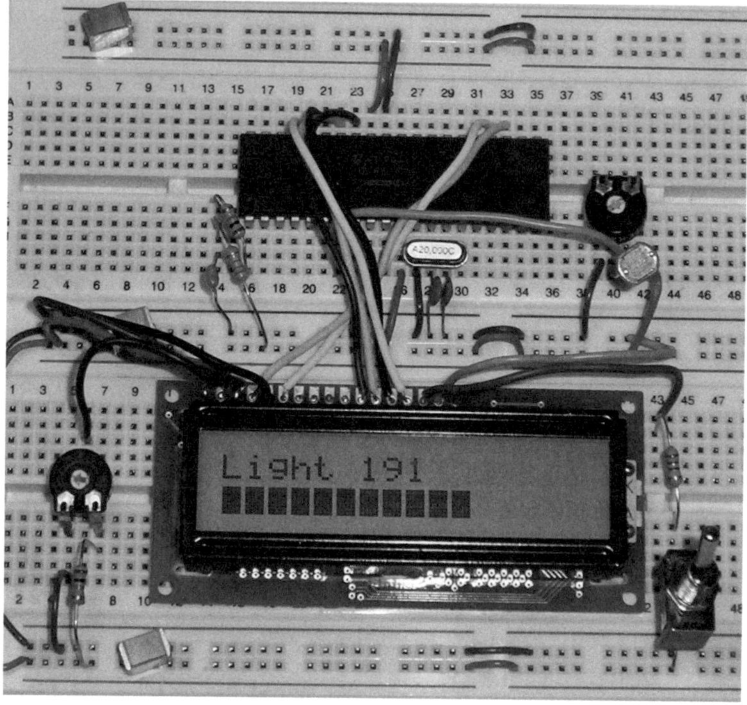

Figure 42. Photometer with LCD display.

5.5 Sampling

This project is a long-term temperature sampler, used to take temperature measurements with an NTC thermistor over an extended period of time. The results are displayed on the PC. This is a great way to monitor your fridge, or the temperature of the room.

Technical background

The purpose of this project is to sample the temperature at regular intervals over an extended period of time. The amount of time between each sample can be as short as 10 milliseconds, as long as 24 hrs…you can even sample every 4000 hours, if you want. The number of samples that can be stored in memory is 7000, so if you take a sample every 4000 hours you won't live to see the day that the memory is full.

The first problem to solve is where to store the measurements. We're going to use the program memory. The details of memory are discussed in Chapter 10. It's not necessary to read that chapter in order to complete this project, but if you intend to modify or expand the program I would certainly advise you read it first.

The memory storage part of the program looks like this:

```
-- take a sample
data = ADC_read_low_res(0)

-- and store
program_eeprom_write(address,data)

counter = counter + 1
address = address + 1

if address > 7000 then
   address = 7000
   counter = counter -1
end if
```

The collected data need to be sent to the PC when requested by the user. If the memory is full the program should not stop, because in that case the stored data would no longer be available. The simplest way to solve this is to overwrite the data on memory location 7000 when there is no more room available.

5 A/D conversion

The variable *counter* keeps track of the number of measurements (samples) that have been recorded. This is necessary so that we know how many samples to transfer to the PC:

```
if pin_d2 then
    while pin_d2 loop end loop
    delay_10ms(1)
    sendcounter = 0
    for counter loop
        program_eeprom_read(startaddress+sendcounter,data)
        serial_sw_write(data)
        sendcounter=sendcounter+1
    end loop
end if
```

A switch is connected to pin d2. In the program code you should recognize the debouncing technique discussed in section 4.2. The switch starts the retrieval of the samples from memory, and sends them to the PC. Afterwards, the program will continue sampling. So you can use the switch to get an idea of the current status without disrupting sampling. During transfer, however, no samples will be taken!

The samples are not taken during every loop, but only as needed:

```
samplecounter = samplecounter + 1
if samplecounter == 60000 then
```

The variable *samplecounter* is increased by 1ms (because of the *delay_1ms(1)* command in the sample loop, which is explained on the next page). In the section above, every 60000 ms (1 minute) a sample is recorded. Since this counter is declared as a word it can contain a maximum value of 65535. And since 7000 measurements can be recorded there is room for 127 hours of data.

If you need a longer period the delay statement can be changed. The disadvantage is that it also takes longer for the program to notice that the user has pressed the switch. If you change the delay to one hour (about a year before you run out of memory), the user may have to wait an hour before the program checks the switch status. The solution would be to use the port B interrupt, but that won't be discussed until section 12.2. So, for the time being, we'll stick with a 1-millisecond delay.

The temperature is recorded using an NTC thermistor.[50] This resistor changes its resistance based on the temperature, typically according to this formula:

$$R = a * e^{(b/T)}$$

Where *a* and *b* are constants that differ for each type of NTC. The following table is an example of a typical NTC:

Temperature (^{o}C)	Resistance (ohm)
-20	22,000
0	7,500
20	2,800
40	1,200
60	600

The software

Adding all the pieces together yields this program:

```
-- JAL 2.0.4
include 16F877_bert

-- define the pins
pin_a0_direction = input
pin_d1_direction = output
pin_d2_direction = input

-- general variable
var byte data
var word address, startaddress, sendaddress, sendcounter
var word samplecounter, counter

startaddress = 1000
samplecounter = 0
counter = 0
address = startaddress

forever loop
```

---

[50] Negative Temperature Coefficient resistor.

```
      -- wait a bit
      delay_1ms(1)

      -- send data to PC
      if pin_d2 then
         while pin_d2 loop end loop
         delay_10ms(1)
         sendcounter = 0
         for counter loop
            program_eeprom_read(startaddress+sendcounter,data)
            serial_sw_write(data)
            sendcounter=sendcounter+1
         end loop
      end if

      samplecounter = samplecounter + 1
      if samplecounter == 60000 then     -- sample every minute
         samplecounter = 0

         -- take a sample
         data = ADC_read_low_res(0)

         -- and store
         program_eeprom_write(address,data)

         counter = counter + 1
         address = address + 1

         if address > 7000 then
            address = 7000
            counter = counter -1
         end if

         -- and flash to show that we're still alive⁵¹
         pin_d1 = !pin_d1

      end if

   end loop
```

---

[51] Using pin_d1 = !pin_d1 is elegant, but involves a risk. See section 4.2 for an explanation.

Once the program has run for a while you can request the sampled data by pressing the button (after setting up an RS232 connection to the PC). If you use the Wisp628 programmer, you must <u>disconnect the yellow wire</u> before you start MICterm, otherwise the PIC™ will be reset and you will lose all of the data. In section 6.1 you can find more information on RS232 connections with a PC.

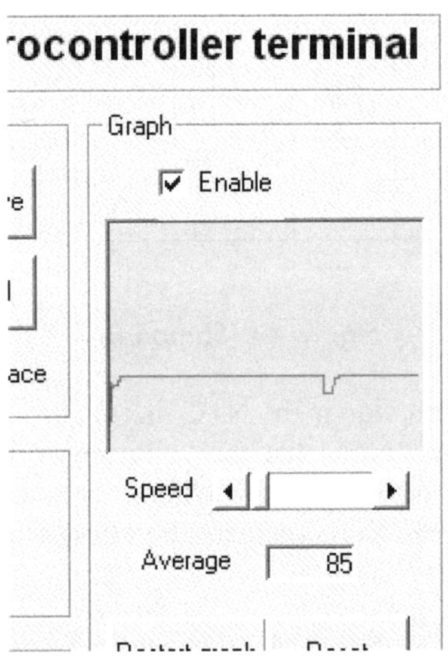

Figure 43. Temperature sampling (3 hour run).

If you enable the graph in MICterm you will get a nice overview of all the collected data. In Figure 43 you can see that the temperature rose in the morning and then stayed constant, except for the moment I touched the NTC.

The hardware

The NTC is connected as a voltage divider with a 2k2 resistor on pin 2.

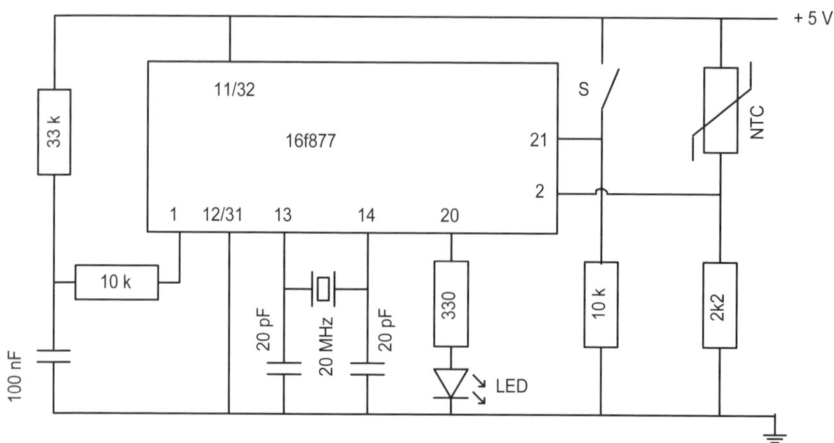

Figure 44. Sampling.

The gray blob on the bottom left side is the NTC thermistor. The blue and green wires are from the Wisp628 programmer. Note that the yellow wire is not connected, so that the programmer can be switched to pass-through without resetting the PIC™. If you want to reprogram the PIC™ you'll need to reconnect the yellow wire (and the white one, which isn't shown on the photograph).

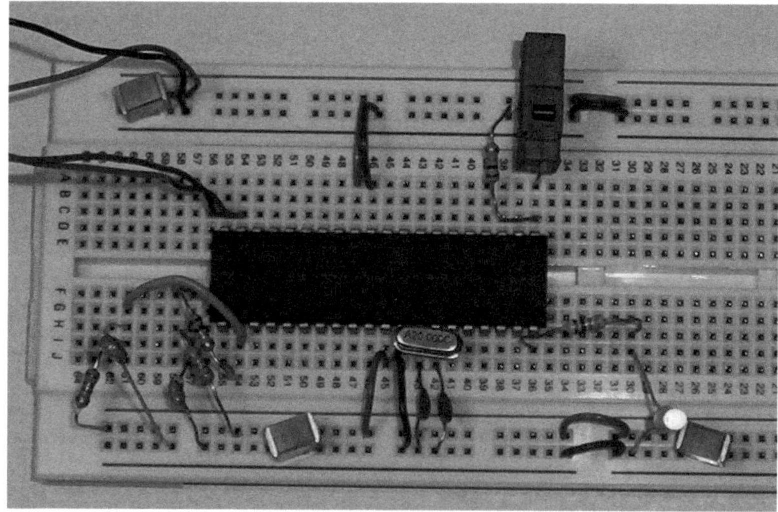

Figure 45. Sampling.

6 RS232 communication

In this chapter we will discuss a few projects that make use of a serial connection between a PIC™ and a PC. Serial connections are ones in which the data are sent one bit at a time. We will be using the standard protocol for short distances called RS232.[52]

On the PC the received data can be processed and used in other applications. This is very convenient for home automation projects where you have multiple modules (PIC™'s) connected to one PC. The settings and measurements of these different modules can then be handled centrally. When the PC is switched off all of the modules will continue working. A simple example of this is the silent alarm in section 6.2.

All of the projects in this book use the pass-through capabilities of the Wisp628 programmer (see section 14.4). This allows you to set up a serial connection with the PIC™ when not in programming mode, without the need for additional hardware. If you use a programmer without this capability you won't be able to do the examples in this book unless you add the hardware discussed in section 6.4.

Project	Description
Serial counter	An example of serial communication between a PIC™ and a PC.
Silent alarm	A silent alarm using a single wire loop through the house.
In-circuit debugging	A great tool to keep PIC™ programs under control and make debugging much easier.
Serial hardware	If you don't want to use the pass-through capabilities of the Wisp628 (or if you simply don't have one) you need this additional hardware.

---

[52] Recommended Standard 232 was originally designed for distances of 15 meters or less.

6 RS232 communication

6.1 Serial counter

The purpose of this project is to set up an RS232 connection to send data from a PIC™ to a PC. To keep it simple the value of a counter is transmitted, but it could be anything.

Technical background

The PIC™ that we use in this project, the 16F877, is equipped with a standard module for RS232 communication (see section 11). We will not be using it however, because it requires pins c6 and c7. Since we want to use the passthrough feature of the Wisp628 programmer it would be much more convenient if the RS232 communications took place over the programming pins b6 and b7. That way we don't need to change any wires.

Since we aren't using the PIC™'s serial module we need to write a program that can emulate the RS232 protocol. Fortunately, this software already exists in the serial_software library, which is part of the standard library, 16F877_bert. By using this library the following commands become available:

Serial_sw_baudrate	Set the baudrate (communication speed) for the RS232 connection.
Serial_sw_invert	Invert the signal.
Serial_sw_write_init	Prepare to send data from the PIC™ over the RS232 connection.
Serial_sw_read_init	Prepare to receive data over the RS232 connection.
Serial_sw_read(data)	Receive data and put into the variable *data*.
Serial_sw_write (data)	Send the contents of the variable *data*.

Let's take a closer look at the settings used in the 16F877_bert.jal library, in case you want to change anything (such as the baud rate).
The library is very flexible and can be used on any pin you want, and at any speed (baud rate). Because the communication has to pass through the programmer the maximum speed is limited. Also, I want to use the same speed for all PIC™'s that I use, even the slower ones. Therefore, we'll use a speed of only 1200 baud, even tough the library itself can handle speeds up to 115.200 baud.

```
const Serial_sw_baudrate = 1200
const Serial_sw_invert  = false
```

Next, the pins need to be defined. During programming b7 is the output and b6 the input, so we need to match that in our pin settings:

```
var volatile bit  Serial_sw_out_pin  is pin_b7
var volatile byte Serial_sw_out_port  is portb
const  Serial_sw_out_nr  = 7
var volatile byte Serial_sw_out_buffer   is _port_b_shadow
var volatile bit  Serial_sw_out_direction is pin_b7_direction
var volatile bit  Serial_sw_in_pin   is pin_b6
var volatile byte Serial_sw_in_port  is portb
const  Serial_sw_in_nr  = 6
var volatile byte Serial_sw_in_buffer  is _port_b_shadow
var volatile bit  Serial_sw_in_direction is pin_b6_direction
```

These are the only settings to be made in the library.

The software

The program consists of a simple loop that increases a counter on each pass, and sends that value to the PC. Since the counter is defined as a byte it will rollover after 255.

```
-- JAL 2.0.4
include 16F877_bert

-- define variables
var byte counter

forever loop

  counter = counter + 1
  serial_sw_write(counter)

end loop
```

The hardware

The circuit is extremely simple since no extra parts are required for using the RS232 pass-through feature of the Wisp628 programmer. This makes it ideal for debugging, as you'll see in section 6.3.

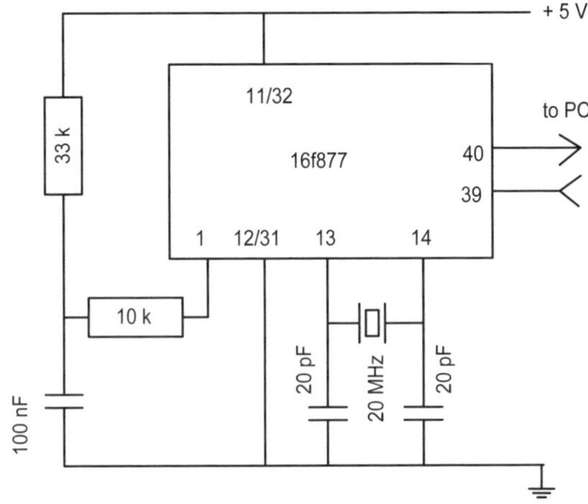

Figure 46. Serial counter.

The long wires on the left hand side on the breadboard are from the programmer, the green and blue wires are used for RS232 communications:

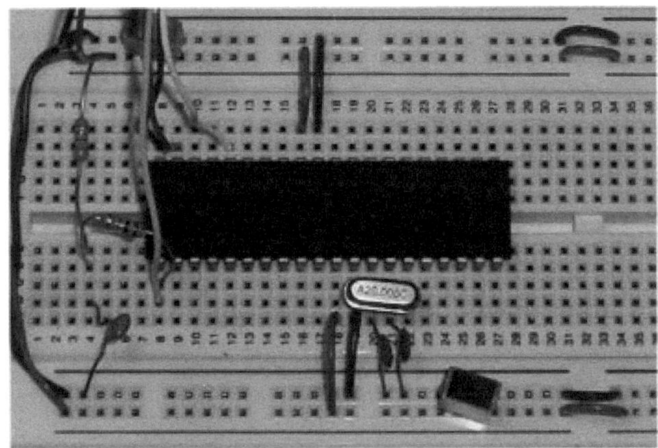

Figure 47. Serial counter on the breadboard.

6.2 Silent alarm

This project is a silent alarm with just a single wire running through the house. The PC is used to display the location of the security breach.

Technical background

The silent alarm is based on measuring the resistance of a loop of wire. At three different locations switches have been installed that open the loop when a door or window is opened. A resistor is mounted across each switch so that if the switch opens the current will have to go through the resistor instead of the switch, thus increasing the resistance of the wire loop. Since all resistors are different a simple resistance measurement of the wire can easily pinpoint which switch (if any) has been opened.

Figure 48. Magnetic switch on a sliding door.

Because the PIC™ can easily measure voltages, the resistors are connected as a voltage divider .

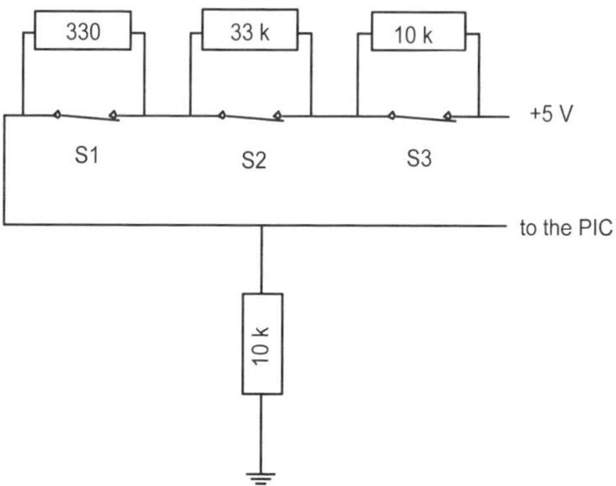

Figure 49. Voltage divider.

If switch S2 is open the voltage divider will consist of 10k to ground and 33k to 5 V. The voltage at the PIC™ pin can be calculated as follows:

$$\frac{10\ k}{33\ k + 10\ k} * 5\ V = 1.14\ V\ (58\ as\ A/D\ signal)$$

A similar calculation can be made for all switches.

Switch	Voltage	Expected A/D value
none	5.00	255
S1	4.84	247
S2	1.14	58
S3	2.50	128

The PIC™ is basically only collecting data "from the field" and relaying it to the PC where the information is displayed. The PIC™ itself only lights an LED in the event of a security breach, to signal that not all of the switches are closed.

```
-- signal broken contact
if resist != 255 then
    pin_d2 = high
else
    pin_d2 = low
end if
```

The PC compares the measured values with the values in the table above. We will do this comparison loosely, by using a range, since the resistors will not be completely accurate and temperature and aging may also affect the resistance. It doesn't have to be too accurate; if 4.5 V is measured it is safe to assume that switch S1 is open.

The software

Apart from lighting an LED when something is wrong, the voltage on pin a0 is measured continuously and sent to the PC:

```
-- JAL 2.0.4
include 16F877_bert

-- define variables
var byte resist

-- define the pins
pin_a0_direction = input
pin_d2_direction = output

pin_d2 = low

forever loop

   -- convert analog on a0 to digital
   resist = ADC_read_low_res(0)

   -- send resistance to PC
   serial_sw_write(resist)
   delay_100ms(1)

   -- signal broken contact
   if resist != 255 then
     pin_d2 = high
   else
     pin_d2 = low
   end if

end loop
```

Of course it would be nice to have a program on the PC to display the measurements. In the download package you'll find a simple program written in Visual Basic (including the source code). It shows a simple map of a living room with two windows and a door. In the middle of the room the alarms are logged. Figure 50 shows a screenshot of the program in action. Window 1 is red (indicating that the switch is open) and the alarm has been logged at 18:45 on September 12th, 2006.[53] If Window 1 is closed again the color will change back to green, but the log will of course remain. If there are a lot of alarms the scroll bar can be used to view the history.

---

[53] American date format is shown in the screenshot.

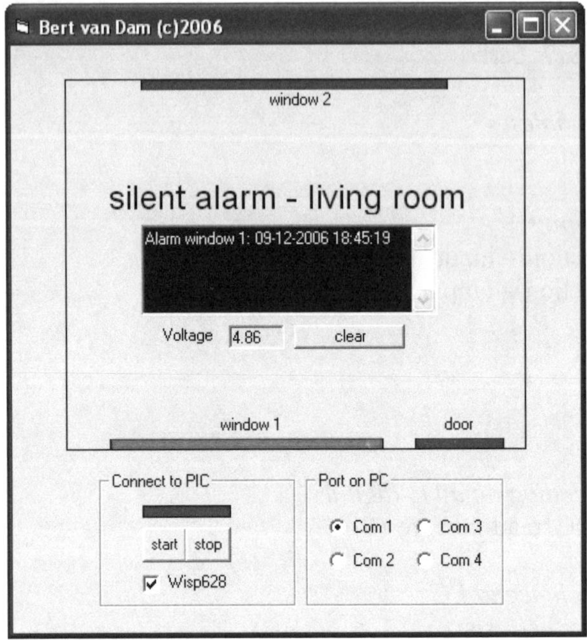

Figure 50. Security breach at Window 1 in the living room.

The hardware

The hardware is located in a central place with a single wire running in a loop around all objects that need to be secured. Switches S1, S2, and S3 could be magnetic door switches, window switches, or even doormat contacts. If you want to secure more objects just expand the loop, or use additional loops. You have, after all, room for seven more loops.

The alarm makes no sound (hence the name "silent alarm"). If you want to make some noise you can replace the LED with a buzzer or siren. Section 12.7 explains how high-power parts like that can be connected to a PIC^{TM}. If the siren can be heard outside local law may require that you restrict the amount of time that the alarm sounds.

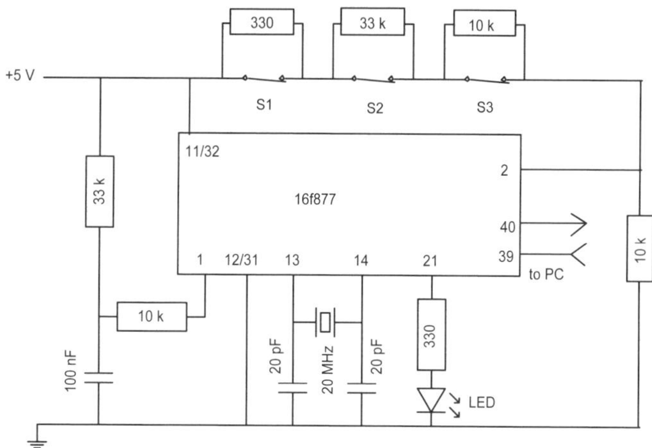

Figure 51. Silent alarm with a single wire loop.

The breadboard shows an example with three switches mounted on the breadboard. The LED is on, because the voltage on pin 1 dropped below 5 volts due to one of the switches opening.

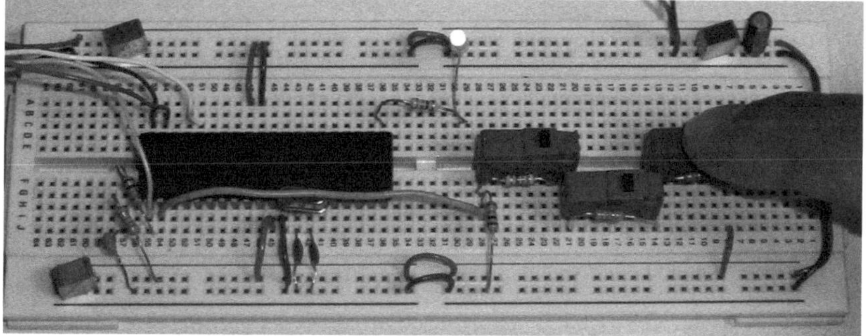

Figure 52. Silent alarm in action.

6.3 In-circuit debugging

Debugging refers to locating bugs in a program (and preferably solving them). We are not talking about syntax errors - JALedit will catch those for you - but logical errors. This means the program works, but doesn't do what you want it to do. There are several different methods that can be used to locate these errors. Which one is most appropriate depends on your needs and the project you are working on.

Debugging Method	When to use
Switch on an LED.	The program gets stuck at a certain location, gets stuck in a loop, or never seems to reach a particular part of the program. You have a free pin available to connect an LED.

At a certain place in the program you insert a command to switch on an LED. If the LED turns on it means that this part of the program has actually run. By moving the command to different locations in the program you can determine where the program gets stuck.

Start at the beginning of the program, by defining the LED and switching it off:

```
pin_d3_direction = Output
pin_d3 = low
```

And at a well-chosen location you switch it on:

```
pin_d3 = high
```

Then, if the LED doesn't light up the error is in the part of the program before this command.

Debugging Method	When to use
serial_sw_write() to display processing flags.	The program gets stuck at a certain location, gets stuck in a loop, or never seems to reach a particular part of the program. You can setup an RS232 connection.

Here, instead of an LED, you insert a command to send a number over a serial connection. On the terminal program on the PC you can see which numbers are sent, and that way keep track of the progress of the program in the microcontroller. For example:

```
serial_sw_write(1)[54]
[ other commands ]
serial_sw_write(2)
```

---

[54] In MICterm use "raw" as the display type so that you'll actually get to see the number. If you use another terminal program you'll need to start counting at 48, the ASCII value of the character "1".

If the PC receives a 1, but not a 2, you'll know the program gets stuck somewhere in between.

Debugging Method	**When to use**
serial_sw_write() to return processing results.	The program runs, but gives the wrong results. You can setup an RS232 connection.

If your program runs but simply gives the wrong results you can send intermediate results of calculations or measurements to the PC for evaluation. If you use MICterm as a terminal program you can graph the data, or even display the values as binary.

Suppose your program needs to do something based on a measurement with the A/D module on AN0. You could use the following loop to determine if this particular value actually occurs:

```
forever loop
    resist = ADC_read_low_res(0)
    serial_sw_write(resist)
end loop
```

Debugging Method	**When to use**
data_eeprom_write(Address,Data) to store processing flags.	The program gets stuck at a certain location, gets stuck in a loop, or never seems to reach a particular part of the program. You can't use an RS232 connection.

If you can't use an RS232 connection (perhaps the program uses the connection for other purposes) an alternative would be to put the debug data in EEPROM. If you erase EEPROM at the start of the program and write numbers to it as the program progresses you can stop the program after it has run for a while and use HEXview to see which numbers have been written.

At the start of the program you write zeros to the part of EEPROM you intend to use, such as addresses 0, 1, and 2:

```
Data_eeprom_write (0,0)
Data_eeprom_write (1,0)
Data_eeprom_write (2,0)
```

At certain points in your program you write the flags to EEPROM:

```
Data_eeprom_write (0,1)
[ other commands ]
Data_eeprom_write (1,1)
[ other commands ]
Data_eeprom_write (2,1)
```

After a while you can use HEXview to look at the EEPROM memory (see section 10.3 for a detailed explanation of how to do this). In our example, if you find the numbers 1,1,0 it means the program got stuck after the second *Data_eeprom_write* command.

EEPROM memory is retained even after the power is switched off.[55] So don't forget to fill the memory with zeros at the start of your program, or you may be looking at data from a previous run.

Debugging Method	**When to use**
Data_eeprom_write (Address,Data) to store processing results.	The program runs, but give the wrong results, and you can't use an RS232 connection.

If your program runs but simply gives the wrong results you can store intermediate results of calculations or measurements in EEPROM. A disadvantage is that you have to stop the program to look at EEPROM memory, and then restart it.

If, for example, your program needs to do something based on a measurement with the A/D module on AN0 you could use the following loop to determine if this particular value actually occurs[56]:

```
forever loop
    resist = ADC_read_low_res(0)
    Data_eeprom_write (0, resist)
end loop
```

Stop the program at the moment that the correct measurement should have been reached and check with HEXview to see if this is indeed the case, which means that the correct value is at address 0.

---

[55] Reprogramming also erases EEPROM memory.
[56] See section 10.3.

Debugging Method	**When to use**
Check register value and change on the fly.	You are not certain of the correct register settings, or would like to try different settings.

In several programs you will be using registers. These are special memory locations that control the behavior of the PIC™. In Chapter 7 this will be discussed in detail.

If your program runs but you suspect you get the wrong results because of incorrect register settings you can use REGedit to check the contents of these registers and change them on the fly from your PC while the PIC™ is still running. This is a handy tool! You can, for example, change interrupt frequencies, change pulse width modulation (PWM) settings, or change pins from analog to digital.

The explanation of this program, along with examples of its use, can be found at the end of section 12.1.

Debugging Method	**When to use**
Use a simulator[57]	In situations where you don't use many parts, and especially no unusual parts.

An alternative is to run the program in a simulator. This will give you a quick insight into all internal variables so that you can easily see what went wrong. This method has two major disadvantages that have caused me to stop using it:

1. It is not always clear if the program doesn't work because of a logical error (which is something the simulator could find). It may very well be that the program waits for a condition that you expect to happen, but in real life simply never takes place. For example, you measure the analog value on AN0, and switch on a LED if this value is larger than 200. If this value cannot be that large (perhaps you're using a voltage divider that limits the maximum value to 127) your program "doesn't work" in real life but it will work just fine in the simulator.

2. If the program doesn't work in the simulator it is not always clear whether this is because the program doesn't work or the simulator needs to be set up differently. Auxiliary parts such as LEDs and switches can cause problems. It is questionable whether setting up and checking the simulator is more time consuming than simply trying the program in real life and using other ways of debugging.

---

[57] There are several JAL simulators available such as JALss (a new Python based version is being worked on) and PICshell. Alternatively, you can use MPLAB® from Microchip; you'll just need to compile the program first and use the .asm file in the simulator.

Debugging Method	When to use
Multiple serial_sw_write() commands at one place.	The program runs, but gives the wrong results. The results depend on multiple variables, and you can setup an RS232 connection to a PC.

It tends to get complicated when your program doesn't work like it should, and is dependent on multiple variables. When you send them all to the PC the terminal program will not be able to group them together and will therefore simply display them all in one long list. In this project a method is discussed to display multiple values at the same time, and even control the speed of the PIC™ from your PC so you get enough time to evaluate the results.

Technical background

It is not very complicated to send data from a PIC™ to the PC. To get the value from the variable *demo* onto the PC it's just a matter of switching the programmer to pass-through mode[58] and using this command:

Serial_sw_write(demo)

The beauty is that it is possible to stop the PIC™ until it gets a signal back from the PC. Once the PIC™ encounters the *Serial_sw_read* command AND there is an actual open RS232 connection the program will simply wait to receive the signal.

The software

As a demonstration we will use the program of section 5.1, the variable speed flashing light.

The command

Serial_sw_read (dummy)

is added in order to wait for the PC. Note that the actual value received from the PC is not used for anything, hence the name *dummy*.

Also added is a command to send data to the PC that appears interesting, in this case that might be the value of the A/D conversion of pin a5 and the situation of the LED on pin

---

[58] This technique can also be used if you do not use the Wisp628 programmer. In that case you need to use the method from Chapter 11 to set up a separate serial connection to the PC.

d0. In the program, the LED is always on when the resistance is measured, which would be a bit boring from a debugging point of view, so we will change this:

```
-- and flash
delay_1ms(resist)
pin_d0 = low
delay_1ms(resist)
pin_d0 = high
```

to this:

```
-- and flash
delay_1ms(resist)
pin_d0 = ! pin_d0
```

This changes the status of the LED at each loop, because it is flipped by the NOT operator. So *on* becomes *off* and *off* becomes *on*.[59]

This is the completed program:

```
-- JAL 2.0.4
include 16F877_bert

-- define the pins
pin_a5_direction = input
pin_d0_direction = output

-- general variable
var byte resist, dummy

forever loop

  -- take a sample
  resist = ADC_read_low_res(3)
  Serial_sw_read(dummy)
  serial_sw_write(resist)
  serial_sw_write(pin_d0)
  -- convert to a suitable range
  resist = (resist / 2 ) + 30
```

---

[59] The use of pin_d0 = !pin_d0 is elegant, but has its drawbacks. See section 4.2 for an explanation.

> *-- and flash*
> delay_1ms(resist)
> pin_d0 = ! pin_d0
>
> end loop

When the program is downloaded to the PIC™ it will run as it normally would. The LED will flash and you can control the speed with the variable resistor. This is because an RS232 connection has not been enabled, so there is nothing to wait for. But as soon as the PC program sets up an RS232 connection the PIC™ program will immediately stop at the *Serial_sw_read* command. When the Visual Basic program sends something, anything, the PIC™ program will resume until it encounters the *Serial_sw_read* command again. This way the PC can control the speed of the PIC™. On the PC, a Visual Basic program collects the data sent by the PIC™ and displays it on the screen.

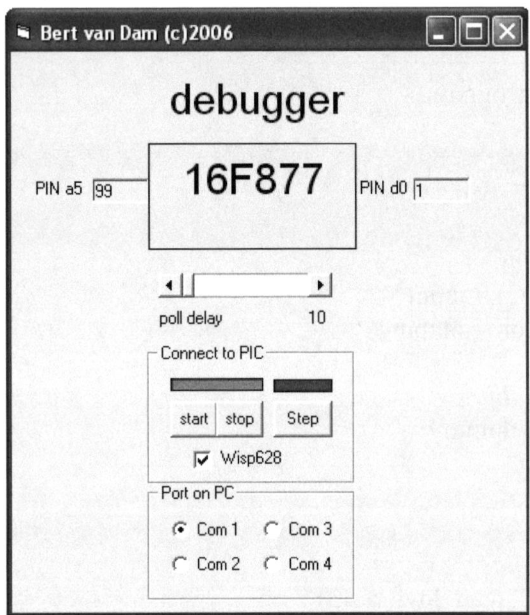

Figure 53. Debugger controlled by the PC.

Debugger operation:

Start	Send a trigger signal to the PIC™ and collect data. How often the trigger is sent (and thus how fast the PIC™ runs) is determined by the "poll delay" control.
Stop	Stop the communication (and therefore the PIC™).
Step	Send a single trigger signal to the PIC™, resulting in a single loop through the program.
Poll delay	Control the speed at which the program in the PIC™ receives trigger signals.

The hardware

The hardware is identical to the project in section 5.1. Just remember that this very helpful debugging method can be used with any program, in any setting, as long as you have a live connection to a PC.

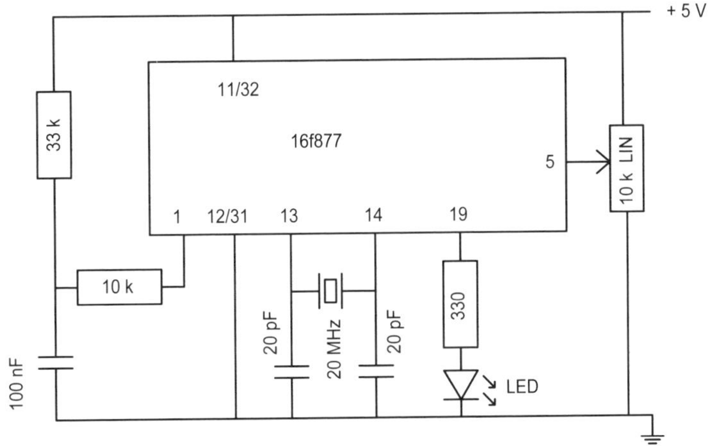

Figure 54. Variable speed flashing light.

The circuit on the breadboard:

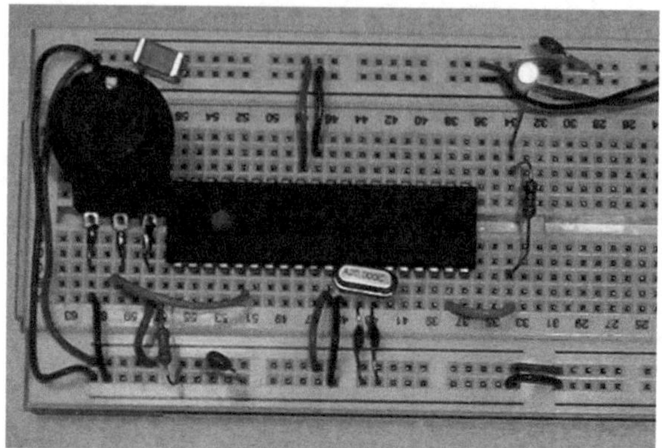

Figure 55. Variable speed flashing light.

You'll need to modify the program on the PC for each PIC™ program you want to debug, but using Visual Basic to add a few pins to the display is very easy. By showing all relevant data on the screen you can study the behavior of your PIC™ program at your leisure. The source code for the Visual Basic 5.0 program is included in the download package. Check out section 14.4.2 if you need help using the communication module in Visual Basic.

6.4 Serial hardware

If you use the Wisp68 programmer you can use the pass-through function to make an RS232 connection between the PC and the PIC™. The required hardware is built into the programmer, so you don't need anything else.

But there can be a number of reasons for you to make an additional connection with separate hardware:

1. You don't have a Wisp628 programmer. You may have opted for another programmer, or a bootloader[60].
2. You have built the project on a circuit board in a box and want to have an RS232 connection without having to use the programmer.
3. You want to use pins c6/c7 for a hardware RS232 connection to a PC.[61]
4. You want to communicate with multiple PCs from just one PIC™.

---

[60] See section 12.9 for more information on bootloaders.
[61] See section 11.1 for more information on using the hardware serial capabilities of the 16F877.

Technical background

It is not possible to generate a true RS232 signal with a PIC™. According to the protocol, a "0" is represented by a signal between +3 V and +12 V, and a "1" by a signal between -3 V and -12 V. Negative voltages are, of course, impossible for a PIC™.

In reality, many (but not all) PCs have a rather relaxed implementation of this protocol. On the Internet you will find many schematics that use just a few simple parts to create the connection between PIC™ and PC. Apart from their low price and simplicity all have one thing in common: they work on some PCs, but not on others.

We won't bother ourselves with this and instead opt for a robust solution that works according to the official protocol. And it only costs just a few dollars in parts.

The chip we will use is the MAX202E by Dallas Semiconductors.[62] This is the pin layout:

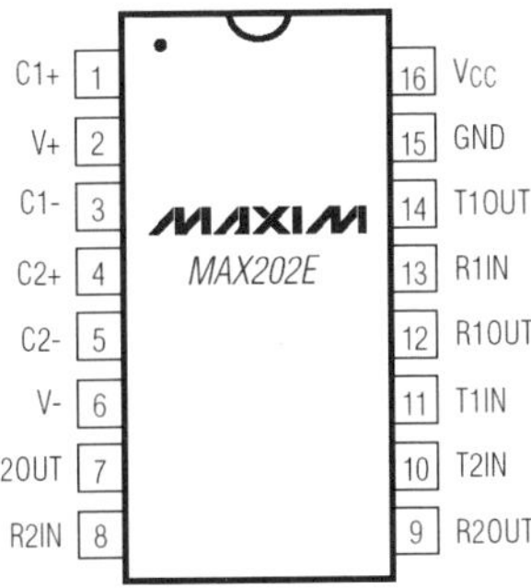

Figure 56. Pin layout of the MAX202.

---

[62]More information and the datasheet of this chip can be found on their website, http://www.maxim-ic.com.

The function of these pins is as follows:

Pin	Description
1 thru 6	Connections for capacitors
7, 14	RS232 output
8,13	RS232 input
9,12	Output to PIC
10,11	Input from PIC
15	Ground (0 V)
16	Vdd (+5 V)

This gives you the ability to set up two RS232 connections with just one MAX202. In total five capacitors are needed to generate the +10 V and -10 V for the signals.

In some applications the signal is inverted, which means the "0" and "1" are switched. The MAX202 uses such an inverted signal, but the Wisp programmer doesn't. If you want to use the MAX202 instead of the Wisp pass-through you'll need to make a modification to the 16F877_bert library. The best way to do it is to follow these steps:

1. Copy the 16F877_bert.jal library from the library directory [63] on your hard disk to the directory where you keep the files that belong to this project, such as the JAL source[64].
2. Start JALedit and open the library (File – Open…)
3. Search for the command *const Serial_sw_invert = false*. Change the word *false* to *true*, so that the command looks like this: *const Serial_sw_invert = true*.
4. Save the file (Ctrl-S).

When the JAL compiler searches for included libraries it first checks the directory containing the JAL program. Here it would find the modified library. If the library is not found it then checks the library directory. A library that is stored with the JAL program is called the "local copy". You can change these local copies to your liking and it won't have any effect on the other programs on your computer (because the library in the library directory is not changed).

---

[63] If you have installed the software package according to the instructions your library directory is c:\picdev\jal\libraries.

[64] This is the directory where you store your PIC™ program.

You can now transfer RS232 data with any communications package on the PC, because you don't need to use the pass-through option. If you use MICterm you can remove the checkmark for "W*isp 628"*.

The software

To demonstrate that the hardware works this program is used to send the position of a variable resistor to the PC:

```
-- JAL 2.0.6
include 16F877_bert

-- define variables
var byte resist

-- define the pins
pin_a0_direction = input

forever loop

    -- convert analog on a0 to digital
    resist = ADC_read_low_res(0)

    -- send resistance to PC
    serial_sw_write(resist)
    delay_100ms(1)

end loop
```

Remember to make the changes to the library as discussed in the technical background.

The hardware

The value of the capacitors for the MAX202E is not critical. The manufacturer recommends a minimum of 0.1 uF and a maximum of 10 uF. The capacitor across the power supply pins should be at least the same capacity as the other four. This is to take care of noise on the power line, which could interfere with the proper operation of the PIC^{TM}.[65] In this project 1 uF capacitors rated at 25 V are used. The positive and negative

---

[65] The MAX202E has to increase the voltage from 5 volts to 10 volts. The mechanism used to do this, a charge pump, can easily cause nasty spikes on the power line. The capacitor prevents this. If

leads of the capacitors on pins 2 and 6 are displayed correctly in the schematic; they have to be mounted in reverse.

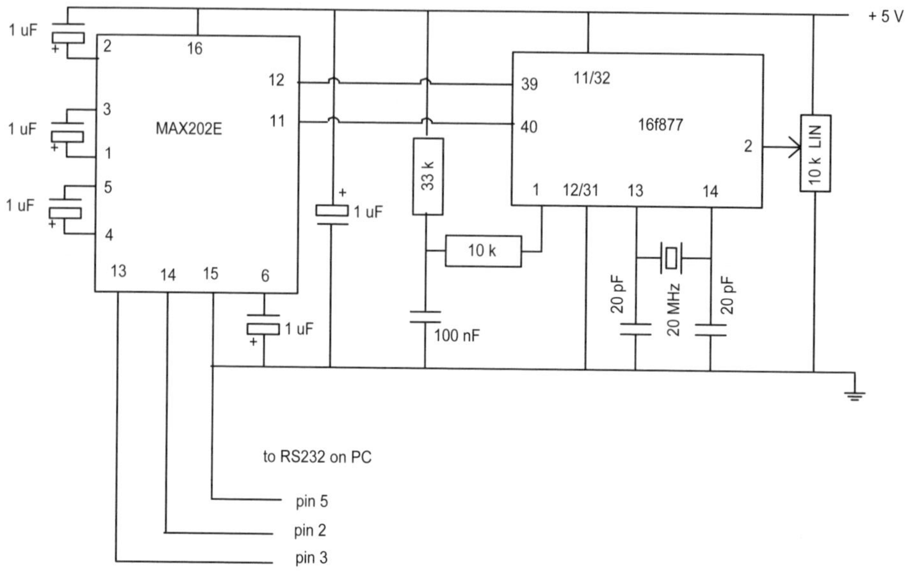

Figure 57. Connection of the MAX202.

On the PC side you only need to connect three wires. The numbers in the schematic refer to the pins on the (female) plug that you need to use. You will find these numbers on the inside of the plug.

you build this project on a circuit board don't forget the small capacitors in the power line close to the PIC^{TM}.

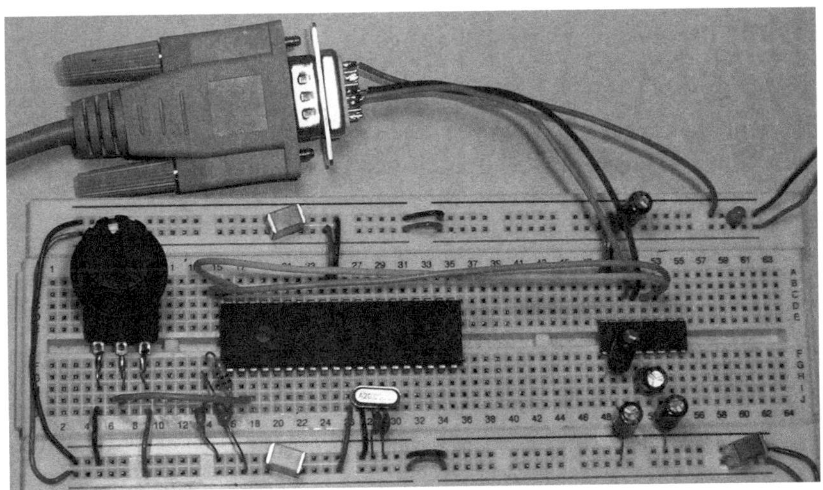

Figure 58. MAX202 (right hand side).

If you need the MAX202 often (for example because you don't have a Wisp628) I would recommend you build this on a circuit board. Building it on the breadboard every time you need it can get boring real quick.

You only get strange characters on the PC

This means you forgot to modify the library as discussed in the technical background section.

7 Electric motor

This chapter contains projects that use an electric motor. The specific problems that you will encounter when using electric motors, such as different supply voltage, high power requirements, and speed control, are all discussed.

Project	Description
Electric motor control	Basic control of a small 9 V electric motor.
Pulse Width Modulation	Control the speed of a small 9 V motor.
Constant motor speed through feedback	Maintain an electric motor at a constant speed, even when the load on the motor varies.
Tachometer	Create a tachometer using the PIC™'s TIMER1 interrupt.

7.1 Electric motor control

The purpose of this project is to demonstrate basic control of a small 9 V electric motor from a PIC™.

Technical background

The motor used in this project is the 71427[66] by the Lego Company, but in principle you could use any small electric motor. This particular motor operates at 9 V and consumes too much power to connect it directly to a PIC™.[67] One solution is to use the TC4427A MOSFET driver IC from Microchip.[68]

---

[66] Technical data: max. 360 rpm, 3.5 mA power consumption without load, 360 mA stalled power consumption and 6 Ncm stalled torque, according to measurements made by Philippe (Philo) Hurbain: http://www.philohome.com.

[67] The PIC™ can deliver 25 mA per pin, with a maximum of 200 mA per port.

[68] Download the datasheet TC4426A-27A-28A from http://www.microchip.com.

It has the following specifications:

Peak output current	1.5 A
Voltage	4.5 - 18 V
Delay	30 ns
Reverse current	max. 500 mA

This chip is a MOSFET driver, but the specs are more than enough for our motor so we don't even need the MOSFETs themselves. The high allowable reverse current means we don't need diodes to protect the chip.

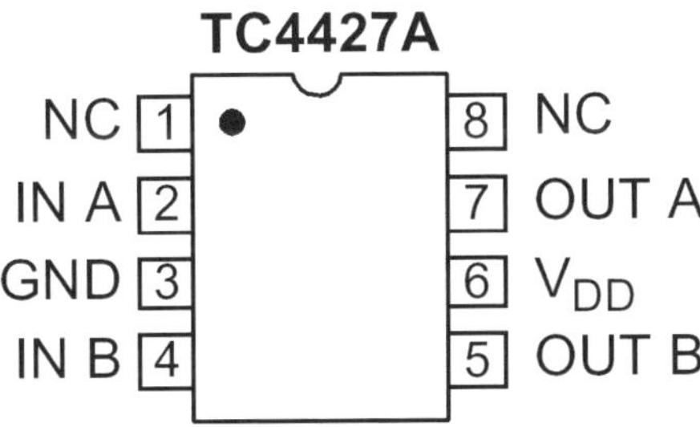

Figure 59. Pin layout of the TC4427A.

From the pin layout you can see that pin 2 (*IN A*) connects to pin 7 (*OUT A*). Since pin 2 is connected to the PIC™ it will switch between 0 V and 5 V. The voltage at pin 7 depends on the power supply voltage of the TC4427 (*Vdd*, pin 6). The maximum is 18 V, so once pin 2 has been made high pin 7 will be at 18 V.

The same applies to pins 4 and 5. Pin 3 (*GND*) is connected to the ground (0 V) of the power supply. Note that when you run the TC4427 on a voltage different than your microcontroller the ground leads of both power supplies must be connected. Pins 1 and 8 are not in use (NC = not connected). So at least the following pins need to be connected:

Pin	Name	Description
3	GND	Connect to the ground (0 V) of the power supply. Note that when you run the TC4427 on a different voltage than your microcontroller the ground leads of both power supplies <u>must</u> be connected to each other.
6	V$_{DD}$	Motor power supply (4.5 to 18 V)

7 Electric motor

The software

The control of a motor has basically three functions: stop, forward and reverse. We will use a variable resistor to do the controlling:

Resistance	LED1	LED2	Action
< 50	0	0	stop
50 - 150	1	0	forward
150 - 200	0	1	reverse
> 200	1	1	stop

When both contacts of the motor driver chip carry the same signal the motor is stopped and braked. This means rotating it manually takes effort. Coast (stopped without braking) would be a fourth motor option, but is not possible with this setup.

After the definition of the pins and variables the program starts by measuring the resistance[69]:

```
-- take a sample of pin a0 (analog 0)
resist = ADC_read_low_res(0)
```

Nested *if...then...else* statements determine which action is to be taken based on the resistance measured:

```
if resist < 50 then
    LED0 = low
    LED1 = low
else if
    resist > 200 then
     LED0 = high
     LED1 = high
   else if
      resist < 150 then
       LED0 = high
       LED1 = low
     else
        LED0 = low
        LED1 = high
```

---

[69] See Chapter 5 for more information on this subject.

```
      end if
    end if
  end if
```

Since both LEDs are connected to the same pins as the TC4427, switching on the LEDs also switches on the motor.

Not required, but fun anyway, is to send the data to the PC over an RS232 connection using the programmer pass-through (see Chapter 6):

```
-- and send to PC
serial_sw_write(resist)
serial_sw_write(LED0)
serial_sw_write(LED1)
```

You can use the Visual Basic debugger software from section 6.3; just remember to add the relevant pins.

Putting it all together yields this program:

```
-- JAL 2.0.4
include 16F877_bert

-- define the pins
pin_a0_direction = input
pin_c4_direction = output
pin_c5_direction = output

-- general variable
var byte resist

var bit LED0 is pin_c4
var bit LED1 is pin_c5

forever loop

  -- take a sample of pin a0 (analog 0)
  resist = ADC_read_low_res(0)

  if resist < 50 then
    LED0 = low
    LED1 = low
```

```
        else if
           resist > 200 then
              LED0 = high
              LED1 = high
           else if
              resist < 150 then
                 LED0 = high
                 LED1 = low
              else
                 LED0 = low
                 LED1 = high
           end if
         end if
      end if

      -- and send to PC
      serial_sw_write(resist)
      serial_sw_write(LED0)
      serial_sw_write(LED1)

      -- give the computer time to react
      delay_100ms(1)

   end loop
```

The hardware

Since the TC4427A has to drive the 9 V electric motor, it has to be connected to a 9 V power supply. We will get the 5 V power supply for PIC™ and the other parts of the project from the same supply, using a UA7805 with a 0.1 uF stabilizing capacitor.

The motor can be directly connected to the MOSFET driver IC, along with a small 0.1 uF noise reduction capacitor across the motor leads.[70]

---

[70] The Lego motor has an internal PTC to protect it against overheating. So an overheating motor will run slower.

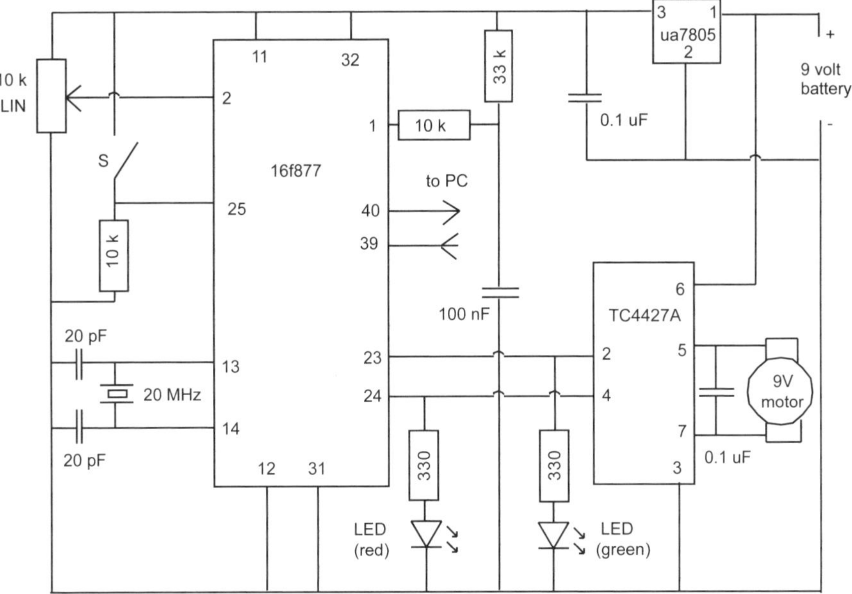

Figure 60. Connecting an electric motor to a PIC™.

The next figure shows the circuit on the breadboard. The top power rail is 9 volts and the bottom power rail is 5 volts. Conversion between the rails is handled by the UA7805 on the right hand side. The long wires on the left side belong to the programmer and are used to send data to the PC.

Figure 61. Connecting an electric motor to a PIC™.

The power supply wires are soldered to the inside of the Lego battery box to prevent accidental power reversal when engaging battery power.

7 Electric motor

Upon closer inspection you may notice a diode in the ground lead between the 9 V and 5 V rail. This turned out to have no useful contribution so it has been left out in later projects. In the schematic, the diode is not shown and you do not need to use it.

7.2 Pulse Width Modulation control of an electric motor

The purpose of this project is to control the speed of a small 9 V electric motor between 0 and 100%. In order to supply the power and higher voltage a TC4427A MOSFET motor driver chip will be used.

Technical background

The simplest way to control the speed of an electric motor would be to vary the voltage between 0 and 9 volts. Unfortunately this doesn't work. First of all, the motor needs a minimum voltage to get started, so it will immediately go from off to fast. Secondly, the torque at low speeds is extremely low. The solution is to keep the voltage constant at 9 volts - which eliminates starting problems - and simply switch the power on and off. If you do that quickly enough the motor will run very smoothly, even at low revolutions.

Two different methods can be used:

1. Increase the on-off pulses to make the motor go faster. The length of the pulses remains the same, but the frequency increases. This is technically the simplest solution, but smooth low-speed operation is difficult to attain.
2. Keep the number of pulses constant, but vary the duration of the pulse. This is technically more difficult, but produces much better results.

We will use method 2, which is called Pulse Width Modulation (PWM). The next figure shows how PWM works. In the top graph the width of the pulses is 10% of the period (the time between the start of two consecutive pulses). This is called the duty cycle, and is the part of the period where power is actually delivered.

In the middle graph the duty cycle is 50%. The bottom graph shows 100%. The latter, of course, means that the power is always on and the motor runs at full speed.

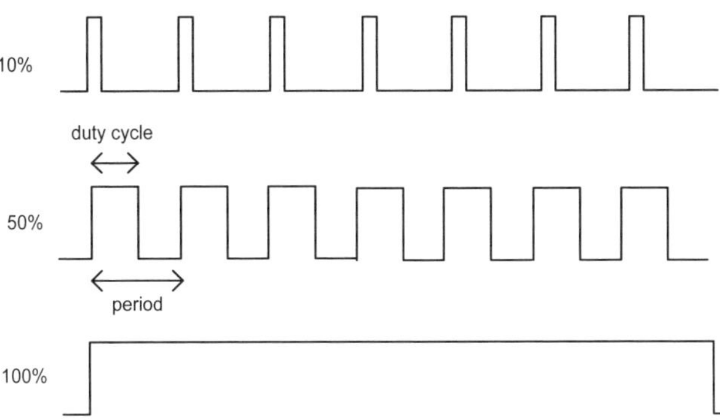

Figure 62. PWM duty cycles.

The PIC™ 16F877 is equipped with two Pulse Width Modulation modules, which are connected to pins c1 and c2. Note that module 1 is connected to pin c2 and module 2 is connected to pin c1. Once connected, the only thing that needs to be done is to initialize the PWM modules and apply the proper values to them.

For standard values the 16F877_bert library can be used, since it contains the pwm_hardware library. However, we may need to use different settings for other projects (PWM has many uses), so we will set the PWM module manually here as a learning experience.

Since all of the variables we are using are 8 bits (max. value 255) it would be convenient if we could use this directly in the PWM module. That would mean we get 256 different speeds (stopped is also a speed), which would appear to be enough.

The PWM module can handle 10-bit speed control, with the two lowest bits being in a different register (CCP1CON). So if we want to use 8-bit speeds we need to split the speed up and spread it over two registers with two bits in CCP1CON and the remaining 6 bits in CCPR1L. That would be rather inconvenient, and the question is how useful would it be?

Let's assume we simply ignore the two lowest bits and just set them to 0. This would mean that any value less than 4 couldn't be selected. A value of 4 would be a duty cycle of 1.6%. This is such a small value that it would be no problem to "jump" right from 0% to 1.6% as the first step.

So if we ignore the lowest two bits we can use the 10-bit setting after all. The lowest two bits in CCP1CON can be set to 0, and the highest 8 bits in CCPR1L will be used for the speed. Looking at the datasheet, the table shows that the highest frequency at 10-bit resolution is 19.53 kHz.

7 Electric motor

TABLE 8-3:   EXAMPLE PWM FREQUENCIES AND RESOLUTIONS AT 20 MHz

PWM Frequency	1.22 kHz	4.88 kHz	19.53 kHz	78.12kHz	156.3 kHz	208.3 kHz
Timer Prescaler (1, 4, 16)	16	4	1	1	1	1
PR2 Value	0xFFh	0xFFh	0xFFh	0x3Fh	0x1Fh	0x17h
Maximum Resolution (bits)	10	10	10	8	7	5.5

Figure 63. PWM frequencies.

This can easily be verified. According to the datasheet the PWM period can be calculated with the following formula:

$$(PR2 + 1) * 4 * Tosc * TMR2prescaler$$

where:

PR2 = FF = 255
Tosc = 1 / 20 MHz = 50 ns
TMR2prescaler = 1

So the period is 0.0000512, which is a frequency of 19.531 kHz.

This frequency is a bit high for a PWM application, but in this case it works like a charm and the electric motor (a Lego motor type 71427 [71]) runs exceptionally smooth. Should your motor not run smoothly or make a lot of noise it is best to reduce the frequency. This is not a problem, because at 10-bit resolution 4.88 kHz and 1.22 kHz are also available.

To get our frequency of 19.53 kHz the TIMER2 prescaler must be set to 1 and PR2 must be set to 0xFFh. PR2 is the TIMER2 period register; the timer will count up to this number and then start at 0 again. It can be assigned like this:

    PR2 = 0xFF

The clock signal is divided by the prescaler and results in a longer period, since it will now take longer before the preset value is reached. The prescaler is hidden in the T2CON register:

---

[71] Technical data: max. 360 rpm, 3.5 mA power consumption without load, 360 mA stalled power consumption and 6 Ncm stalled torque according to measurements made by Philippe (Philo) Hurbain: http://www.philohome.com.

T2CON: TIMER2 CONTROL REGISTER (ADDRESS 12h)

U-0	R/W-0	R/W-0	R/W-0	R/W-0	R/W-0	R/W-0	R/W-0
—	TOUTPS3	TOUTPS2	TOUTPS1	TOUTPS0	TMR2ON	T2CKPS1	T2CKPS0

bit 7   bit 0

bit 7   **Unimplemented:** Read as '0'

bit 6-3   **TOUTPS3:TOUTPS0**: Timer2 Output Postscale Select bits
0000 = 1:1 Postscale
0001 = 1:2 Postscale
0010 = 1:3 Postscale
•
•
•
1111 = 1:16 Postscale

bit 2   **TMR2ON**: Timer2 On bit
1 = Timer2 is on
0 = Timer2 is off

bit 1-0   **T2CKPS1:T2CKPS0**: Timer2 Clock Prescale Select bits
00 = Prescaler is 1
01 = Prescaler is 4
1x = Prescaler is 16

Figure 64. T2CON Register.

To set the prescaler to a value of 1 bits 0 and 1 of T2CON must be set to 0. This is, of course, only useful if the timer is actually switched on, so bit 2 must be set to 1. The postscaler is not needed, so these bits will remain 0. The result is:

T2CON = 0b000_0100

The only thing we need to do now is send the signal to pin c2 (CCP1). This pin has many functions, as can be seen in figure 65. To put it into PWM mode bits 2 and 3 of CCP1CON must be set to 1 (the other bits are irrelevant).

Since we opted not to use the two lowest bits of resolution we need to set them to 0. Otherwise, we won't be able to stop the motor (bits 4 and 5 of CCP1CON).

CCP1CON = 0x0F

CCP1CON REGISTER/CCP2CON REGISTER (ADDRESS: 17h/1Dh)

U-0	U-0	R/W-0	R/W-0	R/W-0	R/W-0	R/W-0	R/W-0
—	—	CCPxX	CCPxY	CCPxM3	CCPxM2	CCPxM1	CCPxM0

bit 7   bit 0

bit 7-6   **Unimplemented:** Read as '0'

bit 5-4   **CCPxX:CCPxY**: PWM Least Significant bits

<u>Capture mode</u>:
Unused

<u>Compare mode</u>:
Unused

<u>PWM mode</u>:
These bits are the two LSbs of the PWM duty cycle. The eight MSbs are found in CCPRxL.

bit 3-0   **CCPxM3:CCPxM0**: CCPx Mode Select bits

0000 = Capture/Compare/PWM disabled (resets CCPx module)
0100 = Capture mode, every falling edge
0101 = Capture mode, every rising edge
0110 = Capture mode, every 4th rising edge
0111 = Capture mode, every 16th rising edge
1000 = Compare mode, set output on match (CCPxIF bit is set)
1001 = Compare mode, clear output on match (CCPxIF bit is set)
1010 = Compare mode, generate software interrupt on match (CCPxIF bit is set, CCPx pin is unaffected)
1011 = Compare mode, trigger special event (CCPxIF bit is set, CCPx pin is unaffected); CCP1 resets TMR1; CCP2 resets TMR1 and starts an A/D conversion (if A/D module is enabled)
11xx = PWM mode

Figure 65. CCP1CON register.

Putting the settings together we have:

```
PR2 = 0xFF
T2CON = 0b000_0100
CCP1CON = 0x0F
```

And obviously the pin must be defined as an output.

```
pin_c2_direction = output        -- actual PWM output pin
```

Because we use JAL we can accomplish the same thing using simple JAL statements, even though you do need knowledge of the datasheet in order to know what to enter.

The relevant commands are:

const pwm_frequency = number	This sets the PWM frequency. You can only chose the frequencies listed in the datasheet and as you have seen this has consequences for the available resolution.
const pwm1_dutycycle = number1 const pwm2_dutycycle = number2	If you use frequency modulation (FM) instead of PWM this is where you set the desired duty cycle. In later sections we will see that this is a fun way to make sounds.
PWM_init_frequency (boolean, boolean)	Engage the PWM modules.
PWM_set_dutycycle (var, var)	Set the duty cycle. When using PWM this is the variable that controls the power output (if an electric motor is used this controls the speed).

The software

We are using a variable resistor to control the speed of the motor. Since we have opted for 8-bit resolution the duty cycle for the motor can be copied directly from the measurement of the A/D converter. Notice that variable *resist* needs to be defined as a byte to hold the 8-bit value:

```
-- convert analog on a0 to digital
resist = ADC_read_low_res(0)

-- set actual PWM duty cycle
PWM_set_dutycycle (resist, resist)
```

The PIC™ cannot deliver enough power to directly drive any kind of motor. Our motor also needs 9 volts, which the PIC™ is unable to provide. For these reasons a TC4427 MOSFET motor driver chip is used, just like in the previous project.

The motor driver chip has two inputs. One will be used for the speed (this is where the PWM signal will be fed into) and the other is for the rotation direction. Unfortunately, if you switch direction you also switch speed. If the duty cycle is 20% with the motor running forward, then changing the direction to reverse will change the duty cycle to 80% (this is due to the inner workings of the TC4427, the 16F877 of course doesn't change). So whenever the direction is reversed the duty cycle also needs to be "reversed". We do this by simply "reversing" the measured resistance.

```
-- if the switch is pressed reverse direction
if pin_c7 == high then
    pin_c4 = high
    -- and reverse reading to maintain speed
    resist = 255 - resist
else
    pin_c4 = low
end if
```

Putting this all together yields this program:

```
-- JAL 2.0.4
include 16F877_bert

-- define variables
var byte resist

-- define the pins
pin_a0_direction = input      -- variable resistor (speed)
pin_c7_direction = input      -- forward/reverse switch

-- enable pulse width modulation
PWM_init_frequency (true, true)

pin_c4_direction = output
var bit direction1 is pin_c4 = true

forever loop

        -- convert analog on a0 to digital
        resist = ADC_read_low_res(0)

        -- send resistance to PC
        serial_sw_write(resist)
        delay_100ms(1)
```

-- if the switch is pressed reverse direction
if pin_c7 == high then
      pin_c4 = high
      -- and reverse reading to maintain speed
      resist = 255 - resist
   else
      pin_c4 = low
end if

-- set actual PWM duty cycle
PWM_set_dutycycle (resist, resist)

end loop

The hardware

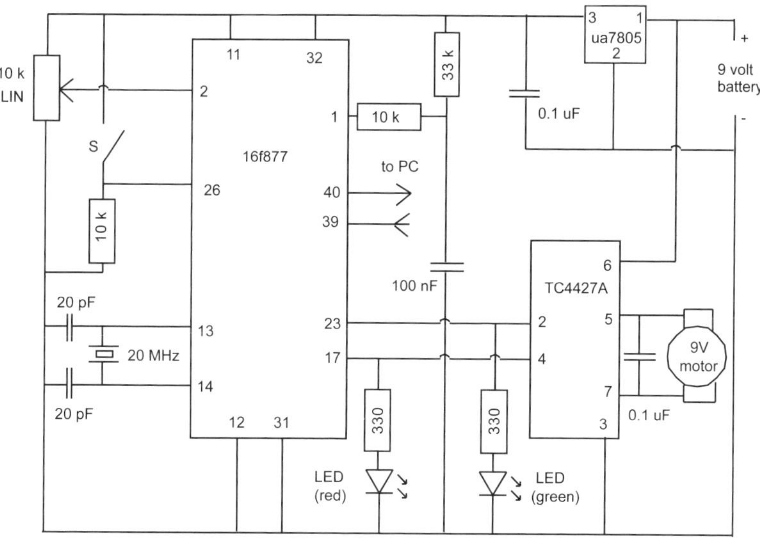

Figure 66. PWM project schematic.

The schematic is identical to the previous project, except that a switch has been added to reverse the direction of the motor and the B input of the 4427 is now connected to the CCP1 output of the 16F877.

The next figure shows the breadboarded circuit. The top power rail is 9 V and the bottom power rail is 5 V. Conversion between the rails is handled by the UA7805 on the right side. The long wires on the left belong to the programmer and are used to send data to the PC.

7 Electric motor

Even at the lowest setting (just 1.6% duty cycle) the motor runs and needs a whopping 14 seconds to make one rotation. Impressive! The Lego motor has a built in gearbox with a ratio of 14:1, so internally the motor makes one revolution per second.

Figure 67. Pulse Width Modulation.

When in-circuit programming with the Wisp628 the motor (and everything else) can remain connected. It may make a strange sound and small movements, but these do not affect the programming in any way.

An option

If you want you can display the PWM data on a PC. It has no impact of the functionality; it's just for fun. If you're not interested the commands:

```
-- send resistance to PC
serial_sw_write(resist)
delay_100ms(1)
```

can be removed from the program.

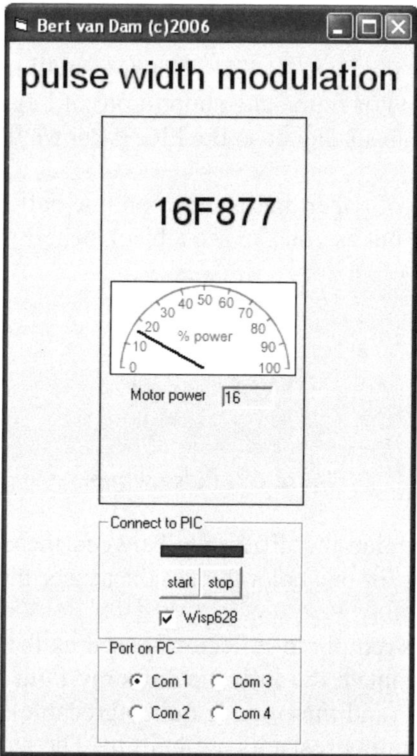

Figure 68. VB program

After powering up the project, start communications by clicking the "start" button. The term "motor power" really means the value being sent to the PWM module. The "percentage power" on the dial is the duty cycle that varies between 0 and 100%.

7.3 Constant motor speed through feedback

The purpose of this project is to maintain an electric motor at a constant speed, even when the load on the motor changes.

Technical background

The speed of an electric motor is measured. Based on that measurement the power to the motor is varied using the PWM module. If the motor slows down for some reason (such as when you pinch the axle between your fingers) the PIC™ will detect this and increase the power until the measured speed matches the desired speed again.

The motor we'll be using is the Lego 71427[72], but any small motor could be used. It may be convenient to build the motor frame and support out of Lego as well. But first we need to generate some sort of feedback signal so the PIC™ knows the speed of the motor.

We start with a small circle of paper that is black on one half and glued to a Lego wheel. A black marker works well, but as you can see a black pencil works just fine too.

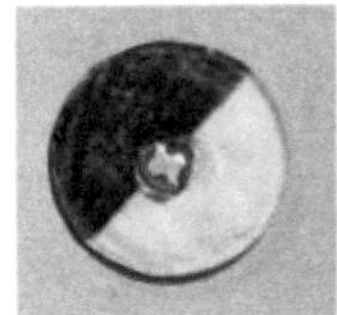

Figure 69. Pulse wheel.

We'll use a sensor to determine the difference between the black and white halves. By measuring how long it takes for one color to pass the sensor the speed can be calculated.

The Fairchild QRB134 infrared photo reflector is used as the sensor. It comes equipped with a daylight filter to eliminate the influence of stray light as much a possible. It also has a built-in infrared LED (and the price is quite agreeable). The datasheet is not quite clear on whether current limiting resistors are built in. The answer is "no" as I found out when I fried the first one.

---

[72] Technical data: max. 360 rpm, 3.5 mA power consumption without load, 360 mA stalled power consumption and 6 Ncm stalled torque according to measurements made by Philippe (Philo) Hurbain: http://www.philohome.com.

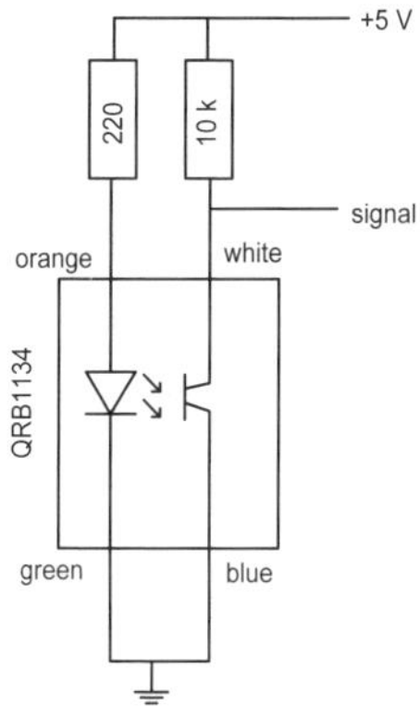

Figure 70. Connecting the QRB1134.

The sensor needs to be mounted at a distance of about 2 to 4 mm (5/64 to 5/32 in.) from the pulse wheel. Figure 71 shows how that can be done using standard Lego parts. The sensor is about 2/3 of a Lego brick high; so two angled 1/3 bricks hold it in place.

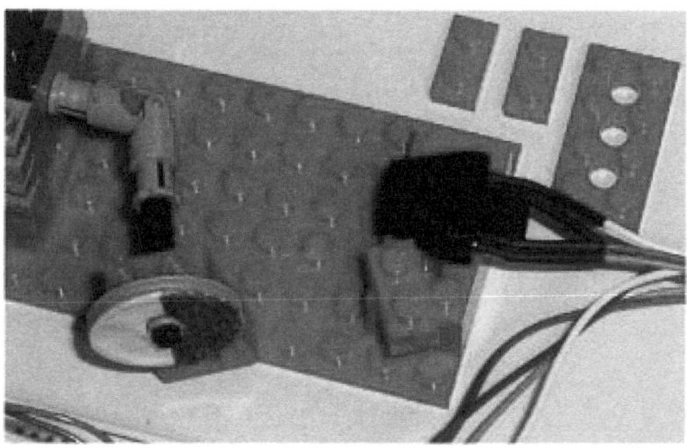

Figure 71. Sensor construction.

Now we need to measure how long it takes for the sensor to "see" a color change. The 16F877 is equipped with a timer for purposes such as this: *TIMER1*[73]. This timer can be controlled using T1CON, the TIMER1 control register. The only thing we need to do is switch it on

    T1CON = 0b_0000_0001

This way we also set bit 1 to zero, which indicates that the internal clock is used.

---

[73] You may recall that there is also a TIMER2, but it is being used for the PWM module.

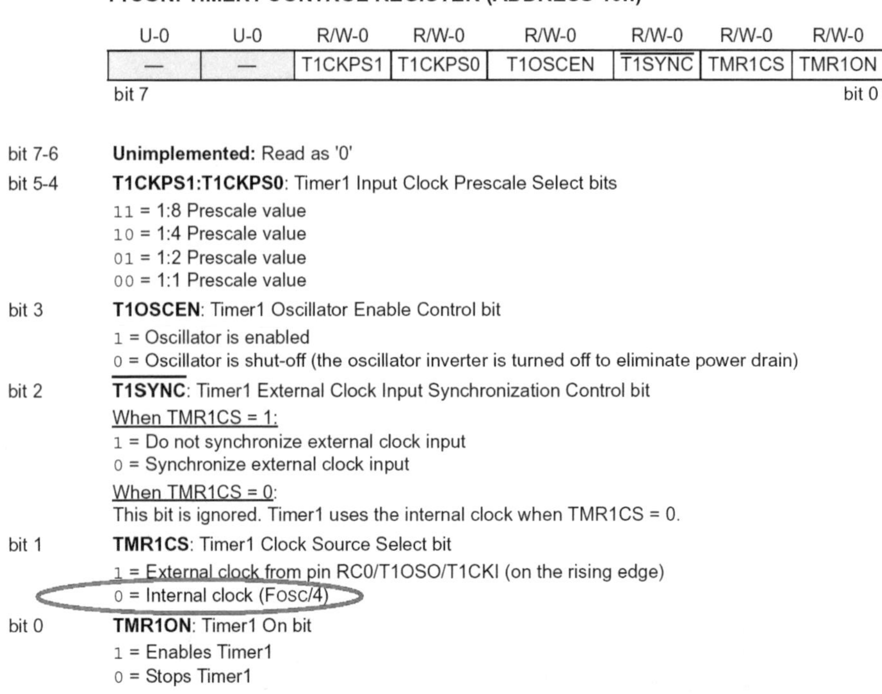

U-0	U-0	R/W-0	R/W-0	R/W-0	R/W-0	R/W-0	R/W-0
—	—	T1CKPS1	T1CKPS0	T1OSCEN	T1SYNC	TMR1CS	TMR1ON

bit 7   bit 0

bit 7-6	**Unimplemented:** Read as '0'
bit 5-4	**T1CKPS1:T1CKPS0**: Timer1 Input Clock Prescale Select bits

11 = 1:8 Prescale value
10 = 1:4 Prescale value
01 = 1:2 Prescale value
00 = 1:1 Prescale value

bit 3   **T1OSCEN**: Timer1 Oscillator Enable Control bit

1 = Oscillator is enabled
0 = Oscillator is shut-off (the oscillator inverter is turned off to eliminate power drain)

bit 2   **T1SYNC**: Timer1 External Clock Input Synchronization Control bit

When TMR1CS = 1:
1 = Do not synchronize external clock input
0 = Synchronize external clock input

When TMR1CS = 0:
This bit is ignored. Timer1 uses the internal clock when TMR1CS = 0.

bit 1   **TMR1CS**: Timer1 Clock Source Select bit

1 = External clock from pin RC0/T1OSO/T1CKI (on the rising edge)
0 = Internal clock (Fosc/4)

bit 0   **TMR1ON**: Timer1 On bit

1 = Enables Timer1
0 = Stops Timer1

Figure 72. TIMER1 control register

Note that the external oscillator controls this internal clock, with the frequency being that of the external oscillator <u>divided by four</u>. This is overlooked quite easily, hence the red circle.

The 16F877 is connected to an external crystal of 20 MHz. The clock frequency (Fosc) is 20 MHz, so one "tick" takes 50 ns[74]. Since the timer only counts one in every four ticks a timer tick takes 200 ns. The maximum number of ticks this timer can hold is 256 for the high byte and 256 for the low byte so in total 256 * 256 = 65,535 ticks. At 200 ns per tick this takes just 0.0131 second. Not enough by a long shot. It's incredible how fast these microcontrollers are!

If we add an extra byte (the eXtra High byte) the maximum time would increase to 3.35 seconds (256 x 0,013 seconds). Just for fun we will add yet another byte, the eXtra eXtra High byte resulting in a maximum time of 858 seconds, which is enough for even the slowest motors!

---

[74] $m = 10^{-3}$, $u = 10^{-6}$, $n = 10^{-9}$, $p = 10^{-12}$, so 1 second is 10^{9} ns, or 1.000.000.000 ns.

In JAL it looks like this:

```
if TMR1H == 255 then
    if counterXH == 255 then
        counterXXH = counterXXH + 1
    end if
    counterXH = counterXH + 1
    while TMR1H == 255  loop end loop
end if
```

When the high byte of the timer is 255 the program needs to take action. At the next increment the high byte will rollover to 0 again.[75] This is a good place to increment the eXtra High byte (counterXH) by one.

```
if TMR1H == 255 then
    counterXH = counterXH + 1
```

This will have to be done only once so we will wait until the high byte has indeed rolled over.

```
    while TMR1H == 255  loop end loop
```

In fact, the eXtra High byte counts a bit too early; specifically when the high byte of the timer is 255 instead of when it actually rolls over. You won't really notice this because the loop above will correct for it. Unless of course the process is stopped (because the sensor color changes) right at this very moment. That would cause an error of 1 tick of the high byte, which is 0.051 ms. I think we can live with that.

When the eXtra High byte rolls over the eXtra eXtra High byte needs to be increased by one:

```
    if counterXH == 255 then
        counterXXH = counterXXH + 1
    end if
    counterXH = counterXH + 1
```

Now all we need to do is start and stop counting at the right moment, when the sensor detects a color change on the pulse wheel. We will stop the program until the pin that is connected to the sensor (*inputpin*) drops from high to low[76]:

---

[75] A byte can hold a maximum value of 255. If you add 1 it will start at zero again, so 255+1=0. This is called a rollover.

[76] Note that it makes no difference whether the color changed from white to black or black to white since they both have the same length.

        while inputpin loop end loop

When that happens TIMER1 is reset by setting the high and low bytes to zero:

        TMR1H = 0x00
        TMR1L = 0x00

The counter loop runs as long as the color of the pulse wheel remains the same:

        while ! inputpin loop

Now that we know how long it took for the motor to make half of a turn we need to add a feedback mechanism. Here's where we need a reality check. We are talking about a toy electric motor with a hand drawn pulse wheel. It is completely useless to measure speed to hundredths of a second. The TIMER1 low byte can thus be completely ignored. Whether the high byte is of use could be a matter of discussion, but in this project we assume that the eXtra High byte is the lowest meaningful value.

As an example, the setpoint for the speed in this project is 10 for the eXtra High byte. Which means one color takes $(10/256)*3.35 = 0.13$ seconds to pass the sensor. So one complete revolution would take 0.26 seconds, which is equivalent to 231 revolutions per minute.[77]

The most essential part of the software - which uses the measured speed to adjust the power to the motor - has now become quite simple.

If the motor runs too slowly (the counter value is <u>too high</u>) the PWM setting is increased by five. If the motor runs too fast the PWM setting is reduced by five.

        if counterXH < 10 then
            CCPR1L = CCPR1L - 5
          end if
          if counterXH > 10 then
            CCPR1L = CCPR1L + 5
          end if

---

[77] In this project the setpoint is a fixed value. You can make the setpoint a variable by connecting a variable resistor to the PIC™ and using the measurement to control the speed. If you divide the measurement by 10 you will get a nice control range. Please be aware that if you stop the motor you won't get it started again because the program will wait for a pulse which will never come. The solution is to add a timeout to the waiting loop to limit the maximum waiting time.

The software

It is not necessary (but really quite interesting) to graph the data from the PIC™ on a PC. Try pinching the motor axle to feel the power increase, and then see the readings on the PC change accordingly.

The red line in the graph of Figure 73 represents the power sent to the motor. You can see that I pinched the motor axle at two different times. The PIC™ immediately increased the power to the motor (the red line went up) until the speed was correct again. When I released the axle the motor ran too fast so the PIC™ corrected for this by reducing motor power.

The actual motor power is shown on the dial and in numbers below. The contents of all counters are also shown.

This Visual Basic program is part of the free download package, and includes the source code.

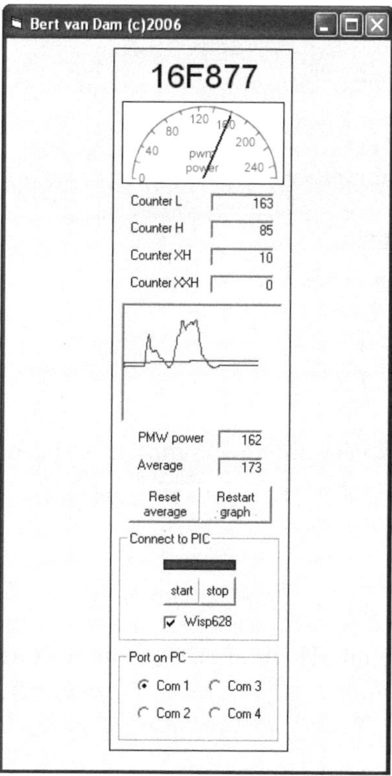

Figure 73. Pinching the motor axle.

7 Electric motor

In order to display these data we do need to actually send them. To keep them separate on the PC side they are preceded by a number.

Prefix	Data content
1	TIMER1 low byte[78]
2	TIMER1 high byte
3	eXtra high byte
4	eXtra eXtra high byte
5	PWM module pulse length

In JAL this is handled as follows:

```
serial_sw_write("1")
serial_sw_write(counterL)
delay_1ms(10)
serial_sw_write("2")
serial_sw_write(counterH)
delay_1ms(10)
serial_sw_write("3")
serial_sw_write(counterXH)
delay_1ms(10)
serial_sw_write("4")
serial_sw_write(counterXXH)
delay_1ms(10)
serial_sw_write("5")
serial_sw_write(CCPR1L)
```

All important parts of the software are now complete and can be put together:

```
-- JAL 2.0.4
include 16F877_bert

-- define variables
var byte counterL, counterH, counterXH, counterXXH
pin_d2_direction = input                    -- motor feedback pulse
```

---

[78] This is, of course, TMR1L. But between the moment it is measured and the moment it is sent to the PC the counter changes value, and so does TMR1L. So right after the measurement the value is put into a separate variable (counterL) to preserve it. The same applies to TMR1H.

```
var bit direction1 is pin_c4 = false        -- motor direction
pin_c4_direction = output
var bit inputpin is pin_d2                   -- signal from the photo reflector
pin_d3_direction = output                    -- yellow led
var bit yellowled is pin_d3


-- enable pulse width modulation
PWM_init_frequency (true, true)
CCPR1L = 138                                 -- set actual PWM duty cycle to 138


T1CON = 0b_0000_0001                         -- TIMER1 enabled

forever loop

   while  inputpin loop end loop             -- wait for high to low transition
          TMR1H = 0x00                        -- initialize TIMER1
          TMR1L = 0x00
   yellowled = high                          -- high pulse turns led on
   while ! inputpin  loop                    -- wait for low to high transition

     if TMR1H == 255 then                     -- meanwhile count overflows
       if counterXH == 255 then
         counterXXH = counterXXH + 1
       end if
       counterXH = counterXH + 1
       while TMR1H == 255  loop end loop
     end if

   end loop

   -- counting completed
   counterH = TMR1H
   counterL = TMR1L
   yellowled = low

   -- adjust the power to the motor if needed
   if counterXH < 10 then
     CCPR1L = CCPR1L - 5
   end if
   if counterXH > 10 then
     CCPR1L = CCPR1L + 5
```

7 Electric motor

```
end if

-- send data to the PC (for information purposes only)
serial_sw_write("1")
serial_sw_write(counterL)
delay_1ms(10)
serial_sw_write("2")
serial_sw_write(counterH)
delay_1ms(10)
serial_sw_write("3")
serial_sw_write(counterXH)
delay_1ms(10)
serial_sw_write("4")
serial_sw_write(counterXXH)
delay_1ms(10)
serial_sw_write("5")
serial_sw_write(f877_CCPR1L)

-- reset all counters
counterL = 0
counterH = 0
counterXH = 0
counterXXH = 0

end loop
```

The hardware

The circuit looks a lot like the PWM project of section 7.2. The Fairchild QRB1134 infrared photo reflector needs to be added of course. If you compare the schematic with the breadboard photograph you will notice a few small differences. The setup on the breadboard works perfectly, however in applications where power is scarce and voltage is lower than anticipated (such as battery applications) the set up in the schematic will function better (such as in battery powered robots).

The diode in the ground lead between the 5 V and 9 V power rails is removed, and the resistor between the PIC™ and the MOSFET driver chip is relocated to the LED (which was what they were meant for in the first place). These changes have been incorporated into the circuit in Figure 74.

The long wires on the left side of the breadboard are from the Wisp628 in-circuit programmer.

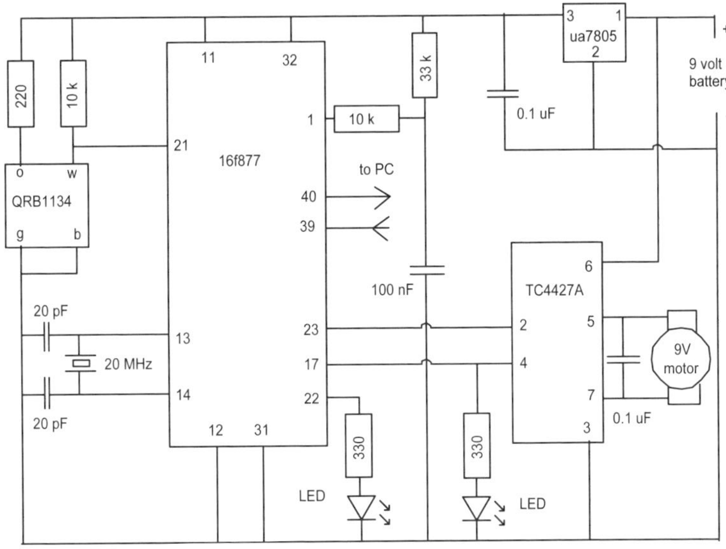

Figure 74. Constant speed with feedback.

Figure 75. Constant speed with feedback.

7.4 Tachometer

In this project a tachometer is made, based on the previous project, but with accurate timing by use of the TIMER1 overflow bit.

Technical background

In the previous project the feedback on the motor speed was based on counters. By dividing the sensor count by the time needed to reach this value the speed of the motor can be calculated.

Counter	Time (per "tick")[79]
counterL	200 nS
counterH	51 uS
counterXH	13 mS
counterXXH	3.35 sec

In that project it was important that the speed remain constant, but the exact value of the speed was irrelevant. For a tachometer, however, the exact value is important so measuring the time that has passed must be done much more accurately.

This is the loop that was used to measure time:

```
if TMR1H == 255 then
    if counterXH == 255 then
        counterXXH = counterXXH + 1
    end if
    counterXH = counterXH + 1
    while TMR1H == 255  loop end loop
end if
```

The first line, *if TMR1H == 255 then*, only works if *TMR1H* is indeed 255 at <u>the exact moment</u> that this test is performed. The counters are always running - even when other commands are being executed - so chances are that *TMR1H* reaches 255 while a different command is executed. This means the rollover goes unnoticed and *counterXH* and *counterXXH* are not incremented. The result is that with short measuring times (high

---

[79] $m = 10^{-3}$, $u = 10^{-6}$, $n = 10^{-9}$, $p = 10^{-12}$

rpms) the measurement seriously deviates from the true value by as much as a factor of 2. Since this deviation is constant it didn't matter in the previous project.

It does matter now, however, so we will use a different counting mechanism. The TIMER1 register contains a variable that is set to 1 each time *TMR1H* rolls over to 0, which is called *TMR1IF*. If we use this in the counting loop the *TMR1H* rollover will never be missed:

```
if TMR1IF then
    -- clear TMR1IF
    TMR1IF = 0
    if counterXH == 255 then
        counterXXH = counterXXH + 1
    end if
    counterXH = counterXH + 1
end if
```

Each time the loop is executed a rollover that has already passed can still be counted because *TMR1IF* is still set. To prevent the rollover from being counted twice the variable is reset to 0 after processing.

Since we are focused on working accurately this would be a good time to reset the timer the official way, meaning we will stop the timer first, set it to 0, and then restart.

Like this:

```
T1CON = 0b_0000_0000        -- timer off
TMR1L = 0x00
TMR1H = 0x00
T1CON = 0b_0000_0001        -- timer on again
```

So the complete counting loop looks like this:

```
while  inputpin loop end loop
T1CON = 0b_0000_0000
TMR1L = 0x00
TMR1H = 0x00
T1CON = 0b_0000_0001
```

```
    while ! inputpin  loop
      if TMR1IF then
         -- clear TMR1IF
         TMR1IF = 0
         if counterXH == 255 then
             counterXXH = counterXXH + 1
         end if
         counterXH = counterXH + 1
      end if
    end loop

    counterH = TMR1H
    counterL = TMR1L
```

This way we will get an accurate time measurement.

The software

The program is much simpler than the previous project, because only the measuring part
is required. Which means you can mount the pulse wheel on basically any axle to
measure the rpms.

Putting it all together yields this program:

```
    -- JAL 2.0.4
    include 16F877_bert

    -- define variables
    var byte counterL, counterH, counterXH, counterXXH
    pin_d2_direction = input
    var bit inputpin is pin_d2    -- signal from the photo reflector

    forever loop

      while  inputpin loop end loop
      T1CON = 0b_0000_0000
      TMR1L = 0x00
      TMR1H = 0x00
      T1CON = 0b_0000_0001

        while ! inputpin  loop
          if TMR1IF then
```

```
        TMR1IF = 0
        if counterXH == 255 then
           counterXXH = counterXXH + 1
        end if
        counterXH = counterXH + 1
      end if
   end loop

   counterH = TMR1H
   counterL = TMR1L

   -- send data to the PC
   serial_sw_write("1") delay_1ms(10)
   serial_sw_write(counterL)
   delay_1ms(10)
   serial_sw_write("2")
   serial_sw_write(counterH)
   delay_1ms(10)
   serial_sw_write("3")
   serial_sw_write(counterXH)
   delay_1ms(10)
   serial_sw_write("4")
   serial_sw_write(counterXXH)

   -- reset all counters
   counterL = 0
   counterH = 0
   counterXH = 0
   counterXXH = 0

 end loop
```

On the PC, the data are received and, with a simple formula, the total time elapsed is calculated:

$$time = counterL*200 \; 10^{-9} + counterH*51 \; 10^{-6} + counterXH*13 \; 10^{-3} + counterXXH*3.35$$

7 Electric motor

The number of revolutions per minute then becomes:

$$\text{revolutions per minute} = \frac{60}{\text{time}}$$

Which is displayed like this:

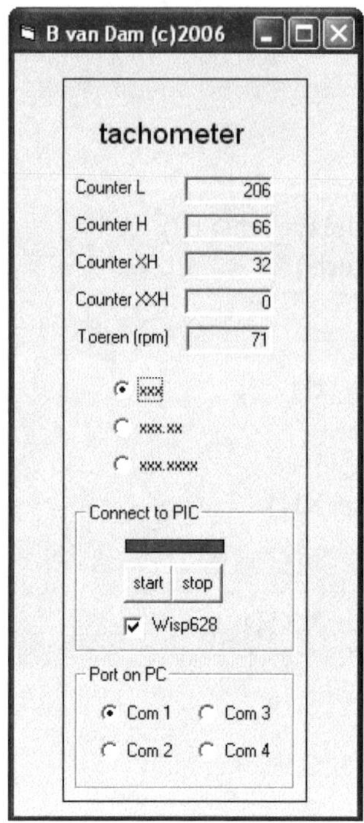

Figure 76. Tachometer.

The Hardware

A lot of parts can be removed, making it much simpler:

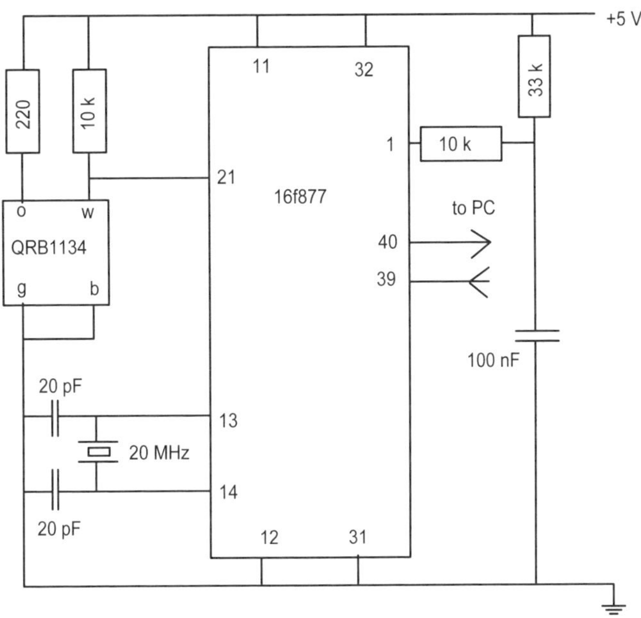

Figure 77. Tachometer.

On the breadboard you can see that the sensor is now connected using a plug, but that doesn't have any impact on the functionality.

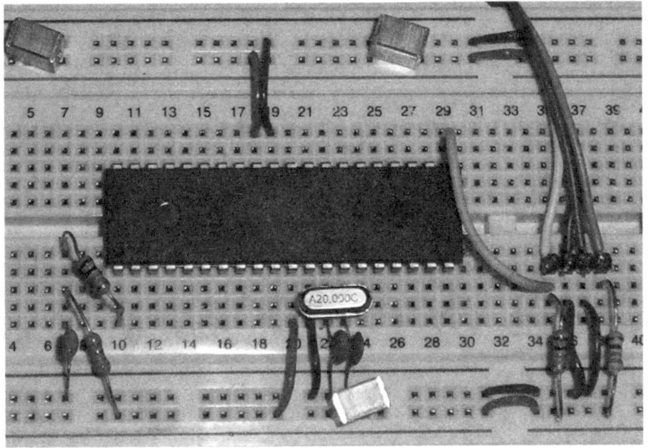

Figure 78. Tachometer.

8 Sensors

In this chapter you will find a series of projects with different kinds of sensors that can be connected to a PIC™.

Sensor	Mechanism	Purpose
GP2Y0D340K infrared object detector	Infrared	Used to detect objects, but incapable of determining their distance.
SRF04 Ultrasonic Range Finder	Ultrasonic	Used to detect objects and their distance from the sensor.
Byte Craft Limited touch sensor design	People	Used to detect people or other conductive objects without touch.
Sharp GP1S036HEL tilt sensor	Tilt	Used to determine an object's position relative to the horizontal plane, i.e. the tilt of an object.

These are not the only sensors discussed in this book; several of them have already been discussed in other sections.

Sensor	Mechanism	Purpose	Section
LDR	light	Used to determine the quantity or presence of visible light.	5.2, 9.2
Fairchild QRB134 infrared photo reflector	Infrared	Used to detect color changes, such as on a code wheel or line follower.	7.3, 7.4
		A bizarre use of this sensor in an infrared RS232 connection.	13.3.5
Switch	Contact	Used to detect the proximity of objects.	4

Sensor	Mechanism	Purpose	Section
NTC	Temperature	Used to measure temperature.	5.5
Keypad	Contacts	Used to enter data, in this case numbers.	4.4

8.1 Infrared object detection

In this project a Sharp GP2Y0D340K infrared object detector is used to detect objects.

Technical background

Infrared light is invisible to humans, but is reflected by objects just like visible (regular) light. By measuring reflected infrared light the presence of an object in front of the sensor can be determined.

Figure 79. Sharp infrared detector.

The drawback to using this sensor is obvious: an object with good reflective properties appears to be closer than an object with poor reflective properties. In one test, a black shiny object was detected at 23 cm (9 in.) while an identical non-shiny white object was detected at 59 cm (23 in.). The price of the sensor, however, is very attractive.[80]

---

[80] Approximately US$ 6

8 Sensors

The software

The sensor is basically a switch that is turned off (yes, off) when an object is detected. By inverting the signal and adding a single LED a working project can be made:

```
-- check sensor
  greenled = ! sensor
```

A second LED is used to show that the system is active. Aside from that the program mainly consists of pin definitions:

```
-- JAL 2.0.4
include 16F877_bert

-- define variables
var bit blueled is pin_c4        -- blue led
var bit greenled is pin_d3       -- green led
var bit sensor is pin_d2         -- sensor
pin_c4_direction = output
pin_d3_direction = output
pin_d2_direction = input

-- turn blue led on
blueled = high

forever loop

    -- check sensor
    greenled = ! sensor

    -- flash blue led
    blueled = ! blueled
    delay_100ms(1)

end loop
```

The hardware

The infrared sensor must be equipped with a small resistor and capacitor. The value of the resistor is not an error; 1.5 ohm is the correct value.

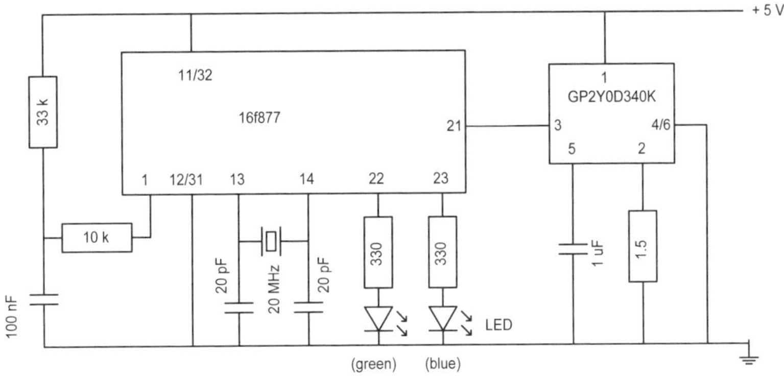

Figure 80. Infrared sensor.

And here is the breadboarded circuit:

Figure 81. Infrared sensor.

The long wires on the left hand side are from the Wisp628 programmer. The green LED is on, so the infrared sensor has detected the photographer!

Complications

During the construction of a large subsumption robot equipped with a series of these sensors the accompanying small resistors and capacitors were soldered directly to the sensors. The sensors themselves were connected by long wires to the PIC™. As a result, the PIC™ stopped running immediately. The (software) oscilloscope[81] showed that the sensors caused so much noise on the power line that the PIC™ couldn't run anymore.

---

[81] Oscilloscope for Windows v. 2.51 written by Konstantin Zeldovich.

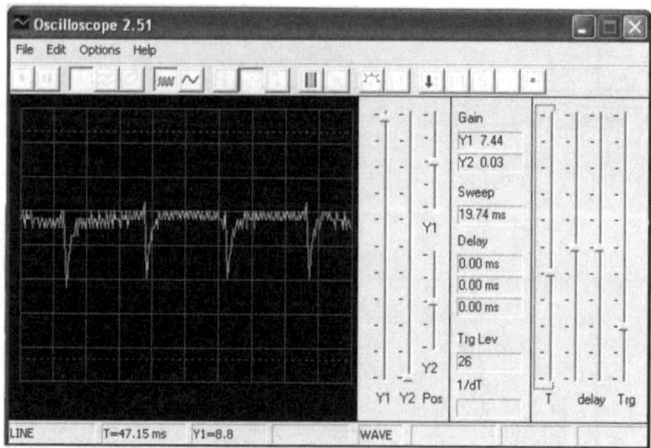

Figure 82. Noise on the power line.

A 100 uF capacitor across the power lines of each sensor solved this problem. In the schematic you will not find this capacitor since the problem only occurs when using long wires.

8.2 Ultrasonic sensor

The purpose of this project is to demonstrate the use of a Devantech SRF04 Ultrasonic Range Finder to measure the distance to various objects. In section 12.6 this sensor is modified and used as ultrasonic radar.

Technical background

The SRF04 is a relatively cheap[82] ultrasonic sensor that uses sound waves to measure the distance of objects. The detection cycle is started by the PIC™ with a pulse of 10 uS or more on the "pulse trigger" line. As soon as this line goes low again the ultrasonic module sends a burst of 8 pulses of 40 kHz sound. To avoid direct coupling between transmitter and receiver the unit waits a bit and then sets the "echo line" to high. This is the signal for the PIC™ to start a time measurement. The first ultrasonic echo to be received switches the "echo line" back to low again. The distance can be calculated based on the elapsed time.

---

[82] About US$ 18.

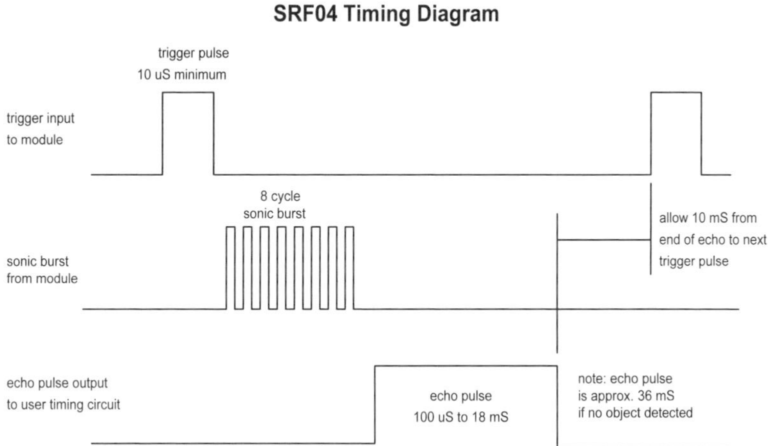

Figure 83. How the ultrasonic sensor works.[83]

The next Figure shows some measurements done with this sensor. You can see that the graph is a perfectly straight line with a minimum detection range of about 1 cm (3/8 in.). A moving pencil can be detected as far away as 50 cm (20 in.). Very impressive!

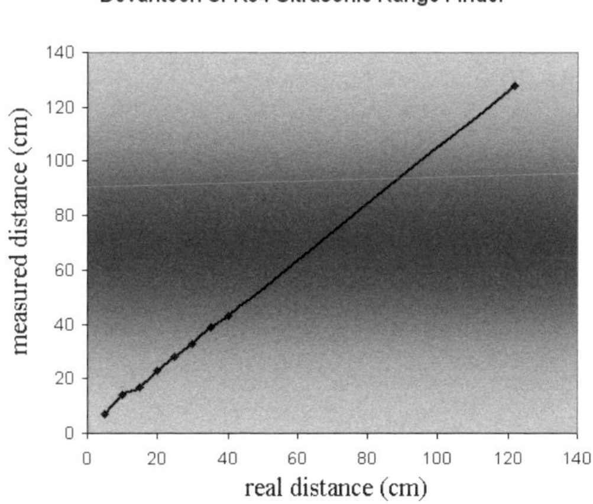

Figure 84. Measurements with the ultrasonic sensor.

---

[83] This diagram is copyrighted by Daventech. The company doesn't have it's own website, but technical information can be found at http://www.robot-electronics.co.uk/htm/srf05tech.htm.

8 Sensors

Based on the elapsed time measured by the PIC™ the distance can be easily calculated. The speed of sound through the air at room temperature is about 342 m/s (765 mph).[84]

```
-- wait for echo pulse (line will go low)
  while echo loop
     distance = distance + 1
     delay_10uS(4)
  end loop
```

At a distance of 10 cm the measured "distance" is 15 program loops. Since each loop takes 4 times 10 uS this means 600 uS elapsed time At the speed of sound this translates to a distance of 0.205 meters. Since the sound has to go to the object and back the distance to the object is half of the distance measured, or 0.103 meter (10 cm). Incredibly accurate!

The software

First the pins need to be defined:

```
-- define variables
var byte distance

-- define pins
var bit pulse is pin_d0          -- pulse trigger
var bit echo is pin_d1           -- echo signal
pin_d0_direction = output
pin_d1_direction = input
```

Then we follow the steps from the manual as closely as possible. The first step is to submit a pulse of at least 10 uS to the pulse trigger line, so we opt for 40 uS, which should be long enough:

```
-- send pulse
  pulse = high
  delay_10uS(4)
  pulse = low
```

---

[84] I conserve energy: the temperature in my office is about 19 degrees C. The formula is c = 20 * square root(T) where T is the air temperature (in Kelvin) and c is the estimated speed of sound at that temperature. Note that degrees Kelvin can be calculated by adding 273.15 to the temperature in degrees C.

As soon as the echo line is high a counter must be started until the line is low again:

```
-- wait for echo circuitry to switch on
  while ! echo loop
  end loop

-- wait for echo pulse (line will go low)
  while echo loop
    distance = distance + 1
    delay_10uS(4)
  end loop
```

The measured value is sent to the PC for processing. Then we wait a while (1 second) for any stray signals to disappear before everything is repeated.

```
-- send distance to PC
  delay_100ms(10)
  serial_sw_write(distance)
```

Putting everything together yields:

```
-- JAL 2.0.4
include 16F877_bert

-- define variables
var byte distance

-- define pins
var bit pulse is pin_d0        -- pulse trigger
var bit echo is pin_d1         -- echo signal
pin_d0_direction = output
pin_d1_direction = input

pulse = low

forever loop

    -- reset distance
    distance = 0

    -- send pulse
    pulse = high
```

```
delay_10uS(4)
pulse = low

-- wait for echo circuitry to switch on
while ! echo loop
end loop

-- wait for echo pulse (line will go low)
while echo loop
   distance = distance + 1
   delay_10uS(4)
end loop

-- send distance to PC
delay_100ms(10)
serial_sw_write(distance)

end loop
```

A Visual Basic program on the PC will use the data to calculate the distance.

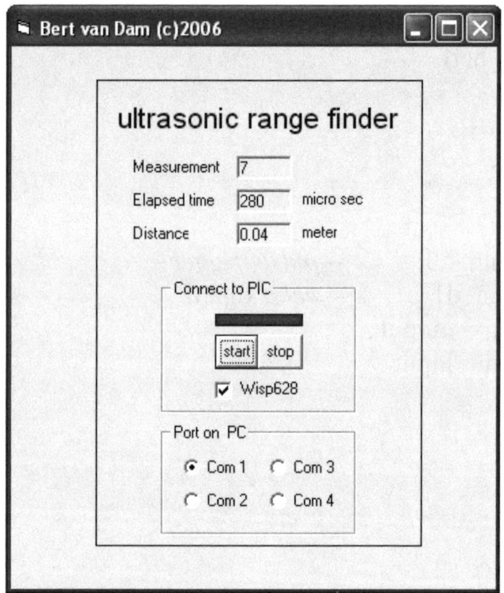

Figure 85. Ultrasonic range finder on the PC.

You can see the measured value, the elapsed time to the first echo, and the calculated distance. The maximum distance that can be measured is 1.74 m (because the *distance* variable has a maximum value of 255).

The hardware

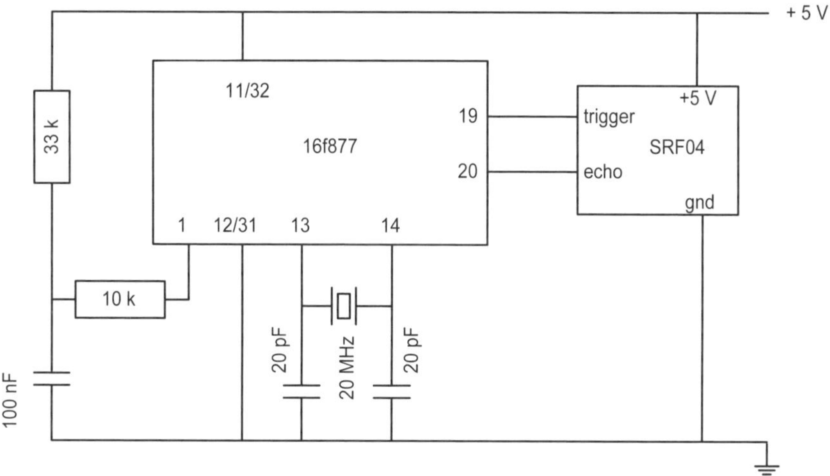

Figure 86. Ultrasonic sensor.

With actual parts it looks like this:

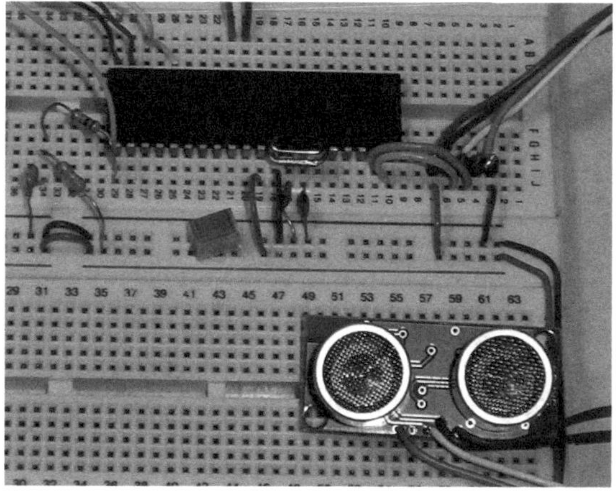

Figure 87. Ultrasonic sensor in action.

The sensor is pointed straight at the photographer. During operation the sensor makes a soft clicking sound (each time a radar burst is emitted), so you can hear whether it is working or not.

The ultrasonic sensor needs to be connected as shown in the accompanying instruction booklet. This is very simple and the instructions are quite clear, with the exception that the drawing shows a bottom view. I missed that and connected it with the power reversed. It did survive, but just be careful.

The power consumption of the entire unit is approximately 24.2 mA, which is good to know if you intend to use battery power.

8.3 People sensor

In Byte Craft Limited[85], Walter Banks wrote an interesting article in which he described a touch sensor based on a capacitor. He used a small touch pad, but if the sensor is made larger it will react as soon as somebody gets near it, even without touching it. This makes it a contact-free people sensor that reacts to anything that conducts electricity.

Technical background

The technique is very interesting. Two pins of a PIC™ are connected together with a large resistor of, say, 470k ohms. One of them is connected to a piece of metal with an insulating layer, such as a piece of aluminum foil in a plastic bag.

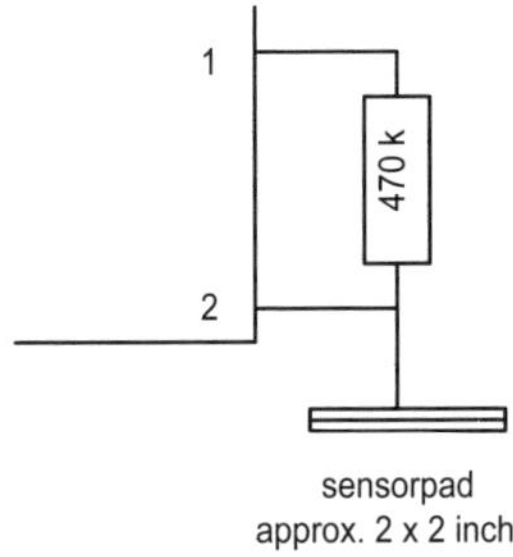

Figure 88. Principle schematic of the people sensor.

---

[85] The website is http://www.bytecraft.com, and Walter Banks article can be found at http://www.bytecraft.com/touchsw.html.

This insulated piece of metal is, in fact, one half of a capacitor. When someone holds his hand near the insulated metal his hand becomes the other side of the capacitor. The hand is the conductor and the air is the insulator.

Charging a capacitor takes a certain amount of time, depending on the capacity. Without a person near it the charging will be fast. But when a body is present, a true capacitor is formed and charging takes much longer (here "much longer" means longer than 3 ms).

The sensitivity of the sensor depends on the size of the metal foil, the length of the wire, and also on the PIC™ itself. In this project the pin combination d1/d2 is used, but in some cases different combinations work better (such as c6/d1). If the sensor lacks sensitivity you might try different pin combinations.

The use of this sensor can be dangerous (to the PIC™, not to you). Should you accidentally be statically charged when your hand gets near the foil a spark may jump across. These sparks always destroy the most expensive component in sight, which in this case is the PIC™. It hasn't happened to me, but use it at your own risk.

The software

The program has to execute the following steps:

- Make pin 1 (in Figure 88) low, to discharge the capacitor
- Wait a bit
- Charge the capacitor by making pin 1 high again
- Wait 4 to 5 ms
- Check if pin 2 is high

If pin 2 is high the charge of the capacitor is small (loading was fast) so no person was near it. If the pin is still low it means the charge is much greater, so a person (or other conductive object) is close by. Note that pins 1 and 2 refer to the pins in Figure 88 and not the 16F877.

Here's what the test looks like:

```
TOUCHOUT = low
delay_1ms(1)
TOUCHOUT = high
delay_4us

if TOUCHIN == high then
    LED0 = low
```

```
    else
        LED0 = high
    end if
```

Rather than waiting a fixed time you could simply measure the amount of time it takes to charge the capacitor, and base your conclusions on that. Unfortunately, those measurements vary wildly so the fixed waiting period is advisable. The program looks like this:

```
-- JAL 2.0.4
include 16F877_bert

-- define the pins
pin_c4_direction = output
pin_d2_direction = output
pin_d1_direction = input

-- general variables
var bit LED0 is pin_c4
var bit TOUCHOUT is pin_d2
var bit TOUCHIN is pin_d1

forever loop

  TOUCHOUT = low
  delay_1ms(1)
  TOUCHOUT = high
  delay_4us

  if TOUCHIN == high then
      LED0 = low
  else
      LED0 = high
  end if

  -- and send to PC
  serial_sw_write( LED0 )
  delay_100ms(1)

end loop
```

The use of this sensor would be well suited for alarms (just remember the static electricity warning). A small Visual Basic program could be used on the PC to display the result of the measurement. This program is part of the download package.

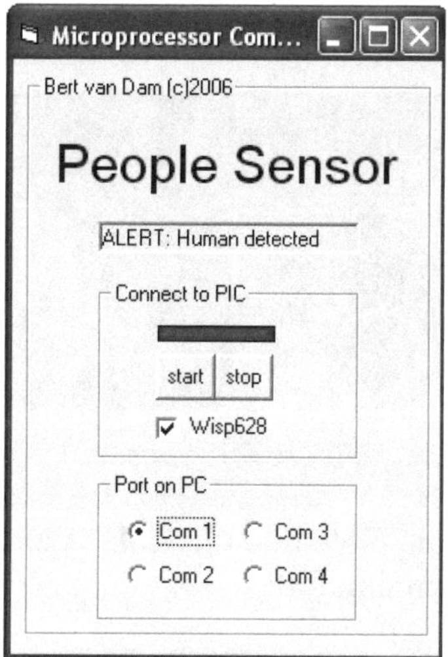

Figure 89. People sensor on the PC.

The hardware

The schematic is rather simple.

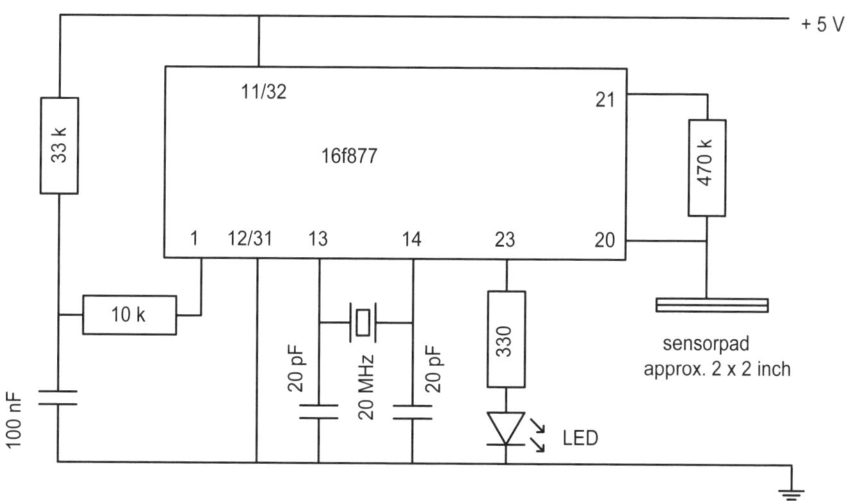

Figure 90. Schematic of the people sensor.

Be careful to connect the sensor to the correct side of the resistor, at pin 20 (the input).

The sensor itself is shown in Figure 91. It is placed inside a sturdy plastic sleeve, such as used by card collectors. The sensitivity can be controlled by changing the size of the aluminum foil.

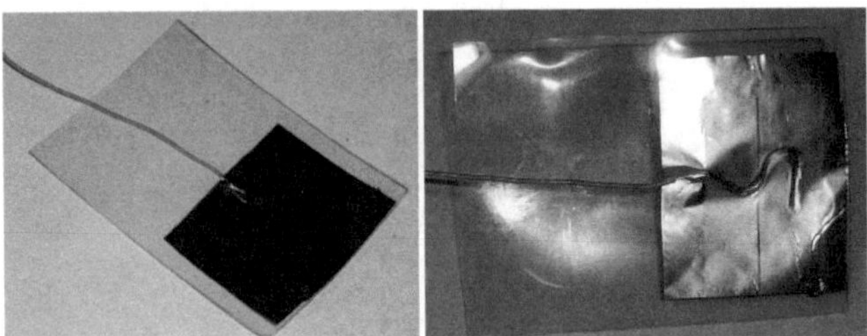

Figure 91. Sensor.

And here is the sensor in action. Note that the LED is already on while the hand is still centimeters away from the aluminum foil!

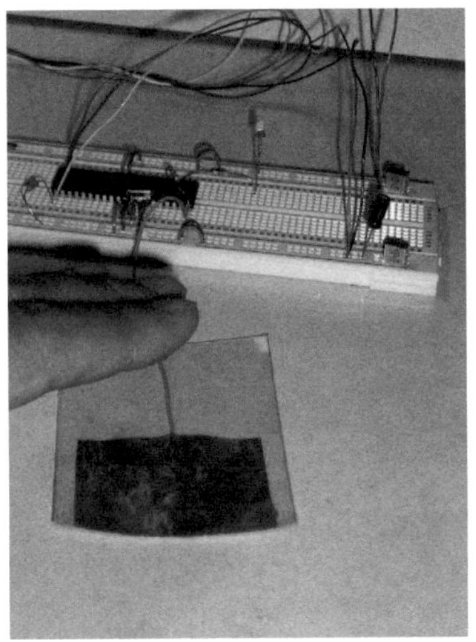

Figure 92. The people sensor in action.

8.4 Tilt sensor

The purpose of this project is to demonstrate the use of a Sharp GP1S036HEL tilt sensor.

Technical background

The GP1S036HEL tilt sensor has a tiny ball inside. On one side of the ball is an LED and on the other side are four light sensitive sensors. When you move the tilt sensor the little ball moves, thereby blocking (or rather, interrupting) the light to one or more of the internal sensors. For that reason Sharp calls this device the "Photointerrupter for Detecting Tilt Direction".

This sensor can also be used to detect vibration, assuming the vibrations are a bit "wild". An ideal application is a battery powered bicycle light that remains switched on as long as the bicycle is moving.[86]

---

[86] Real vibration controlled bicycle lights are also equipped with a light sensor which allows them to only switch the light on when the bicycle is being used in the dark.

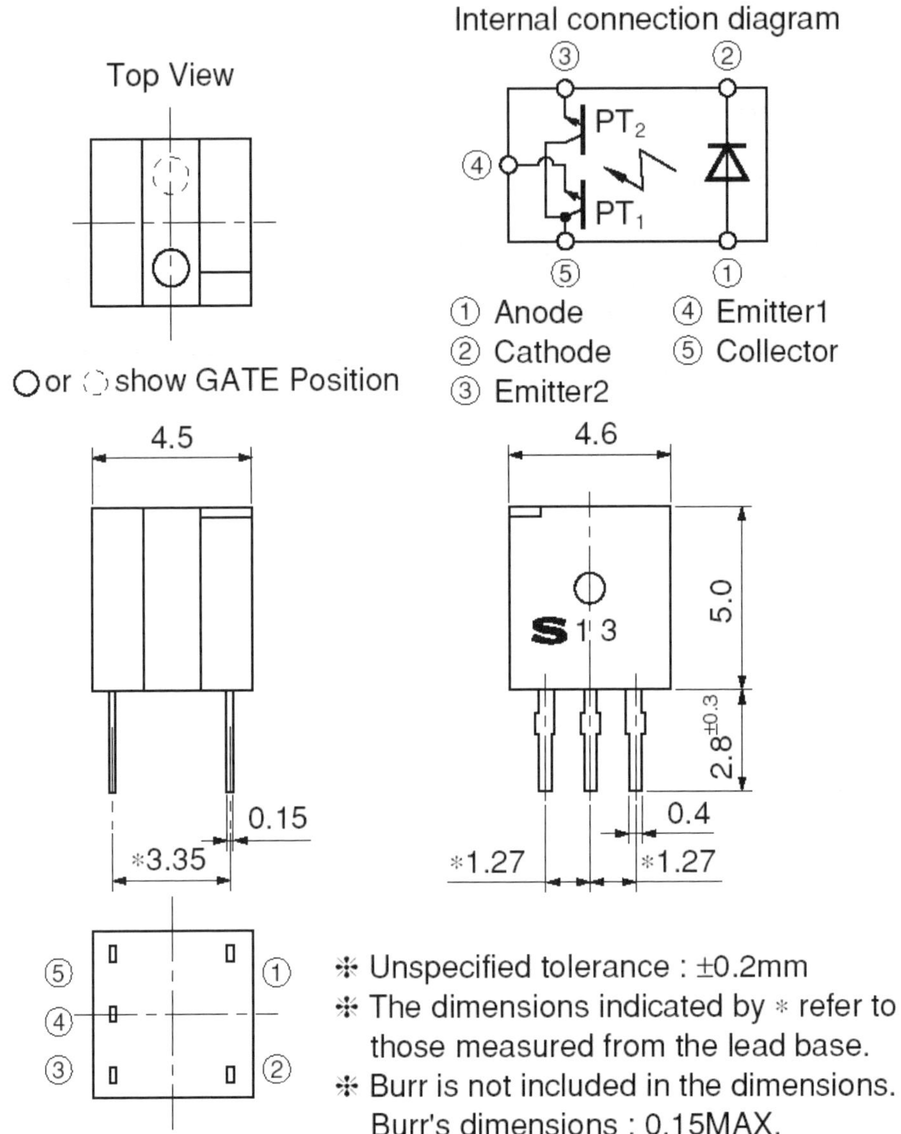

Figure 93. Datasheet for the tilt sensor, __bottom__ view.

Connecting the sensor is easy with the only exception being that the datasheet diagram says "top view', but should read "bottom view". So pay attention when soldering.

Make sure the sensor doesn't get too hot while soldering; otherwise the little ball inside will melt and destroy the sensor.

The software

The software is very simple, because this is a static sensor. All you need to do is keep an eye on the pins that are connected to the sensor and relay its status to a couple of LEDs.

```
forever loop

    pin_d4 = pin_d1
    pin_d5 = pin_d0

end loop
```

And the program with the pin definitions:

```
-- JAL 2.0.4
include 16F877_bert

pin_d1_direction = input     -- sensor
pin_d0_direction = input     -- sensor
pin_d4_direction = output    -- green LED
pin_d5_direction = output    -- red LED

forever loop

  pin_d4 = pin_d1
  pin_d5 = pin_d0

end loop
```

The hardware

According to the datasheet the sensor can handle a maximum current of 100 mA. At 5 V this translates to a current limiting resistor of 100 ohms. To be on the safe side a 330 ohm resistor is used. The output collector has a maximum current of 20 mA, which would require a 250 ohm resistor. We will use a 1 k resistor.

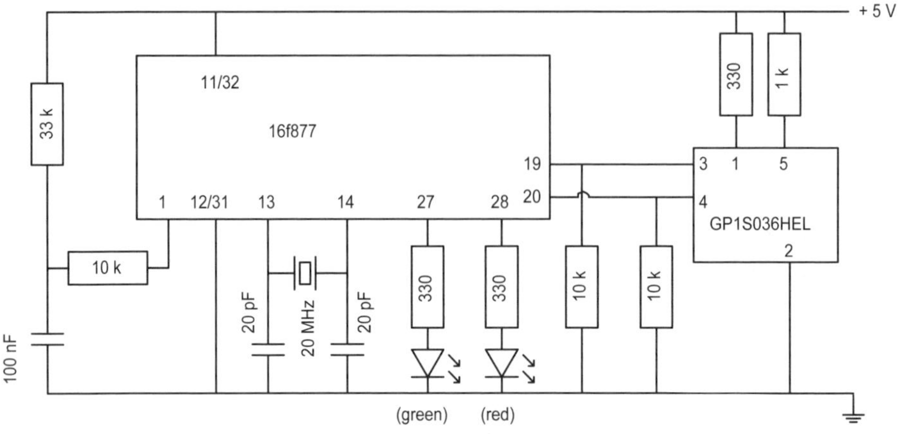

Figure 94. Tilt sensor schematic.

This is what the breadboard looks like:

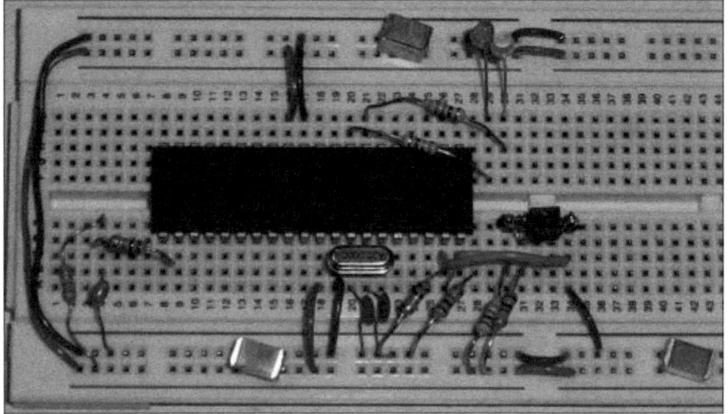

Figure 95. Tilt sensor.

The tilt sensor can detect four directions. Unfortunately, these are not forward, reverse, left and right, but are just a rotation in one plane.

The LEDs display the different positions the sensor can detect as shown in the table:

Sensor position	Red LED	Green LED
Level, in front of you (connections facing down)	0	0
Rotated 90 degrees to the right (connections facing left)	0	1
Rotated 180 degrees (connections facing up)	1	1
Rotated 270 degrees (connections facing right)	1	0

In addition to determining its position the sensor can also indicate acceleration . The little ball inside is flung to one of the sides if the sensor is accelerated (or decelerated).

Acceleration	Red LED	Green LED
To the right	1	0
To the left	0	1

9 Sound

Sound consists of vibrations in the air that our ears can detect. In this chapter a number of different techniques are used to generate or record sound.

Project	Description
Beep	A simple beep made using the PWM module.
Night buzzer	A small project to really annoy someone with nightly noises
Frequency generator	Flipping a pin continuously between high and low in a simple program loop.
A simple melody	Music made using the TIMER0 interrupt.[87]
Recording sounds	Convert the sound of a cricket and store it in program memory.
Super compression	A special technique to store 8 times more sound in a PIC™ with an acceptable sound quality.

Sound is also discussed at other places in the book:

Project	Description	Section
Frequency generator	Flipping a pin continuously between high and low, controlled by the TIMER0 interrupt.	12.1
VU meter	An 8 LED VU meter to display sound volume using a 16F876A.	13.3.4

---

[87] It is advisable to read section 12.1 first, otherwise the technical background may be hard to understand. Besides, it will also show you a nice frequency generator.

9.1 Beep

In this project the PWM module (introduced in section 7.2) is used to generate a beep.

Technical background

A beep consists of a single audio frequency. This means that a speaker must receive a voltage that fluctuates to that frequency. An obvious way to achieve this is to use the PWM module. This module works independently of the rest of the program. So once the proper conditions for the beep are set the program doesn't have to concern itself with it anymore; it will just continue to beep all by itself. This can be a major advantage in large or complicated programs.

The most complicated part of this project is to select and set the proper frequency. The audible frequency range is between 20 Hz and 20 kHz.[88] The sensitivity of our ears is highly frequency dependent, as you can see in the next figure.

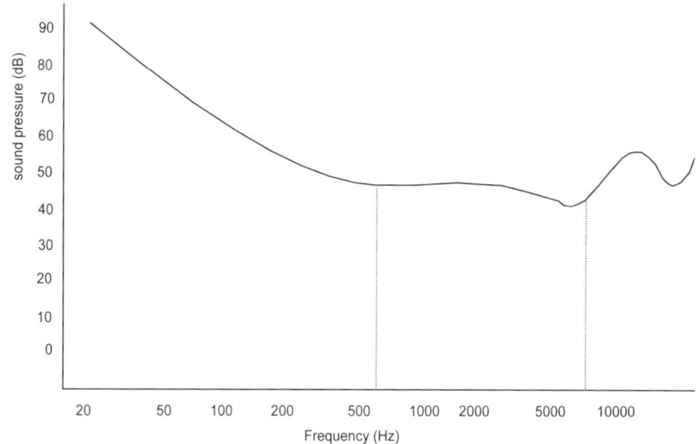

Figure 96. ISO226 equal loudness contour (approximation).

All frequencies on this line sound equally loud to the human ear. The highest sensitivity is therefore in the area between 500 to 6000 Hz, assuming you were careful with your headphone volume.

The standard library has the PWM frequency set to 19.53 kHz, which is much too high.

---

[88] James Boyk has shown in his May 2004 article "*There's Life Above 20 Kilohertz! A Survey of Musical Instrument Spectra to 102.4 kHz*" that people react to sounds above 26 kHz even if they can't consciously hear them.

TABLE 8-3:   EXAMPLE PWM FREQUENCIES AND RESOLUTIONS AT 20 MHz

PWM Frequency	1.22 kHz	4.88 kHz	19.53 kHz	78.12kHz	156.3 kHz	208.3 kHz
Timer Prescaler (1, 4, 16)	16	4	1	1	1	1
PR2 Value	0xFFh	0xFFh	0xFFh	0x3Fh	0x1Fh	0x17h
Maximum Resolution (bits)	10	10	10	8	7	5.5

Figure 97. Available PWM frequencies.

The datasheet shows that two frequencies are conveniently located within the desired range. We opt for 1.22 kHz. To get this frequency the timer prescaler must be set to 16.

T2CON: TIMER2 CONTROL REGISTER (ADDRESS 12h)

U-0	R/W-0	R/W-0	R/W-0	R/W-0	R/W-0	R/W-0	R/W-0
—	TOUTPS3	TOUTPS2	TOUTPS1	TOUTPS0	TMR2ON	T2CKPS1	T2CKPS0

bit 7   bit 0

bit 7   **Unimplemented:** Read as '0'

bit 6-3   **TOUTPS3:TOUTPS0**: Timer2 Output Postscale Select bits
0000 = 1:1 Postscale
0001 = 1:2 Postscale
0010 = 1:3 Postscale
•
•
•
1111 = 1:16 Postscale

bit 2   **TMR2ON**: Timer2 On bit
1 = Timer2 is on
0 = Timer2 is off

bit 1-0   **T2CKPS1:T2CKPS0**: Timer2 Clock Prescale Select bits
00 = Prescaler is 1
01 = Prescaler is 4
1x = Prescaler is 16

Figure 98. TIMER2 control register.

The timer prescaler is located in the TIMER2 control register, in bits 0 and 1, and will need to be set to 1 to achieve a prescaler of 16. In the 16F877_bert library this timer has already been switched on (otherwise the PWM module wouldn't work), so we must avoid switching it off accidentally. Therefore bit 2 also needs to be set to 1, like this:

```
T2CON = 0b000_0111
```

The software

A pulsating beep is a bit more interesting than a constant beep, so the PWM module is alternated between 0% and 59% duty cycle (values of 0 and 150):

```
-- turn beep on and off
if alternate then
   PWM_set_dutycycle (0,0)
else
   PWM_set_dutycycle (150,150)
end if
```

Putting it all together yields the following program:

```
-- JAL 2.0.4
include 16F877_bert

-- define variable
var bit alternate

-- start PWM module
PWM_init_frequency (true, true)

-- set an audible frequency
T2CON = 0b000_0111

forever loop

   -- wait a bit
   delay_100ms(2)

   -- turn beep on and off
   if alternate then
      PWM_set_dutycycle (0,0)
   else
      PWM_set_dutycycle (150,150)
   end if

   -- invert control variable
  alternate = ! alternate

end loop
```

The hardware

The speaker is scavenged from an old headphones set. It only uses about 1.54 mA, so it can be connected directly to the PIC™. If your speaker consumes more power you'll need to be careful; the coil in the speaker can cause a reverse current that damages the pin. In that case a current limiting resistor of 100 ohms in series with the speaker is recommended. In this project this resistor is not used. A 1 k variable resistor takes care of volume control.

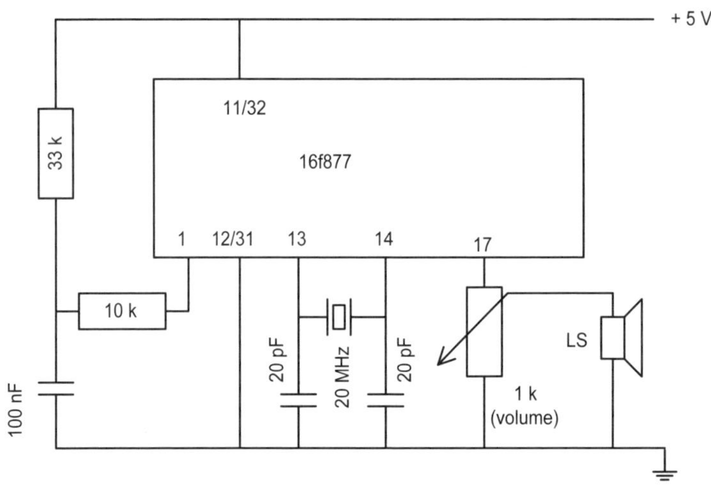

Figure 99. Beep.

On the breadboard it looks like this (the wires on the left belong to the Wisp628 programmer).

Figure 100. Beep.

9.2 Night buzzer

On the Internet I found a small project by a guy who calls himself Zach the Terrible, and with reason as you are about to find out. The purpose of this project is to really annoy someone with nightly noises.[89]

Technical background

You hide this little apparatus in the bedroom of your victim. Once it has been dark for a while the apparatus will make soft noises. As soon as your victim turns on the light to see where these strange buzzing noises are coming from they immediately stop. Your victim will think it was just his imagination and turn off the light, which triggers the apparatus to start its noises again. Hence the name, night buzzer.

The Software

Once the power is switched on the amount of light is measured. If this drops below a certain threshold (apparently it is dark), a noise is made. If the light measurement is above the threshold value the noise is switched off and the program will wait 30 seconds:

```
-- turn beep on and off
if resist < 100 then
   PWM_set_dutycycle (150,150)
else
   PWM_set_dutycycle (0,0)
   delay_1s(30)
end if
```

This means that depending on the moment that the victim switches off the light the beep will start after 0 to 30 seconds. You can modify this time period, but if you make it too long your victim may fall asleep before the beeping starts.

The program itself is quite simple and uses the PWM technique to make sound, as discussed in the previous section.

---

[89] Zach didn't use a PIC™ microcontroller, so the electronics and software design are mine; I just used his idea for this annoying device.

```
-- JAL 2.0.4
include 16F877_bert

-- define variables
var byte resist

-- define the pins
pin_a0_direction = input

-- enable pulse width modulation
PWM_init_frequency (true, true)

-- set an audible frequency
T2CON = 0b000_0111

forever loop

   -- convert analog on a0 to digital
   resist = ADC_read_low_res(0)

   -- turn beep on and off
   if resist < 100 then
     PWM_set_dutycycle (150,150)
   else
     PWM_set_dutycycle (0,0)
     delay_1s(30)
   end if

end loop
```

The hardware

The amount of light is measured with an LDR. The 10k variable resistor connected across the LDR enables you to adjust the threshold so it will not switch on until it is dark enough.

The 1k variable resistor controls the volume of the beep. It should be set low enough so that it is only just audible. If it is too loud the device can easily be located.

The speaker is scavenged from an old headset and makes enough noise for this purpose.

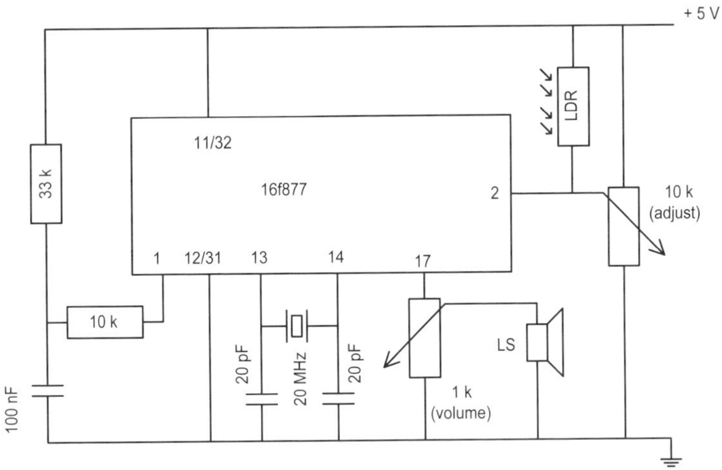

Figure 101. Night buzzer.

This is the setup on the breadboard:

Figure 102. Night buzzer.

9.3 Frequency generator

This frequency (tone) generator arguably uses the simplest method to make a sound: switching a pin between high and low in a continuous loop (see section 12.1 for a similar program using an interrupt).

Technical background

Switching a pin between high and low generates the tone. The PIC™ can do this so quickly that you wouldn't hear a thing. So we will use a delay statement to slow things down a bit:

```
forever loop

    delay_[something]us([something else])

    pin_d1 = ! pin_d1

end loop
```

In section 4.2 it was shown that *pin_d1* = *! pin_d1* will cause problems if a "slow" load is connected to the pin, such as a capacitor or a coil. The little speaker we use in this project has a very tiny coil, but it is a coil nonetheless. So instead of changing the pin directly we will use an intermediate variable called *flag*:

```
flag = ! flag
pin_d1 = flag
```

Now back to our sound loop. The question is what we need to use instead of "something" and "something else" in the delay statement to generate certain frequencies. Of course we can calculate for each delay what the resulting frequency would be. This will however not be correct, because the program has to do other things as well, such as running the loop. The easiest way to find out is to simply fill in values and measure the result with a frequency counter [90].

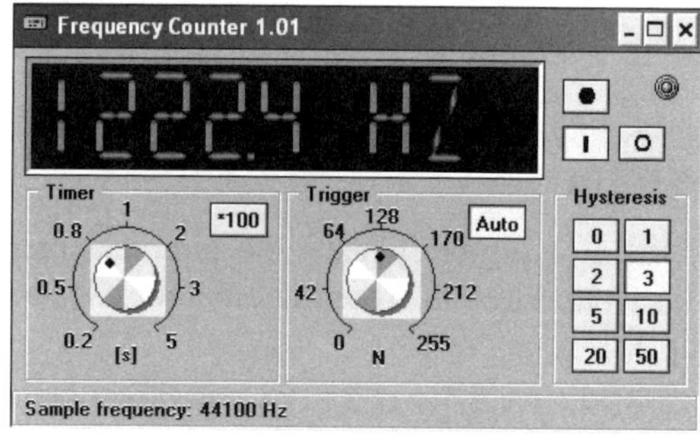

Figure 103. Frequency counter.

---

[90] This simple frequency counter is included in the download package.

Delay 50 uS

Value in delay command	Frequency (Hz)	
	Calculated	Measured
$1^{[91]}$	20000	7824
10	2000	982
50	400	213
100	200	108
255	78	44

Except for *value = 1*, the relationship between calculated and measured frequency is rather linear. So now the program overhead can be taken into account:

actual frequency = 5.93 + calculated frequency * 0.49 (deviation is less than 6%)

And the calculated frequency is determined using this formula:[92]

$$\text{calculated frequency} = \frac{1}{\text{total delay time}}$$

For *delay_20uS* the same table can be generated:

Delay 20 uS

Value in delay command	Frequency (Hz)	
	Calculated	Measured
1	50000	17214
10	5000	2408
50	1000	529
100	500	269
255	196	105

---

[91] So this would be *delay_50us(1)*, in the next table it would be *delay_20uS(1)*
[92] $m = 10^{-3}$, $u = 10^{-6}$, $n = 10^{-9}$, $p = 10^{-12}$

9 Sound

Which yields the exact same formula, again with the exception of a value of 1.

If we use a variable resistor to control the frequency the time required to measure an analog signal (20 uS) should be added to the total delay time. The formula remains exactly the same, except that 20 uS needs to be added to the total delay time.

Delay(uS)	Total time (uS)	Analog value	Frequency (Hz)	
			Calculated	Measured
50	70	1	14286	4530
50	70	50	286	208
50	70	255	55	44

Based on this you could add a scale to the knob of the variable resistor that controls the frequency (the one connected to pin a0).

The software

The program is very simple. After measuring the variable resistor this value is used in a delay statement. The operating range is a sound frequency between 44 and 4530 Hz.

```
-- JAL 2.0.4
include 16F877_bert

var byte resist
var bit flag

pin_d1_direction = output

forever loop

   resist = ADC_read_low_res(0)
   delay_50us(resist)

   flag = ! flag
   pin_d1 = flag

end loop
```

The result is a very nice square wave. The deformation is caused by the capacitor in the input circuit of the PC soundcard:

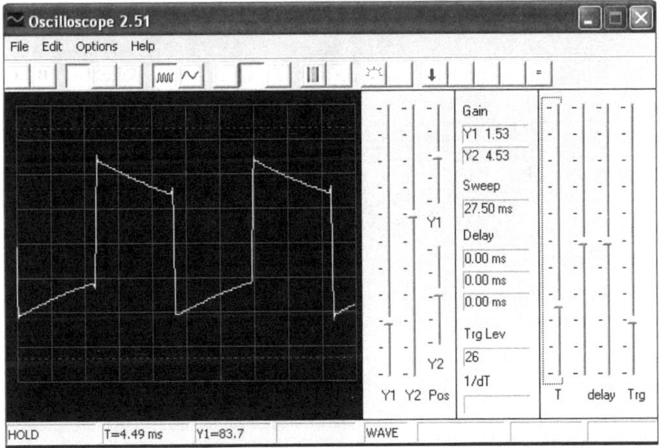

Figure 104. Result of the frequency generator on a software oscilloscope.

The hardware

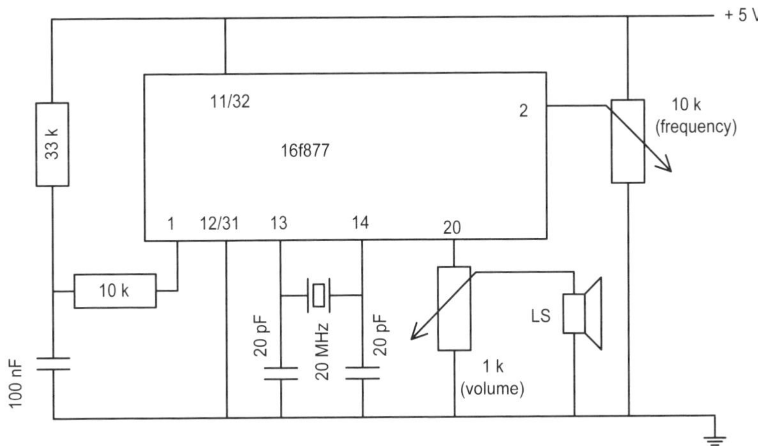

Figure 105. Frequency generator.

9 Sound

In the breadboard, the variable resistor on the left side controls the frequency and the one on the right side controls the volume.

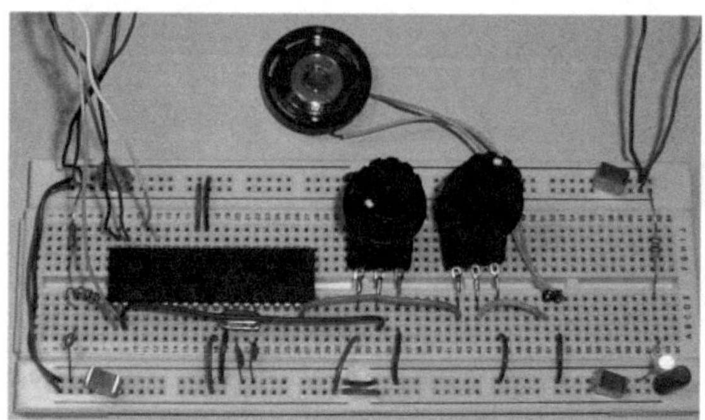

Figure 106. Frequency generator.

9.4 A simple melody

Here we use the microcontroller to play a simple melody. You can use this technique for a Christmas decoration or a door chime (in the latter case you will have to add an amplifier).

Technical background

Before you start reading the technical background it is advisable (or even necessary) to read section 12.1 first. That project explains the TIMER0 interrupt, and the description here continues where that one leaves off.

You have seen that changing the TIMER0 starting point changes the frequency of the sound. What frequency that will be can easily be calculated. Normally the interrupt will occur after 256 increments of the TIMER0 counter, and each increment takes 0.2 uS. As in section 12.1 we will set the prescaler to 2, which means that it will take <u>eight</u> times as long before the interrupt occurs. So in total it takes 256 * 0.2 * 8 = 409.6 uS, which equals a frequency of 2441 Hz.

So, when the starting point of the TIMER0 counter is 50, the interrupt will occur after (256 - 50) * 0.2 * 8 = 329.6 uS, which is a frequency of 3034 Hz.

This is the formula:

$$\text{frequency} = \frac{1{,}000{,}000}{(256 - x) * 0.2 * 8}$$

If we rearrange the formula a bit it will be more useful, because we can calculate the starting point for the TIMER0 counter for the desired frequency:

$$\text{starting point} = 256 - \frac{1{,}000{,}000}{\text{frequency} * 0.2 * 8}$$

There is one small catch, though. The calculated frequency is the frequency of the interrupt itself. For each interrupt the pin only changes once (high to low, or low to high):

    flag = ! flag
    pin_d1 = flag

This is only half a sound wave. Which means the sound frequency is half of the calculated frequency.

The frequency we need depends on the tuning system being used.[93] In this project we use the Equally Tempered Scale, which is designed especially for keyboards.

In the following table[94] the TIMER0 starting pint is calculated for each note:

Note	Frequency	TIMER0 start
-	1220	0
$D^{\#}_6/E^{b}_6$	1244.51	5
E_6	1318.51	19
F_6	1396.91	32
$F^{\#}_6/G^{b}_6$	1479.98	45
G_6	1567.98	57
$G^{\#}_6/A^{b}_6$	1661.22	68
A_6	1760	78
$A^{\#}_6/B^{b}_6$	1864.66	88
B_6	1975.53	98

---

[93] For example, the Pythagorean scale, the Mean-tone scale, Werckmeister scale, Equally Tempered Scale.

[94] The left two columns were made by professor Bryan H. Suits of the Physics Department of MTU (Michigan Tech University) using A4 = 440 Hz with C4 as middle C. The right hand column is calculated with the formula.

Note	Frequency	TIMER0 start
C_7	2093	107
$C^{\#}_7/D^{b}_7$	2217.46	115
D_7	2349.32	123
$D^{\#}_7/E^{b}_7$	2489.02	130
E_7	2637.02	137
F_7	2793.83	144
$F^{\#}_7/G^{b}_7$	2959.96	150
G_7	3135.96	156
$G^{\#}_7/A^{b}_7$	3322.44	162
A_7	3520	167
$A^{\#}_7/B^{b}_7$	3729.31	172
B_7	3951.07	177
C_8	4186.01	181
$C^{\#}_8/D^{b}_8$	4434.92	186
D_8	4698.64	189
$D^{\#}_8/E^{b}_8$	4978.03	193

Using an array the notes can be put into the program:

var byte notes[26] = {0, 5, 19, 32, 45, 57, 68, 78, 88, 98, 107, 115, 123, 130, 137, 144, 150, 156 ,162, 167 ,172, 177, 181, 186, 189, 193}

Now we are ready to write our song (remember the array starts counting at 0). In addition to a note we also need the duration of the note, which we will do in 50mS intervals.

So, to produce 1397 Hz for 1/2 second it would be:

note index	3
duration	10

We'll put all of the data into two separate arrays. The first containing all of the song notes and the second containing the durations of the notes. The following arrays contain the children's song "Brother John":

var byte songnotes[32] = {3, 5, 7, 3, 3, 5, 7, 3, 7, 8, 10, 7, 8, 10, 10, 12, 10, 8, 7, 3, 10, 12, 10, 8, 7, 3, 3, 0, 3, 3, 0, 3} var byte songdurations[32] = {10, 10, 10, 10, 10, 10, 10, 10, 10, 10, 20, 10, 10, 20, 5, 5, 5, 5, 10, 10, 5, 5, 5, 5, 10, 15,15 ,15 ,15 ,15 ,15}

The song is interrupt controlled. So if we want a small pause at the end before the song restarts a delay statement will only work if the interrupt is temporarily switched off. In section 12.1 you can see that the INTCON register is used for this:

```
interrupt off:          INTCON = 0b_0010_0000
interrupt back on:      INTCON = 0b_1010_0000
```

The Software

In the main loop of the program the right note must be pulled from the array:

```
note = songnotes[index]
```

Based on that the TIMER0 starting point must be pulled from the notes array. We will do this in the interrupt procedure so that the value can be put into the index right away:

```
TMR0 = notes[note]
```

Once the song is completed, a one second delay is inserted with the interrupt temporarily disabled:

```
INTCON = 0b_0010_0000
delay_1s(1)
INTCON = 0b_1010_0000
```

How the interrupt procedure works and why it looks like this is explained in section 12.1.

This is the completed program:

```
-- JAL 2.0.4
include 16F877_bert

var bit flag
var byte note
var byte index = 0
pin_d1_direction = output

var byte notes[26] = {0,5,19,32,45,57,68,78,88,98,107,115,123,130,137,
144,150,156,162,167,172,177,181,186,189,193}
```

```
var byte songnotes[32] =
{3,5,7,3,3,5,7,3,7,8,10,7,8,10,10,12,10,8,7,3,10,12,10,8,7,3,3,0,3,3,0,3}
var byte songdurations[32] =
{10,10,10,10,10,10,10,10,10,10,20,10,10,20,5,5,5,5,10,10,5,5,5,5,10,
15,15,15,15,15,15}

-- the actual interrupt routine
procedure make_a_sound is
   pragma interrupt

   if T0IF then

      -- switch pin to make sound
      flag = ! flag
      pin_d1 = flag

      -- use correct frequency
      TMR0 = notes[note]

      -- clear TOIF to re-enable timer interrupts
      T0IF = 0
   end if

end procedure

-- enable timer 0
OPTION_REG= 0b_0000_0010

-- enable interrupts
INTCON =  0b_1010_0000


forever loop

   -- get the next note from the array
   note =  songnotes[index]

   -- wait as specified in the duration array
   delay_50ms(songdurations[index])

   -- increase index
   index = index +1
```

```
    -- if the end of the song has been reached
    if index > 31 then

        -- reset index
        index = 0

        -- disable interrupts
        INTCON =  0b_0010_0000

        -- pause between songs
        delay_1s(1)

        -- enable interrupts
        INTCON =  0b_1010_0000

    end if

end loop
```

The hardware for this project is identical to that of section 9.1, except the speaker needs to be connected to pin 20 instead of pin 17. .

9.5 Recording sounds

In this project the sound of a cricket is converted to a digital format and stored in the program memory of the PIC™.

Technical background

The principle of this program is really simple. A short sound that has been recorded onto the PC as a WAV file, is stored in the PIC™ and played back using the PWM module.[95] For storage, we will use program memory, which is discussed more thoroughly in section 10.2. The TIMER0 interrupt also plays a major role here, and is covered in section 12.1 due to the complexity. Neither of these features will be given much explanation in this project, but are assumed to exist and be functioning; so read those sections first if you want more information.

---

[95] The maximum storage is approximately 0.8 seconds at a 9766 Hz bit rate.

9 Sound

Sound can be stored on the PC in many different formats. The best known at the moment is undoubtedly MP3[96], because it is heavily compressed to take up less space, making for quicker downloads and room for more music on your portable player. We will be using a different well-known format, however, the WAV file.[97] A WAV file is made by converting sound from analog to digital using an A/D converter (just like the one in a PIC™). So a WAV file just consists of a long row of numbers. These can be made analog (and thus audible) again using the PWM module of a PIC™.

Sound takes up a lot of space. The only place that we could possibly have enough room for sound is in program memory[98]. The designers of the microcontroller never envisioned anyone wanting to store data in program memory, so writing is relatively slow - too slow, in fact, to record a sound directly into it. A good alternative is to record the sound on a PC and then send it over an RS232 connection to the PIC™ at a more convenient pace.

Playback has to be done at a consistent rate; you will be able to hear the tiniest deviation. The best way to achieve this is to use the TIMER0 interrupt[99]. The faster you can send data to the PWM module the better the sound quality, but also the more room you need (per second of sound you need more data). As a compromise we have opted for 9766 Hz, a frequency that can be easily realized with the TIMER0 interrupt. This frequency is called the bit rate.

So now we need to record a sound on the PC and store it in a WAV file, with a bit rate of 9766 Hz. Unfortunately, this is much more complicated than it sounds. Many programs can record at this bit rate (sampling rate), but when they store the file they automatically use a more standard bit rate. The sound program Cool Edit can handle this, but it's not exactly freeware.[100] The download package includes a WAV file you can use, so that you don't need additional software to complete this project.

To convert the WAV file to data that can be sent to the PIC™ the WAVconvert program is used. This Visual Basic program is also included in the download package.

---

[96] Formally named MPEG-1 Audio Layer 3, after the Moving Picture Experts Group, for developing compression techniques to transfer sound and video over the Internet. Strangely enough they didn't develop MP3, which was actually done by European engineers working on the Eureka project. MP3 is a highly compressed audio file, where all frequencies inaudible to the human ear have been removed. It also uses a variable bit rate, which makes it a bit too complex for this book.

[97] Windows Wave, the standard sound format used by Microsoft Windows.

[98] See section 10.1

[99] See section12.1

[100] Cool Edit was purchased by Adobe and has become five times as expensive (from 69 to 349 dollars). Perhaps you can find an old version on the Internet, or another program that is capable of custom bit rates.

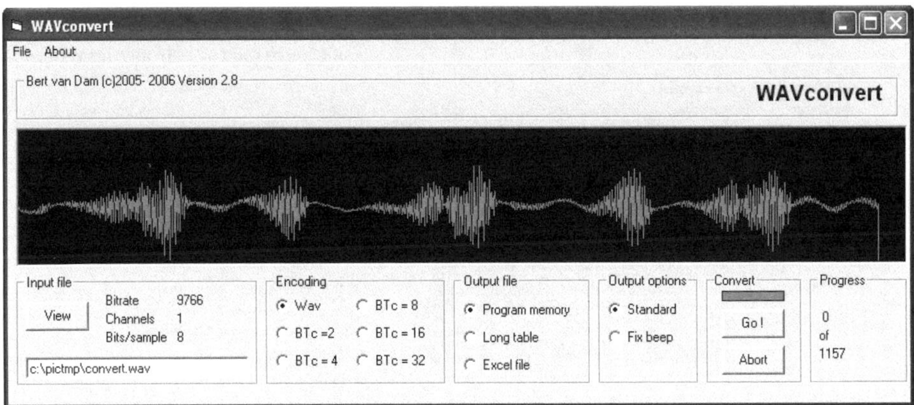

Figure 107. WAVconvert.

At the bottom left you enter the name of the WAV file (including the path). Click "view" to display the file. It will also display the bit rate, so if you made the file yourself this is a good time to check if the software you used actually stored the file at 9766 Hz. The length of the file is displayed at the bottom right corner.[101]

Note that there is only room for 7000 bytes; the cricket sound we are using only takes up 1157 bytes. Be sure to use the following settings:

Encoding	Wav
Output file	Program memory
Output Options	Standard

The other options will be discussed in later projects. When you click "go" the convert light will turn green and in the "progress" section the progress is shown. When the program is done a new file is created in the same directory where the original WAV file is located, with the extension of .prg. This is the file that needs to be loaded into the PIC™.

You can load the file using MICterm.

---

[101] In the progress section it says "0 of 1157" where 1157 is the length of the file. If you loaded a different file you will of course see a different length.

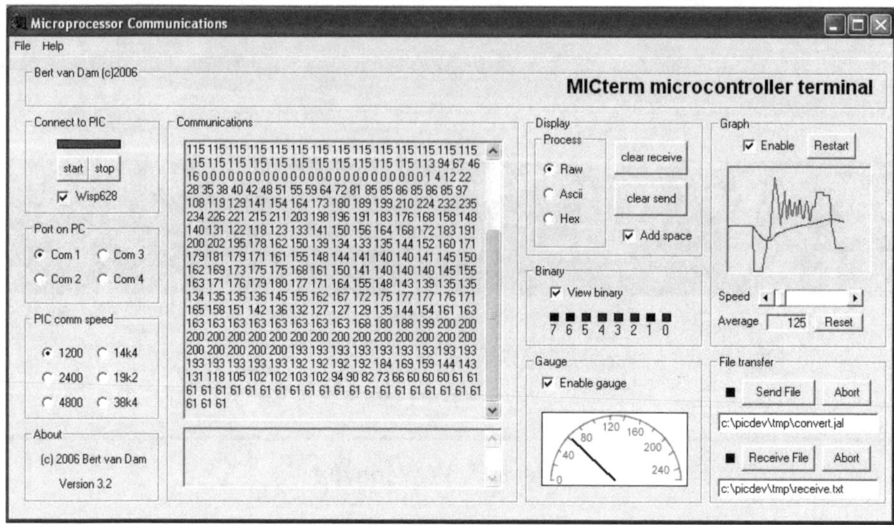

Figure 108. MICterm.

At the bottom right, just below the *Send File* button, you enter the name of the file including the path and the .prg extension. Then you connect to the PIC™ (remove the checkmark next to "Wisp628" if you do not use this programmer) and click on "*Send File*". In the "send" display you will see all the bytes of the file. This will take a while because we want to give the PIC™ sufficient time to store the data. The PIC™ will echo all of the data back, so in the "receive" display you should see the same numbers appear.

We are actually going a bit too fast, because we haven't even written a PIC™ program yet! So let's do that now.

The first question is how much data will be sent from the PC. WAVconvert has recorded this information at the beginning of the file with the sound data (the prg file):

Byte position in file	Value	Meaning
1	4	high byte
2	97	low byte
3	128	data
4	123	data
etc.		

The first step is to receive two bytes:

```
Serial_sw_read (hi)
Serial_sw_read(lo)
```

Then we can calculate how much data will have to be stored. We will also need this information during playback, so let's store it in program memory too.

```
-- calculate file length, echo and store
length = 256 * hi + lo

Program_eeprom_write( 999, lo )
Program_eeprom_write( 998, hi)
```

All of the data will be stored in the same memory that our program is. If you want to change this program please read section 10.1 first to see how you can prevent your program from being overwritten by data. If you don't change the program you don't need to worry about this. We will start writing in memory location 998 with the file size, and the data will start at location 1000, well clear of our program.

Now all that is needed is a simple loop to read the data coming in over the RS232 connection and store it in program memory:

```
for length + 1 loop
   Serial_sw_read (data)
   address = address + 1
   Program_eeprom_write( Address, Data )
end loop
```

Perhaps you noticed that the loop is executed once more than calculated. That is because the computer starts counting at 0 and we don't. So if you count to three that would be three numbers for humans (1, 2, 3) but four for computers (0, 1, 2, 3).

Playback of the sound is done by reading the data from memory and then sending it to the PWM module (see section 7.2 for an explanation of this module).

```
address = startaddress
for length +1 loop

    Program_eeprom_read( Address, Data )
    address = address + 1

    while ! interrupted loop
    end loop
    interrupted = false

    CCPR1L = data

end loop
```

The original WAV file was recorded with a bitrate of 9766 Hz, so play back needs to be done at the same speed. We will use the TIMER0 interrupt to achieve this. Each time a number has been retrieved from program memory using *program_eeprom_read* the program will wait for an interrupt to occur:

```
while ! interrupted loop
end loop
interrupted = false
```

These interrupts have a frequency of 9766 Hz, so it's exactly the right speed. The interrupt routine sets the variable *interrupted* to *true*. As long as the interrupt hasn't occurred, the variable will remain false and the program will wait in the loop. Once the interrupt occurs the program can escape from the loop. It will set the *interrupted* flag back to *false* in preparation for the next loop and send the data to the PWM module.

In the source code you can see the interrupt routine. It is described in detail in section 12.1, so at this point we will simply take it at face value.

This all sounds terribly complicated, but it's really not that bad.

The Software

If we were to put all of the parts together like this you would have to load the sound file into the PIC™ each time you switch it on. Of course this is not necessary because once the sound file is in program memory it will remain there even when the PIC™ is switched off (just like the program itself is retained). So we will add two push buttons, one for "recording" sound for when you use the program for the first time or want to change the sound, and one for playback.

A simple loop at the beginning of the program watches these two switches and awaits your choice:

```
while oke == 0 loop
    if record then oke = 1 end if
    if play then oke = 2 end if
end loop
```

The variable *oke* is used to check if a button has been pressed. As long as no buttons have been pressed (*oke* = 0) the program will remain in the loop. Further down in this section the steps you need to take to actually use this program are shown in a table.

The sound file in this project is that of a cricket. These animals don't chirp continuously, only every once in a while with (seemingly) random pauses…so we will do the same.

```
pause = random_byte
if pause > 200 then
    delay_1s(2)
else
    delay_1ms(random_byte)
end if
```

We draw a random value between 0 and 255. If it is smaller than 200 then that will be the time in milliseconds that we will wait before playing the sound again. If the value drawn is larger than 200 (22% of the draws) we will wait 2 seconds. This way the cricket sounds quite realistic! Play with these numbers to see for yourself.

To indicate that the PIC™ is ready for recording (which means you can start the file transfer on MICterm) an LED will be switched on once you have pressed the record push button. You only need to press it momentarily.

All of the data received from the PC is send back to the PC so any errors can be spotted. Sending back the same data is called echo. This is done by using a *serial_sw_write* command after each *serial_sw_read*.
This is the complete program:

```
-- JAL 2.0.4
include 16F877_bert

-- define variables
var byte data , pause, oke
var word length, startaddress, address, hi, lo
var bit interrupted

pin_d1_direction = output
pin_d2_direction = input
pin_c4_direction = input


var bit led is pin_d1
var bit play is pin_d2
var bit record is pin_c4

-- the interrupt routine
procedure make_a_sound is
   pragma interrupt

   if T0IF then

      -- signal that the interrupt has occurred
      interrupted = true

      -- clear T0IF to re-enable timer interrupts
      T0IF = 0
   end if

end procedure

-- init PWM
PWM_init_frequency (true, true)

-- record or play?
oke = 0
```

```
led = low

-- compilation memory length was 431
startaddress = 1000
address = startaddress

while oke == 0 loop
   if record then oke = 1 end if
   if play then oke = 2 end if
end loop


if oke == 1 then
   -- record
   led = high

   -- wait till character received, echo
   Serial_sw_read (hi)
   Serial_sw_write (hi)
   Serial_sw_read(lo)
   Serial_sw_write (lo)

   -- calculate the amount of data
   length = 256 * hi + lo

   -- remember length of data
   Program_eeprom_write( 999, lo )
   Program_eeprom_write( 998, hi)

   -- read data and store
   for length + 1 loop
      Serial_sw_read(data)
      Serial_sw_write (data)
      address = address + 1
      Program_eeprom_write( Address, Data )
   end loop

   led = low
end if

if oke == 2 then
   -- play
```

```
      -- retrieve length of data
      Program_eeprom_read( 999, lo )
      Program_eeprom_read( 998, hi)
      length = 256 * hi + lo
   end if

   -- enable TIMER0
   OPTION_REG= 0b_0000_0000

   -- enable interrupts
   INTCON =  0b_1010_0000

   forever loop
      address = startaddress
      for length +1 loop

         Program_eeprom_read( Address, Data )
         address = address + 1

         -- wait for the interrupt before playing the next sound value
         while ! interrupted loop
         end loop
         interrupted = false

         -- send value to PWM module
         CCPR1L = data

      end loop

      -- insert random pause
      pause = random_byte
      if pause > 200 then
         delay_1s(2)
      else
         delay_1ms(random_byte)
      end if

   end loop
```

The Hardware

The circuit is basically identical to the Beep project in section 9.1, which also uses the PWM module for sound. New are the two switches to allow record and play, and an LED to indicate "recording in progress".

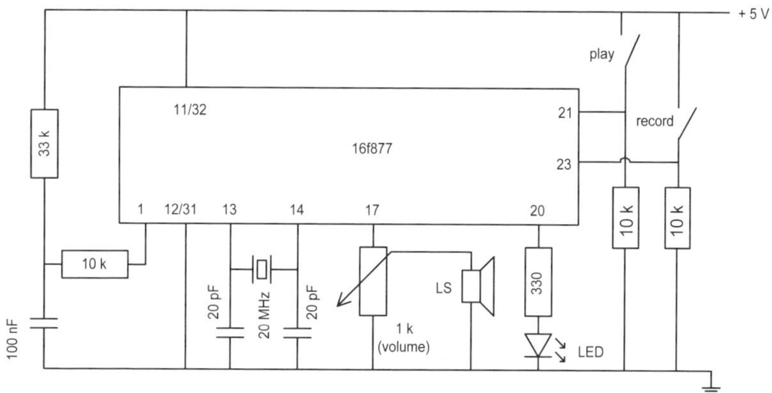

Figure 109. Recording brief sounds.

On the left side of the picture you can see the wires of the Wisp628 in-circuit programmer. These are the same wires used to transfer the data to the PIC™. So if you use this programmer you can leave the wires connected.

The two push button switches in the middle are for recording the sound file (left), in fact receiving a file from the PC, and for playback (right).

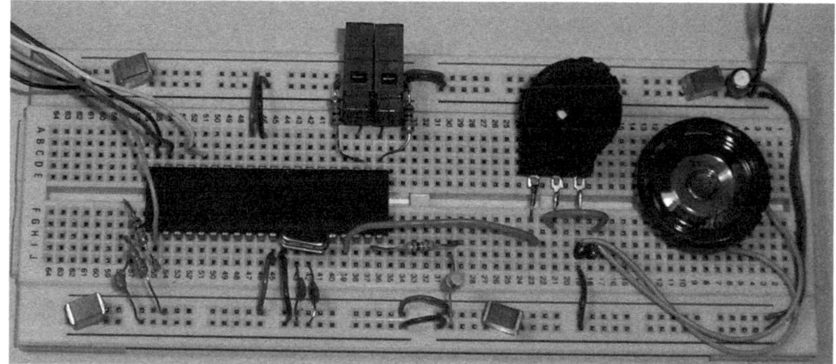

Figure 110. Recording brief sounds.

9 Sound

Using the device

Now we will discuss the steps you need to take to get this project to work once the hardware is built. There are three sets of instructions:

Quick start	Get the project working as quickly as possible with the ready-made files in the download package.
Do the conversion	Go through all the steps using the basic files in the download package.
Record your own	Record and use your own sound.

Quick start

This gets the project working with a minimum of fuss, by using the sound files from the download package.

1. Connect the programmer and download the program from section 9.5 into the PIC™ (0905.jal from the download package).
2. Start MICterm on the PC and enter the name of the converted file from the download package (with the .prg extension) into the box at the lower left hand corner (cricket.prg). Make sure you use the correct path to the file.
3. Connect to the PIC™ by clicking on the "start" button on the top left hand side. You will see a few numbers appear in the receive window, but this is normal.
4. Momentarily press the left push button on your project. The LED will now switch on.
5. Send the file to the PIC™ by clicking on the "Send File" button on MICterm. In the "send" display (the bottom display) you will see the data from the file which is being sent. You should see the same numbers (with a short delay) appear in the top display as they are being echoed back. If this doesn't happen there is no connection with the PIC™; check the wiring and start over.
6. Once the LED turns off the transfer is complete and the sound is now stored in the PIC™. It will start automatically.

If you want you can now switch the PIC™ off. Turn it back on, and if you want to hear the stored sound again press the push button on the right.

Doing the sound file conversion

Using the basic files in the download package to generate the data file, this requires just a bit more work.

1. Start the WAVconvert program on the PC and enter the name of the sound file from the download package into the window at the bottom left hand side (cricket.wav). Make sure you use the correct path.
2. Click on the "view" button to view the file.
3. Use the following settings:

Encoding	Wav
Output File	Program memory
Output Options	Standard

4. Click on "Go!" and wait for the green rectangle above the button to turn red again.
5. Connect the programmer and download the program from section 9.5 into the PIC™ (0905.jal from the download package).
6. Start MICterm on the PC and enter the name of the converted file from the download package (with the .prg extension) into the box at the lower left hand corner (cricket.prg). Make sure you use the correct path to the file.
7. Connect to the PIC™ by clicking on the "start" button on the top left hand side. You will see a few numbers appear in the receive window, but this is normal.
8. Momentarily press the left push button on your project. The LED will now switch on.
9. Send the file to the PIC™ by clicking on the "Send File" button on MICterm. In the "send" display (the bottom display) you will see the data from the file which is being sent. You should see the same numbers (with a short delay) appear in the top display as they are being echoed back. If this doesn't happen there is no connection with the PIC™; check the wiring and start over.
10. Once the LED turns off the transfer is complete and the sound is now stored in the PIC™. It will start automatically.

If you want you can now switch the PIC™ off. Turn it back on, and if you want to hear the stored sound again press the push button on the right.

9 Sound

Recording your own sound

If you want to use a sound of your own just follow these steps:

1. The sound is being played back multiple times and at irregular intervals (to emulate the behavior of a cricket). If that is your intention you can leave the software as it is. If you want something else (such as playing the file just once when the playback button is pressed) you need to change the PIC™ software.
2. Record a sound with a bit rate (sometimes called sampling rate) of 9766 Hz, or use an existing sound file and convert to this bit rate. There is room in the PIC™ for a sound of slightly less than one second (in section 9.6 a technique is discussed for longer sounds, though at a lower quality). Save the file as a WAV file.
3. Start the WAVconvert program on the PC and enter the name of the sound file in the window at the bottom left hand side. Make sure you use the correct path.
4. Click on the "view" button to view the file. If you don't see anything your sound file is not in order. If you do see the graphical display check the bit rate (left side). Also check if the total length is less than 7000 (bottom right hand side). Note that many programs will record at any bit rate but insist on writing at a more standard bit rate.
5. Use these settings:

Encoding	Wav
Output File	Program memory
Output Options	Standard

6. Click on "Go!" and wait for the green rectangle above the button to turn red again.
7. Connect the programmer and download the program from section 9.5 into the PIC™ (0905.jal from the download package), or the version that you modified. .
8. Start MICterm on the PC and enter the name of the converted file from the download package into the box at the lower left hand corner. It is the same name and path as your sound file, but with the .prg extension. Make sure you use the correct path to the file.
11. Connect to the PIC™ by clicking on the "start" button on the top left hand side. You will see a few numbers appear in the receive window, but this is normal.
12. Momentarily press the left push button on your project. The LED will now switch on.
13. Send the file to the PIC™ by clicking on the "Send File" button on MICterm. In the "send" display (the bottom display) you will see the data from the file which is being sent. You should see the same numbers (with a short delay) appear in the

top display as they are being echoed back. If this doesn't happen there is no connection with the PIC™; check the wiring and start over.

14. Once the LED turns off the transfer is complete and the sound is now stored in the PIC™. It will start automatically.

If you want you can now switch the PIC™ off. Turn it back on, and if you want to hear the stored sound again press the push button on the right.

9.6 Sound super-compression

Here is a special technique to get eight times more sound into a PIC™, and with quite reasonable quality. It isn't suited for music but there is room for about 11 seconds of speech.

Technical background

Storing sound takes a lot of memory, which is why external memory is usually used. In section 9.5 a WAV file was stored in a PIC™ and even with the low bit rate of 9766 Hz there was room for just 0.8 seconds. Mind you, the cricket sound only lasted 0.12 seconds, so there is still a lot you can do with that 0.8 seconds!

In this project we will use a little known but very smart and yet simple technique that only takes 1/8 of the room, and still has a quite acceptable intelligibility: BTc8.

Storage mechanism	Bytes needed per second	Time in 16F877 flash[102]
WAV 9766 Hz	9766	0.8 sec
BTc8 9766 Hz	1221	11.0 sec
BTc8 19531 Hz	2442	5.6 sec

In the table you can see that the available time with BTc8 is more than 8 times the available time with the WAV file. That is because the WAV file in the previous project was stored in 8-bit numbers. Program memory, however, is 14 bits wide. With BTc8 the entire memory width can be used which results in an additional 75% capacity.

This technique was first described by Roman Black and called the BTc (Binary Time constant) methodology[103].

---

[102] Based on a JAL program of 500 bytes with the rest of program memory available for sound.

[103] Roman Black, December 2001, http:\\www.romanblack.com

In a WAV file each point of the sound wave is accurately described by an 8-bit number. All of these numbers in a row describe the entire sound wave. When using the BTc8 method, however, this is not the case.

This is the concept: an RC network is connected to a pin of the PIC™. When the pin is for example changed from high to low the RC network is incapable of following this behavior immediately, so the signal will be lower but not completely low (ground). What does happen at the exit of the RC network can be predicted mathematically. By flipping the pin from high to low in a certain way the output of the RC network will mimic the shape of the original sound file.

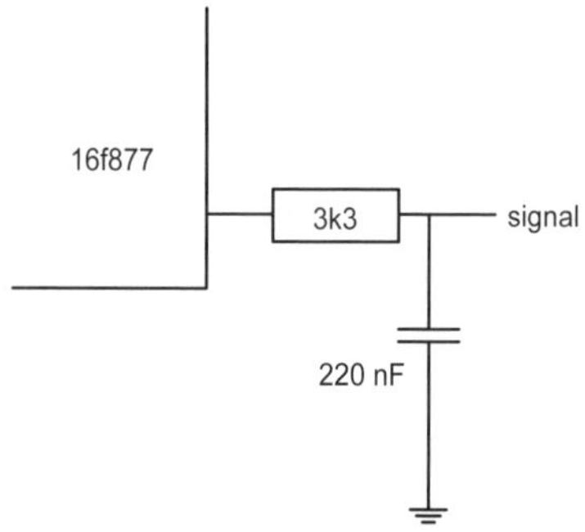

Figure 111. The RC network.

If the bit rate is high enough this can result in good sound quality. But the interesting thing is that even with a low bit rate the quality is still very reasonable. It's good enough, anyway, for simple speech, such as "You pressed button one". In this project we will push the BTc8 technique to its limits by choosing a very low bit rate. This will have quite an impact on the quality, of course, but it does show how much sound can be stored in a 16F877.

Writing the code is the hard part, because a row of zeros and ones must be selected which mimics the sound file as closely as possible. The difficulty is that the voltage at the output of the RC network doesn't always change by the same amount at every zero or one transition of the pin.

The behavior can be predicted using a simple formula:

Tc=RC

where   R = resistance
        C = capacitor
        Tc = time constant

The time constant is the amount of time needed to charge the capacitor through the resistor to 63.2%.[104] By choosing a convenient time constant (or rather a resistor and capacitor combination), the voltage on the capacitor - and thus the output of the RC network - will increase exactly 1/8 of the maximum possible voltage increase during the time that the pin is high. This convenient time constant is called the "binary time constant" 8, or BTc8.

Of course that also means that the sound curve can never rise faster than 1/8 of the maximum possible rise per bit. Should you choose BTc2 (where the voltage increases 1/2 of the maximum possible increase) the more subtle wave fluctuations cannot be followed. So there is an optimum combination of the type of sound you want to encode, the BTc value you choose, and the bit rate (in this case, the frequency with which you can set the pin high or low). For the best results you will need to experiment a little.

These are the time constants as calculated by Roman Black:

BTc2 = 0.6931 x Tc
BTc4 = 0.2877 x Tc
BTc8 = 0.1393 x Tc
BTc16 = 0.0645 x Tc
BTc32 = 0.0317 x Tc
BTc64 = 0.0157 x Tc

Encoding is handled by the WAVconvert program, which was also used in the previous section. It supports BTc2 to BTc32 and uses a series of steps to encode the signal.

---

[104] Or discharge to 36.8%, depending on whether the pin is set high or low.

9 Sound

1. The model for the voltage on the output of the RC network has to start somewhere. It is logical to start in the middle of the curve since most sound files begin with silence. In Visual Basic[105] this is handled as follows:

    > *'set voltages (where 255 = 5 volts)*
    > Vmax = 255
    > Vmin = 0
    > *'start at the middle of the model*
    > Vmodel = (Vmax - Vmin) / 2

2. In order to determine the next value we need to predict what would happen if the pin is made high, and what would happen if the pin is made low. From these two values we pick the one closest to the original value in the WAV file.

    a. The maximum increase the voltage can make is the difference between the current (model) voltage and the maximum voltage (5 V). This number is divided by 8 (because we use BTc8) and the result is added to the model voltage. This becomes the new model value for when the pin is made high.

    b. For the maximum decrease that the voltage can make the same calculation is made, but now using the difference between the current (model) voltage and the minimum voltage (ground). Note that the maximum possible increase and decrease are not the same (unless the model is at exactly 2.5 V). This is the new value of the model for when the pin is made low.

3. Now we compare both model values with the real value in the WAV file. The closest one is selected as the new model value. The corresponding pin status (high or low) is recorded.

In the next table this has been calculated for 6 values of a WAV file as an example. In the first line the voltage is 4 V. The model starts at 2.5 V. We see that if the pin is made high the new model voltage would be 2.8125 V. If the pin is made low the new model value would be 2.1875 V. The value for making the pin high is closest to the actual value, so this one is selected and in the last column a "1" is added.

---

[105] WAVconvert is written in Visual Basic. If you don't own Visual Basic and you want to write your own program you can use the code bits discussed in this section. The download package also contains the executable version if you simply want to follow the book without Visual Basic.

	Voltage		Pin		BTc8 Code
	Actual	Model	High	Low	
1	4.000	2.5000	**2.8125**	2.1875	1
2	4.000	2.8125	**3.0859**	2.4610	1
3	4.000	3.0859	**3.3250**	2.8470	1
4	3.525	3.5250	**3.7094**	3.0840	1
5	3.000	3.7094	3.8707	**3.2457**	0
6	2.990	3.2457	3.4650	**2.8400**	0

It sounds more complicated than it is. In Visual Basic it would be handled like this:

```
'calculate High (Bhi) and Low bit (Blo)
Bhi = ((Vmax - Vmodel) / BTc) + Vmodel
Blo = Vmodel - ((Vmodel - Vmin) / BTc)

'find closest one and use it
If Abs(Vact - Bhi) < Abs(Vact - Blo) Then
    'Hi bit was closest
    Vmodel = Bhi
    Boutput = 1
Else
    'Lo bit was closest
    Vmodel = Blo
    Boutput = 0
End If
```

The question of course is how closely this resembles the original WAV file. The next Figure shows a part of the original file and the BTc8 conversion, both at a bit rate of 9766 Hz.

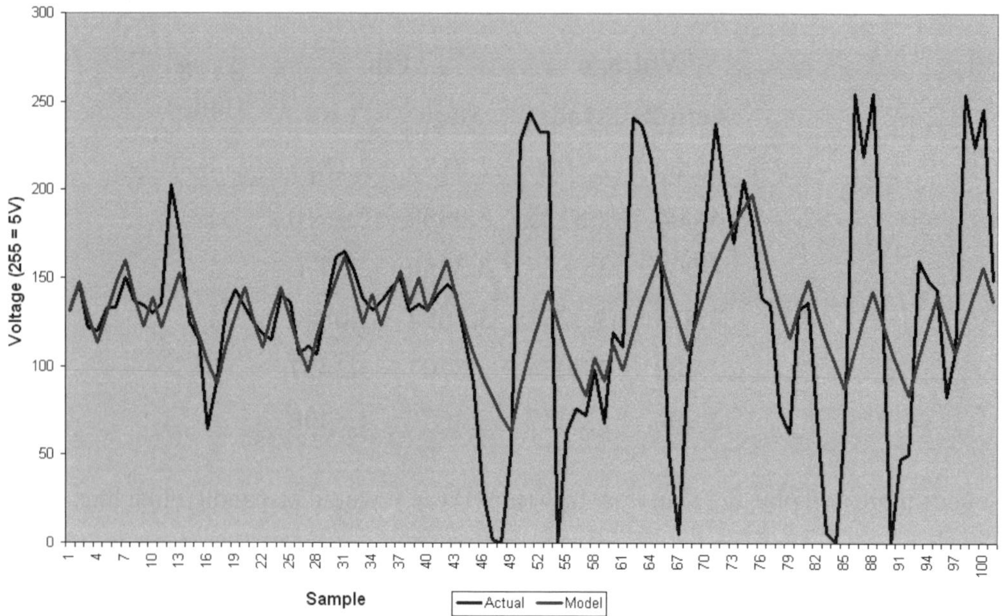

Figure 112. Comparing actual and BTc8 model at a 9766 Hz bit rate.

You can see that the model follows the original sound file quite reasonably when the voltage swings are low, but at higher voltage swings it completely loses track. This is to be expected, because the maximum possible change in voltage is only 1/8 of the possible change while the real sound file has no limitations. The bottom line, of course, is how this will sound.

Just like in the previous project we will use a bit rate of 9766 Hz.[106] From this we know how long a pin will be high:

$$\frac{1}{9766 \text{ Hz}} = 1.02 \ 10^{-4}$$

In order to calculate the time constant fot BTc8 it needs to be divided by 0.1393.

So Tc = 1.02 10^{-4} / 0.1393 = 7.35 10^{-4}

---

[106] With the combined knowledge of sections 9.4 and 10.1 you should be capable of using almost any bit rate you want.

Now we just have to find a combination of resistor and capacitor values that obeys:

$$R * C = 7.35 \ 10^{-4}$$

In the table below the resistor values are calculated for a number of capacitors from my parts box. Unfortunately, not all resistors actually exist, so in a separate column the closest commercially available value is shown, along with the calculated error.

Capacitor (C)		Resistor (R)		Error
Value	in F	Value	closest available	%
220nF	$2.2 \ 10^{-7}$	3341	*3k3*	1.22
0.1uF	$1 \ 10^{-7}$	7350	7k5	2.04
47nF	$4.7 \ 10^{-8}$	15.638	15k	4.07
22nF	$2.2 \ 10^{-8}$	33.409	33k	1.23
10nF	$1 \ 10^{-8}$	73.500	75k	2.04
1nF	$1 \ 10^{-9}$	735.000	750k	2.04
470pF	$4.7 \ 10^{-10}$	1.563.830	1m6	2.31

The combination I chose is a capacitor of 220nF with a resistor of 3k3. The resulting error is just 1.2 %. The RC network will only behave as predicted when it carries no load and, of course, a speaker is considered a load. So we will need to use an amplifier that follows the voltage and can supply power to a speaker, without loading the RC network. The 741 Operational Amplifier (Opamp[107]) will work well, since it has a very high input impedance ("resistance") resulting in almost no current being drawn from the RC network.

---

[107] Opamps were originally developed for carrying out calculations ("operations") in analog computers. Modern computers are digital and don't use Opamps anymore. Opamps have found use in places where signals have to be amplified and are very low in price.

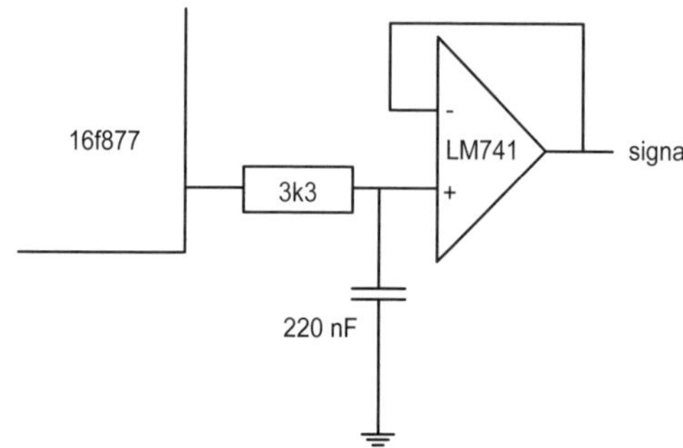

Figure 113. The 741 Opamp as a non-inverting voltage follower.

This setup with the Opamp is only useful at higher bit rates and higher BTc's, such as a bit rate of 32kHz and BTc32. At low values - like in this project - you can connect the pin directly to the speaker since the sound quality is so bad that it will not make much difference.

The software

The program is roughly identical to the previous project with a few significant changes.

WAVconvert has generated a file with a series of numbers. Contrary to a WAV file these numbers have no meaning; they are just individual bits that happen to be grouped in sets of 8 in order to be transferable using MICterm.

The data are stored in the 16F877 in 14-bit numbers, because we are not using the "normal" data memory but the 14-bits-wide program memory instead (although it was never meant for data). In order not to waste any space all incoming bits are re-grouped into sets of 14 and stored:

```
for length + 1 loop
   Serial_sw_read(data)



   for 8 loop
      -- store data bit by bit in value
      value = value << 1
      value = value + inbit
      data = data << 1
      outcount = outcount + 1

      if outcount == 14 then
```

```
        -- outgoing word completed write to memory
        address = address + 1
        Program_eeprom_write( Address, value )
        outcount = 0
      end if
    end loop

      -- show empty data to PC
      Serial_sw_write (data)
    end loop
```

The variable *value* will eventually be put into memory and the variable *data* has just arrived from the PC. The variable *inbit* is defined as:

```
    var byte data
    var bit inbit at data : 7
```

…Which makes it the 7th (leftmost) bit of the incoming number *data*. We start by shifting all bits in *value* one position to the left:

```
    value = value << 1
```

Then we add *inbit*:

```
    value = value + inbit
```

Since *inbit* is only one bit long this addition only changes the rightmost bit of *value*. So *value* now contains the leftmost bit of *data*. We then repeat for the next bit of *data*:

```
    data = data << 1
```

Continuing this way all bits from *data* are put into *value* one by one. When we finish all 8 bits in *data* a new number is read from the PC. And when *value* contains 14 bits of data it is written to memory.

If after the PC is done sending data there are still empty memory bits left over they will be filled with zeros and written to memory as well:

```
    if  outcount != 0 then
        -- last byte read, complete word and write to memory
        value = value << (14 - outcount)
        address = address + 1
        Program_eeprom_write( Address, value )
    end if
```

Playback is also a bit different. The bits must be played from left to right because we have just stored them that way. By defining the variable *codec* like this:

```
    var word value
    var bit codec at value : 13
```

...It contains the leftmost bit of *value*, the variable that was pulled from memory. Before an interrupt takes place *value* is shifted one position to the left so the next bit ends up in *codec*:

```
    value = value << 1
```

In the interrupt routine, *codec* is send to the output pin:

```
    -- send signal to pin
    sound = codec
```

Which means it will change status in exactly the right rhythm. The completed program is shown below:

```
    -- JAL 2.0.4
    include 16F877_bert

    -- define variables
    var byte pause, outcount
    var word startaddress, address , hi, lo
    var bit interrupted

    var byte data
    var bit inbit at data : 7

    var word value
    var bit codec at value : 13

    var word length
```

```
var byte leng[2] at length

pin_c2_direction = output
pin_d1_direction = output
pin_d2_direction = input
pin_c4_direction = input


var bit led is pin_d1
var bit play is pin_d2
var bit record is pin_c4
var bit sound is pin_c2

-- the interrupt routine
procedure make_a_sound is
  pragma interrupt

  if T0IF then

     -- send signal to pin
     sound = codec

     -- signal that the interrupt has occurred
     interrupted = true

     -- clear T0IF to re-enable timer interrupts
     T0IF = 0
  end if

end procedure

-- record or play?
led = low

-- program length at compilation 675
startaddress = 1000
address = startaddress

forever loop

  if record then
```

```
while record loop
  delay_10ms(1)
end loop

-- disable interrupts
INTCON =  0b_0000_0000

-- record
led = high

-- wait till character received, echo inverted
Serial_sw_read (hi)
Serial_sw_write (hi)
Serial_sw_read(lo)
Serial_sw_write (lo)

-- calculate the amount of data
length = 256 * hi + lo

-- read data and store
for length + 1 loop
  Serial_sw_read(data)


  for 8 loop
    -- store data bit by bit in value
    value = value << 1
    value = value + inbit
    data = data << 1
    outcount = outcount + 1

    if outcount == 14 then
      -- outgoing word completed write to memory
      address = address + 1
      Program_eeprom_write( Address, value )
      outcount = 0
    end if
  end loop

  -- show empty data to PC
  Serial_sw_write (data)
end loop
```

```
if  outcount != 0 then
  -- last byte read, complete word and write to memory
  value = value << (14 - outcount)
  address = address + 1
  Program_eeprom_write( Address, value )
end if

length = address - startaddress

-- remember length of data
Program_eeprom_write( 999, leng[1] )
Program_eeprom_write( 998, leng[0])
Serial_sw_write (leng[1])
Serial_sw_write (leng[0])

-- done switch led off
led = low

end if

if play then
  -- play

  -- enable timer 0
  OPTION_REG= 0b_0000_0000

  -- enable interrupts
  INTCON =  0b_1010_0000

  -- retreive length of data
  Program_eeprom_read( 999, hi )
  Program_eeprom_read( 998, lo)
  length = 256 * hi + lo
  address = startaddress

for length + 1 loop

    -- retrieve values from memory
    Program_eeprom_read( Address, Value )
    address = address + 1
    for 14 loop
```

```
    -- wait for the interrupt before playing the next sound value
    while ! interrupted loop
    end loop
    interrupted = false

    -- prepare next value
    value = value << 1

  end loop

 end loop

end if
end loop
```

You may have noticed that the main loop is a bit different than usual. At playback the sound is only played once. The loop has been modified so that the push button remains enabled; so you can playback whenever you want.

The hardware

In the schematic you can see the RC network connected to the LM741 Opamp. As always, pins not shown in the schematic are not in use. The volume control variable resistor is not really necessary, because the sound is not very loud. Between the Opamp and the variable resistor a capacitor is connected to block DC from going to the speaker.

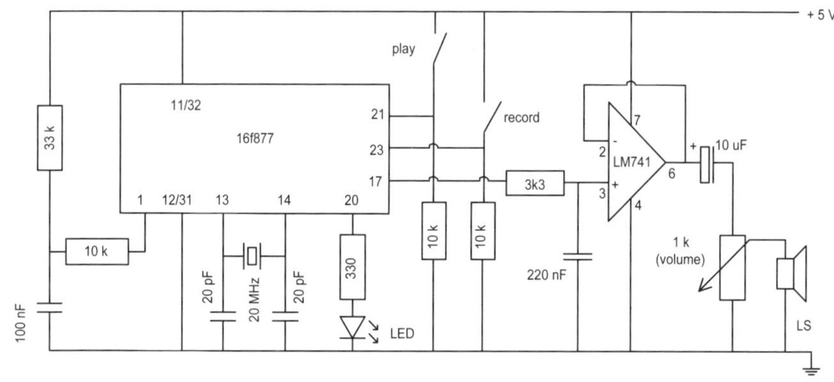

Figure 114. Super compression.

This setup with the Opamp is only useful at higher bit rates and higher BTc's, such as a bit rate of 32kHz and BTc32. At low values, like in this project, you can connect pin 17 directly to the speaker since the sound quality is so bad that it will not make much difference.

The circuit on the breadboard:

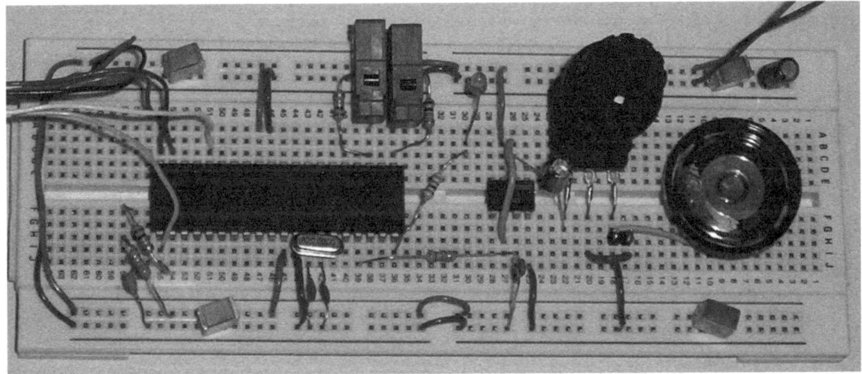

Figure 115. Super compression.

The left push button is for recording from the PC and the right push button is for playback. The long wires on the left hand side are from the Wisp628 in-circuit programmer, which is also used (in pass-through mode) to send the sound data to the 16F877 using MICterm. For transfer you only need the green and blue wires, but the others can remain connected.

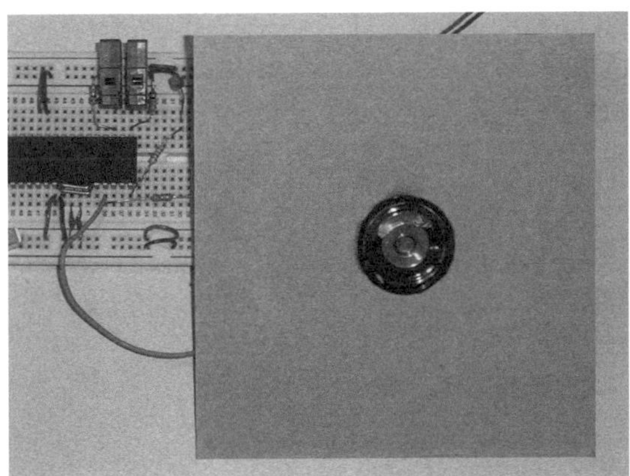

Figure 116. Cardboard sounding board.

The sound is significantly improved when a simple piece of cardboard is used as a sounding board for the speaker. The intelligibility is very much improved, as is the warmth of the sound.

The beep

Buried in the sound you can hear a soft beep or whistle, which is particularly noticeable during silent parts.

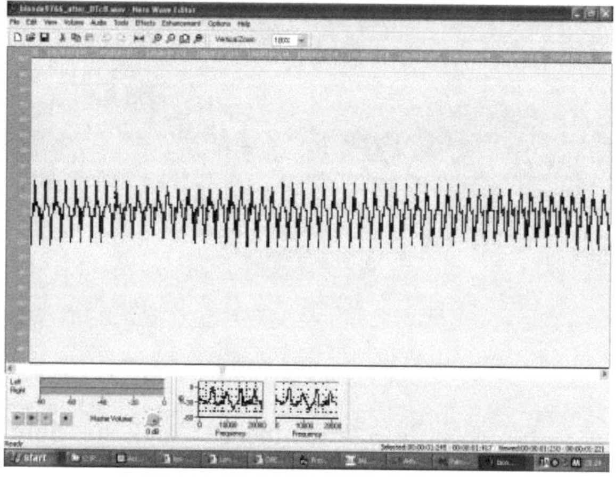

Figure 117. Whistle during a silent part.

In Figure 117 you see a strong magnification of a silent part of the file, with the whistle clearly visible. The frequency is around 5 kHz, which is the highest possible frequency you can make with an interrupt at 9766 Hz. Apparently this is a row of alternating zeros and ones. It appears that the coding mechanism has a problem with coding a constant voltage. Since it is a row of 01010 the best solution would be to suppress rows like this during conversion. WAVconvert has a special function for this that you can enable by checking "Fix Beep" in the output options.

Considering the technology used the sound quality is quite reasonable once the whistle is removed and a cardboard sounding board is used. Perhaps could be even better with a quality speaker!

Using the device

Now we will discuss the steps you need to take to get this project to work once the hardware is built. There are three sets of instructions:

Quick start	Get the project working as quickly as possible with the ready-made files in the download package.
Do the conversion	Go through all the steps using the basic files in the download package.
Record your own	Record and use your own sound.

Quick start

This gets the project working with a minimum of fuss, by using the sound files from the download package.

1. Connect the programmer and download the program from section 9.6 into the PIC™ (0906.jal from the download package).
2. Start MICterm on the PC and enter the name of the converted file from the download package (blonde9766.prg) into the box at the lower left hand corner. Make sure you use the correct path to the file.
3. Connect to the PIC™ by clicking on the "start" button on the top left hand side. You will see a few numbers appear in the receive window, but this is normal.
4. Momentarily press the left push button on your project. The LED will now switch on.
5. Send the file to the PIC™ by clicking on the "Send File" button on MICterm. In the "send" display (the bottom display) you will see the data from the file which is being sent. You should see numbers (with a short delay) appear in the top display. If this doesn't happen there is no connection with the PIC™; check the wiring and start over.
6. Once the LED turns off the transfer is complete and the sound is now stored in the PIC™.
7. Press the push button on the right to start the playback.

If you want you can now switch the PIC™ off. Turn it back on, and if you want to hear the stored sound again press the push button on the right.

Doing the sound file conversion

Using the basic files in the download package to generate the data file, this requires just a bit more work.

1. Start the WAVconvert program on the PC and enter the name of the sound file from the download package into the window at the bottom left hand side (blonde9766.wav). Make sure you use the correct path.
2. Click on the "view" button to view the file.
3. Use the following settings:

Encoding	BTc8
Output File	Program memory
Output Options	Fix Beep

4. Click on "Go!" and wait for the green rectangle above the button to turn red again.
5. Connect the programmer and download the program from section 9.6 into the PIC™ (0906.jal from the download package).
6. Start MICterm on the PC and enter the name of the converted file (with the .prg extension) into the box at the lower left hand corner (blonde9766.prg). Make sure you use the correct path to the file.
7. Connect to the PIC™ by clicking on the "start" button on the top left hand side. You will see a few numbers appear in the receive window, but this is normal.
8. Momentarily press the left push button on your project. The LED will now switch on.
9. Send the file to the PIC™ by clicking on the "Send File" button on MICterm. In the "send" display (the bottom display) you will see the data from the file which is being sent. You should see numbers (with a short delay) appear in the top display. If this doesn't happen there is no connection with the PIC™; check the wiring and start over.
10. Once the LED turns off the transfer is complete and the sound is now stored in the PIC™.
11. Press the push button on the right to start the playback.

If you want you can now switch the PIC™ off. Turn it back on, and if you want to hear the stored sound again press the push button on the right.

Recording your own sound

If you want to use a sound of your own just follow these steps:

1. Record a sound with a bit rate (sampling rate) of 9766 Hz, or use an existing sound file and convert to this bit rate. There is room in the PIC™ for a sound of about 11 seconds. Save the file as a WAV file.

2. Start the WAVconvert program on the PC and enter the name of the sound file into the window at the bottom left hand side. Make sure you use the right path.
3. Click on the "view" button to view the file. If you don't see anything your sound file is not in order. If you do see the graphical display check the bit rate (left side). Also check if the total length is less than 13000 (bottom right hand side). Note that many programs will record at any bit rate but insist on writing at a more standard bit rate.
4. Use these settings:

Encoding	BTc8
Output File	Program memory
Output Options	Fix Beep

5. Click on "Go!" and wait for the green rectangle above the button to turn red again.
6. Connect the programmer and download the program from section 9.6 into the PIC™ (0906.jal from the download package), or the version that you modified.
7. Start MICterm on the PC and enter the name of the converted file from the download package into the box at the lower left hand corner. It is the same name and path as your sound file, but with the .prg extension. Make sure you use the correct path to the file.
8. Connect to the PIC™ by clicking on the "start" button on the top left hand side. You will see a few numbers appear in the receive window, but this is normal.
9. Momentarily press the left push button on your project. The LED will now switch on.
10. Send the file to the PIC™ by clicking on the "Send File" button on MICterm. In the "send" display (the bottom display) you will see the data from the file which is being sent. You should see numbers (with a short delay) appear in the top display. If this doesn't happen there is no connection with the PIC™; check the wiring and start over.
11. Once the LED turns off the transfer is complete and the sound is now in the PIC™.
12. Press the push button on the right to start the playback.

If you want you can now switch the PIC™ off. Turn it back on, and if you want to hear the stored sound again press the push button on the right.

10 Memory

The 16F877 has three different types of memory available:

Memory	Quantity	Purpose
Program memory (FLASH)	8192 words (14 bits)	This is where the program is stored.
RAM	368 bytes (8 bits)	This is where all the variables of the program are stored.
EEPROM	256 bytes (8 bits)	This is where the programmer (you) can store data.

In this chapter we will discuss how to use each type of memory. We will also discuss external EEPROM, which will allow you to increase the available memory almost without limit.

Memory	Quantity	Purpose
External EEPROM with I2C	64k bytes, 8 bits	In this project two EEPROM chips are connected to a PIC™ using the I2C serial protocol. A software I2C library is used.

10.1 FLASH program memory

We will start with the most difficult type of memory, because this is just about the last place where you are supposed to store your data. Also take a look at section 12.8 where JAL shows it's true power with the *long table* - a unique way to store data in program memory.

Technical background

Program memory is the largest memory the 16F877 has available, so it is a very attractive location for your data. This is also the memory that contains your program, so how much room is actually available remains to be seen and depends on the size of your program.

Which means that

1. We don't have the total memory capacity available.
2. We should avoid writing over the program itself.

Fortunately, this is easier than it would appear. According to the datasheet of the 16F877 the memory map is organized as follows:

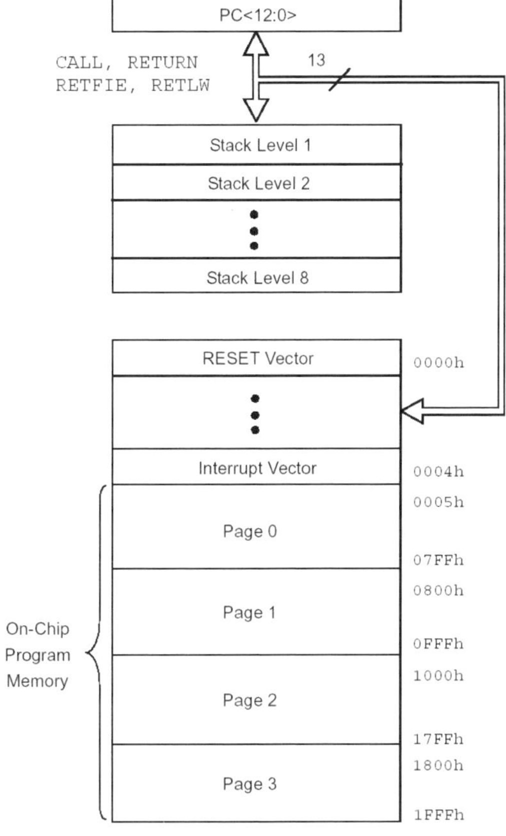

Figure 118. Memory map of the 16F877.

A total of 8192 14-bit words[108] are available. If you use an address higher than this the counter will rollover to zero and you will end up in the middle of your program, which is not a good idea.

---

[108] A 14-bit word consists of a low byte of 8 bits and a high byte of 6 bits. So the highest value that the high byte can hold is 63 (0b111111 = 63).

There is also a lower limit. Once the program has been compiled with JALedit the size is shown. In Figure 20 you can see that this particular program has a size of 269 words (this is the "code area"). In the memory map you can see that a program is stored starting at address 5h. So the total memory usage of this program is 5h + 269 = 274 words.

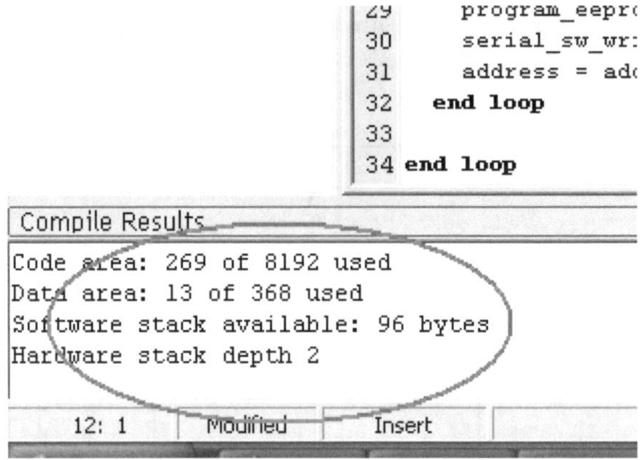

Figure 119. Compiler result.

In this situation you can use all memory between addresses 274 and 8192 without any danger to the program.[109]

If you want to use program memory you should take the following steps:

1. Write the program.
2. Compile it and note the amount of space used (code area).
3. Add five to this number.
4. Use this value in your program as the lower limit
   (and 8192 as the upper limit).

The standard library contains a few commands for the use of program memory.[110] The details of how these commands work are very complicated and outside the scope of this book.[111] So we will just limit ourselves to their use:

---

[109] If you use a bootloader (see section 12.9) you also have to take into account the amount of memory used by the bootloader.

[110] Standard JAL also contains a command for the use of program memory: the long table (see section 12.8).

[111] The library is pic_program_eeprom by Stef Mientki, part of the 16F877_bert standard library.

program_eeprom_read(address, data)	Read the program memory *address* and store the result in *data*. The command is safe; you could even write a program that reads itself.
data = program_eeprom(address)	A different way to achieve the same result.
program_eeprom_write(address, data)	Write the value in *data* to program memory location *address*. You can accidentally overwrite your program with this command.[112]

The software

Now that the upper and lower limits of the available program memory have been determined the program itself is perhaps not very exciting. Right above the program in memory, a row of numbers is stored:

```
address = 274
for 255 loop
   program_eeprom_write (address,data)
   data = data + 1
   address = address + 1
end loop
```

And subsequently read back:

```
address = 274
for 255 loop
   program_eeprom_read (address,data)
   serial_sw_write(data)
   address = address + 1
end loop
```

To prove that it works the results are sent to the PC. As you can see the numbers arrive intact and the program keeps working so we have indeed succeeded in avoiding overwriting the program.

---

[112] You can also overwrite your program on purpose, which would be a self-modifying program.

Communications

```
0 1 2 3 4 5 6 7 8 9 10 11 12 13 14 15 16 17 18 19 20 21 22 23
24 25 26 27 28 29 30 31 32 33 34 35 36 37 38 39 40 41 42 43
44 45 46 47 48 49 50 51 52 53 54 55 56 57 58 59 60 61 62 63
64 65 66 67 68 69 70 71 72 73 74 75 76 77 78 79 80 81 82 83
84 85 86 87 88 89 90 91 92 93 94 95 96 97 98 99 100 101
102 103 104 105 106 107 108 109 110 111 112 113 114 115
116 117 118 119 120 121 122 123 124 125 126 127 128 129
130 131 132 133 134 135 136 137 138 139 140 141 142 143
144 145 146 147 148 149 150 151 152 153 154 155 156 157
158 159 160 161 162 163 164 165 166 167 168 169 170 171
172 173 174 175 176 177 178 179 180 181 182 183 184 185
186 187 188 189 190 191 192 193 194 195 196 197 198 199
200 201 202 203 204 205 206 207 208 209 210 211 212 213
214 215 216 217 218 219 220 221 222 223 224 225 226 227
228 229 230 231 232 233 234 235 236 237 238 239 240 241
242 243 244 245 246 247 248 249 250 251 252 253 254
```

Figure 120. The result in MICterm.

Just for fun you could use a value lower than 274 and see what happens if you write in the middle of your program. Don't worry, it's just software; you won't break anything.

This is the completed program:

```
-- JAL 2.0.4
include 16F877_bert

var byte data
var word address

forever loop

  data = 0
  address = 274
  for 255 loop
    program_eeprom_write (address,data)
    data = data + 1
    address = address + 1
  end loop

  address = 274
  for 255 loop
    program_eeprom_read (address,data)
    serial_sw_write(data)
    address = address + 1
```

end loop

end loop

The hardware

This application only uses the internal 16F877 memory so the required hardware is minimal. We only need the parts that are required to run the PIC™:

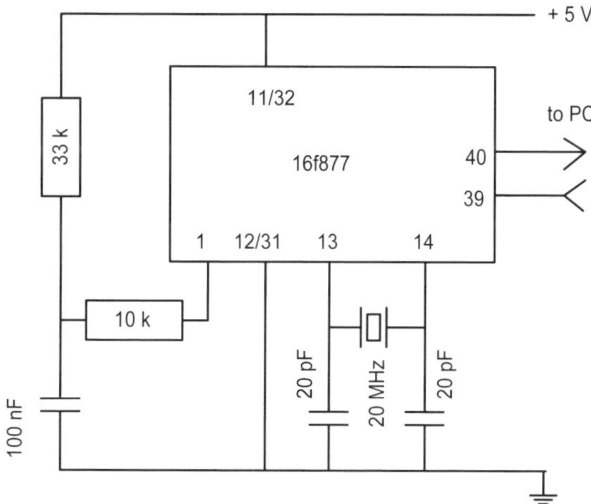

Figure 121. FLASH memory test.

Which looks like this on the breadboard.

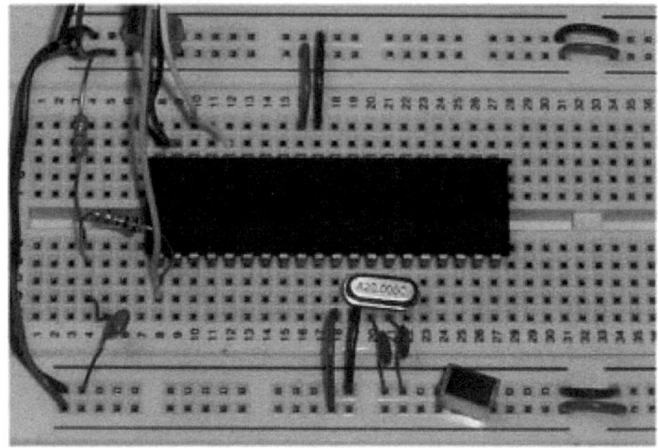

Figure 122. Memory test.

10.2 RAM

RAM is the simplest memory to use, because it is specifically meant for data storage.

Technical background

With the simple command

demo = 5

the number 5 is stored in RAM with "demo" as the name of that address. It gets a bit more exciting when arrays are used.

Normally a variable has only one value. With an array a variable can be given a whole range of values. In the following example the array *demo* is assigned a row of five values.[113]

var byte demo[5] = {11,12,13,14,15}

---

[113] If you declare the array along with the contents you don't need to enter the length, because the compiler can figure it out. So this is a valid declaration: var byte demo[] = {11,12,13,14,15}. As well as: var byte demo[5] where you add the values later.

To get a value out of the array the number between square brackets indicates the position that you want. Remember that computers start counting at 0, so the first position in the array is 0. This means that *demo[0]* is 11.

The next command selects the fourth number in the array, which contains the value 14.

> a = demo[3]

Adding a value to an array (or modifying one) is done in a similar manner. With the next command the fourth position in the array is assigned the value in variable *a*:

> demo[3]= a

Your program can use the *count* statement to determine the length of an array:

> a = count(demo)

But there is a limitation. The RAM memory of the 16F877 is divided into four different parts, called banks. Each of these banks contains special variables called registers that control the behavior of the PIC™. In section 7.2, for example, we have used the T2CON register to set the PWM[114] module. Each bank has some empty space that is used as RAM, as shown in the Register File Map of the datasheet:

---

[114] PWM Pulse Width Modulation

PIC16F877/876 REGISTER FILE MAP

Bank 0	File Address	Bank 1	File Address	Bank 2	File Address	Bank 3	File Address
Indirect addr.[*]	00h	Indirect addr.[*]	80h	Indirect addr.[*]	100h	Indirect addr.[*]	180h
TMR0	01h	OPTION_REG	81h	TMR0	101h	OPTION_REG	181h
PCL	02h	PCL	82h	PCL	102h	PCL	182h
STATUS	03h	STATUS	83h	STATUS	103h	STATUS	183h
FSR	04h	FSR	84h	FSR	104h	FSR	184h
PORTA	05h	TRISA	85h		105h		185h
PORTB	06h	TRISB	86h	PORTB	106h	TRISB	186h
PORTC	07h	TRISC	87h		107h		187h
PORTD[1]	08h	TRISD[1]	88h		108h		188h
PORTE[1]	09h	TRISE[1]	89h		109h		189h
PCLATH	0Ah	PCLATH	8Ah	PCLATH	10Ah	PCLATH	18Ah
INTCON	0Bh	INTCON	8Bh	INTCON	10Bh	INTCON	18Bh
PIR1	0Ch	PIE1	8Ch	EEDATA	10Ch	EECON1	18Ch
PIR2	0Dh	PIE2	8Dh	EEADR	10Dh	EECON2	18Dh
TMR1L	0Eh	PCON	8Eh	EEDATH	10Eh	Reserved[2]	18Eh
TMR1H	0Fh		8Fh	EEADRH	10Fh	Reserved[2]	18Fh
T1CON	10h		90h		110h		190h
TMR2	11h	SSPCON2	91h		111h		191h
T2CON	12h	PR2	92h		112h		192h
SSPBUF	13h	SSPADD	93h		113h		193h
SSPCON	14h	SSPSTAT	94h		114h		194h
CCPR1L	15h		95h		115h		195h
CCPR1H	16h		96h		116h		196h
CCP1CON	17h		97h	General Purpose Register 16 Bytes	117h	General Purpose Register 16 Bytes	197h
RCSTA	18h	TXSTA	98h		118h		198h
TXREG	19h	SPBRG	99h		119h		199h
RCREG	1Ah		9Ah		11Ah		19Ah
CCPR2L	1Bh		9Bh		11Bh		19Bh
CCPR2H	1Ch		9Ch		11Ch		19Ch
CCP2CON	1Dh		9Dh		11Dh		19Dh
ADRESH	1Eh	ADRESL	9Eh		11Eh		19Eh
ADCON0	1Fh	ADCON1	9Fh		11Fh		19Fh
	20h		A0h		120h		1A0h
General Purpose Register 96 Bytes		General Purpose Register 80 Bytes		General Purpose Register 80 Bytes		General Purpose Register 80 Bytes	
			EFh		16Fh		1EFh
		accesses 70h-7Fh	F0h	accesses 70h-7Fh	170h	accesses 70h - 7Fh	1F0h
	7Fh		FFh		17Fh		1FFh

Figure 123. Register File Map of the 16F877.

An array should fit into a single bank. Which means you have the following space available for arrays:

- 2 x 16 bytes
- 3 x 80 bytes
- 1 x 96 bytes

So an array can never be longer than 96 bytes, otherwise you will have to split it.[115] And if you want to use all of the RAM you need to use (at least) six arrays.

The software

As a demonstration we will write a small program that sends a few letters over a serial connection to a PC. First, we declare the array:

```
var byte demo[] = {"B","e","r","t"}
```

Then we read the data and send it to the PC. Since we don't want to count the length of the array ourselves we let JAL take care of it with the *count(demo)* command.

```
index = 0
 for count(demo) loop

    data = demo[index]
    serial_sw_write(data)
    delay_100ms(1)
    index = index + 1

 end loop
```

Please note that the counter (*index*) starts at zero.[116]

This is what the completed program looks like:

---

[115] If you need more space you can use the longtable, see section 12.8.
[116] After all of these warnings, can you guess how many times I've made a mistake with this?

```
-- JAL 2.0.4
include 16F877_bert

var byte data, index
var byte demo[] = {"B","e","r","t"}

forever loop

 index = 0
 for count(demo) loop

  data = demo[index]
  serial_sw_write(data)
  delay_100ms(1)
  index = index + 1

 end loop

 end loop
```

The hardware for this project is identical to project 10.1.

10.3 EEPROM

Just like RAM, EEPROM was designed to store data, but it is a bit more complicated. The advantage of EEPROM is that any data stored in it will stay there even if the PIC™ is switched off. To demonstrate this we will store a two-dimensional array.

Technical background

EEPROM is an abbreviation for Electronically Erasable Programmable Read Only Memory, which is of course a contradiction. If it is "read only" it means you cannot write to it, let alone erase it. So basically it is an erasable unerasable memory.

In principle only two types of memory exist. ROM (read only memory) can only be written once. After that you cannot change it, but the data is retained even after the power is removed. The other type of memory is RAM (Random Access Memory). You can read and write to this memory an "infinite" number of times, but the data is lost when the power is removed. Other memory types are derived from this, even though the name wasn't always logical. EEPROM is derived from EPROM (Erasable Programmable Read Only Memory), which in fact means the chip can only be programmed once. Because once isn't very often this chip could be erased by exposing it to UV light, but this wasn't very convenient. EEPROM does not need UV light and can be erased electronically, hence the extra "E" in the name.

The 16F877 is equipped with 256 bytes of EEPROM. And the standard library contains a few commands to use it:

data_eeprom_write(address, data)	Write the value in *data* to the *address* memory location in EEPROM.
data_eeprom_read(address, data)	Read the *address* memory loction in EEPROM and put the contents into the *data* variable.
data = data_eeprom(address)	The same as above, but written as a function.

You see that you need to provide an address as the location of your data. You cannot overwrite your program (which is in a different memory), but you can overwrite your own data so care should be taken. The first usable address is location 0.

If you know what you want to store in EEPROM during programming you can let the JAL compiler worry about assigning the proper address by using the following commands:

pragma eedata data1, data2, etc.	Let the compiler store data such as *data1, data2* in EEPROM. No need to mess with addresses and you can fit a lot of data on a single line.
data_eeprom_read(address, data)	Read EEPROM data. The address is obtained by a count of the pragma data (just remember to start at 0).

This project has two software sections, the second one demonstrating the use of *pragma eedata*.

10 Memory

Although we intend to store a two-dimensional array, JAL can only handle one-dimensional arrays by default (see section 10.2). A two-dimensional array is usually depicted as a matrix, but in memory the data is all in a single row.[117]

	y1	2	3	4	5
x1	1	2	3	4	5
2	6	7	(2,3) or 8	9	10
3	11	12	13	14	15
4	16	17	18	19	20

So, position (2,3) in the matrix is the same as position 8 in the row in memory. The formula to calculate the position in memory is:

position in memory $=$ (row -1)*maxcolumn + column + startingpoint

where:
    maxcolumn = the number of columns in the matrix
    column = the y-position
    row = the x-position
    startingpoint = the first position in memory[118]

If you want to store the number 250 in the matrix at location (2,3) it would translate to position in memory 8:

(2-1) * 5 + 3 + 0 = 8

The command will be

    data_eeprom_write(8,250)

The software (1)

In this program an index going from 0 to 255 is stored in position (2,3) of a two-dimensional array. It is then retrieved and sent to the PC for verification.

---

[117] With a bit of mathematics you can store a two-dimensional array in a one-dimensional JAL array. This is just as simple (or complicated) as the method described here. This will allow you to store a matrix in RAM.

[118] The starting point will allow you to place multiple matrices in memory behind each other.

First we will define the array:

```
maxcolumn = 5
startingpoint = 0
```

set the position of the number to be stored:

```
column = 2
row = 3
```

and store the number:

```
data_eeprom_write((column-1)*maxcolumn+column+startingpoint, counter)
```

In the next step we retrieve the stored number using a different name for the variable. That way we can be sure the value was actually stored and retrieved successfully.

```
data_eeprom_read((column-1)*maxcolumn+column+startingpoint, answer)
```

As a final step the answer is sent to the PC and the loop is repeated indefinitely. On the PC you will see a repeating row from 0 to 255.

And this is the complete program:

```
-- JAL 2.0.4
include 16F877_bert

-- declare variables
var byte column, row, maxcolumn, startingpoint, counter, answer

-- define the two dimensional array
maxcolumn = 5
startingpoint = 0

forever loop

   -- position in the array
   column = 2
   row = 3
```

```
-- calculate the memory position and store
data_eeprom_write((column-1)*maxcolumn+column+startingpoint, counter)

-- calculate the memory position and retrieve
data_eeprom_read((column-1)*maxcolumn+column+startingpoint, answer)

-- send result to the PC
serial_sw_write(answer)

counter = counter + 1

end loop
```

The hardware for this project is identical to project 10.1.

The software (2)

If you already know which data you want to store in EEPROM at the moment of programming you can store it with the *pragma eedata* command:

```
pragma eedata "L","E","D"
```

With this command the letters "L', "E', and "D" are stored in memory in a row, where L is stored in memory position 0. In addition to letters you can also store numbers or control tokens.[119]

The most important control tokens are:

```
const byte ascii_lf  = 10        Line Feed (lf): go to a new line.

const byte ascii_cr  = 13        Carriage Return[120] (cr): go to the first
                                 position of the line.
```

In section 14.2 you will find an overview of all ASCII values.

---

[119] In reality the program stores binary values.

[120] Carriage Return comes from the days when typewriters were in use. The paper was on a rubber roll, and moved left after each letter. At the end of the line the rubber roll with paper (the carriage) had to be pushed back to the right. Line Feed originated from those same days and really means that the rubber roll must be rotated upwards.

We could use this technique to make a virtual flashing light - a project in which a non-existent LED is flashing. It wouldn't surprise me if I were the only person who thinks this is funny.

Anyway, first we store the data in EEPROM:

```
pragma eedata "L","E","D"," "
pragma eedata "o","n"," ",ascii_cr,ascii_lf
pragma eedata "L","E","D"," "
pragma eedata "o","f","f",ascii_cr,ascii_lf
```

Then we read it back in groups of nine (note that after the word "on" a space has been added. You can do without this, but then you would need to first read a group of 8 and then a group of 9).

```
for 9 loop
   data_eeprom_read  (counter, data)
   serial_sw_write (data)
   counter = counter +1
end loop
```

Once all positions have been read we start over.

```
if  counter == 18 then counter = 0 end if
```

The completed program looks like this:

```
-- JAL 2.0.4
include 16F877_bert

-- data to be stored
pragma eedata "L","E","D"," "
pragma eedata "o","n"," ",ascii_cr,ascii_lf
pragma eedata "L","E","D"," "
pragma eedata "o","f","f",ascii_cr,ascii_lf

var byte counter, data

counter = 0
forever loop
```

```
-- show a dataset
for 9 loop
    data_eeprom_read  (counter, data)
    serial_sw_write (data)
    counter = counter +1
end loop

-- wait a bit
delay_100ms(10)

-- out of data so start anew
if  counter == 18 then counter = 0 end if
end loop
```

And this is what you get on the PC:

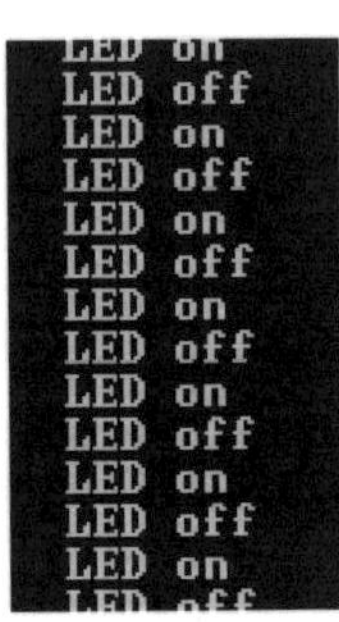

Figure 124. Virtual flashing LED.

To save you time in converting long text to *pragma eedata* statements the download package contains the PEconverter program to do this for you.

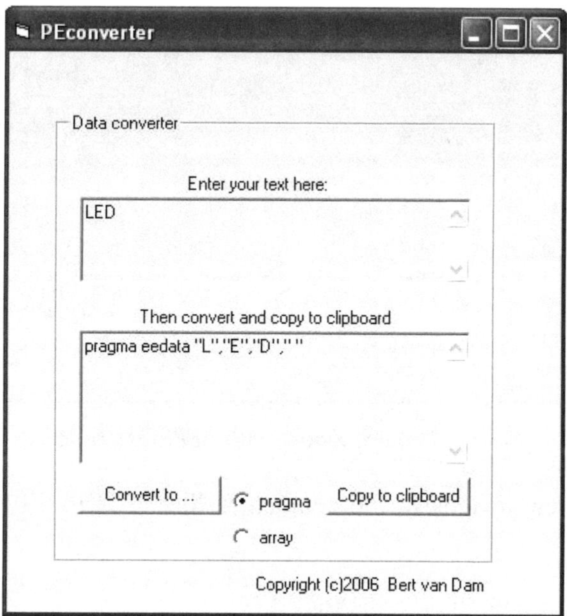

Figure 125. Generate pragma EEPROM statements.

Enter your text in the top window. When you click on "Convert" a *pragma eedata* statement will be generated (if you selected "pragma") and shown in the lower window.[121] With the "Copy to clipboard" button you copy the entire statement and then paste the statement into JALedit (or any other editor) with the Edit-Paste or Control-V command.

The hardware for this project is identical to project 10.1.

HEXview

With the HEXview program and a Wisp628 programmer you can download the PIC™'s program and EEPROM data for viewing. This is particularly useful when you want to upgrade the programmer as discussed in section 13.2.6.

---

[121] The other options will be discussed in section 12.5.

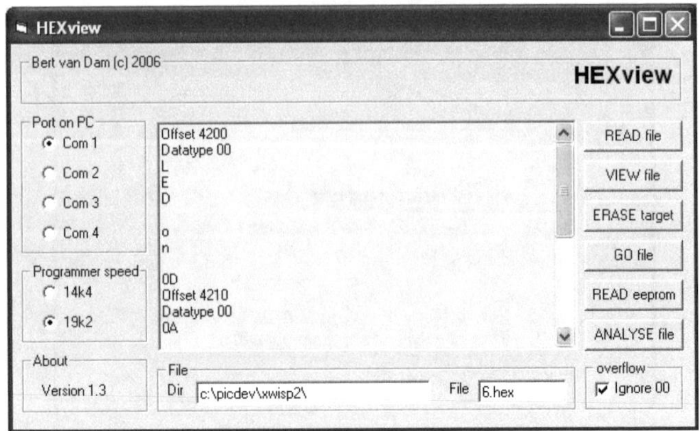

Figure 126. HEXview with EEPROM data.

You can use HEXview to look at the contents of the PIC™'s EEPROM by following these steps:

1. Connect the programmer to the PIC™.
2. Load and run the program from Software (2).
3. Start HEXview.
4. Enter a path and filename in the lower panel where the retrieved data will be stored.
5. Click the "Read EEPROM" button. A black window is displayed in which you can observe the progress, while data is being retrieved from the PIC™ and stored in the file.
6. Click "Analyze File" and the data will be shown, translated to ASCII if relevant, otherwise in hex. If you want to see the untranslated file click "View File".

In this example all letters are shown on a new line. The tokens *carriage return* (ascii_cr) and *line feed* (ascii_lf) are shown in hex (000D and 000A). You will also see where in memory the data was stored (*offset ...*) and what kind of data it is (in EEPROM memory this is always datatype 00).

You can use this technique to debug programs by storing data in EEPROM at certain locations and using HEXview to see the data. See section 6.3 for more information on this method and on debugging in general.

Note that you cannot use HEXview simultaneously with a pass-through RS232 connection. More information on HEXview and the structure of EEPROM data files can be found in section 14.7.

10.4 External EEPROM with I2C

In this project two EEPROM chips are connected to a PIC™ using the I2C protocol. This will give us 64k of additional memory.

Technical background

Microcontrollers can communicate in many different ways with other chips (see also section 11). One of those ways is the I2C protocol developed by Philips. The real name is Inter-IC bus, abbreviated to I2C because of the double I at the beginning (in fact it should be spelled as I^2C but on the Internet the ^{2} is not always easy to make). In every I2C network a single PIC™ has control and is called the master.[122] The master controls traffic over the I2C bus by deciding who gets to talk and when. Every other device on the bus is called a slave.

In this project we will build a bus with one 16F877 master and two EEPROM chips as slaves.

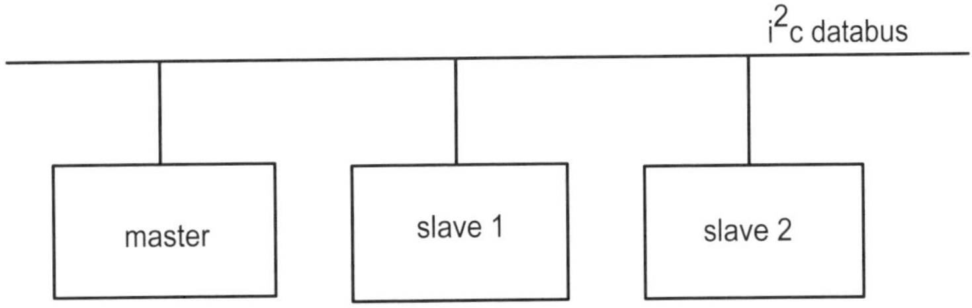

Figure 127. Schematic view of an I2C bus.

The 16F877 uses the bus to communicate with the EEPROM chips to store and retrieve data.

We will use 24LC256 EEPROM chips manufactured by Microchip. These chips have their own datasheet, and it is a good idea to download them from the Microchip website[123]. Each chip contains 256 kbit of memory, which amounts to 32 kB (a byte is 8 bits)[124].

---

[122] Technically it is possible to have multiple masters on a single bus, but that is rather complicated and outside the scope of this book.

[123] http://www.microchip.com

[124] This can be confusing, because memory chips are normally referred to by their capacity in bytes, not bits. Microchip is by the way notorious for their confusing name conventions.

The I2C bus consists of just two wires. One wire is called SCL and is used as a clock. The master switches this wire high and low at the speed necessary to send and receive data. The other wire is called SDA, or data line, and is the wire that the data is transmitted over.

I2C is a very smart system. If there is a pulse on the clock line but not on the data line then the data is a 0. If there is a pulse on the clock line and also on the data line then the data is a 1. Both lines are connected to the power line through a resistor. A chip has to actively pull the line low, or release it (which would cause the line to go high automatically.

Each chip needs its own address. For the EEPROMs this is taken care off by making one or more of the pins A0, A1 or A2 high.

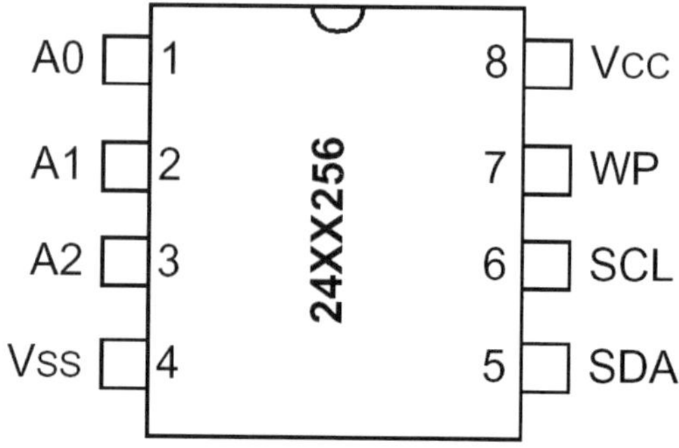

Figure 128. Pin configuration.

These pins have the following functions:

pin	name	description
1,2,3	A0 to A2	Address of the EEPROM chip
4	V_{SS}	Power, ground
5	SDA	I2C data line
6	SLC	I2C clock line
7	WP	Write protect
8	V_{CC}	Power, +5 V

You will need to connect at least pins 4, 5, 6, and 8. To keep it simple, one EEPROM will have none of the address lines pulled high, and the other EEPROM will have just pin A0, the least significant bit, pulled high[125]:

A2	A1	A0	address
0	0	1	001

So the addresses we'll be using are 000 and 001.

If you took a sneak peek at the source code you may have noticed this command:

    chipaddress = 0b_0101_0000

Which may surprise you because you just selected three-bit addresses for the EEPROMs. But this is caused by a rather awkward terminology in the datasheet. In fact, the three-bit address is not an address but a "chip select code'. The complete (7-bit!) address on an EEPROM is the chip select code preceded by a control code.

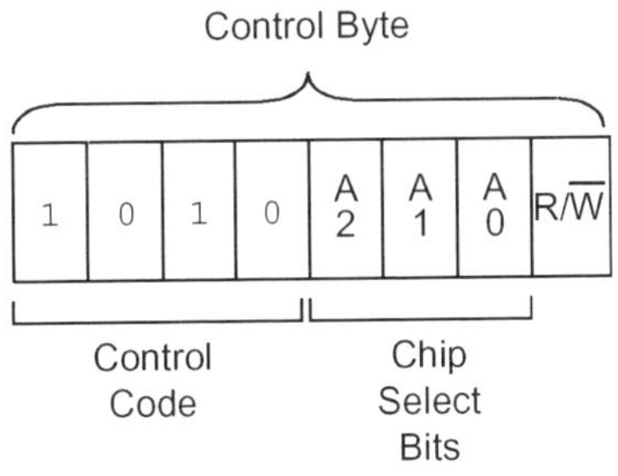

Figure 129. Control byte.

The first seven bits are the address and together with the 8th bit (a read/write flag) they comprise the control byte. At this point we are only interested in the address part of the control byte, which we reference like this:

    chipaddress = 0b_0101_0000

or

    chipaddress = 0b_0101_0001

---

[125] The address pins comprise a three-bit number. With pins A2 and A0 pulled high the address would be thus be 5. This allows you to have 8 of these EEPROMs on a single I2C bus.

When a read or write command needs to be given by the I2C library all it needs to do is add the read/write bit at the right.[126] All bits then move one position to the left which yield:

> chipaddress = 0b_1010_000x

or

> chipaddress = 0b_1010_001x

which is the correct address with "x" as the read/write bit.

Although the 16F877 is equipped with a standard I2C module we will not be using it. First of all, these pins can be used for other protocols as well. So it is convenient to use software I2C which will leave you free in your choice of pins.[127] Perhaps even more important is that using a software I2C library allows you to use I2C with a PIC™ that doesn't have built-in support for it, such as the 12F675.

The standard library 16F877_bert does not contain I2C software routines. So we will use an additional set of libraries (i2c_sw) that are included in the download package.[128]

There are three commands available to work with external memory:

i2c_sw_write(chipaddress,addressH, addressL, value)	Write *value* to *addressH*, *addressL* of the EEPROM having an address of *chipaddress*.
i2c_sw_read(chipaddress,addressH, addressL, value)	Read the contents *(value)* of *addressH*, *addressL* of the EEPROM having an address of *chipaddress*.
i2c_sw_ackpoll(chipaddress)	Wait for an acknowledgement from the EEPROM having an address of *chipaddress*.

The program itself is not very useful. It just fills the entire EEPROM, reads it back, and sends it to the PC over the serial pass-through connection.

---

[126] This is done like this: new address = (address << 1) + 0b_0000_0001 so shift the address left one bit and add one. This means the bit is set to "read".

[127] You can modify this in the file called i2cp.jal, which you can find in the library directory. If you change it you need to copy this file to the same directory where your program is so that the original remains intact and useable for other programs.

[128] This library set consists of three interlinked libraries written by Wouter van Ooijen, Dave Ellis and Bert van Dam.

This takes a long time, by the way. Complete filling an EEPROM with data takes 4 minutes and 8 seconds! That means one write operation (including calculations, loops, and acknowledgement polling) takes 4:08/32768 = 7.57 msec. The datasheet mentions a maximum of 5 ms for just the EEPROM, so that matches nicely.

Reading is even slower - in excess of 10 minutes - because the data is also sent to the PC. During reading and writing an LED flashes to tell that the program is still running.

The software

First we need to load the I2C library:

```
include i2c_sw
```

Basically there are two loops. The first one fills the EEPROM with incrementing numbers. The EEPROM is 256 kbit which means 32768 bytes. The maximum value for the high address byte is, thus, 127 (and for the low byte, obviously, 255):

```
greenled = high
   addressH = 0
   addressL = 0
   for 127 loop
      addressH = addressH + 1
      greenled = ! greenled
      for 255 loop
         addressL = addressL + 1
         value = addressL
         i2c_sw_write(chipaddress, addressH, addressL, value)
         i2c_sw_ackpoll(chipaddress)
      end loop
   end loop
   greenled = low
```

The green LED flashes at a rather low frequency. It takes about four minutes before something happens on the PC. At that point the second loop starts to read the data:

```
-- now read it back and send to the PC
blueled = high
addressH = 0
addressL = 0
for 127 loop
   addressH = addressH + 1
```

```
        blueled = ! blueled
        for 255 loop
           addressL = addressL + 1
            i2c_sw_read(chipaddress, addressH, addressL, value)
           serial_sw_write(value)
        end loop
     end loop
     blueled = low
```

This time the blue LED flashes. Both loops are then repeated for the second EEPROM.

The entire program looks like this:

```
-- JAL 2.0.4
include 16F877_bert
include i2c_sw

-- define variables
var bit blueled is pin_d2         -- blue led
var bit greenled is pin_d3        -- green led
var byte chipaddress, addressL, addressH, value

-- enable i2c
sspcon = 0b_0011_0110

-- define the pins
pin_d2_direction = output
pin_d3_direction = output

-- turn the leds off
blueled = low
greenled = low

-- start data
addressH = 0
addressL = 0
value = 0
chipaddress = 0b_0101_0000

for 2 loop
```

```
-- fill the memory with sequential numbers
greenled = high
addressH = 0
addressL = 0
for 127 loop
   addressH = addressH + 1
   greenled = ! greenled
   for 255 loop
      addressL = addressL + 1
      value = addressL
      i2c_sw_write(chipaddress, addressH, addressL, value)
      i2c_sw_ackpoll(chipaddress)
   end loop
end loop
greenled = low

-- now read it back and send to the PC
blueled = high
addressH = 0
addressL = 0
for 127 loop
   addressH = addressH + 1
   blueled = ! blueled
   for 255 loop
      addressL = addressL + 1
      i2c_sw_read(chipaddress, addressH, addressL, value)
      serial_sw_write(value)
   end loop
end loop
blueled = low

-- next chip
chipaddress = chipaddress + 1

end loop
```

The hardware

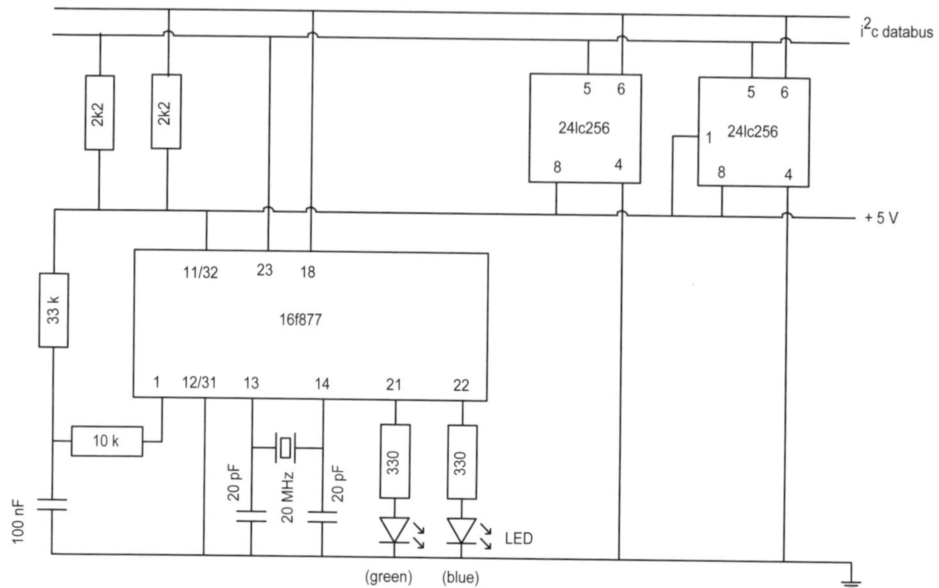

Figure 130. I2C with two EEPROMs.

The I2C bus consists of two wires that are connected to the plus using 2k2 resistors. This means that the lines are normally high, and are pulled low by the chips. Because software I2C routines are used you are free to choose the pins. The library assumes c3/c4, but you can change this in the i2cp.jal file in the library directory. It is advisable to copy the file beforehand to the same directory as the program in order to maintain the original library for other projects.

The left EEPROM has chipselect 0, where none of the three address pins is pulled high. The right EEPROM has chipselect 1.

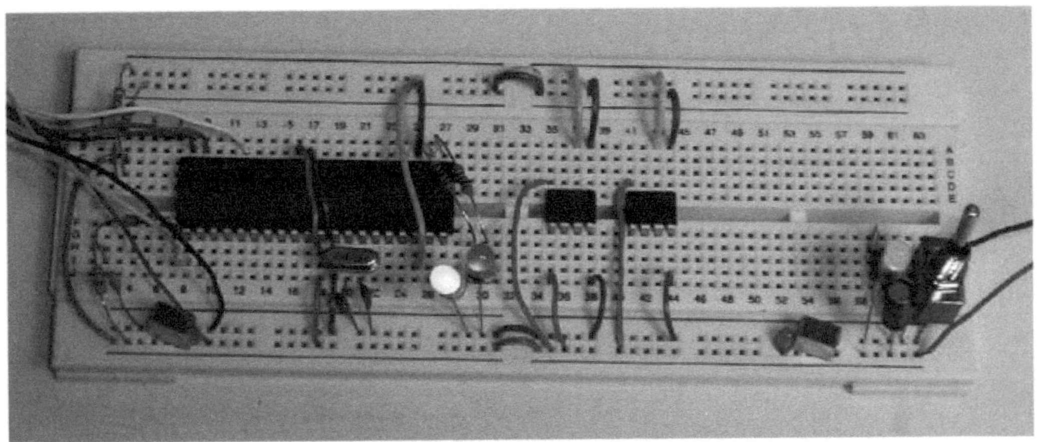

Figure 131. I2C with two EEPROMs.

On the breadboard the upper rail is used for I2C. Beneath the programmer wires on the left hand side you can just barely see the two resistors.

11 Multiple PIC™ microcontrollers

In this chapter we will discuss a few techniques to connect multiple PIC™ microcontrollers to each other. This way you can have more inputs or outputs available or even parallel processing power. Of course the PIC™ microcontrollers don't have to be next to each other. If you have, for example, twenty remote sensors you can use twenty-one wires[129] or add a remote PIC™ and just use four wires (two for the power and two for the communications).

Project	Purpose
Two serial RS232 connections (and a small game)	Two PIC™ microcontrollers are connected using a RS232 serial connection. One of the PIC™ microcontrollers is also connected to a PC.
Serial synchronization	Two PIC™ microcontrollers that "know" each other's status based on smart messages. As a result they can synchronize. One of the PIC™ microcontrollers is also connected to a PC.
A serial network	A very neat way to connect three or more PIC™ microcontrollers to each other using a serial network with a master and multiple slaves.

A serial connection doesn't necessarily need wires as you can see in this project:

Project	Purpose
An infrared transmitter/receiver	A serial connection between two PICs using infrared in section 13.3.5.

---

[129] Twenty for the signals and one for the ground. Sensors with I2C capability can simply be connected to a bus, just like the EEPROM chips in section 10.4.

11.1 Two RS232 connections

Two PIC™ microcontrollers are connected to each other using a serial connection. One of the PIC™ microcontrollers is also connected to the PC. Both PIC™ microcontrollers are equipped with a switch. Pressing any of the switches sends a signal to the PC. This allows a small game to be played.

Technical background

If you haven't read the introduction of Chapter 6 now would be a good time so that you get some background information on RS232 signals and connections.

The 16F877 is equipped with an USART port on pins c6 and c7 (25 and 26).[130] It can be set to two different protocols: RS232 of SPI. In this project we will use the RS232 option (which is the default for the 16F877_bert library).

By connecting the PIC™ microcontrollers with the wires crossed the "transmit" of one becomes the "receive" of the other and, thus, they can communicate with each other. Since the functionality is built into the hardware this is referred to as hardware serial port. In the standard library the following commands are available:

USART_hw_Serial	Set the correct protocol: true = RS232, false = SPI (default is true)
Serial_hw_baudrate	Communication speed is set to 19k2 by default but 1200 or 115k baud is also possible.
Serial_hw_read(data)	Receive something and store it in the variable *data*.
Serial_hw_write(data)	Send the content of the variable *data*.
Serial_hw_data = data	The same as above, but written as a function.

The first two commands are used to establish the correct settings (RS232 or 19k2 baud).

---

[130] USART Addressable Universal Synchronous Asynchronous Receiver Transmitter

The programs in both PIC™ microcontrollers are identical (except for the letter A or B) and do two things in their main loop. First, any signal that comes in on the hardware serial port is relayed to the software serial port, which is only useful for the PIC™ that is actually connected with its software serial port to the PC. We could write separate programs for each PIC™ (and we will in upcoming sections), but then you would have to remember which program goes where.

```
if Serial_hw_read( mydata ) then
    Serial_sw_write(mydata)
end if
```

When you press the switch a letter is sent to the other PIC and to the PC. One PIC will send the letter A and the other the letter B.

```
if switch  then
    Serial_sw_write("A")
    Serial_hw_write("A")
end if
```

Pressing the switches will result in something like this in your PC's terminal program:

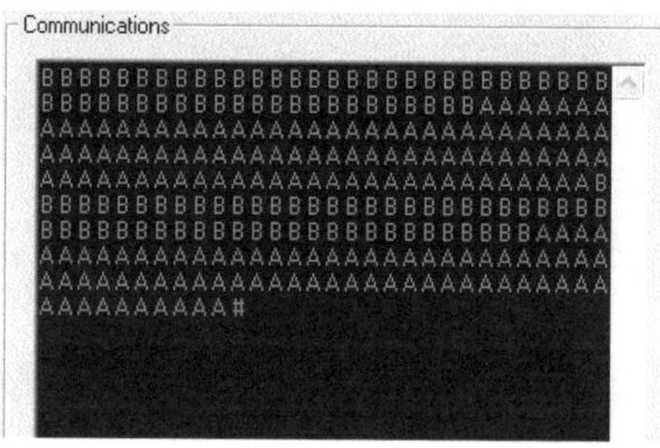

Figure 132. The switches as seen on the PC.

A simple game for two

Whether you realized it or not you have just created a simple game for two. Each person gets to push his/her own button as short as possible. The one with the fewest letters on the PC wins this game.

My best score was 5.

The software

When all the parts are put together this is the resulting program. Use the letter "A" in one PIC™ and the letter "B"in the other one.

```
-- JAL 2.0.4
include 16F877_bert

var byte mydata

-- define the pins
pin_b1_direction = input
var bit switch is pin_b1

forever loop

   -- get byte from serial PIC
   if Serial_hw_read( mydata ) then
      -- echo to PC
      Serial_sw_write(mydata)
   end if

   -- if switch is pressed send A
   if switch  then
      Serial_sw_write("A") -- send to PC
      Serial_hw_write("A") -- send to other PIC
   end if

end loop
```

The hardware

The hardware serial connections are as follows:

Pin number	Pin name	Function	Description
25	c6	TX	transmit
26	c7	RX	receive

To connect two of them together means that pins 25 and 26 of both PIC™ microcontrollers must be connected crossed over, which means that the TX pin from one

PIC™ is connected to the RX pin of the other. The speed between the two PIC™ microcontrollers is 19k2 baud and the speed between the PIC™ and the PC is 1200 baud.

Each PIC™ needs it's own switch.

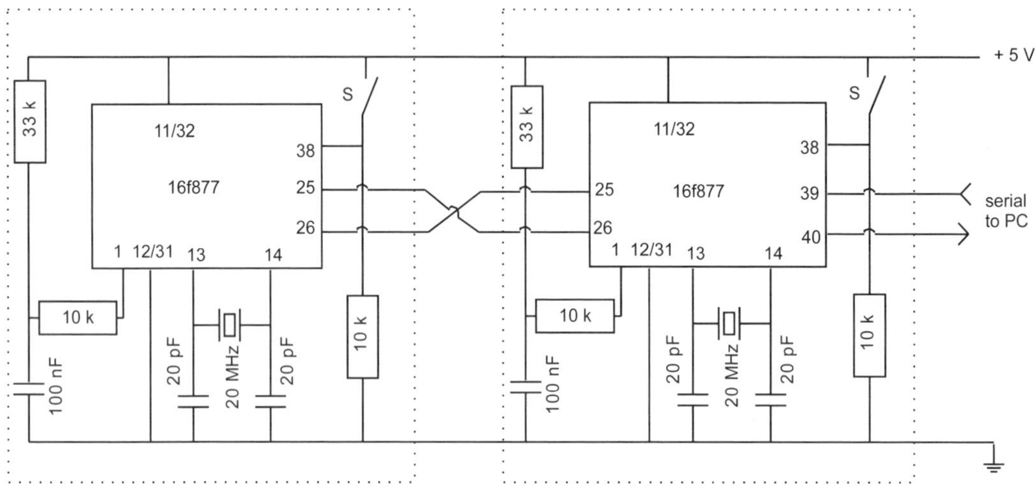

Figure 133. Hardware and software serial connection.

The dotted lines indicate the two units. This is strictly informational; it does not represent wiring or anything else. The two units can theoretically be placed a maximum of 15 meters apart. In practice this is highly dependent on interference from the environment. In your living room you may be able to place the units further apart than in an industrial setting. This is what it looks like on the breadboard:

Figure 134. Hardware and software serial connection.

The blue and green wires are from the Wisp628 in-circuit programmer and make the connection to the PC.

Infrared

Take a look at section 13.3.5 where the communication is done using infrared signals instead of wires.

11.2 Serial synchronization

Two PIC™ microcontrollers that "know" each others status based on smart messages. As a result they can synchronize.

Technical background

When two microcontrollers need to do certain things together (such as process part of a problem in parallel to speed up the process) they need to be synchronized with each other. There are many complicated ways to achieve this, but using the hardware RS232 buffers is a surprisingly simple and effective one.

When a PIC™ receives a message on the (hardware) serial port, but doesn't have time to process it yet the message is put into a buffer.[131] Let us assume that both programs have synchronization points where they wait for each other. If the program reaches that particular point it sends a signal to the other PIC™ and waits for a reply. If the other PIC™ had already arrived at the synchronization point this reply will arrive immediately (from the buffer). If the other PIC™ hasn't arrived at the synchronization point the program will wait until an answer arrives (this time direct instead of from the buffer).

In this project the programs have three synchronization points. One of the programs is significantly slower than the other, because it has one-second delays between each synchronization point. So the fast program needs to wait for the slow one.

---

[131] Don't get your hopes up too high: the buffer can hold just two bytes. It is called *RCREG* in case you want to look for the relevant data in the datasheet.

11 Multiple PIC™ microcontrollers

This is what a synchronization point looks like, with both programs next to each other:

mydata = "0"
Serial_hw_write("B")
while mydata != "A" loop
  Serial_hw_read(mydata)
end loop
	mydata = "0"
	Serial_hw_write("A")
	while mydata != "B" loop
	  Serial_hw_read(mydata)
	end loop

The software

The programs in both PIC™ microcontrollers are basically identical, but differ at a few important points:

PIC™ 1 (left, in the schematic)	**PIC™ 2 (right, in the schematic)**
At a synchronization point send an "A" and wait for a "B".	Send a "B" and wait for an "A".
Fast program	Slow program: wait for 1 second between each synchronization point.
	Send the actual location in the program (0, 1, 2 or 3) to the PC.

The programs start up with a one-second delay. The PIC™ microcontrollers need a bit of time to start up, and during that period the buffers are not active. If one happens to be faster than the other synchronization can not start.

Perhaps it is interesting to view both completed programs next to each other:

Program for the PIC™ that is connected to the PC:	**Program for the other PIC™:**
-- JAL 2.0.4 include 16F877_bert var byte mydata *-- define the pins* pin_b1_direction = output var bit led is pin_b1	*-- JAL 2.0.4* include 16F877_bert var byte mydata *-- define the pins* pin_b1_direction = output var bit led is pin_b1

```
-- give other pic time to start up
delay_1s (1)

forever loop

   -- send current position to the PC
   Serial_sw_write("0")

   -- first synch
   mydata = "0"
   Serial_hw_write("B")
   while mydata != "A" loop
     Serial_hw_read(mydata)
   end loop

   -- send current position to the PC
   Serial_sw_write("1")

   -- wait a bit
   delay_1s(1)

   -- second synch
   mydata = "0"
   Serial_hw_write("B")
   while mydata != "A" loop
     Serial_hw_read(mydata)
   end loop

   -- switch yellow led on
   led = high

   -- send current position to the PC
   Serial_sw_write("2")

   -- wait a bit
   delay_1s (1)

   -- third synch
   mydata = "0"
   Serial_hw_write("B")
   while mydata != "A" loop
     Serial_hw_read(mydata)
```

```
-- give other pic time to start up
delay_1s (1)

forever loop

   -- switch yellow led on
   led = high

   -- first synch
   mydata = "0"
   Serial_hw_write("A")
   while mydata != "B" loop
     Serial_hw_read(mydata)
   end loop

   -- switch yellow led off
   led = low

   -- second synch
   mydata = "0"
   Serial_hw_write("A")
   while mydata != "B" loop
     Serial_hw_read(mydata)
   end loop

   -- switch yellow led on
   led = high

   -- third synch
   mydata = "0"
   Serial_hw_write("A")
   while mydata != "B" loop
     Serial_hw_read(mydata)
```

<table>
<tr>
<td>

```
       end loop

       -- switch yellow led off
       led = low

       -- send current position to the PC
       Serial_sw_write("3")

       -- wait a bit
       delay_1s(1)

   end loop
```

</td>
<td>

```
       end loop

       -- switch yellow led off
       led = low




   end loop
```

</td>
</tr>
</table>

If you use the Wisp628 pass-through feature make sure to disconnect the yellow wire OR connect pin 1 of both PIC™ microcontrollers together. If you enable the pass-through function the programmer uses the yellow wire to reset the PIC™. If you reset one program but not the other synchronization will be lost. So you have to either disconnect the yellow wire (none of the PICs restart) or connect pin 1 of both PICs together (both PICs reset).

The hardware

Please note that the wires between the PIC™ microcontrollers are connected crossed over and that the LED is on a different pin of each PIC™ microcontroller. The dotted lines indicate the two different units and have no other purpose.

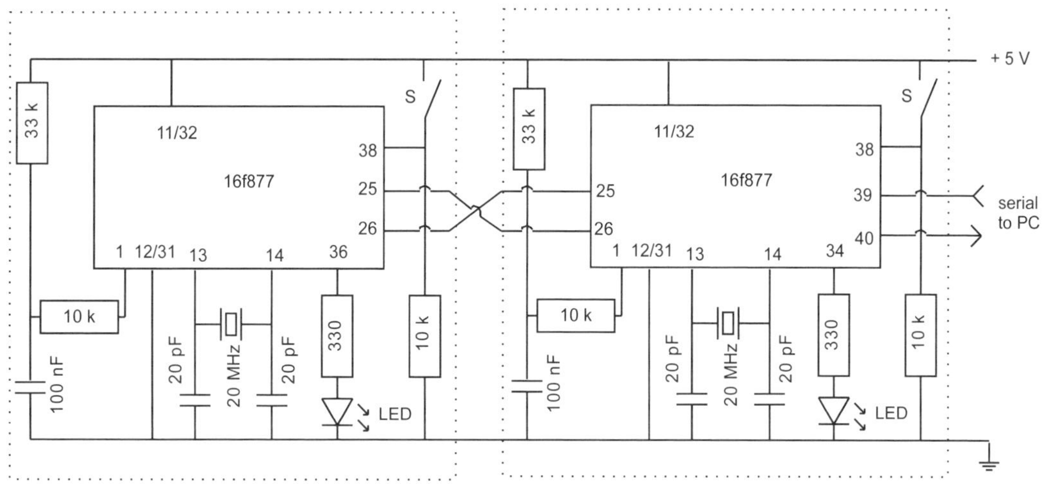

Figure 135. Synchronization.

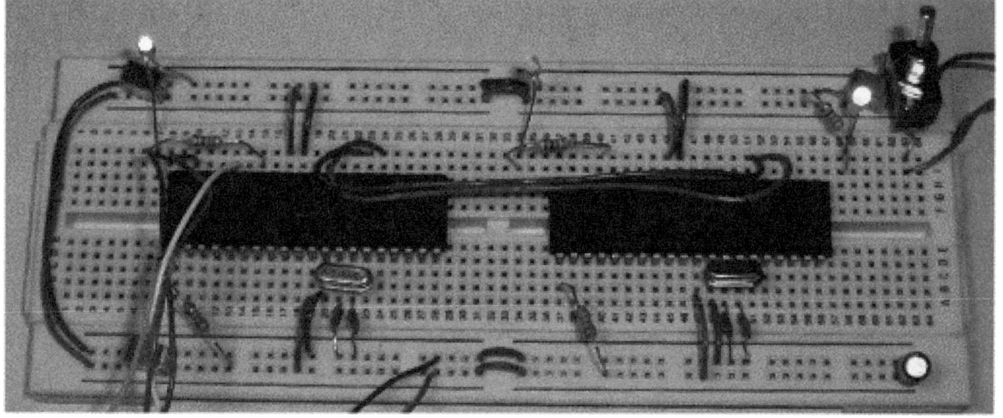

Figure 136. Synchronization.

Be certain to disconnect the yellow wire OR connect pin 1 of both PIC™ microcontrollers together.

11 Multiple PIC™ microcontrollers

11.3 A serial network

Here we have a project to connect three (or more) PIC™ microcontrollers to each other using a serial network with one master and multiple slaves.

Technical background

The output of a PIC™ can easily be connected to multiple inputs of other PICs. So if the transmit pin (TX) of the standard RS232 module is connected to the receive pins (RX) of two other PIC™ microcontrollers then both will receive the same message.

The other way around is a bit more difficult, because connecting the transmit pins together can cause trouble. The solution is simple: add a diode and a resistor. The resistor pulls the line high so that it doesn't float and the diode blocks the transmit signals.

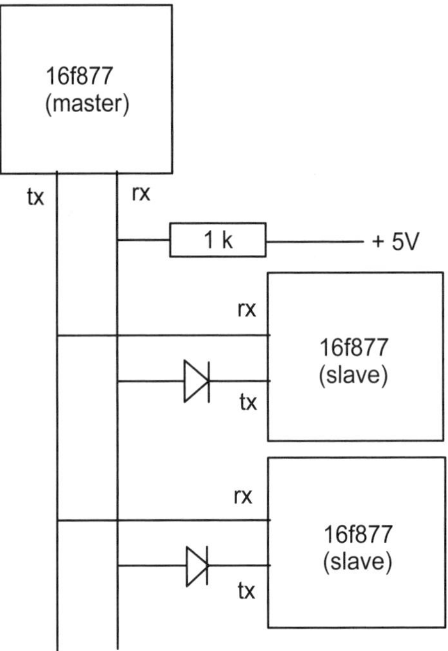

Figure 137. The RS232 pins connected.

In this network the master is the only one sending unsolicited messages. The slaves receive all messages, check to see if any of these messages are addressed to them, and then respond if necessary.

The software

In this system the master sends commands to the slaves, which then reply. The messages sent by the master have the following structure:

bit 7	bit 6	bit 5	bit 4	bit 3	bit 2	bit 1	bit 0
Command				Address			

So both the address and the command are four-bit variables.[132] Suppose command 10 is to be sent to a slave with address 2, the message would be coded like this:

bit 7	bit 6	bit 5	bit 4	bit 3	bit 2	bit 1	bit 0
1	0	1	0	0	0	1	0
Command				Address			

Since we will need this particular piece of software often we may as well turn it into a procedure.

We expect to call this procedure with two variables (address and command) and indicate that these will each be 4 bits long:

procedure serial_net_write(bit*4 in address, bit*4 in command) is

The variable that will be sent is a regular byte:

var byte data2send

First, the command must be put into the variable that will be sent:

data2send = command

It is true that the command is only 4 bits long and *data2send* is 8 bits long, but that doesn't matter. The 4 lowest bits of *data2send* are replaced by the 4 bits of *command*, and the 4 highest bits of *data2send* remain what they were before. To get the command bits on the high side of *data2send* we shift everything 4 bits to the left:

data2send = data2send << 4

---

[132] So you can use a maximum of 16 different addresses and 16 different commands.

Now we can add *address*. This is also a 4-bit variable, which now fits nicely because after the left shift the 4 lowest bits of *data2send* are empty:

    data2send = data2send + address

Now all we need to do is send the data and end the procedure:

    serial_hw_write(data2send)
    end procedure

When you call the procedure you don't need to worry about the fact that *address* and *command* are only 4 bits. If you call the procedure with bytes the highest 4 bits will simply be deleted.

The slaves need to decode the message to see if it is meant for them. They don't need to continually watch the RS232 pin, because incoming data is put in the buffer (the first two bytes anyway).

First, we define the variables for the slaves. This time we take care to define them as 4 bits for easier decoding:

    var byte myaddress, data
    var bit*4 address, command

As soon as a message comes in we will check whom it is for:

    if Serial_hw_read(data) then
        address = data
        if myaddress == address then

You see that we put the 8-bit long *data* into the 4 bit long *address*. Only the lowest 4 bits will actually fit, and that happens to be the *address*. Surely no coincidence. If this *address* matches the PIC™ address the *command* needs to be extracted. We shift all bits in *data* to the right, which causes the *address* to fall out and the lowest 4 bits are now the *command*:

    command = data >> 4

We can now see what the command is that the PIC™ is expected to do.

In this sample program only three commands are in use:

Command	Action to take
0	switch LED off
1	switch LED on
2	send a number

Using the procedure that we have just written we can tell the PIC™ with address 1 to switch off its LED (command 0) like this:

```
serial_net_write(1,0)
```

It is a bit complicated with the 4 bits, 8 bits, and shifts. If you lose track it is a good idea to write the numbers on paper in binary and try out all the things we have done. Once you are used to it you'll see it is much easier than you thought.

Time to put all the commands together:

The master software:

```
-- JAL 2.0.4
include 16F877_bert

-- define variables
var byte data

-- serial network write procedure
procedure serial_net_write (bit*4 in address, bit*4 in command) is
   var byte data2send
   data2send = command
   data2send = data2send << 4
   data2send = data2send + address
   serial_hw_write(data2send)
end procedure


forever loop
```

```
        --switch both remote leds on
        serial_net_write(1,1)
        serial_net_write(2,1)

        --wait a bit
        delay_100ms(3)

        -- switch both remote leds off
        serial_net_write(1,0)
        serial_net_write(2,0)

        -- wait a bit
        delay_100ms(3)

        -- get a number from the remote pic 1
        serial_net_write(1,2)
        serial_hw_read(data)
        -- and send to PC to check
        serial_sw_write(data)

        -- get the number from the remote pic 2
        serial_net_write(2,2)
        serial_hw_read(data)
        -- and send to PC to check
        serial_sw_write(data)

    end loop
```

The slave software:

```
        -- JAL 2.0.4
        include 16F877_bert


        var byte myaddress, data
        var bit*4 address, command
        pin_d1_direction = output
        var bit led is pin_d1 = false

        myaddress = 1

        forever loop
```

```
if Serial_hw_read( data ) then
  address = data
  if myaddress == address then
    command = data >> 4
    serial_sw_write(address)
    serial_sw_write(command)
    if command == 1 then
      led = high
    else
      led = low
    end if
    if command == 2 then
      serial_hw_write(100)
    end if
  end if
end if

end loop
```

Obviously you need to give all slaves a different address.

You may have noticed that messages sent back by the slaves are not coded. That is because the slaves cannot see each other's messages. Only the master can read them, and since the master knows to whom he asked the question it also knows what this incoming data is and whom it is from.

There is no reason to use the same software in every slave; you could have them do totally different things!

The hardware

On the breadboard in Figure 139 the junction of the serial wires (yellow and purple) is clearly visible. At the left top hand side the green and blue wires of the software serial connection to the PC are just visible.

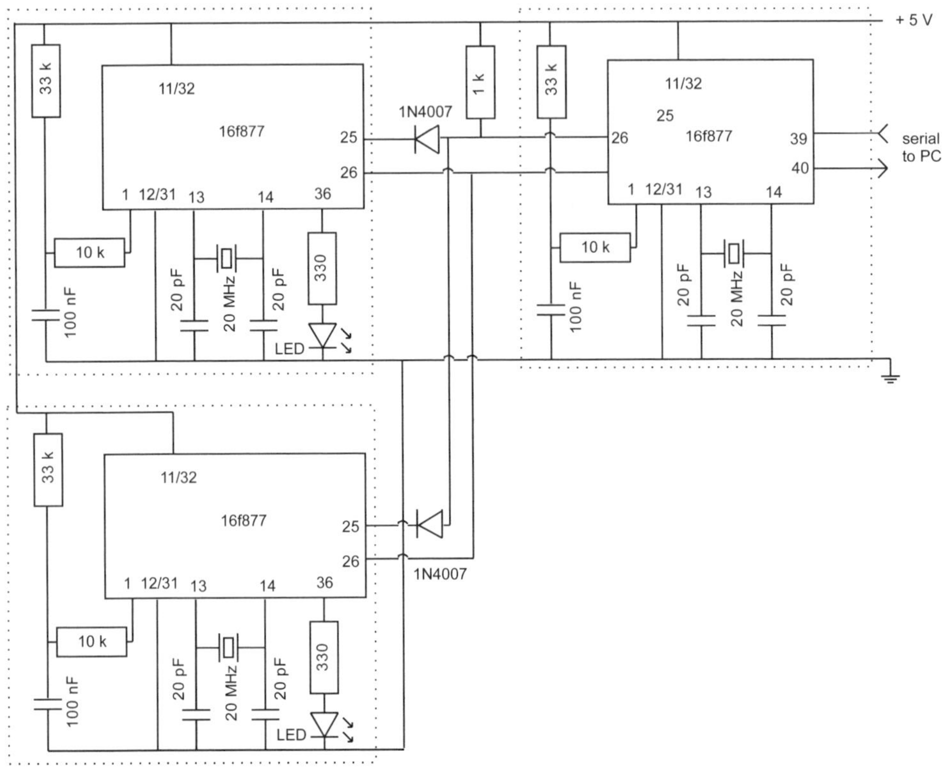

Figure 138. Serial network with 3 PIC™ microcontrollers.

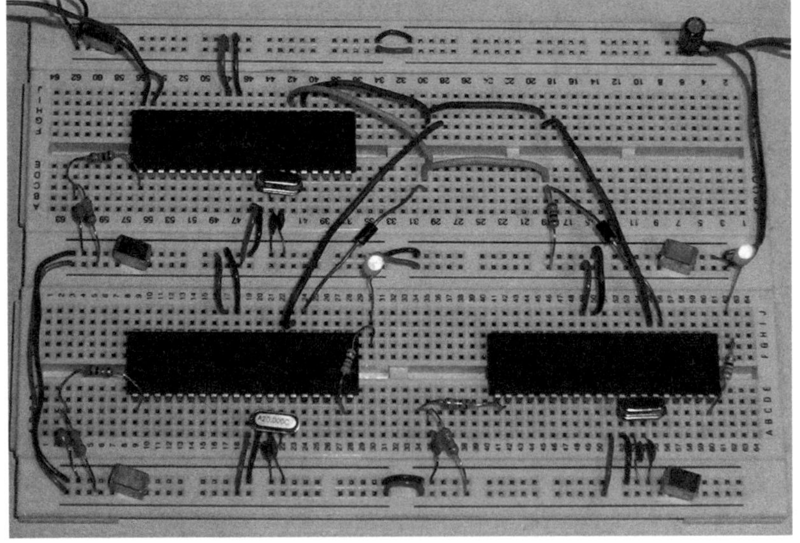

Figure 139. Serial network with 3 PIC™ microcontrollers.

12 Miscellaneous Projects

In this final chapter on the 16F877 we discuss a number of projects that don't quite fit in any category.

Project	**Description**
Timer 0 interrupt	If something needs to happen with regularity the TIMER0 interrupt is a good choice.
Port B interrupt	Catch any signal on port B even when the program is doing something else.
Pictures of light	Our eyes see a fast moving light as a stripe. By flashing lights in a certain rhythm while they move our eyes see a picture.
Digital clock	A digital clock with LCD display and three buttons to adjust the time.
Scrolling display with animation	A scrolling display on an LCD panel with homemade animation.
Ultrasonic radar	A Devantech SRF04 Ultrasonic Range Finder is modified to serve as ultrasonic radar.
Handling larger currents	Three ways to control larger currents with a PIC™.
The poetry box	Playful use of the bizarre *long table* command to display a poem on an LCD screen.
Bootloader	A bootloader is a way to load programs into a PIC™ without using a programmer.

12.1 TIMER0 interrupt

If something needs to happen with regularity the TIMER0 interrupt is a good choice.

Please note that some processes may not be interrupted. If for example serial transmission would be interrupted this would certainly cause a transmission failure[133]. Writers of such routines routinely switch off interrupts before their routine starts and switch it back on at the end. Of course this destroys your "regularity". So when writing programs that use an interrupt you still need to consider which other parts of the chip you are using. A good suggestion (for any software development) is to write in small chunks and test regularly.

Technical background

TIMER0 can stop a program in progress in order to run a small procedure. How often this takes place depends on the settings of the OPTION_REG register.

---

[133] Interrupts will not cause transmission failures when using hardware serial communication.

OPTION_REG REGISTER

R/W-1	R/W-1	R/W-1	R/W-1	R/W-1	R/W-1	R/W-1	R/W-1
$\overline{\text{RBPU}}$	INTEDG	T0CS	T0SE	PSA	PS2	PS1	PS0

bit 7   ...   bit 0

bit 7   **$\overline{\text{RBPU}}$**

bit 6   **INTEDG**

bit 5   **T0CS**: TMR0 Clock Source Select bit
             1 = Transition on T0CKI pin
             0 = Internal instruction cycle clock (CLKOUT)

bit 4   **T0SE**: TMR0 Source Edge Select bit
             1 = Increment on high-to-low transition on T0CKI pin
             0 = Increment on low-to-high transition on T0CKI pin

bit 3   **PSA**: Prescaler Assignment bit
             1 = Prescaler is assigned to the WDT
             0 = Prescaler is assigned to the Timer0 module

bit 2-0   **PS2:PS0**: Prescaler Rate Select bits

Bit Value	TMR0 Rate	WDT Rate
000	1 : 2	1 : 1
001	1 : 4	1 : 2
010	1 : 8	1 : 4
011	1 : 16	1 : 8
100	1 : 32	1 : 16
101	1 : 64	1 : 32
110	1 : 128	1 : 64
111	1 : 256	1 : 128

Figure 140. OPTION_REGregister.

This register can also be used to generate interupts on port B. The RBPU (port B pull-up enable) and INTEDG (interrupt edge select) bits are meant for this purpose (see section 12.2).

T0CS (TIMER0 clock source) indicates whether the clock is internally or externally controlled. We are using a crystal so "externally" would be an obvious answer. In this case, however, "external" refers to pin T0CK1 (pin a6), so we need to choose "internally".

The other bits (PS0, PS1, PS2 and PSA) determine how often the interrupt needs to occur. A bit of mathematics: the crystal has a frequency of 20 MHz. Every <u>fourth</u> pulse TIMER0 is incremented by 1 (because each instruction takes four clock pulses to execute). An interrupt is generated when TIMER0 rolls over, after 256 increments. This means the standard interrupt frequency is

$$20.000.000 / 4 / 256 = 19.531 \text{ Hz}$$

That might be a bit quick, so a prescaler can be used to make the interrupt occur less frequently. This prescaler can be assigned to the WDT (watch dog timer) or the TIMER0 module. The impact of all this is shown in the following interrupt frequency table.

Interrupt frequency	TMR0 assignment	WTD assignment
Prescaler	Frequency (Hz)	Frequency (Hz)
0	9.766	19.531
1	4.883	9.766
2	2.441	4.883
3	1.221	2.441
4	610	1.221
5	305	610
6	153	305
7	76	153

So if you set the prescaler to 2 and assign the result to TMR0 (which results in an OPTION_REG value of 0b_0000_0010) the interrupt frequency will be 2.441 Hz.

It is also possible to increase the frequency. Normally speaking TIMER0 starts counting at 0, but you can also make it start at another value. This means the rollover point will be reached sooner. If you start TIMER0 at 50 instead of 0 the rollover time becomes (256 - 50) * 0.2 uS, which creates a theoretical interrupt frequency of 24.272 Hz.

If you make the interrupt frequency too high the program itself will not have time to do anything. If you make TIMER0 start at 200, for example, only 56 instructions are left over for your entire program to use, including the interrupt routine itself. So for the higher starting values the following table is more theory than reality.

Interrupt frequency	WTD assignment, prescaler = 0
TMR0 start	**Frequency (Hz)**
0 (do nothing)	19.531
50	24.272
100	32.051
150	47170
200	89.286

The procedure that is called during an interrupt is almost identical to a normal procedure, with a few small exceptions:

1. The very first line of the procedure is *pragma interrupt* (a instruction to the JAL compiler to turn this into an interrupt routine). You can make as many interrupt routines as you like; the JAL compiler will notice this and neatly put them together. A very powerfull feature!
2. Interrupt procedures may not be called from the main program or any other procedure.
3. Check to see if it is "your" interrupt calling the procedure.
4. Keep the procedure short.
5. It is considered good programming practice not to read or write pins during an interrupt.

We will get back to rule three later. A typical interrupt procedure would look like this:

```
procedure myInterruptProc is
   pragma interrupt

   [this is where the commands go]

end procedure
```

Now that we have an interrupt procedure and a desired frequency all that is left to do is to switch it on. This is done in the INTCON register[134]. Let's see what the datasheet has to say about this register:

INTCON REGISTER (ADDRESS 0Bh, 8Bh, 10Bh, 18Bh)

R/W-0	R/W-0	R/W-0	R/W-0	R/W-0	R/W-0	R/W-0	R/W-x
GIE	PEIE	T0IE	INTE	RBIE	T0IF	INTF	RBIF

bit 7   bit 0

bit 7   **GIE**: Global Interrupt Enable bit
1 = Enables all unmasked interrupts
0 = Disables all interrupts

bit 6   **PEIE**: Peripheral Interrupt Enable bit
1 = Enables all unmasked peripheral interrupts
0 = Disables all peripheral interrupts

bit 5   **T0IE**: TMR0 Overflow Interrupt Enable bit
1 = Enables the TMR0 interrupt
0 = Disables the TMR0 interrupt

bit 4   **INTE**: RB0/INT External Interrupt Enable bit
1 = Enables the RB0/INT external interrupt
0 = Disables the RB0/INT external interrupt

bit 3   **RBIE**: RB Port Change Interrupt Enable bit
1 = Enables the RB port change interrupt
0 = Disables the RB port change interrupt

bit 2   **T0IF**: TMR0 Overflow Interrupt Flag bit
1 = TMR0 register has overflowed (must be cleared in software)
0 = TMR0 register did not overflow

bit 1   **INTF**: RB0/INT External Interrupt Flag bit
1 = The RB0/INT external interrupt occurred (must be cleared in software)
0 = The RB0/INT external interrupt did not occur

bit 0   **RBIF**: RB Port Change Interrupt Flag bit
1 = At least one of the RB7:RB4 pins changed state; a mismatch condition will continue to set the bit. Reading PORTB will end the mismatch condition and allow the bit to be cleared (must be cleared in software).
0 = None of the RB7:RB4 pins have changed state

Figure 141. INTCON register.

---

[134] You can use this register also to temporarily switch off interrupts for parts of the program that should not be interrupted (such as those dealing with communications). Manipulating this switch will, of course, alter the expected frequency.

This register is very important. It contains both settings and vital information. For us bits 7, 5, and 2 are interesting. Bit 7 is used to switch on interrupts in general (like a main switch if you like), and with bit 5 the the TIMER0 interrupt is switched on, like this:

    INTCON = 0b_1010_0000

You may have noticed that interrupts can be generated by many different souces, not just TIMER0. To be sure that "our" interrupt is actually taking place bit 2 can be used. If this bit (T0IF) is 1 at the moment that an interrupt occurs it means the interrupt is caused by TIMER0. So your interrupt procedure should check for this condition, and reset it to 0 afterwards, like this:

    procedure myInterruptProc is
       pragma interrupt

       if T0IF then

          [this is where the commands go]

          T0IF = 0
       end if

    end procedure

This was rule three from the interrupt rules: Check to see if it is "your" interrupt calling the procedure.

The software

Now that we've thoroughly covered using an interrupt we need to put it to good use. So what could we do with a frequency of 2.441 Hz? Make a sound! If we use the interrupt to toggle a pin high and low we have a sound (in combination with a speaker).

The interrupt routine would look like this:

    procedure make_a_sound is
       pragma interrupt

       if T0IF then
          -- *switch pin to make sound*
          flag = ! flag
          pin_d1 = flag

> *-- clear TOIF to re-enable timer interrupts*
> T0IF = 0
>   end if
>
>   end procedure

After checking if this was a call caused by the TIMER0 interrupt the state of pin d1 is switched. Of course that means that each interrupt we only make half of a sound wave. This pin will go up or down each time, but not both.

So even though the procedure is called at 2.441 Hz the actual sound will have a frequency that is half of that: 1220 Hz. The frequency counter in Figure 143 shows this to be correct..

Figure 142. The actual sound frequency.

The main program looks a bit bizarre because nothing happens:

> forever loop
> end loop

You do need it, however, because without the loop the program will stop and disable the interrupts.

Putting it all together yields this program:

> *-- JAL 2.0.4*
> include 16F877_bert
>
> pin_d1_direction = output
> var bit flag

```
-- the actual interrupt routine
procedure make_a_sound is
   pragma interrupt

   if T0IF then
       -- switch pin to make sound
       flag = ! flag
       pin_d1 = flag

       -- clear T0IF to re-enable timer interrupts
       T0IF = 0
   end if

end procedure

-- enable timer 0
OPTION_REG= 0b_0000_0010

-- enable interrupts
INTCON = 0b_1010_0000

forever loop
end loop
```

You may have noticed that I violated rule 5 because I changed pin status in the middle of an interrupt call. A good exercise for you would be to rewrite the program without violating this rule.

The hardware

The hardware is very simple. A basic setup of the 16F877 with just two extra parts: a speaker and a variable resistor for volume control.

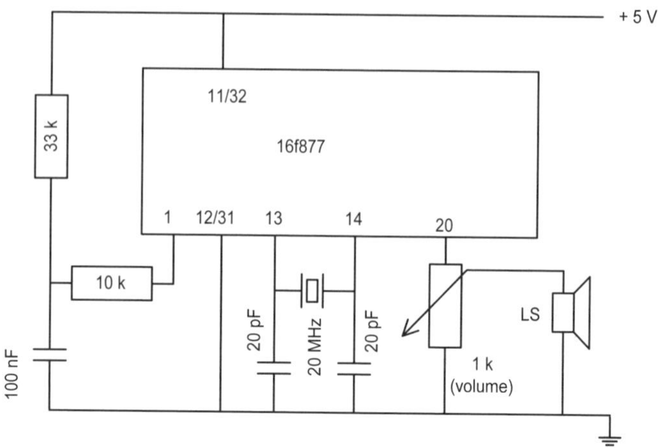

Figure 143. TIMER0 whistle.

Which looks like this in real life:

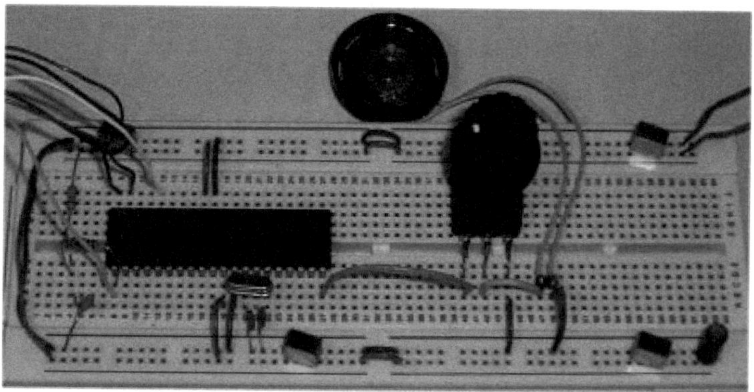

Figure 144. TIMER0 whistle on the breadboard.

Optional

Surely you have wondered by now what would happen to the whistle if TIMER0 would not start counting at zero but a another value. The explanation in the technical background section indicates that the frequency should go up.

It is fun to add a variable resistor to set the starting point of TIMER0. This way you get a frequency generator (or tone generator) with a variable frequency!

In the interrupt routine we add the following line:

    TMR0 = resist

After each interrupt the timer will not start at zero but at the value of the variable resistor. The resistance is measured in the main program (Rule 4: Keep the procedure short)[135]:

    resist = ADC_read_low_res(0)

The complete program looks like this:

```
-- JAL 2.0.4
include 16F877_bert

var byte resist
var bit flag
pin_d1_direction = output

-- the actual interrupt routine
procedure make_a_sound is
    pragma interrupt

    if T0IF then
        -- switch pin to make sound
        flag = ! flag
        pin_d1 = flag

        -- modify frequency
        TMR0 = resist

        -- clear T0IF to re-enable timer interrupts
        T0IF = 0
    end if

end procedure

-- enable timer 0
OPTION_REG= 0b_0000_0010
```

---

[135] Try moving the *resist = ADC_read_low_res(0)* statement from the main program to the interrupt procedure. Slowly increase the frequency and see what happens. Due to the slowness of this command some sort of maximum frequency occurs.

-- enable interrupts
INTCON = 0b_1010_0000

forever loop

  resist = ADC_read_low_res(0)

end loop

Of course you need to add the extra variable resistor to the project:

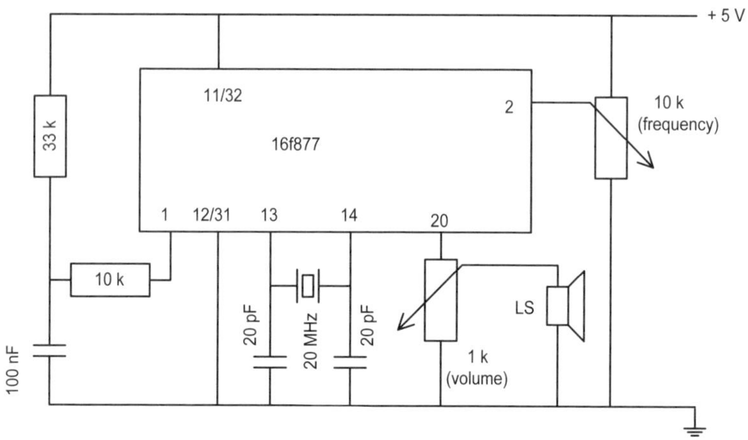

Figure 145. The extra variable resistor is added.

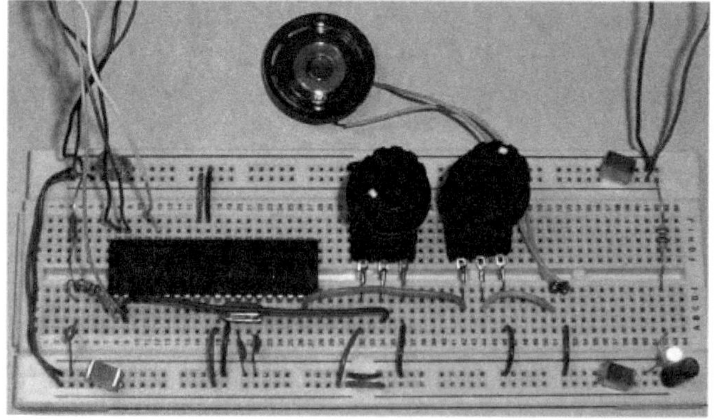

Figure 146. The extra variable resistor is added.

In section 9.4 you can play a simple melody with this technique and perhaps use it as a doorbell or christmas decoration.

Debugging with REGedit

Several times in this book you have used registers - special memory locations which influence the behavior of the PIC™. Whenever you doubt the correct setting you can simply try them all and see what happens in the program.

There is a much simpler way to do this, though, by using the REGedit program. With this program, in combination with a special library you can see the register values on your PC and even modify them while the program in the PIC™ is running!

As an example we will take a look at the OPTION_REG register of the first program of this section and then change it in the running PIC™ program.

To start with we will need to add a switch to pin d2. This switch will be used to sidetrack the main program and allow communication with the PC.

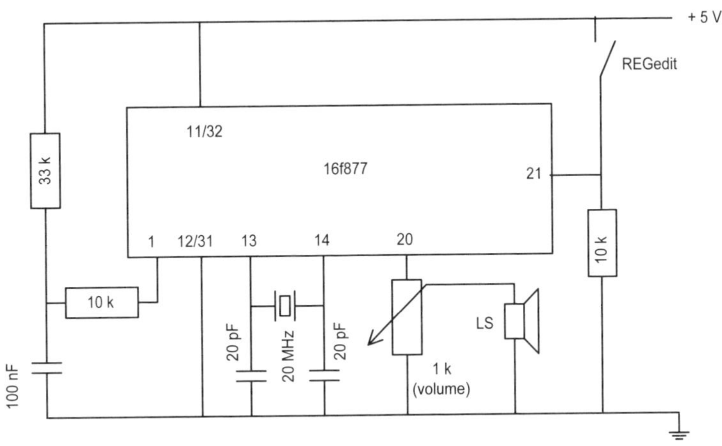

Figure 147. The additional switch.

The program needs to be modified as well. First, the switch is declared:

    pin_d2_direction = input

The special *regedit* library is included:

    -- JAL 2.0.6

```
include 16F877_bert
include regedit
```

And a call to the library is added to the main loop of the program:

```
forever loop

    -- press switch to edit
    if pin_d2 then
      register_debug
    end if

end loop
```

With only these minor changes here is the completed program:

```
-- JAL 2.0.6
include 16F877_bert
include regedit

pin_d1_direction = output
pin_d2_direction = output

var bit flag

-- the actual interrupt routine
procedure make_a_sound is
   pragma interrupt

   if T0IF then
       -- switch pin to make sound
       flag = ! flag
       pin_d1 = flag

       -- clear T0IF to re-enable timer interrupts
       T0IF = 0
   end if

end procedure
```

-- enable interrupts
INTCON = 0b_1010_0000
OPTION_REG= 0b_0000_0010

forever loop

  -- press switch to edit
  if pin_d2 then
    register_debug
  end if

end loop

When you run the program you hear the whistle, as normal. In the free software download package you will find the program REGedit. Connect the Wisp 628 programmer (or at least the black, red, green, and blue wires) and start REGedit:

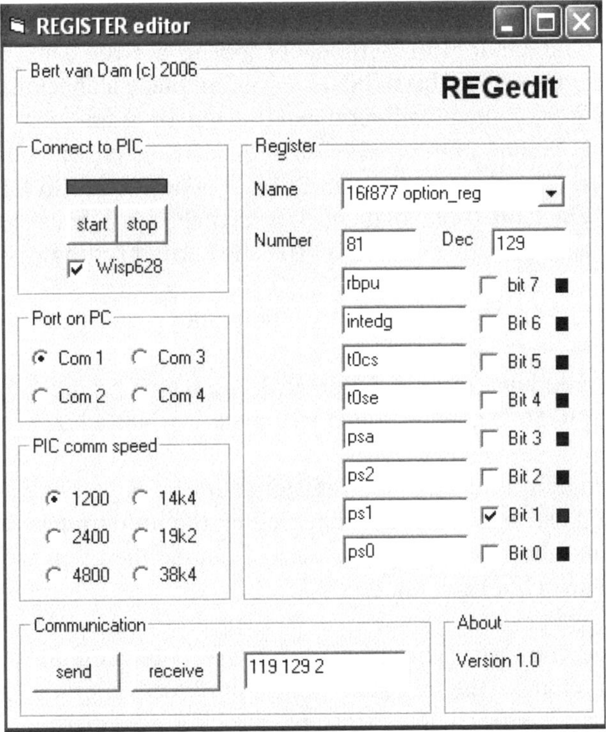

Figure 148. The register editor REGedit.

Now let's change the frequency of the whistle by changing the settings of the *OPTION_REG* register:

1. Start the connection by clicking on the "Start" button. The status bar above the buttons turns green (if needed select another COM port). If you haven't made any changes to the 16F877_bert library the speed is correct by default (1200 baud).
2. Select in the combo box the name of the register, in this case "16F877 option_reg". If all is well this name is already selected when you start the program.
3. First let's check what the current setting of this register is. Press the switch on the breadboard. The program is directed to a side loop and the whistle stops.
4. Click on the "Receive" button. The whistle resumes and to the right of the "bit 0, bit 1..." column the bits that are currently turned on in this register have become blue. In this case the only blue square is next to bit 1, as is to be expected, for the program contains the command:

OPTION_REG = 0b_0000_0010

In the light blue window a few numbers appear, but you can ignore them.
5. On the other side of the "bit 0, bit 1..." column place a checkmark next to bit 0.
6. Press the switch on the breadboard and the whistle stops.
7. Click on the "Send" button. The whistle starts again, but this time the pitch is much higher. The blue square next to bit 0 is now blue, so that means this bit is indeed switched on (note that bit 1 is switched off because you didn't put a checkmark next to it, just next to bit 0). The current setting is:

OPTION_REG = 0b_0000_0001

This means you have just set the prescaler to 0 (see Figure 140). This results in a frequency of 9766 Hz, and a sound frequnency of 4883 Hz.

You can use this program to change the register as much as you like. Other registers can be changed too. You can select those by clicking on the little triangle after the name box. Also fun is to disable the interrupt altogether (of course then you won't have a whistle any more) and then switch it back on.

If you found a value you fancy you need to add it to your program for the PIC^{TM}. With REGedit you only change the register values, not the program itself. This is very fortunate, because you could change registers in such a way that the program won't run anymore. In which case all you need to do is switch the power off and back on and everything is restored.

Of course you can use this technique with any program you like. All you need to do is follow these steps:

1. Add a pushbutton switch to a free pin.
2. Make these changes to the PIC™ program:
   - Add the special regedit library using *include regedit*
   - Define the pin that the switch is connected to. For example:
     pin_d2_direction = input
   - Add the loop to start the editing process. For example:
     -- press switch to edit
     if pin_d2 then
        register_debug
     end if
3. Start the program REGedit.

All registers used in this book are included in the Visual Basic program REGedit. If you want to use other registers you can add them yourself in just two easy steps (assuming you have Visual Basic).

1. In the *Private Sub Combo1_Click()* module add the names of the registers, and the names of the bits in the registers. Some registers may have the same name in different PIC™ microcontrollers but with a different address and possibly different contents. So you also have to add the name of the PIC™, like in the example below of the *OPTION_REG* register of the 16F877. Enter the bits from high to low; so in *Text3(0).Text* you enter bit 7. And don't forget to add the final field, *Text3(8).Text,* with the address of the register as found in the datasheet, but in decimal.

```
If Combo1.Text = "16F877 option_reg" Then
    Text3(0).Text = "rbpu"
    Text3(1).Text = "intedg"
    Text3(2).Text = "t0cs"
    Text3(3).Text = "t0se"
    Text3(4).Text = "psa"
    Text3(5).Text = "ps2"
    Text3(6).Text = "ps1"
    Text3(7).Text = "ps0"
    Text3(8).Text = 129
End If
```

2. Then add the <u>exact same name</u> in *Private Sub Form_Load()* as you had entered in *Combo1.Text,* like in this example:

    Combo1.List(0) = "16F877 option_reg"

Obviously, instead of 0 you would select the first available number.

When you start the program this register is now also available.

12.2 Port B interrupt

In this project the port B interrupt is used to count pulses on a pin while the main program is executing a delay statement.

Technical background

When a program is processing commands, such as a delay statement, signals on pins can go unnoticed. A few pins of port B, however, can be connected to an interrupt routine. At the moment a change takes place on one of these pins (high-to-low as well as low-to-high) an interrupt is generated and the interrupt procedure is executed.

First, two registers need to be set, just like for the TIMER0 interrupt, namely OPTION_REG and INTCON.

OPTION_REG REGISTER

R/W-1	R/W-1	R/W-1	R/W-1	R/W-1	R/W-1	R/W-1	R/W-1
RBPU	INTEDG	T0CS	T0SE	PSA	PS2	PS1	PS0

bit 7   bit 0

bit 7	**RBPU**
bit 6	**INTEDG**

bit 5   **T0CS**: TMR0 Clock Source Select bit
1 = Transition on T0CKI pin
0 = Internal instruction cycle clock (CLKOUT)

bit 4   **T0SE**: TMR0 Source Edge Select bit
1 = Increment on high-to-low transition on T0CKI pin
0 = Increment on low-to-high transition on T0CKI pin

bit 3   **PSA**: Prescaler Assignment bit
1 = Prescaler is assigned to the WDT
0 = Prescaler is assigned to the Timer0 module

bit 2-0   **PS2:PS0**: Prescaler Rate Select bits

Bit Value	TMR0 Rate	WDT Rate
000	1 : 2	1 : 1
001	1 : 4	1 : 2
010	1 : 8	1 : 4
011	1 : 16	1 : 8
100	1 : 32	1 : 16
101	1 : 64	1 : 32
110	1 : 128	1 : 64
111	1 : 256	1 : 128

Figure 149. OPTION_REGregister.

Only the higest bit in this register is of importance. We will connect a switch to a pin and take care of our own pull-down[136] resistor. An internal pull-up resistor is nice, but I find it difficult to remember that 0 means that the switch is closed. Strangely enough this bit has to be set to 1 if you do <u>not</u> want the pull up.

OPTION_REG = 0b_1000_0000

Of course interrupts in general must be enabled in the INTCON register (bit 7). Switching on the "interrupt on port B change" is done with bit 3.

INTCON = 0b_1000_1000

---

[136] A pull-down resistor is connected to ground, thus making the pin normally low ("down") and a switch connected to the power supply voltage can make it high when closed. A pull-up resistor is connected to the power supply voltage. To have both at the same time would be useless.

This interrupt doesn't work on all pins of port B, just pins b4, b5, b6 and b7. And since b6 and b7 are already used for the serial communication through the programmer there are only two pins left over.

Pin b0 can also be used with an interrupt, but it works a bit differently. For this pin you have to choose whether you want an interrupt when the pin goes from low to high or when is goes from high to low.[137]

INTCON REGISTER (ADDRESS 0Bh, 8Bh, 10Bh, 18Bh)

R/W-0	R/W-0	R/W-0	R/W-0	R/W-0	R/W-0	R/W-0	R/W-x
GIE	PEIE	T0IE	INTE	RBIE	T0IF	INTF	RBIF

bit 7   bit 0

bit 7   **GIE:** Global Interrupt Enable bit
1 = Enables all unmasked interrupts
0 = Disables all interrupts

bit 6   **PEIE:** Peripheral Interrupt Enable bit
1 = Enables all unmasked peripheral interrupts
0 = Disables all peripheral interrupts

bit 5   **T0IE:** TMR0 Overflow Interrupt Enable bit
1 = Enables the TMR0 interrupt
0 = Disables the TMR0 interrupt

bit 4   **INTE:** RB0/INT External Interrupt Enable bit
1 = Enables the RB0/INT external interrupt
0 = Disables the RB0/INT external interrupt

bit 3   **RBIE:** RB Port Change Interrupt Enable bit
1 = Enables the RB port change interrupt
0 = Disables the RB port change interrupt

bit 2   **T0IF:** TMR0 Overflow Interrupt Flag bit
1 = TMR0 register has overflowed (must be cleared in software)
0 = TMR0 register did not overflow

bit 1   **INTF:** RB0/INT External Interrupt Flag bit
1 = The RB0/INT external interrupt occurred (must be cleared in software)
0 = The RB0/INT external interrupt did not occur

bit 0   **RBIF:** RB Port Change Interrupt Flag bit
1 = At least one of the RB7:RB4 pins changed state; a mismatch condition will continue to set the bit. Reading PORTB will end the mismatch condition and allow the bit to be cleared (must be cleared in software).
0 = None of the RB7:RB4 pins have changed state

Figure 150. INTCON register.

---

[137] If you want to use this interrupt you need to set bit 6 (intedg) to 1 (low-to-high) or 0 (high-to-low) in OPTION_REG , and in INTCON you need to set bit 4 (inte) to 1.

The software

When the interrupt routine is called we must first check to see if this is indeed a port B generated interrupt. This can be done with RBIF.[138] If this variable is high the next step is to determine which pin is involved. Since the serial connection is also on this port the interrupt might also be caused by signals coming in on those pins.

The switch is connected to pin b5 and is likely to cause bouncing . With a small loop we can wait for the pin to go low again and then another 1 ms to catch the remainder of the bouncing.

It is not a very elegant program (we did say interrupt routines should be as short as possible), but it does work.

So like this:

```
procedure detect_a_pin is
   pragma interrupt

   if RBIF then
     if pin_b5 == 1 then
        counter = counter + 1
     end if
     while pin_b5 loop
     end loop
     delay_1ms(1)

     -- clear RBIF to re-enable timer interrupts
     RBIF = 0

   end if
end procedure
```

In the main program an LED flashes at a leisurely pace of 5 seconds on and 1 second off. The idea of this project is that you press the switch on the breadboard a number of times while the LED is on. Invisible to you the interrupt routine counts this number. When the LED is turned off the result of the count is sent to the PC and the counter is reset to zero.

---

[138] Bit 0 in the OPTION_REG register.

```
        if counter != 0 then
            serial_sw_write(counter)
            counter = 0
        end if
```

Note that an interrupt is generated when this pin goes from low to high (when the switch is pressed), but also from high to low (when the switch is released). When you push the switch just once and release it the counter on the PC will show 2.

The entire program looks like this:

```
-- JAL 2.0.4
include 16F877_bert

pin_b4_direction = input
pin_b5_direction = input
pin_d1_direction = output

var bit led is pin_d1
var byte counter
counter = 0


-- the actual interrupt routine
procedure detect_a_pin is
  pragma interrupt

  if RBIF then
    if pin_b5 == 1 then
      counter = counter + 1
    end if
    while pin_b5 loop
    end loop
    delay_1ms(1)

    -- clear RBIF to re-enable poort B interrupts
    RBIF = 0

  end if
end procedure
```

```
   -- disable pull-up
   OPTION_REG= 0b_1000_0000

   -- enable interrupts
   INTCON =  0b_1000_1000

   forever loop

      -- start test
      led = high
      delay_1s(5)
      led = low


      -- show test results
      if counter != 0 then
         serial_sw_write(counter)
         counter = 0
      end if

      -- short break
      delay_1s(1)

   end loop
```

The hardware

The hardware is simple, just the normal 16F877 setup with one switch and an LED.

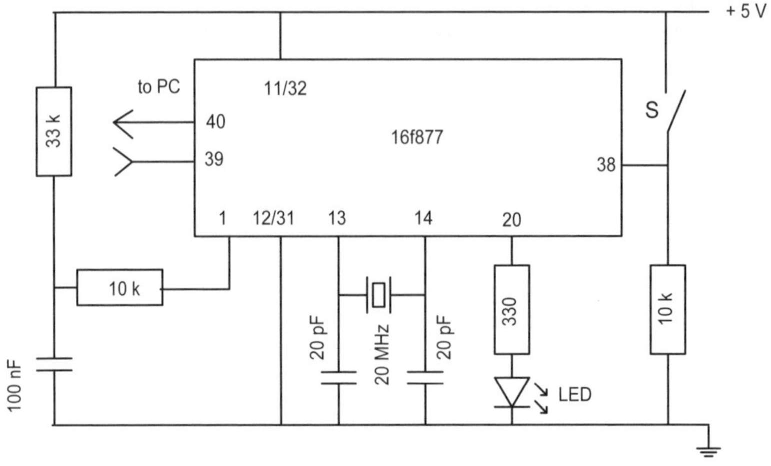

Figure 151. Port B interrupt.

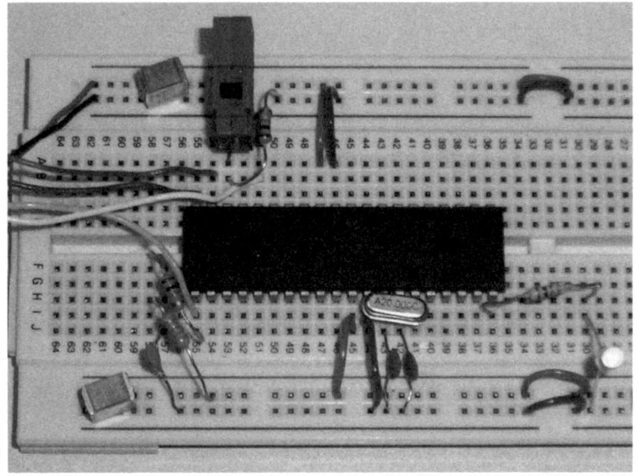

Figure 152. Port B interrupt on the breadboard.

12.3 Pictures of light

Our eyes see a fast moving light as a stripe. By flashing lights in a certain rhythm while they move our eyes see a picture: a picture of light..

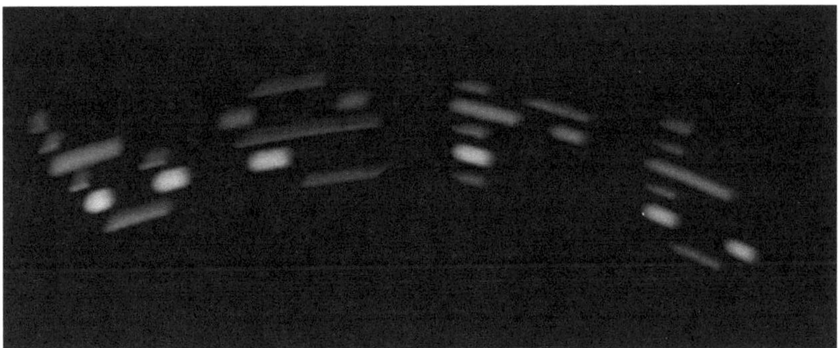

Figure 153. A picture of light.

Technical background

The purpose of this project is to have a row of LEDs flash in such a way that a picture can be seen when the LEDs are moved about quickly. It sounds much more complicated than it is in reality.

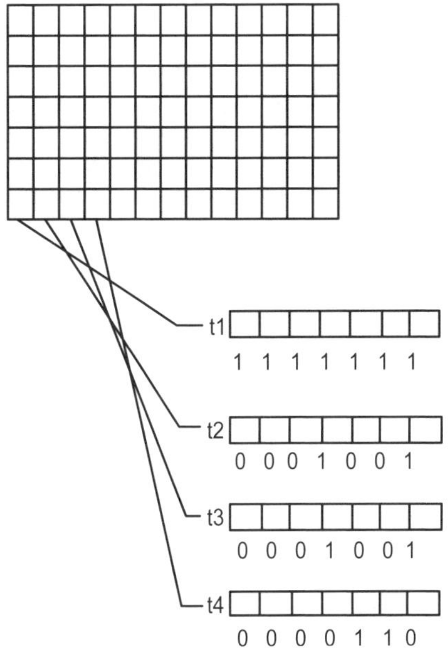

Figure 154. From letters to binary strips.

In the figure above you see the letter "b". The 7 LEDs are aligned in a column. At time t1 all of the LEDs are lit, displaying the first column of the figure, which is the back line of the "b". (A yellow square means that a LED at that position is switched on). A very short time later, at time t2, the LEDs have moved slightly to the right and are lit to display the second column of the "b" up (the first and fourth from the bottom). Two "very short times" later at t4 the last column of the "b" is shown. The slowness of our eyes ensures we can still see the entire "b'even though it is no longer there (and if fact it never even was there in the first place).

Every colored square represents one LED that is switched on. If we connect all LEDs to a single port we can set them all in the correct position (on or off) in one go, like this:

    portd = 0b_0001_1100

Using square ruled paper you can draw a picture and program it column by column. This gets boring real quick, however, so you can simply use the SkyWriter program. When you start the program you see what looks like square ruled paper. Each square represents a single LED. By clicking with the mouse on the squares you can switch them on or off, and make a drawing. When you are done you put a checkmark under every column that is part of the drawing and should be put into the program.

Before you continue you need to enter the name of the JAL program you want to create in the white box on the lower left hand corner, including a path (such as c:\picdev\tmp\sky.jal). Next, click on the "Start new JAL program" button (the square next to the file name turns green). Then click on "Add marked columns". The field next to the file name (Selected) shows how many columns are currently in the program.

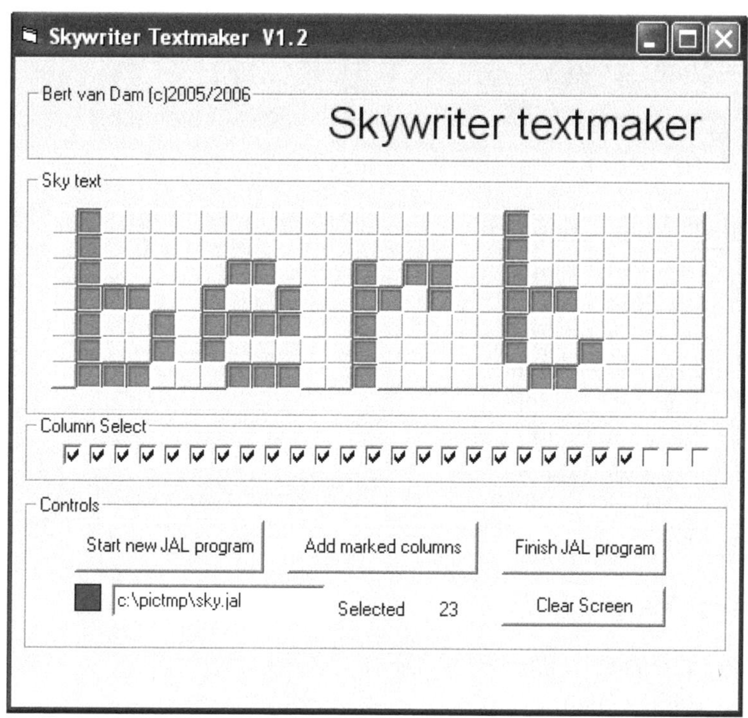

Figure 155. Skywriter in action.

Now you can choose:

1. The screen was too small for your picture. Erase the picture by clicking on the "Clear Screen" button and draw the next part of your drawing just like you drew the first part. When you are done click on "Add marked columns" again. Repeat as needed.
2. You have completed the picture. Click on "Finish JAL program". The square next to the file name turns red again. The JAL program is now completed.

The software

The result of your artistic skills in SkyWriter is a ready-to-run program that can be sent to the PIC™ as it is. At the beginning you will find the variable "watch" that indicates how long the program needs to wait between each port command. This represents the speed at which you need to wave the LEDs about. If you feel you need to move too fast (or too slow) modify the value of "watch".

```
-- JAL 2.0.4
include 16F877_bert

var byte watch
watch = 50

pin_d0_direction = output
pin_d1_direction = output
pin_d2_direction = output
pin_d3_direction = output
pin_d4_direction = output
pin_d5_direction = output
pin_d6_direction = output
pin_d7_direction = output

forever loop

   -- sweep forward

   portd = 0b_0000_0000
   delay_100us(watch)
   portd = 0b_1111_1110
   delay_100us(watch)
   portd = 0b_0001_0010
   delay_100us(watch)
   portd = 0b_0001_0010
   delay_100us(watch)
   portd = 0b_0000_1100
   delay_100us(watch)
   portd = 0b_0000_0000
   delay_100us(watch)
   portd = 0b_0001_1100
   delay_100us(watch)
   portd = 0b_0010_1010
   delay_100us(watch)
   portd = 0b_0010_1010
   delay_100us(watch)
   portd = 0b_0001_1010
   delay_100us(watch)
   portd = 0b_0000_0000
   delay_100us(watch)
   portd = 0b_0000_0000
```

```
    delay_100us(watch)
    portd = 0b_0011_1110
    delay_100us(watch)
    portd = 0b_0001_0000
    delay_100us(watch)
    portd = 0b_0010_0000
    delay_100us(watch)
    portd = 0b_0011_0000
    delay_100us(watch)
    portd = 0b_0000_0000
    delay_100us(watch)
    portd = 0b_0000_0000
    delay_100us(watch)
    portd = 0b_1111_1100
    delay_100us(watch)
    portd = 0b_0001_0010
    delay_100us(watch)
    portd = 0b_0001_0010
    delay_100us(watch)
    portd = 0b_0000_0100
    delay_100us(watch)
    portd = 0b_0000_0000
    delay_100us(watch)

  -- sweep back

    for ( 23  * watch) loop
      delay_100us(1)
    end loop

  end  loop
```

The return pass (with the LEDs off) takes exactly as long as the forward pass. So try to use an even rhythm.

The hardware

This project runs on battery power to prevent problems with short power leads. A voltage regulator is used (the 7805), which runs off of a small 9 volt battery.

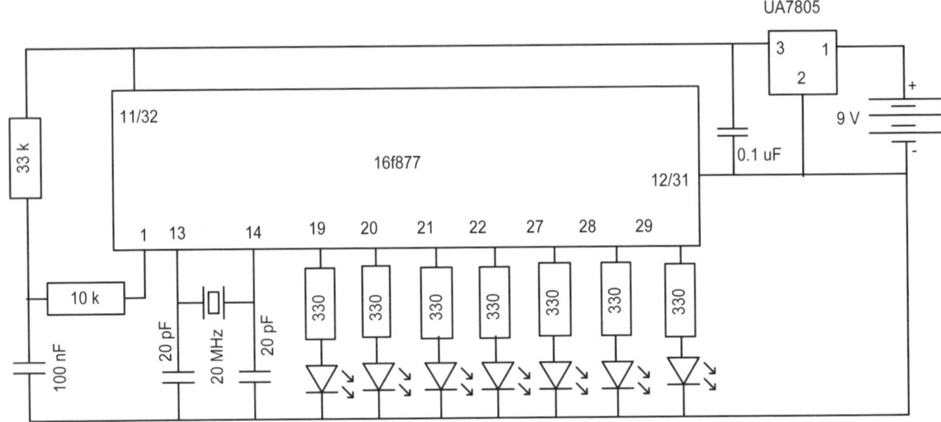

Figure 156. Pictures in light.

By now you have probably questioned why seven LEDs have been used when eight might have been more logical. Using just seven LEDs allows you to borrow designs from an LCD screen, because that also uses seven lines (the 8th is for the cursor); see section 12.5. The eighth pin is configured as an output so that we can set the entire port at once.

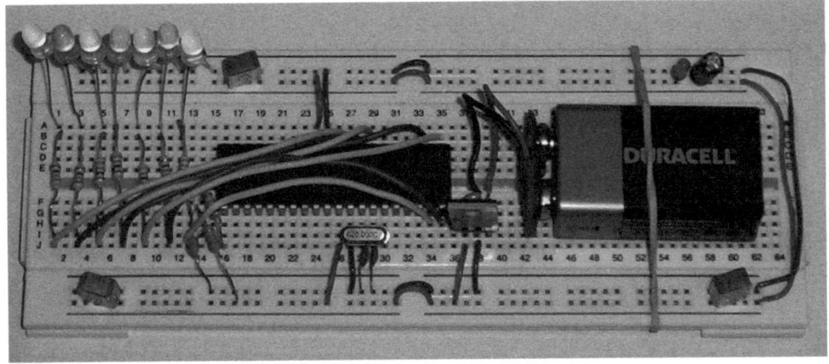

Figure 157. Pictures in light with battery power.

The instructions are very simple. Hold the breadboard at the battery side and wave it back and forth, preferrably in the dark. Look at the letters and adjust your swinging motion as needed. It takes a bit of practice to get it right, but the result is absolutely amazing: a picture of light out of nowhere!

Keep a firm grip on the battery and don't remove your fingers from it. Otherwise the battery will immediately be launched in the direction of the most expensive object; that tiny rubberband isn't going to hold it in place.

12.4 Digital clock

A digital clock with an LCD display.

Technical background

In principle this program consists of two interlocking loops

Main loop (select = 0)	1.	Wait 1 second.
	2.	Increment the relevant counters.
	3.	See if any button has been pushed.
	4.	Return to step 1.

Secondary loop (select != 0)	1.	Skip the "wait 1 second" statement.
	2.	Do not increment the counters.
	3.	See if any button has been pushed.
	4.	Display the text that goes with the selected function.
	5.	Make sure the up/down buttons modify the correct counters.
	6.	Return to step 1.

The 16F877_bert library doesn't have LCD commands so we will load the extra library, lcd_44780. The commands to put numbers and letters on the LCD display have already been discussed in section 5.4.

This, however, is a new command:

    LCD_clock_line_pos(number, line, position)

This is a special command for clock applications. The number is displayed on two positions with preceding zeros. That means it will display the number 4 as "04" It also means that any number higher than 99 will only show the last two positions (so 255 would be displayed as "55"), but for a clock that is not relevant.

The software

The switches in this project are push buttons, and every time you press them they should give just one pulse (this is done by the debouncing technique discussed in section 4.3). The hours are displayed from 0 to 23. If you want to display the hours in the American format you'll have to modify the program, and add "am" and "pm".

This piece of the program may surprise you:

```
if hour == 0 then hour = 24 end if
hour = hour - 1
```

It would seem more appropriate to write:

```
hour = hour - 1
if hour < 0 then hour = 23 end if
```

But *hour* has been defined as a byte, so it can never be smaller than 0. And declaring *hour* as an sbyte (which does allow negative numbers) is not possible either, because the LCD library cannot handle it.

The rest of the program contains no surprises:

```
-- JAL 2.0.4
include 16F877_bert
include lcd_44780

-- define variables
var byte second = 0
var byte minute = 0
var byte hour = 0
var byte counter = 0
var byte selected= 0

-- define switches
var bit select is pin_d2
var bit up is pin_d1
var bit down is pin_d0

-- define texts
var byte TimeText[4]={"T","i","m","e"}
var byte HourText[12]={"A","d","j","u","s","t"," ","h","o","u","r","s"}
var byte MinuteText[14]={"A","d","j","u","s","t"," ","m","i","n","u","t","e","s"}
```

```
-- set text line 0
counter = 0
for 4 loop
   LCD_char_line_pos(TimeText[counter],0,counter)
   counter = counter + 1
end loop

-- switch the cursor off
LCD_cursor = off

forever loop

  if selected == 0 then
    -- only run if not adjusting time
    delay_1s(1)
    second = second + 1
    if second == 60 then
      second = 0
      minute = minute + 1
      if minute == 60 then
        minute = 0
        hour = hour +1
        if hour == 24 then
          hour = 0
        end if
      end if
    end if
  end if

  -- display time
  LCD_clock_line_pos(hour, 0,6)
  LCD_clock_line_pos(minute, 0,9)
  LCD_clock_line_pos(second, 0,12)
  LCD_char_line_pos(":",0,8)
  LCD_char_line_pos(":",0,11)
```

```
-- function select
if select then
  while select loop
  delay_10ms(1)
  end loop
  selected = selected + 1
end if

-- adjusting hours
if selected == 1 then
  counter = 0
  for 12 loop
    LCD_char_line_pos(HourText[counter],1,counter)
    counter = counter + 1
  end loop
end if
if up & selected == 1 then
  while up loop
  delay_10ms(1)
  end loop
  hour = hour + 1
  if hour > 23 then hour = 0 end if
end if
if down & selected == 1 then
  while down loop
  delay_10ms(1)
  end loop
  if hour == 0 then hour = 24 end if
  hour = hour - 1
end if

-- adjusting minutes
if selected == 2 then
  counter = 0
  for 14 loop
    LCD_char_line_pos(MinuteText[counter],1,counter)
    counter = counter + 1
  end loop
end if
```

```
        if up & selected == 2 then
          while up loop
          delay_10ms(1)
          end loop
          minute = minute + 1
          if minute > 60 then minute = 0 end if
        end if
        if down & selected == 2 then
          while down loop
          delay_10ms(1)
          end loop
          if minute == 0 then minute = 60 end if
          minute = minute - 1
        end if

        -- done adjusting
        if selected == 3 then
          counter = 0
          for 14 loop
            LCD_char_line_pos(" ",1,counter)
            counter = counter + 1
          end loop
          selected = 0
        end if

      end loop
```

The hardware

The variable resistor on pin 3 is used to adjust the brightness of the display. If you run this project and you don't see anything on the display (or just black blocks) try adjusting this variable resistor.

The regular switch is just to light the display. This uses quite a bit of power. In the next table you see an estimate how long the clock can run using 1.5 volt AA batteries:

Display	Power consumption	Battery life[139]
off	8.4 mA	200 hours
on	51.6 mA	40 hours

---

[139] Predicted battery life using Duracell AA MN1500 alkaline batteries.

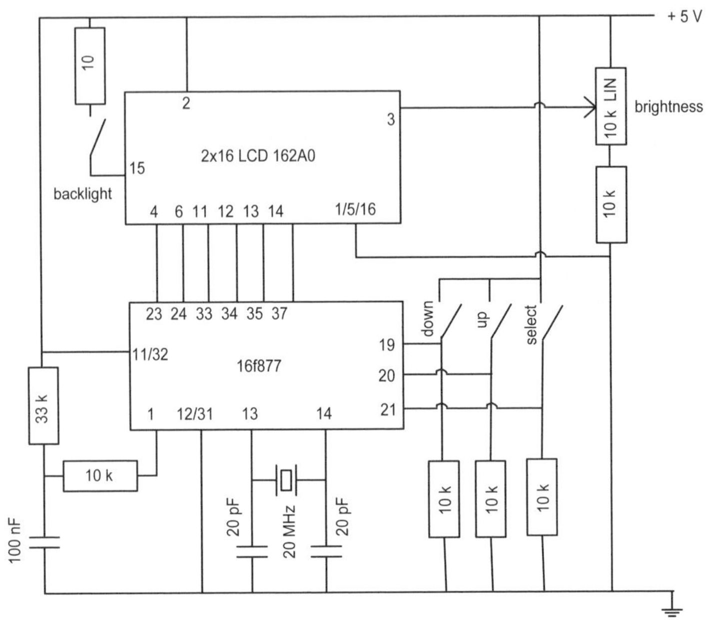

Figure 158. Digital clock.

Figure 159. The digital clock is operational.

The operation is very simple. Connect the power to the project. The display will show "Time 00:00:00', where the seconds start running immediately. Press the "select" push button (the left one on the breadboard). Press it long enough to see one second pass (you need to get beyond the *delay_1s(1)* statement) and then release it. On the bottom line the words "Adjust hours" are displayed and the clock will stop running. Use the other two push buttons to increase (middle button) or decrease (right button) the hours. Once the hours are correct press "select" again. This time the delay_1s(1) command is not in the loop so you don't have to wait. Now the words "Adjust minutes" are displayed. Set the correct minutes similarly to the way you adjusted the hours. When you are done press "select" again. The lower line on the display will clear and the clock will start running.

12.5 Scrolling display with animation

A scrolling display with custom animation.

Technical background

A scrolling display consists of letters that appear on the right side of the LCD screen, scroll to the left, and then disappear off the left side. In section 5.4 it was briefly mentioned that you can print outside the visible area of the LCD screen. In this project we will make good use of this technique, since it allows us to shift a row of 40 characters back and forth past the display while only the sixteen characters "in" the display area are actually visible.The rest protrudes off the sides and is invisible. This means we can write all of the characters right next to the display in one go and then shift them left one character at a time to get a scrolling motion.

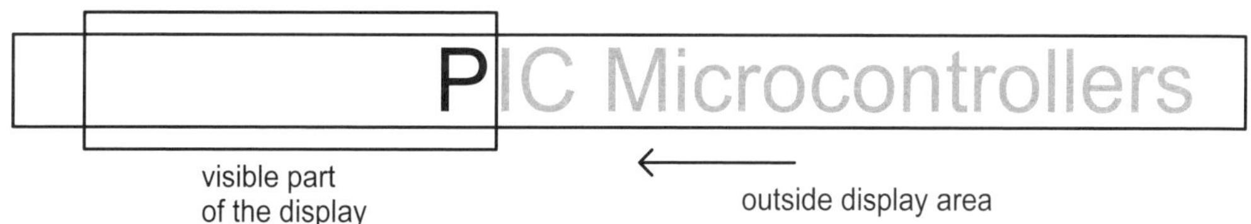

Figure 160. Character appearing from the right side.

What disappears on the left while shifting eventually shows up on the right again. So if we simply keep on scrolling left the same characters will display endlessly.

A convenient way to store the text you want to display is in an array. You can make such an array with the same program that we used in section 10.3 to make *pragma* commands. Except this time you select "array" instead of "pragma".

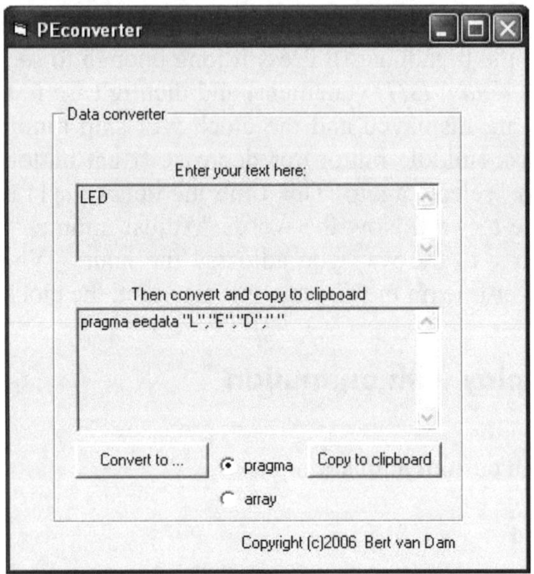

Figure 161. Making arrays with PEconvertor.

The result is a ready-made array called "Demo". You can rename it if you want and turn it into a declaration, like this:

```
var byte news[22] = {"P","I","C"," ","-"," ","M","i","c","r","o","c","o","n","t","r",
"o","l","l","e","r","s"}
```

The entire content of this array is now placed to the right of the LCD screen, starting at position 17 (remember the display only has 16 positions):

```
counter = 0
for 22 loop
   LCD_char_line_pos(news[counter],0,counter+17)
   counter = counter + 1
end loop
```

If we scroll left continuously in the main loop all of the text will scroll through the visible area of the LCD:

```
delay_100ms(4)
LCD_shift_left
```

The command *LCD_shift_left* is part of the lcd_44780 library. What's confusing is that the position numbers also shift left. That means position 0, the leftmost position on the screen when the project starts, becomes position 1 after one left shift. So when you write something to position 0 you won't see it. You can restore the entire LCD screen to the starting position by re-initiallizing it with the *LCD_init* command.

During scrolling you need to add a short delay, otherwise it will go much too fast for you to read. And while this scrolling is fun, it would be even more interesting if it would stop every once in a while and show a small animation, such as a spinning clock.

In the datasheet[140] of the 44780 you can see that a number of positions in the character memory of the LCD screen are empty. The first eight (circled red in Figure 162) can be used to store custom characters.

---

[140] This is considered the LCD standard, which is also applicable to the display used in this book. You can download the datasheet of the industry standard, Hitachi hd47780, from http://www.hitachi-ds.com/en/download/brochures/

Lower 4 Bits \ Upper 4 Bits	0000	0001	0010	0011	0100	0101	0110	0111	1000	1001	1010	1011	1100	1101	1110	1111
xxxx0000	CG RAM (1)			0	@	P	`	p				ー	タ	ミ	α	p
xxxx0001	(2)		!	1	A	Q	a	q			。	ア	チ	ム	ä	q
xxxx0010	(3)		"	2	B	R	b	r			「	イ	ツ	メ	β	θ
xxxx0011	(4)		#	3	C	S	c	s			」	ウ	テ	モ	ε	∞
xxxx0100	(5)		$	4	D	T	d	t			、	エ	ト	ヤ	μ	Ω
xxxx0101	(6)		%	5	E	U	e	u			・	オ	ナ	ユ	σ	ü
xxxx0110	(7)		&	6	F	V	f	v			ヲ	カ	ニ	ヨ	ρ	Σ
xxxx0111	(8)		'	7	G	W	g	w			ア	キ	ヌ	ラ	g	π
xxxx1000	(1)		(	8	H	X	h	x			ィ	ク	ネ	リ	√	x̄
xxxx1001	(2)		)	9	I	Y	i	y			ゥ	ケ	ノ	ル	⁻¹	y
xxxx1010	(3)		*	:	J	Z	j	z			ェ	コ	ハ	レ	j	千
xxxx1011	(4)		+	;	K	[	k	{			ォ	サ	ヒ	ロ	ˣ	万
xxxx1100	(5)		,	<	L	¥	l	|			ャ	シ	フ	ワ	¢	円
xxxx1101	(6)		-	=	M	]	m	}			ュ	ス	ヘ	ン	£	÷
xxxx1110	(7)		.	>	N	^	n	→			ョ	セ	ホ	゛	ñ	
xxxx1111	(8)		/	?	O	_	o	←			ッ	ソ	マ	゜	ö	█

Figure 162. Character set of the LCD screen.

You can design the custom characters by hand, but you can also use the CHARmaker program which is in the free download package.

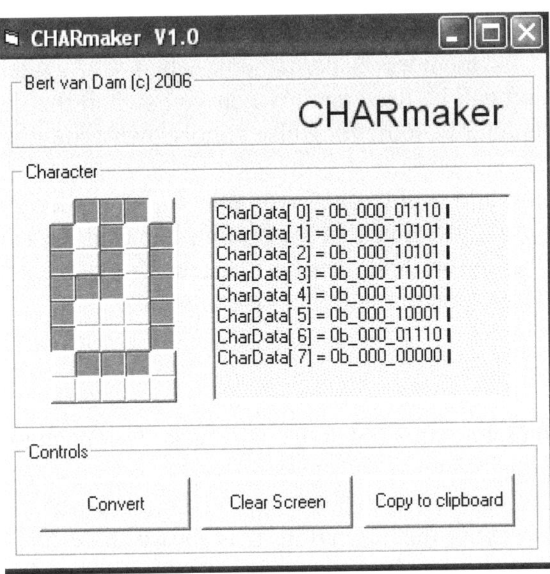

Figure 163. Design of a clock in CHARmaker.

The program works as follows: on the left you can design your character by clicking the squares on and off with your mouse. Then you click the "Convert" button to turn your design into an array. With "Copy to clipboard" the array is copied, which you can then paste into your program editor with the Edit-Paste (or Control-V) command. In your Jal program it will look like this:

```
CharData[ 0] = 0b_000_01110
CharData[ 1] = 0b_000_10101
CharData[ 2] = 0b_000_10101
CharData[ 3] = 0b_000_11101
CharData[ 4] = 0b_000_10001
CharData[ 5] = 0b_000_10001
CharData[ 6] = 0b_000_01110
CharData[ 7] = 0b_000_00000
```

You don't need to declare this array, this has already been taken care of in the LCD library. IMPORTANT: you cannot give the array another name!

Now we can transfer the entire array to the LCD memory:

```
LCD_custom(3)
```

In this case the custom character is put at the fouth memory location from the top (the counter starts at 0). This memory is permanent; when you switch off the display the character is retained and can be used again when you switch the display back on. If you want to change the character to something else simply overwrite it with your new design.

There are five columns and eight rows available for your design. If you look at the existing character set you will notice that the bottom line is always empty. This is because the cursor flashes on the bottom line. It is best to keep this line empty on your designs as well, unless you are certain that you will not be using the cursor.

The software

One clock is not much of an animation so we will make four custom characters, each with different minute hand positions.

The show starts by displaying the animation. It is shown three times (the *for 3* loop) and consists of four different custom characters (the *for 4* loop). By playing with the counters a bit we can display eight animated clocks on the screen at the same time, each turning three times around.

```
for 3 loop
    counter = 0
    for 4 loop
      counter2 = 0
      for 8 loop
        LCD_char_line_pos (counter,0,counter2)
        counter2 = counter2 + 2
      end loop
      delay_100ms(4)
      counter = counter + 1
    end loop
  end loop
```

After that the scrolling of the text starts. This has to stop at exactly the right moment. One reason is that otherwise there would be no room for the animations. But more importantly we want the first position on the screen to be zero again so the whole text scrolling can start over. Since there are 40 characters in the scrol-marquee we shift left 40 times:

```
for 40 loop
    delay_100ms(4)
    LCD_shift_left
  end loop
```

Perhaps good to note is that the new characters must be in the array CharData[]. You are not allowed to change that name. That means every custom character has to be stored in the LCD memory before you can define a new character. Otherwise the arrays would overwrite each other.

This is the completed program:

```
-- JAL 2.0.4
include 16F877_bert
include lcd_44780

var byte counter, counter2
var byte news[22] = {"P","I","C"," ","-"," ","M","i","c","r","o","c","o"
,"n","t","r","o","l","l","e","r","s"}

-- switch the cursor off
LCD_cursor = off

-- write character, also outside display area
counter = 0
for 22 loop
   LCD_char_line_pos(news[counter],0,counter+17)
   counter = counter + 1
end loop

-- custom character
CharData[ 0] = 0b_000_01110
CharData[ 1] = 0b_000_10101
CharData[ 2] = 0b_000_10101
CharData[ 3] = 0b_000_10101
CharData[ 4] = 0b_000_10001
CharData[ 5] = 0b_000_10001
CharData[ 6] = 0b_000_01110
CharData[ 7] = 0b_000_00000
-- load custom character in LCD memory location 0
LCD_custom(0)

-- custom character
CharData[ 0] = 0b_000_01110
CharData[ 1] = 0b_000_10101
CharData[ 2] = 0b_000_10101
```

```
CharData[ 3] = 0b_000_10111
CharData[ 4] = 0b_000_10001
CharData[ 5] = 0b_000_10001
CharData[ 6] = 0b_000_01110
CharData[ 7] = 0b_000_00000
-- load custom character in LCD memory location 1
LCD_custom(1)

-- custom character
CharData[ 0] = 0b_000_01110
CharData[ 1] = 0b_000_10101
CharData[ 2] = 0b_000_10101
CharData[ 3] = 0b_000_10101
CharData[ 4] = 0b_000_10101
CharData[ 5] = 0b_000_10101
CharData[ 6] = 0b_000_01110
CharData[ 7] = 0b_000_00000
-- load custom character in LCD memory location 2
LCD_custom(2)

-- custom character
CharData[ 0] = 0b_000_01110
CharData[ 1] = 0b_000_10101
CharData[ 2] = 0b_000_10101
CharData[ 3] = 0b_000_11101
CharData[ 4] = 0b_000_10001
CharData[ 5] = 0b_000_10001
CharData[ 6] = 0b_000_01110
CharData[ 7] = 0b_000_00000
-- load custom character in LCD memory location 3
LCD_custom(3)

forever loop
  -- show clock 4 frame animation 3 times
  for 3 loop
    counter = 0
    for 4 loop
      counter2 = 0
      for 8 loop
        LCD_char_line_pos (counter,0,counter2)
        counter2 = counter2 + 2
      end loop
```

```
      delay_100ms(4)
      counter = counter + 1
   end loop
 end loop

 -- move left continuously, will wrap around
 for 40 loop
    delay_100ms(4)
    LCD_shift_left
 end loop

   end loop
```

The hardware

The schematic is more or less identical to the one from section 12.4, but without the switches.

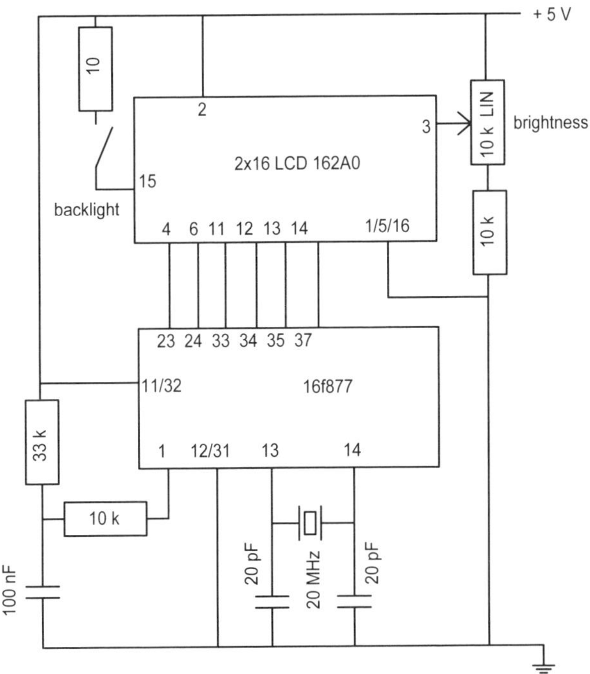

Figure 164. Scrolling display.

In the breadboard picture you can see that the animation has just finished and scrolling has begun.

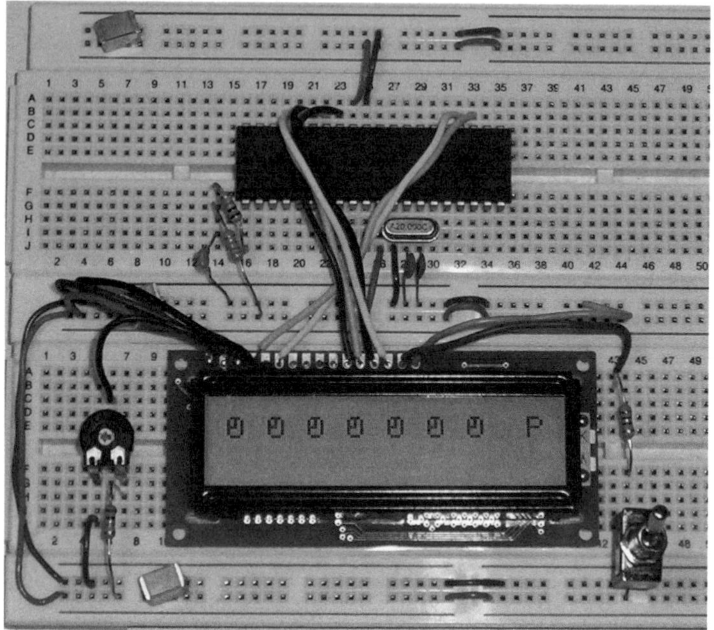

Figure 165. Scrolling display with animation.

12.6 Ultrasonic radar

In this project a Devantech SRF04 Ultrasonic Range Finder is modified so it can function as radar.

Technical background

The Devantech SRF04 Ultrasonic Range Finder measures the distance to the closest object in its path. Any ultrasonic echoes that arrive later are processed, but subsequently ignored and not passed to the PIC^{TM}.

Time to fire up the soldering iron and adapt the sensor a little bit. We will add a new wire, the "raw signal line', and we will process any signals on that line ourselves, bypassing the sensor's microcontroller.

WARNING: You void the manufacturer's warranty by modifying the sensor. And you will be soldering wire to an SMD component. So don't make the modification unless you have the skill to do so.

Figure 166. The yellow wire in the circle is new.

The figure above shows the bottom of the printed circuit board of the sensor. The yellowish wire needs to be soldered to pin 5 of the 12C508 chip. I have wrapped a piece of wire around the tip of my soldering iron, and by extending it a little bit I created a very small tip. Using a magnifying glass I was just able to solder a wire to that pin. The chip rose up a little bit, but fortunately that had no impact on performance.

On this new wire all incoming ultrasonic echoes are received, not just the first one. So the 16F877 needs to "listen" to this wire. Since it is normally high it needs to wait for the line to go low (*!radar*). We will use a counter called *distance* to register how long it takes for an echo to come in.

```
procedure GetSignal (byte out distance) is begin
  distance = 0
  while radar & distance < 254 loop
    distance = distance + 1
    delay_10uS(2)
  end loop
  distance = distance - 1
  -- wait until radar is positive again
  dummy = 0
  while ! radar & dummy < 254 loop
    dummy = dummy + 1
  end loop
end procedure
```

Since it is possible that there is no echo at all we need a way for this loop to time out. This will happen as soon as *distance* exceeds 254.

The same applies for the end of the signal. We need to wait for the signal to finish to make sure we are not repeatedly counting the same signal. It may, for whatever reason, never end. So a time out is used here as well.

Of course this is just one signal; there may be others. In fact, we hope there are others or the modification would have been pointless. So we will call this procedure multiple times - in this project five times. It's rare to see more than five signal echoes.

Meanwhile the PC is busy turning the radar unit in the proper direction. We will need to wait for the unit to be in position before sending a radar pulse. The PC informs the 16F877 about this by sending the letter "s" (for "start").

```
Procedure GetRadar  (byte in angle) is begin
  -- wait for the PC to signal a start (s)
  dummy = "0"
  while dummy != "s" loop
    serial_sw_read(dummy)
  end loop
  -- send pulse
  pulse = high
  delay_10uS(4)
  pulse = low
  -- wait for echo circuitry to switch on
  while ! echo loop
  end loop
  GetSignal(distance1 )
  GetSignal(distance2 )
  GetSignal(distance3 )
  GetSignal(distance4 )
  GetSignal(distance5 )
  -- send distance to PC
  serial_sw_write(angle)
  serial_sw_write(distance1)
  serial_sw_write(distance2)
  serial_sw_write(distance3)
  serial_sw_write(distance4)
  serial_sw_write(distance5)
end procedure
```

As a next step the distances measured are sent to the PC for processing.

The ultrasonic sensor is mounted on a contraption made with Lego Technic and controlled by a motor:

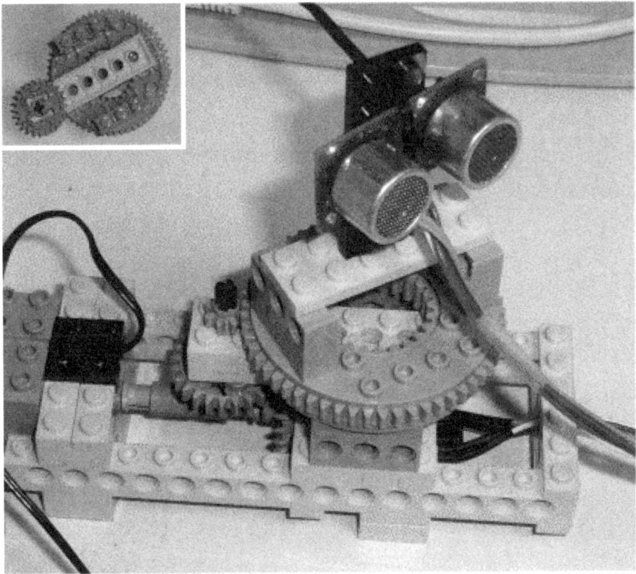

Figure 167. Mounting the sensor.

The pulse wheel is located at the bottom, just like in section 7.3, and with a Fairchild QRB134 infrared photo reflector to detect the black/white transitions. In this case, a pulse wheel is used with 16 sections (8 white and 8 black).

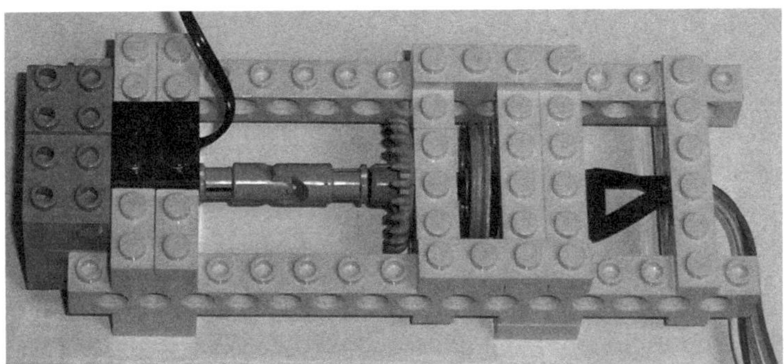

Figure 168. Construction of the base unit.

Rotating the unit is done by waiting until the infrared sensor measurement changes, indicating a different color is now in front of the sensor:

```
CCPR1L = speed
-- wait for color change on sensor wheel
while rotation loop
  yellowled = rotation
end loop
CCPR1L = 0
```

After 180 degrees the unit must be stopped (otherwise the wires to the ultrasonic sensor will wrap themselves around the unit). Then the unit will be rotated back 180 degrees to the starting position:

```
if rotpulse > 56 then
    -- go back to start otherwise the wire will get entangled
    direction = true
    CCPR1L = 175
    for rotpulse / 2 loop
      while ! rotation loop
        yellowled = rotation
      end loop
      while rotation loop
        yellowled = rotation
      end loop
    end loop
    direction = false
    rotpulse = 0
  end if
```

The data that is been transmitted to the PC requires some math for it to be useful.

The pulse wheel is divided into 16 sections, so each section the motor rotates translates to $360/16 = 22{,}5$ degrees.

The gears from the horizontal axle to the vertical axle have a ratio of 1 to 1, but from the vertical axle to the plaform is a ratio of 8 teeth to 56 teeth (1 to 7). So the radar unit will rotate 22,5/7 or 3,2 degrees per pulse wheel section. This means 56 pulses from the PC to rotate (*rotpulse*) will turn the unit approximately 180 degrees.

The PIC™ will send a rotation angle and a distance to the PC. In order to know where in the screen the corresponding dot needs to be placed the data must be converted to horizontal (x) and vertical (y) screen coordinates:

$$x = distance * \cos (angle)$$
$$y = distance * \sin(angle)$$

To complicate matters (in case you don't think it is complicated already), the x = 0 position of graph paper is at the bottom, but on a computer screen it is at the top. So we need to compensate for the size of the screen. And finally, it would be nice if the center of our half circle would be in the middle of the screen all the way at the bottom.

In Visual Basic it looks like this:

```
yt = Form1.Picture1.ScaleHeight - (d * Sin(alpha)) *
(Form1.Picture1.ScaleHeight / range)
xt = (d * Cos(alpha) * Form1.Picture1.ScaleWidth / (range * 2)) +
Form1.Picture1.ScaleWidth / 2
```

Nothing is ever simple, because Visual Basic works in radians and not in degrees so that needs to be converted as well:

```
alpha = anglefrompic * 3.2143
alpha = alpha * (3.1415692 / 180)
```

Fortunately the picture is worth all this trouble:

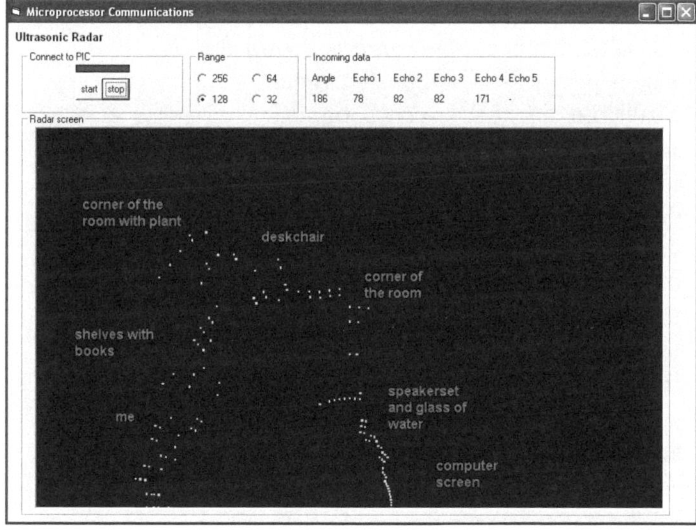

Figure 169. Radar image of my office.

On the ultrasonic radar image of my office I have noted what the radar was pointed at when that particular signal was received. At the top of the screen the measurements received from the PIC™ are displayed. Apart from that you can select a range (the scale of the radar image on the PC). The shorter the range the more the image is magnified. Measurements outside the screen are not shown.

You can see that reading this image is not very easy. Most of the objects in my office are hard, so stray ultrasonic echoes appear to be bouncing about. For indoor use the decision of the manufacturer only to process the first incoming echo was a wise one.

The software

Since all of the important parts have already been discussed all that is left is to put them together:

```
-- JAL 2.0.5
include 16F877_bert

var byte rotpulse, speed , angle, dummy
var byte distance1, distance2, distance3, distance4, distance5

-- define the pins
var bit rotation is pin_c0      -- rotation sensor
var bit direction is pin_c3     -- motor direction
var bit yellowled is pin_c4     -- rotation sensor led
var bit pulse is pin_d0         -- pulse trigger
var bit echo is pin_d1          -- echo signal
var bit radar is pin_d2         -- additional wire

pin_c0_direction = input
pin_c3_direction = output
pin_c4_direction = output
pin_d0_direction = output
pin_d1_direction = input
pin_d2_direction = input

procedure GetSignal (byte out distance) is begin
    -- wait for negative (!) signal on the radar line
    distance = 0
```

```
-- while radar & distance < 254 loop
while radar & distance < 254 loop
  distance = distance + 1
  delay_10uS(2)
end loop
distance = distance - 1
-- wait until radar is positive again
dummy = 0
while ! radar & dummy < 254 loop
  dummy = dummy + 1
end loop
end procedure


Procedure GetRadar  (byte in angle) is begin
  -- wait for the PC to signal start (s)
  dummy = "0"
  while dummy != "s" loop
    serial_sw_read(dummy)
  end loop
  -- send pulse
  pulse = high
  delay_10uS(4)
  pulse = low
  -- wait for echo circuitry to switch on
  while ! echo loop
  end loop
  GetSignal(distance1 )
  GetSignal(distance2 )
  GetSignal(distance3 )
  GetSignal(distance4 )
  GetSignal(distance5 )
  -- send distance to PC
  serial_sw_write(angle)
  serial_sw_write(distance1)
  serial_sw_write(distance2)
  serial_sw_write(distance3)
  serial_sw_write(distance4)
  serial_sw_write(distance5)
end procedure

pulse = low
-- enable pulse width modulation
```

```
PWM_init_frequency (true, true)

rotpulse = 0
direction = false
speed = 100

forever loop

  CCPR1L = speed
  -- wait for color change on sensor wheel
  while ! rotation loop
    yellowled = rotation
  end loop
  CCPR1L = 0
  rotpulse = rotpulse + 1
  GetRadar (rotpulse)
  CCPR1L = speed
  -- wait for color change on sensor wheel
  while rotation loop
    yellowled = rotation
  end loop
  CCPR1L = 0
  rotpulse = rotpulse + 1
  GetRadar (rotpulse)
  -- if half a circle has been made
  if rotpulse > 56 then
    -- go back to start otherwise the wire will get entangled
    direction = true
    CCPR1L = 175
    for rotpulse / 2 loop
      while ! rotation loop
        yellowled = rotation
      end loop
      while rotation loop
        yellowled = rotation
      end loop
    end loop
    direction = false
    rotpulse = 0
  end if

end loop
```

In the download package you will find the Visual Basic radar program for the PC.

The hardware

On the breadboard you may have noticed the BS170 MOSFET in the ground wire between the 5 and 9 volts sections. This part is not necessary and has been omitted from the schematic.

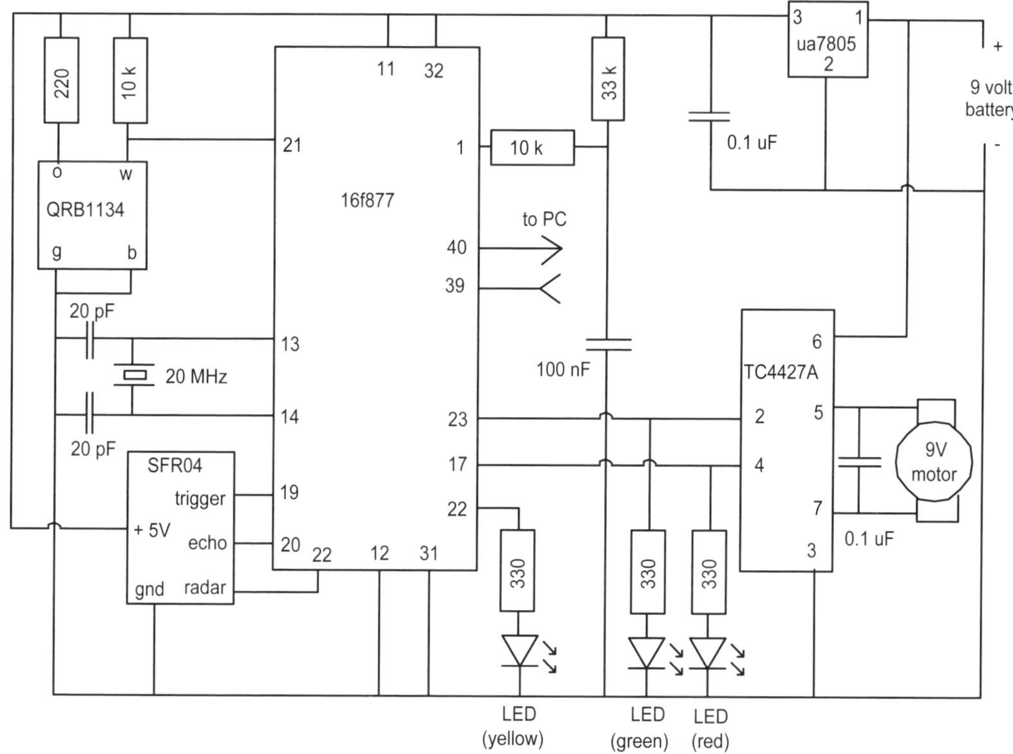

Figure 170. Ultrasonic radar schematic.

On the breadboard several capacitors are shown in the power lines. Small ones of 0.1 uF and larger ones of 470 uF. These may be required to prevent disturbances to and from the different sensors. They are not shown in the schematic, because the layout of the components determines how many are needed and where. The right side of the upper rail is 9 volts, the rest is 5 volts.

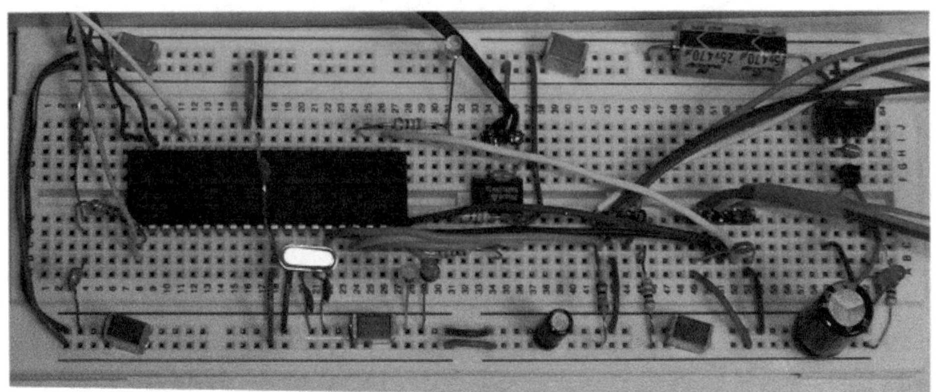

Figure 171. Ultrasonic radar on the breadboard.

12.7 Handling larger currents

It will happen periodically that you want to connect something to a PIC™ that consumes too much power. A siren from a burglar alarm, a 110 V or 240 V light bulb for a darkness activated switch, or even a simple Lego motor.

A PIC™ can drive a maximum of 25 mA per pin with a maximum of 200 mA per port. If you need more power (or a higher voltage) you will need to use a transistor, a TC4427A MOSFET driver, or a relay. In this chapter these three methods are discussed. In the table below you can see the applications for each method.

Method	Reversible power direction	Adjustable power quantity	Handles dangerous voltages or currents
Transistor		x	
MOSFET driver	x	x	
Relay			x

12.7.1 Transistor

Using a transistor is quite simple, but selecting the right type is a bit more complicated. The method described here was devised by John Hewes[141] of the Kelsey Park Sports College Electronics Club.

There are two basic types of transistors: NPN and PNP. An NPN transistor will conduct when a small positive voltage[142] is applied to the base, which in microcontroller terms is a "1". Only a very small current is required, because the transistor can amplify the current.

In addition to switching and amplifying current, you can also increase the voltage to your device, simply by connecting the transistor to a higher voltage. The ground wires of the PIC™ and the power source of the transistor must in that case be connected to each other. NPN is the type you will be using most, because it seems logical to switch the device on using a "1" from the microcontroller.

The following steps will help select and use the proper NPN transistor:

1. The maximum allowable current through the collector ($I_{c\,max}$) must be larger than the current consumed by the load (I_c).

2. The minimum current amplification (gain) of the transistor ($h_{FE,min,}$), must at least be 5 times larger than the collector current (I_c), devided by the maximum current the PIC™ can deliver.

3. Select a transistor from the table in section 14.5 that matches these criteria and make a note of its properties $I_{c,max}$ and $h_{FE,\ min}$.

4. Calculate the value for the base resistor, R_B, using the formula:

$$R_B = \frac{V_c * h_{FE,min}}{5 * I_{c,max}}$$

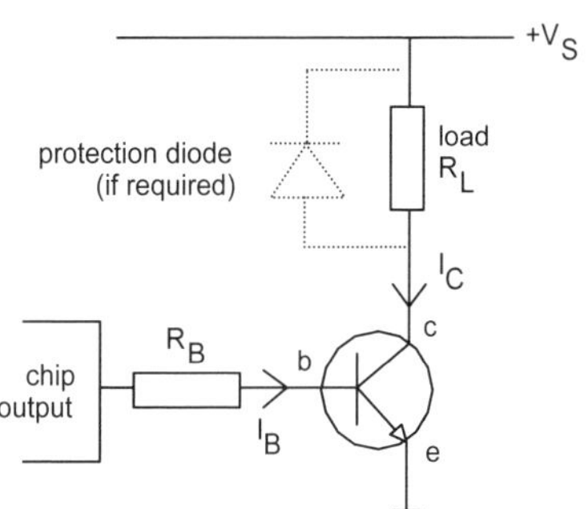

Figure 172. NPN transistor.

---

[141] Used in adapted format with permission from the author. For more information see the website http://www.kpsec.freeuk.com/index.htm

[142] Here is an easy to remember rule of thumb applicable to any electronic component: when conducting, the arrow in the symbol always points to the ground lead.

where V_c is the voltage that the PIC™ delivers.

In a simple situation where all voltages are the same you can use the simplified formula:

$$R_B = 0.2 \times R_L \times h_{FE,min}$$

5. Choose the closest available standard value for R_B.

6. If the load contains a coil (such as a relay or motor) you need to use a protective diode.

The PNP type works just the opposite way, where the transistor will conduct when the base is connected to ground (low in microcontroller terminology). Since this is less intuitive from the PIC™ point of view (you would expect something to go on when you make a pin high) you will not use a PNP type very often.

Selecting a PNP transistor is done using the same steps as above, except it needs to be connected differently.

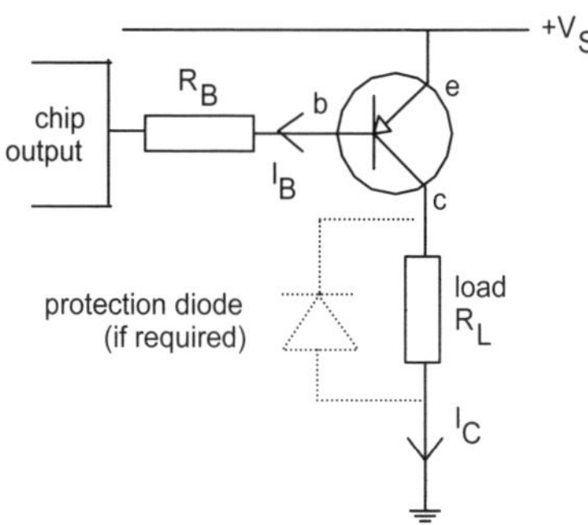

Figure 173. PNP transistor.

To clarify, this let's take a practical application. We want to run a 6 V 50 mA light bulb from a microcontroller and use PWM to vary the light intensity. The power consumption of the light bulb is almost double what the pin can handle so a transistor is required.

1. The light bulb uses 50 mA, so the transistor needs to have an $I_{c\,max}$ of at least 50 mA.

2. The load resistance, R_L, of the light bulb is 100 ohm (5 V / 0.05 A).

3. The maximum current that the PIC™ can deliver is 25 mA, so the transistor needs a h_{FE} of at least 10 (5 * 50mA / 25 mA).

4. The transistor will be connected to the PWM pin so it is probably a good idea to select a fast one, such as one designed for audio applications.

5. We choose the BC547B with $I_{c,max}$ = 100 mA and $h_{FE,min}$ = 200.

6. Since both the microcontroller and the light bulb will be run off of 5 volts the simplified formula can be used to calculate the value of R_B:
   $$R_B = 0.2 * R_L * h_{FE,min} = 0.2 * 100 * 200 = 4000 \text{ ohm}$$

7. A suitable standard value would be 3k3 (orange-orange-red).

The parts must be connected like this:

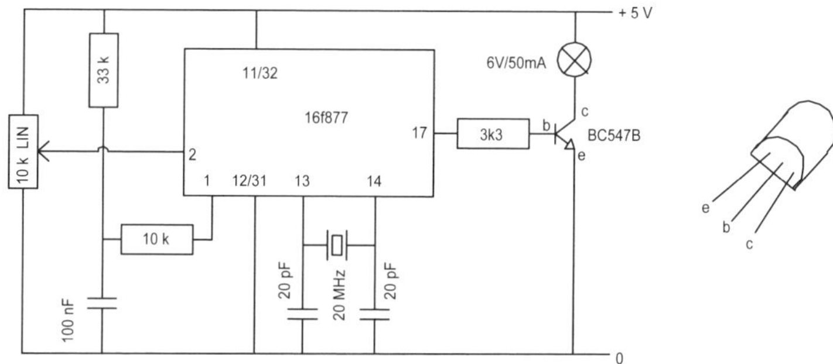

Figure 174. Connecting a 50 mA light bulb to a PIC™.

The project works perfectly (no smoke from the PIC™), but the light bulb is not very bright because it is a 6 V bulb running on 5 V. And the transistor has a typical power drop of 0.7 volt, so the light bulb only gets 4,3 volt, or 72%, of the design voltage.

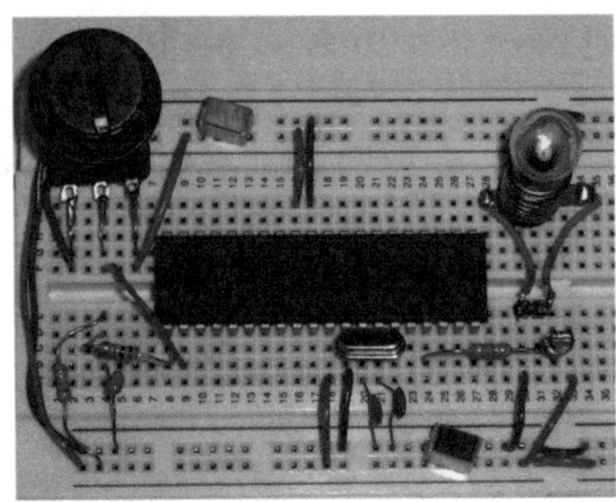

Figure 175. Connecting a 50 mA light bulb to a PIC™.

The program is very straightforward:

```
-- JAL 2.0.3
include 16F877_bert

var byte resist
PWM_init_frequency(true,true)

forever loop

  resist = ADC_read_low_res(0)
  CCPR1L = resist

end loop
```

Another example of the use of a transistor can be found in section 13.2.4.

12.7.2 TC4427A MOSFET driver

The TC4427A MOSFET driver manufactured by Microchip[143] has already been used in section 7 to drive a Lego motor.

---

[143] Download the TC4426A-27A-28A datasheet on http://www.microchip.com

The datasheet shows it has the following specifications:

Peak power out	1.5 A
Voltage	4.5 - 18 V
Delay	30 ns
Reverse current	max 500 mA

And that was more than enough for our little motor that had a maximum consumption of 260 mA. The high reverse current resistance means you don't need to use a protective diode.

These are the connections:

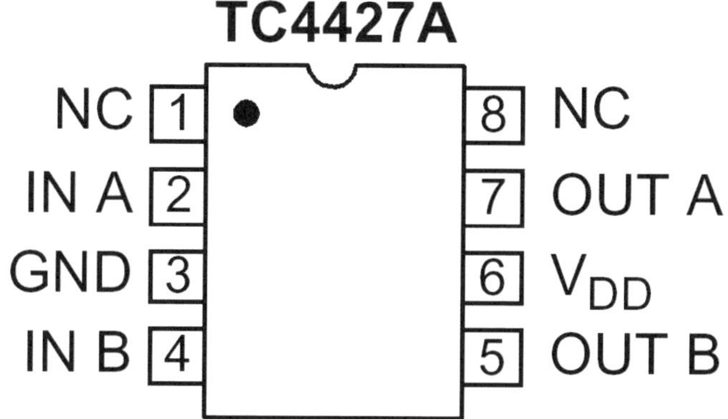

Figure 176. Connections of the TC4427A.

What it basically boils down to is that pin 2 (IN A) is "connected" with pin 7 (OUT A). Pin 2 is connected to the PIC™ and will thus carry 5 V. Which voltage is on pin 7 depends on the voltage you use as power for the TC4427, which is the voltage on pin 6 (Vdd). You can use a maximum of 18 V, in which case pin 7 will also carry 18 V, assuming it has been made high by pin 2.

The same applies to pins 4 and 5. Pin 2 (GND) is connected to the ground of the power supply just like the PIC. If you use a different voltage for the PIC™ and the TC4427A you will need to connect the ground connections together. Pins 1 and 8 are not in use (NC = not connected). So you need to at least connect the following pins:

Pin	Name	Description
3	GND	Connect to the ground of the power supply. Both the ground from the PIC™ power supply as well as the ground from the TC4427 power supply (if these are not the same) must be connected together.
6	V_{DD}	Power supply: +4,5 V to 18 V

So in principle the TC4427 is connected as follows:

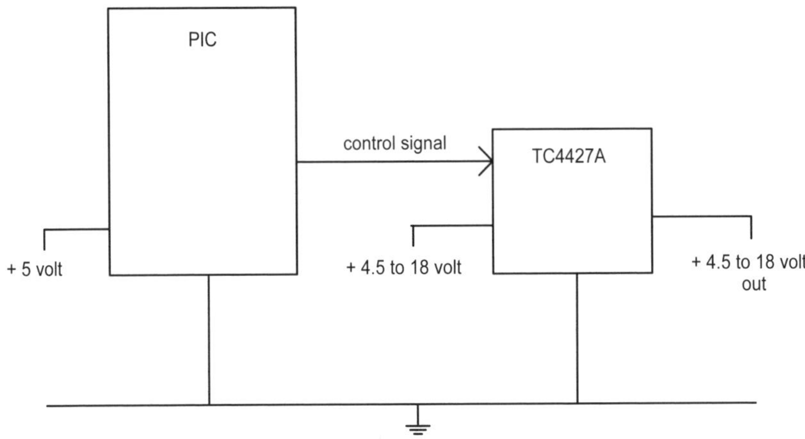

Figure 177. Connection of a TC4427A to a PIC.

Practical schematics can be found in sections 7.1, 7.2 and 7.3

12.7.3 Relay

The PIC™ can handle a maximum of 25 mA per pin with a maximum of 200 mA per port. Even though it is possible to find a relay that matches these specifications in most cases you will need to amplify the current. You can use a transistor as described in section 12.7.1. And you'll need to add the diode as described in the text to protect the transistor and the PIC™ against reverse current.[144]

---

[144] The current through a coil is persistent. If the power is removed the current will continue running for a bit. Since it cannot go anywhere the voltage will rise, easily high enough to destroy the transistor and the PIC™. The diode ensures that the current can flow away to prevent the voltage from rising.

Even easier would be to use a TC4427 MOSFET driver to drive the relay. You'll have ample power available for a huge relay and will not be bothered by reverse currents (you can still add the diode if you want). A MOSFET driver is more expensive than a simple transistor, so in a lot of commercial applications you will find a transistor and diode.

The advantage of a relay is that you can switch high voltages such as 110 V or 240 V. Be extremely careful, though. High voltages like this can kill!

12.8 The poetry box

A very unusual project: here we write a poem to an LCD screen.

Technical background

As one of the final projects in this chapter we will demonstrate one of the most bizarre commands of the JAL language, the long table, in an even more bizarre program.

In section 5.4 the array was introduced as a means of storing a collection of letters and numbers in memory. In section 10.2 you saw the limitations of this, because arrays are stored in empty blocks of RAM memory, thus limiting the maximum length of arrays considerably.

An exception to this is the long table. The programmer and designer of JAL version 2, Kyle York, explained the long table to members of the beta test group as follows: *"A long table is a constant array which is accessed at least once using a non-constant expression; whereas an array is non-constant and assigned at least one value."*

If these conditions are met the long table is stored in the program memory (FLASH) of the 16F877. Depending on the size of your program (which is also in program memory) a long table can be a whopping 8000 bytes long!

This is the syntax:

```
const byte demo[7591] = {"a", 67, "b", 45,56,...}
```

By definition of the long table these are constants, so this:

```
{"a","b","c","d","e","f","g","h"}
```

is identical to this:

        {"abcdefgh"}

Don't make these fragments too long, though, because if JALedit truncates your line you will get an error as JAL assumes each command to only take one line.

When you can store this much information we can do a playful project, like displaying a poem. You can mount the poetry box on the wall, or make it part of an Object d'Art. There is room for multiple poems, but in this project we will use only one, *"Berlin 1975, at the wall"*.[145]

You cannot display the entire text in one go, so we will start writing at position 16 (just to the right of the visible screen). Then we move the entire screen one position to the left and write again next to the screen.

```
counter = 0
position=16
LCD_char_line_pos (demo[counter],0,position)
delay_100ms(4)
LCD_shift_left
counter = counter + 1
position = position +1
```

Since the display moves the positions also move. That means position 16, which was originally next to the screen, is now visible. To write to the screen the next time we need to write to position 17. And to remain next to the screen the write position must be incremented with each shift.

With this LCD position 40 is not on the first line, but on the second. Which means that after 40 steps we are back at zero and need to write there as well:

```
if position == 40 then position = 0  end if
```

Not all displays are the same length. So it is possible that you need to change this value, in some cases even to 80.

---

[145] From the Dutch book *op drift geraakt* (let adrift) by *Bert van Dam*, page 12, published http://www.kirja.nl

The software

The entire poem has been converted to an array using the PEconverter program. The array is renamed to a long table.

This is the completed program:

```c
const byte demo[572] = {"b","e","r","l","i","n",","," ","1","9","7","5"," "," "," "," "," "," "," "," "," "," "," "," "," "," "," "," "," "," ",
"a","t"," ","t","h","e"," ","w","a","l","l"," "," "," "," "," "," "," "," "," "," "," "," "," "," "," "," "," "," "," "," ",
"i","n"," ","t","h","e"," ","d","a","r","k"," "," "," "," "," "," "," "," "," "," "," "," "," "," "," "," "," "," "," "," ",
"a","n","o","t","h","e","r"," ","w","o","r","l","d"," ","u","n","f","o","l","d","s"," "," "," "," "," "," "," "," "," "," ",
"a","n","d"," ","I"," ","d","o","n","'","t"," ","k","n","o","w"," ","w","h","o"," ","I"," ","a","m"," "," "," "," "," "," "," ",
"w","h","e","n"," ","I"," ","s","l","e","e","p"," "," "," "," "," "," "," "," "," "," "," "," "," "," "," "," "," "," "," ",
"w","h","e","n"," ","I"," ","d","r","e","a","m"," "," "," "," "," "," "," "," "," "," "," "," "," "," "," "," "," "," "," ",
"I"," ","a","m"," ","i","n","v","i","n","c","i","b","l","e"," ","a","n","d"," ","p","o","w","e","r","f","u","l"," "," "," "," ",
"g","e","t"," ","e","v","e","r","y","t","h","i","n","g"," ","m","y"," ","w","a","y"," "," "," "," "," "," "," "," "," "," ",
"t","e","n"," ","s","w","e","e","t"," ","g","i","r","l","s"," ","a","t"," ","e","v","e","r","y"," ","h","a","n","d"," "," "," ",
"o","r"," ","I"," ","m","a","k","e"," ","o","n","l","y"," ","w","r","o","n","g"," ","d","e","c","i","s","i","o","n","s"," "," ",
"a","n","d"," ","I"," ","a","m"," ","a"," ","l","o","s","e","r",","," ","a"," ","n","o","b","o","d","y"," "," "," "," "," ",
"i","n"," ","t","h","e"," ","m","o","r","n","i","n","g"," "," "," "," "," "," "," "," "," "," "," "," "," "," "," "," "," ",
"t","h","e"," ","t","r","u","t","h"," ","e","m","e","r","g","e","s"," "," "," "," "," "," "," "," "," "," "," "," "," "," ",
"a","n","d"," ","I"," ","a","m"," ","b","a","c","k"," "," "," "," "," "," "," "," "," "," "," "," "," "," "," "," "," "," ",
"a","n","d"," ","w","a","i","t"," ","f","o","r"," ","t","h","e"," ","n","e","x","t"," ","n","i","g","h","t"," "," "," "," ",
" "," "," "," "," "," "," "," "," "," "," "," "," "," "," "," "," "," "," "," "," "," "," "," "," "," "," "," "," "," ",
" "," "," "," "," "," "," "," "," "," "," "," "," "," "," "," "," "," "," "," "," "," "," "," "," "," "," "," "," "}
```

```
-- JAL 2.0.6
include 16F877_bert
include lcd_44780

var byte position
var word counter

forever loop

   -- switch the cursor off
   LCD_init
   LCD_cursor = off

   counter = 0
   position=16
   for 572 loop

      LCD_char_line_pos (demo[counter],0,position)
      delay_100ms(4)
      LCD_shift_left
      counter = counter + 1
      position = position +1
      if position == 40 then position = 0  end if
   end loop
end loop
```

The hardware

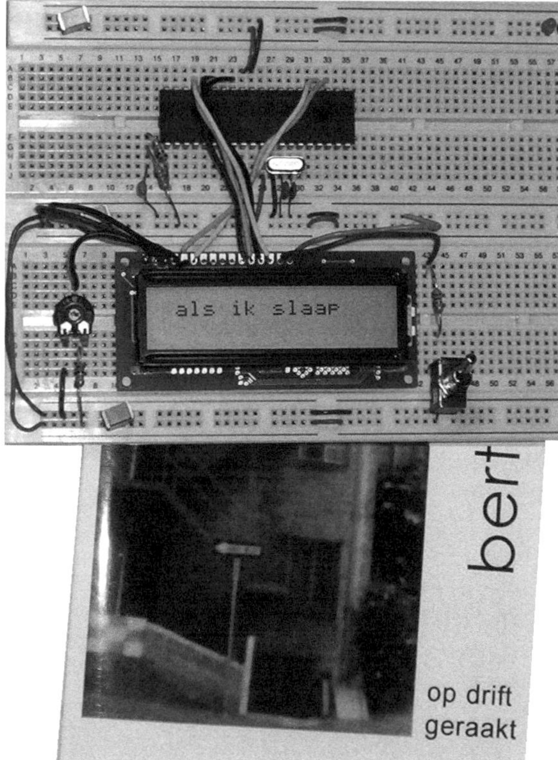

Figure 178. The poetry box with book.

The hardware is identical to section 12.5. In the picture of the breadboard you can see part of the poem (the original Dutch version) scroll by and underneath the breadboard a part of the poetry book is visible.

12.9 Bootloader

A bootloader is a way to load programs into a PIC™ without using a programmer.

Technical background

A bootloader is a small program in the PIC™ memory. As soon as the PIC™ is switched on this program will wait for a certain amount of time (in our case 1 second) to see if a hardware serial connection is being made by special program on a PC. If that doesn't happen the normal program in the PIC™ is started.

If, however, a hardware connection is made the PC can send a regular PIC™ program over the hardware serial connection, which will then be stored in the memory of the PIC™. This unusual way of programming seems quite handy at first, because it doesn't require a programmer. But, of course, you do need a programmer to get the bootloader into the PIC™!

Also, the bootloader will only work with PIC™ microcontrollers that are capable of writing to their own program memory. The 16F877 can do this, but many other PIC™ types cannot. The 12F675 and 16F628, which will be discussed in section 13, do not have this capability. For these types you will always need a programmer.

For home use the bootloader is not very useful: if you can get the bootloader into the PIC™ surely you can get other programs in there as well. If you sell your projects to other people, and especially in the professional market, bootloaders are much more useful. Simply add a MAX202E chip to your printed circuit board and your customers can install upgrades using a regular PC with some simple software. They don't need to buy and operate a programmer.

Since a bootloader is always in the PIC™ memory and doesn't do anything useful most of the time it is a good idea to use the smallest one available.[146] In this section we use the Tiny Bootloader written by Claudiu Chiculita.[147] This one is just 100 words[148] long (the 16F877 memory consists of over 8000 words) and has all the capabilities you need.

---

[146] You may have other criteria for selecting a bootloader, such as the ability to use certain pins, to start a bootloader from the PC, or to buy a PIC™ with preloaded bootloader.

[147] More information on this bootloader can be found on the website of the author at http://www.etc.ugal.ro/cchiculita/software/picbootloader.htm

[148] According to research by the programmer this is the smallest bootloader currently available on the Internet. The next smallest bootloader is double that size. Another advantage is that this bootloader uses the hardware serial port and thus achieves high programming speed of up to 115k2.

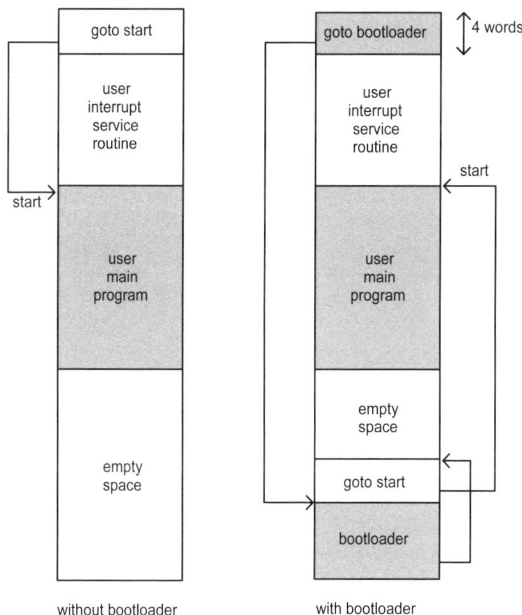

Figure 179. Memory map with bootloader.[149]

Bootloaders are located at the very end of program memory, not the beginning. This means that the regular PIC™ program should not start with a reference to itself (left side of the Figure above), but instead refer to the bootloader (right side). The JAL compiler calls this a *long start*. If you execute a program that is compiled with the *long start* option without a bootloader in memory then it will still work. For ease of use JALedit is configured with a *long start*.

The bootloader consists of two parts: a small program for the PIC™, and a small program for the PC. The first thing to do is load the bootloader into the PIC™. Create a simple hardware setup, such as in section 10.1, and connect your normal programmer. In the *c:\picdev\tools\tinyboot* directory on the harddrive of your PC you will find a program with the somewhat threatening name of *burnboot*.[150] Switch the power to your project on and double-click on that program. You will now see the normal black window that you are used to with JALedit, and the program will transfer to the 16F877. The PIC™ is now ready to be used in this project.

---

[149] Copied with permission from the author, Claudiu Chiculita.

[150] If you installed the download package in a different location you need to use the directory you selected at that point. You also need to modify the program burnboot.bat and enter the proper directory to the path where you stored the xwisp2w program.

12 Miscellaneous Projects

The software

To test the bootloader we will use a small program that reads the position of a variable resistor and sends it to the PC.

```
-- JAL 2.0.6
include 16F877_bert

-- define variables
var byte resist

-- define the pins
pin_a0_direction = input

forever loop

    -- convert analog on a0 to digital
    resist = ADC_read_low_res(0)

    -- send resistance to PC
    serial_hw_write(resist)
    delay_100ms(1)

end loop
```

Enter this program into JALedit in the usual way and store it with an easy to remember name, such as "demo". Use F9 (or the button with the green arrow) to compile the program without sending it to the programmer (we are not using our programmer!).[151]

Now would be a good time to build the hardware. You have already installed the PIC™ in order to download the bootloader using *burnboot*, so the rest can be added easily.

The hardware

The bootloader will communicate directly to the RS232 port of the PC so we need some additional hardware to generate the RS232 signals (see section 6.4 for more information on this subject).

---

[151] It is important that the JALedit compiler settings include "-long-start -d". If you haven't touched them after installing the download package you are all set. Otherwise, change them back using Compile - Environment Options - General - Additional commandline parameters.

The value of the capacitors for the MAX202E is not critical. The manufacturer recommends a minimum value of 0.1 uF and a maximum value of 10 uF. The capacitor that is mounted across the power line (to the right of the MAX202E in the schematic) needs to be at least the same size as the other ones. This capacitor has to eliminate stray signals on the power lines that could interfere with the proper operation of the PIC™.[152] We will use 1 uF / 25 V capacitors. Note that the positive and negative leads of the capacitors on pins 2 and 6 are correct; they are mounted differently that you might perhaps expect!

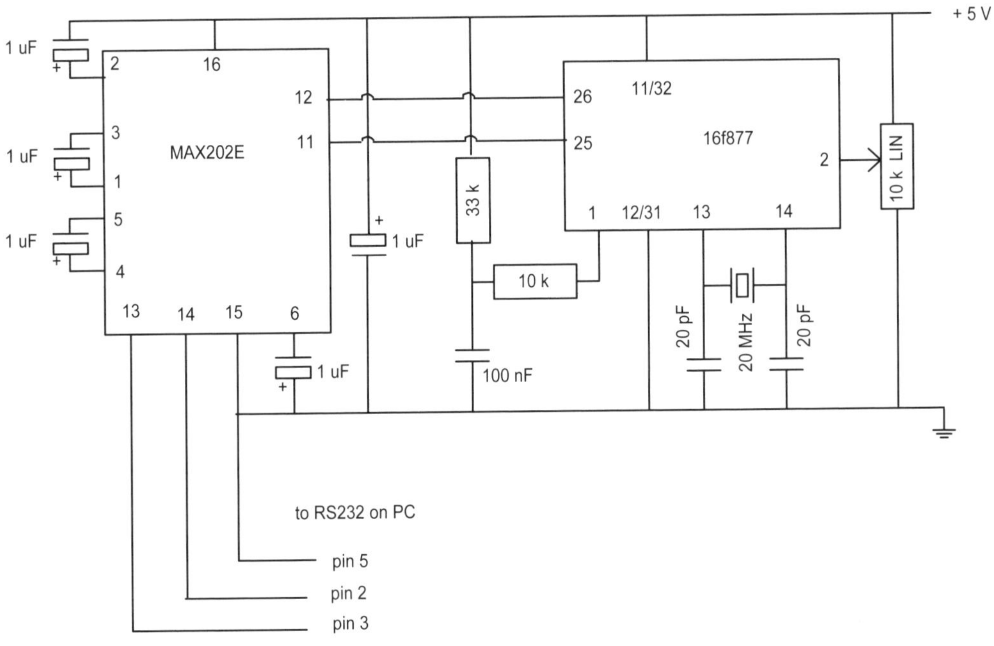

Figure 180. Bootloader setup.

You only need to connect three wires on the PC side. The pin numbers in the schematic are the numbers you will find on the (female) RS232 plug.

---

[152] The MAX202E has to increase the voltage from 5 V to 10 V. The mechanism used to do this (a charge pump) can easily cause nasty spikes on the power line. The capacitor prevents this. If you build this project on a circuit board don't forget the small capacitors in the power line close to the PIC™.

This is the set up on the breadboard:

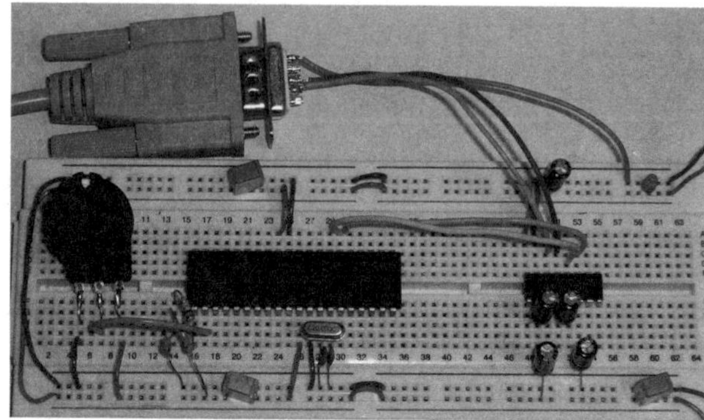

Figure 181. Bootloader setup.

Using the bootloader

Now that the software and hardware have been completed it is time to try out the bootloader.

Start the *tinybldwin.exe* program. You will find this program in the *c:\picdev\tools\tinyboot* directory of the download package. You will get this screen:

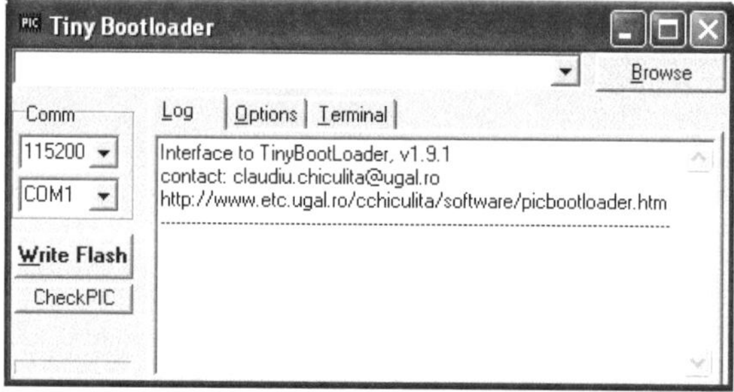

Figure 182. Startup screen tiny bootloader.

The communication speed is set by default to 115k2, which is the correct value (note that you are communicating with the bootloader and not with a JAL program that uses the standard library). You may need to change the COM port depending on where you plugged in the RS232 plug.

Now use the "browse" button to search on your harddrive for the program you have just compiled using JALedit. You must look for the hex file and not the JAL file (these are in the same directory). At this point timing is everything. When you switch on the power to your project, you have one second to click on the "Write Flash" Button. If you are not vary handy with the mouse you can opt to press the "w" key on your keyboard. If you are too early you get a "PIC™ not found" error. No problem, just switch the power to your project off and then on and try again. It's not as difficult as it sounds.

If all goes well you will see the program pass very quickly followed by the message "Write OK". It will go a lot faster than you are used to. The Wisp628 programs at 19k2 and the Tiny Bootloader at 115k2, so six times faster. The program that you downloaded is started automatically.

The bootloader program on your PC has a small built-in terminal package that you can start by clicking the "Terminal" tab. You need to adjust the speed (this time you are communicating with the JAL program) and set it to 19k2, the speed of the standard 16F877_bert library used for communication over the hardware serial port. NOTE: do not forget to reset the speed to 115k if you want to download another program!

Next steps

You can use the bootloader for any program you want. As long as you use the bootloader to load programs into the PIC™ it will remain in memory. If you use a regular programmer, such as the Wisp628, the bootloader will be overwritten because it will use the full memory of the PIC™.

If you intend to use the bootloader you can change the settings of JALedit to make this the default programmer. Remember that the bootloader cannot program PIC™ types such as the 12F675 and 16F628, which will be discussed in the following sections.

In JALedit select the "Compile" menu, then "Environment Options', followed by "Programmer". Write down the current settings to make sure you can easily go back to the Wisp628.[153] At the executable path enter:

    C:\PICdev\tools\tinyboot\tinybldWin.exe

And at the command line parameters:

    %F

Remember that you will still have to start the download within 1 second of powering up your project. The easiest way is to use F9 to compile the program, then power up the

---

[153] If you installed the download package according to the instructions the programmer executable path is set to *"c:\picdev\xwisp2\xwisp2w.exe"* and the command line parameters to *"go %F"*.

project, and then press Shift-F9. If you prefer to use the mouse click on the green triangle, power up the project, and then click on the button with the downward arrow.

Even easier is to let the bootloader control the reset pin of the PIC^{TM}. This way the timing is always correct. Instructions on how to do this are in the download package.

13 Other PIC™ microcontrollers

It is important to work with just one microcontroller as much as you can, so that you really get to know it inside out. For that reason all of the projects we have discussed so far are built using the 16F877. By now you should have a lot of knowledge and experience with this PIC. However, it is sometimes convenient to use other types as well, such as when you have limited space or a limited budget. In this section we will discuss three other microcontrollers.

PIC™	**Description**
12F675	The 8-pin 12F675 is popular with model train enthusiasts who have little room available and still want to use a PIC™.

Sample projects:
1. Railroad crossing
2. RGB fader

16F628	This PIC™ is pin-compatible with the 16F84, an old PIC™ for which a lot of legacy software is still available. It is popular with people who want to recreate an old project, even though all 16F84 software will have to be re-written before it can be used in the 16F628.

Sample projects:
1. Electric candle
2. Adjustable clock frequency
3. Wisp628 programmer upgrade

16F876	The little brother of the 16F877. This PIC™ has all the functionality of the 16F877, but in a 28-pin package and without ports D and E.

Sample projects:
1. VU meter
2. Infrared RS232

In section 13.5 the portability of programs between these microcontrollers is discussed. This is where you can see the true power of JAL and the standard libraries.

13 Other PIC™ microcontrollers

13.1 The 12F675

13.1.1 Introduction

The 12F675 is one of the smallest PICs available, with only 8 pins, but is still very powerful. All of the pins have multiple functions and because there are so few pins you'll need to know how to switch between the different functions.

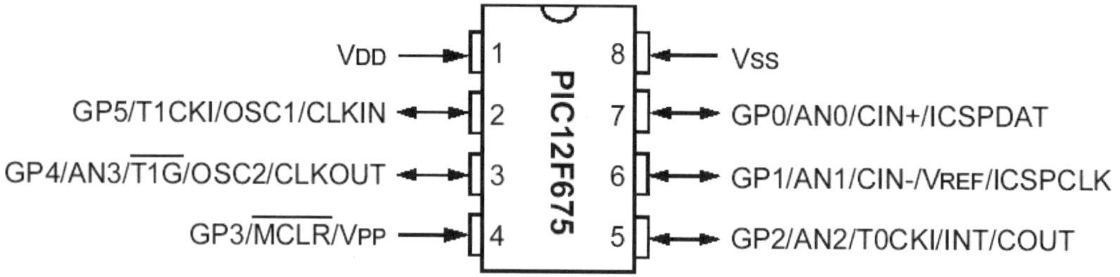

Figure 183. Pin layout of the 12F675.

Pay close attention to the bizarre numbering of the pins. For example, AN0 (or GP0) is connected to pin 7. These are the properties of this small PIC™:

Item	Specification
Program memory	1024 words (14 bit)
RAM	64 bytes
EEPROM	128 bytes
I/O pins	6
A/D pins	4 (of 8 or 10 bits each)
USART	no
Speed	5 mips
Cost	US$ 1 to 2
PWM	no
I2C	no
Integrated oscillator	yes

It may be less impressive than the 16F877, but it also has a smaller size and price.

The following pins must always be connected:

Pin	Name	Description
1	V_{DD}	Power supply +5 V
4	MCLR/Vpp	Master clear pin and programmer voltage input. This pin requires a 33k resistor to +5 V.
8	V_{SS}	Power supply ground (0 V)

If you use the Wisp628 programmer the wires must be connected as follows:

Wire	Connects to
yellow	pin 4
blue	pin 7
green	pin 6
white	not in use
red	+ 5 V
black	ground (0 V)

Note that you need the dongle described in section 2.2.

13.1.2 12F675_bert library

The standard library for this microcontroller is 12F675_bert.[154] This library enables a lot of the functionality discussed in this book (RS232, A/D conversion, delays, etc.). It will also set the pins to a default configuration, which is suitable for many applications (note that without this library for example all A/D converters are switched on, a very complicated hurdle for the novice programmer).

---

[154] You will find this file in the library directory; it is part of the download package.

13 Other PIC™ microcontrollers

This is the default pin configuration with the 12F675_bert library loaded:

12F675 pin	RS232	Analog in	Digital in	Digital out
GP0 / pin_a0	X	X		X
GP1 / pin_a1	X		X	X
GP2 / pin_a2		X		X
GP3 / pin_a3			X	
GP4 / pin_a4		X		X
GP5 / pin_a5			X	X

The table indicates the functionality that is switched on after loading the 12F675_bert library. So, for example, you can use pin a0 for an RS232 connection, an analog input, or a digital output.

Using pins a0 and a1 you can make an RS232 connection. Of course it is no coincidence that these are the pins the programmer is connected to so that the pass-through functionality of the programmer can be used.

You also have two analog and two digital inputs available, or three digital outputs. Usually this default setting will do just fine. If not, you can use the *disanalog()* command to switch analog pins to digital. Note that analog inputs can be used as digital outputs without switching them to digital.

Officially the pins are called GP0 to GP5. To allow portability between different microcontrollers we have chosen to call these pins a0 to a5 as if they belong to an imaginary port A.

An important command that has not been discussed for the 16F877 is *disanalog()*, because the larger PIC™s have so many pins that you normally don't need to change the analog pin settings.[155] For the small 12F675 this is not the case. For many novices setting the analog pins to digital is a major stumbling block, so lets take a look at the hidden functionality behind the *disanalog()* command.[156]

---

[155] It can be done using the 16F877 library, by modifying the pin assignment as a group with *no_ADC = X*.

[156] You can still use this command even if you don't know how it works. If you are not interested you can skip the rest of this section.

ANSEL (analog select) is one of two registers involved in making a pin digital:

ANSEL — ANALOG SELECT REGISTER (ADDRESS: 9Fh)

U-0	R/W-0	R/W-0	R/W-0	R/W-1	R/W-1	R/W-1	R/W-1
—	ADCS2	ADCS1	ADCS0	ANS3	ANS2	ANS1	ANS0

bit 7   bit 0

bit 7   **Unimplemented:** Read as '0'.

bit 6-4   **ADCS<2:0>:** A/D Conversion Clock Select bits

000 = Fosc/2
001 = Fosc/8
010 = Fosc/32
x11 = FRC (clock derived from a dedicated internal oscillator = 500 kHz max)
100 = Fosc/4
101 = Fosc/16
110 = Fosc/64

bit 3-0   **ANS3:ANS0:** Analog Select bits
(Between analog or digital function on pins AN<3:0>, respectively.)

1 = Analog input; pin is assigned as analog input[1]

0 = Digital I/O; pin is assigned to port or special function

> **Note 1:** Setting a pin to an analog input automatically disables the digital input circuitry, weak pull-ups, and interrupt-on-change. The corresponding TRISIO bit must be set to Input mode in order to allow external control of the voltage on the pin.

Figure 184. ANSEL register of the 12F675.

Here, bits 0 to 3 are important. The default value for each is 1, and must be set to 0 to switch off the analog function and make the pin digital. Bits 4 to 6 are used for the A/D settings so it is better to leave these alone. So, to set AN0 (on pin a0) to digital you would use the following command:

ANSEL = ANSEL & 0b_1111_1110

By using the AND operator (&) all bits that are AND-ed with a 1 are not changed. Bits that are AND-ed with a 0 are flipped from 1 to 0 or 0 to 1, depending on whatever they were before the command was executed.

You can check this in the AND truth table:

A	B	Out (A & B)
1	1	1 & 1 = 1
1	0	1 & 0 = 0
0	1	0 & 1 = 0
0	0	0 & 0 = 0

The second important register is CMCON (comparator module).

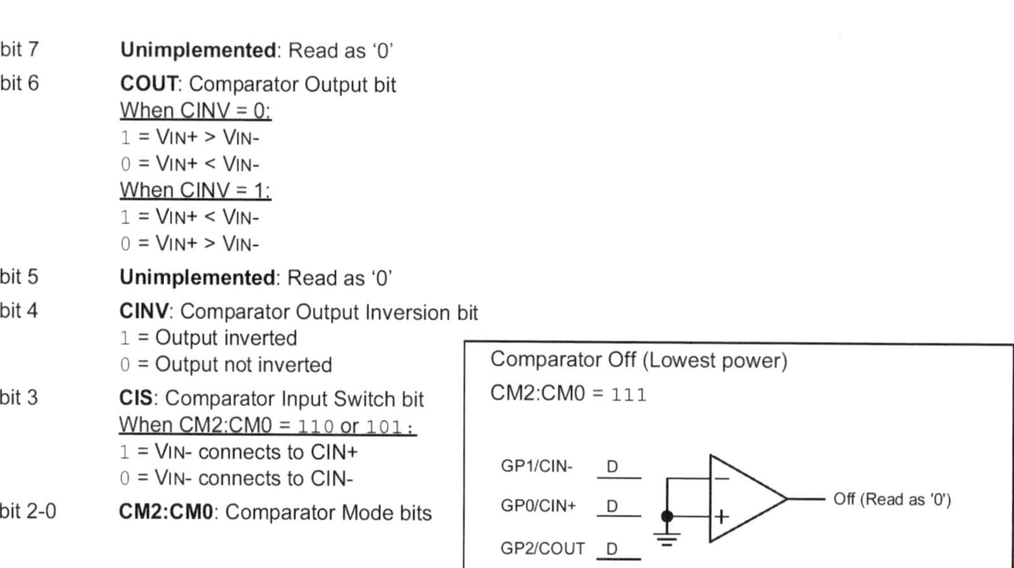

Figure 185. CMCON register of the 12F675.

In addition to the A/D converters the 12F675 is also equipped with a comparator that uses the same pins.[157] In the datasheet you can see that the comparator can be switched off by setting each of the lowest three bits to 1 (the other possible configurations are not relevant):

---

[157] The comparator can be used to compare different voltages and perform certain actions based on the difference. Of course this can also be done with an A/D converter, but a comparator is faster.

CMCON = 0x07

Since 7 hexadecimal = 7 decimal = 111 binary. So the procedure should be:

```
procedure disanalog (byte in x) is
   CMCON = 0x07
   if x == 0 then ANSEL = ANSEL & 0b_1111_1110 end if
   if x == 1 then ANSEL = ANSEL & 0b_1111_1101 end if
   if x == 2 then ANSEL = ANSEL & 0b_1111_1011 end if
   if x == 3 then ANSEL = ANSEL & 0b_1111_0111 end if
end procedure
```

You will find this procedure in the 12F675_bert library. In section 14.2 all of the library functions are discussed. In this table you can see which library functions are applicable for the 12F675. If the 12F675 column has an x this means you can use the exact same command as you do for the 16F877, just with the limitations of the smaller PIC™.

Functionality (using the standard library)	16F877	12F675
Serial communication - hardware	x	
Serial communication - software	x	x
Pulse width modulation PWM	x	
A/D conversion	x	x
Program memory	x	
EEPROM	x	x
ASCII	x	x
Delay	x	x
Registers and variables	x	x
Setting pins to digital		x
Random numbers	x	x

13 Other PIC™ microcontrollers

13.1.3 Demo program

As a demonstration of the capabilities of the 12F675 and the 12F675_bert library a small sample program is discussed.

Technical background

This program contains the following functionality:

- A/D conversion
- RS232 communication
- Setting a pin to digital
- Reading a digital signal
- Writing a digital signal

This program will read the voltage on pin a2 and send it to the PC over a serial connection.

```
-- take a sample on AN2 (pin_a2)
resist = ADC_read_low_res(2)

-- and send over RS232 to the PC
serial_sw_write(resist)
```

The LED on pin a5 will flash as long as the switch on a4 is pressed.[158]

```
-- flash the led if the switch is pressed
if switch  then
   led = ! led
else
   led = low
end if
```

If you look at the table you can see that pin a4 is set to analog after loading the 12F675_bert library. This means the pin cannot detect a switch being pressed, so it will have to be set to digital:

---

[158] Using *led = ! led* is elegant, but does have its risks, as discussed in section 4.2.

```
-- disable analog function of AN3 (pin_a4)
disanalog(3)
```

The software

The completed program looks like this. Please note that you need the dongle described in section 2.2 in order to program this PIC™:

```
-- jal 2.0.6
include 12F675_bert

-- general variables
var byte resist
var bit led is pin_a5
var bit switch is pin_a4

-- disable analog function of AN3 (pin_a4)
disanalog(3)

-- define the pins
pin_a4_direction = input
pin_a5_direction = output

forever loop

   -- take a sample on AN2 (pin_a2)
   resist = ADC_read_low_res(2)

   -- and send over RS232 to the PC
   serial_sw_write(resist)

   -- flash the led if the switch is pressed
   if switch  then
     led = ! led
   else
     led = low
   end if

   -- wait a bit otherwise the led flashes a bit fast...
   delay_100ms(1)

end loop
```

13 Other PIC™ microcontrollers

The hardware

Although the 12F675 is capable of running with a 20 MHz crystal it requires two pins (a4 and a5) and there are not very many to start with. So the standard library assumes we will be using the internal oscillator, at 4 MHz, instead of the crystal. And this is the reason it uses a relatively low RS232 speed of 1200 baud.

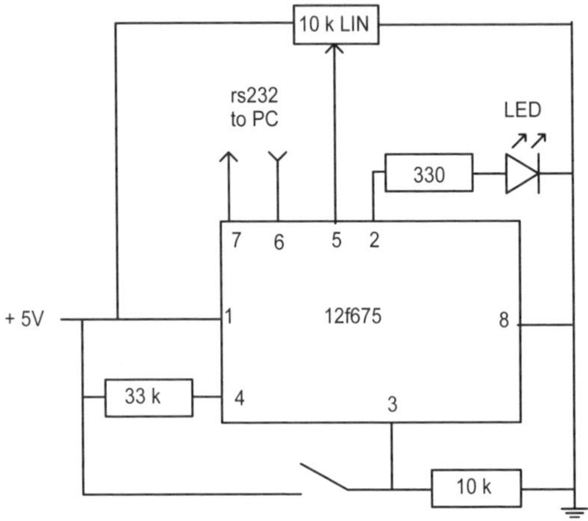

Figure 186. Demo program for the 12F675.

The hardware is rather simple.

Figure 187. Demo program for the 12F675.

This program is almost identical to one for a 16F877. So you can see that by using the 12F675_bert and 16F877_bert libraries programs can be transferred relatively easy from one PIC™ to the next, assuming you pay attention to the limitations of each PIC™. This is an important advantage that you would not have had without JAL and the standard libraries!

13.1.4 Railroad crossing

Here we have a small project for the model railroad lovers, a Dutch AKI. An AKI (Automatische Knipperlicht Installatie, or automatic flashing lights installation) is becoming a bit rare in the Netherlands, because they are all being replaced by crossings using barriers, for safety reasons.

Technical background

Three lights are mounted on a triangular black board. The top light is white, the lower two lights are red. The white light is less bright than the red lights.

In the normal situation the white light flashes slowly. This indicates that the installation is fully functional and it is safe to cross (though at your own risk, since it isn't a green light). When a train approaches, the white light is switched off and the two red lights start flashing alternately at a faster rate. You will also hear a loud bell, which is not part of this project.

The software

This is the completed program. Please note that you need the dongle described in section 2.2 in order to program this PIC™:

```
-- jal 2.0.6
include 12F675_bert

-- general variables
var bit led0 is pin_a0
var bit led1 is pin_a1
var bit led2 is pin_a5

var bit switch is pin_a4
```

13 Other PIC™ microcontrollers

```
    -- disable analog function of AN3 (pin_a4)
    disanalog(3)

    -- define the pins
    pin_a0_direction = output
    pin_a1_direction = output
    pin_a5_direction = output

    forever loop

        -- flash the led if the switch is pressed
        if switch  then
          -- danger, flash red leds159
          led0 = ! led0
          led1 = ! led0
          led2 = low
        else
          -- flash led2 for all  clear signal
          led2 = ! led2
          led0 = low
          led1 = low
          delay_100ms(6)
        end if

        -- wait a bit otherwise the led flashes a bit fast...
        delay_100ms(3)

    end loop
```

The hardware

The white LED has a larger resistor to make it dimmer than the red ones. The switch is actually a rail contact that engages as long as a train is near the railroad crossing. Alternatively, you could use a contact that is engaged only once as the train approaches, and then use a delay to control the amout of time the red LEDs flash.

---

[159] Using *led = ! led* is elegant, but does have its risks, as discussed in section 4.2.

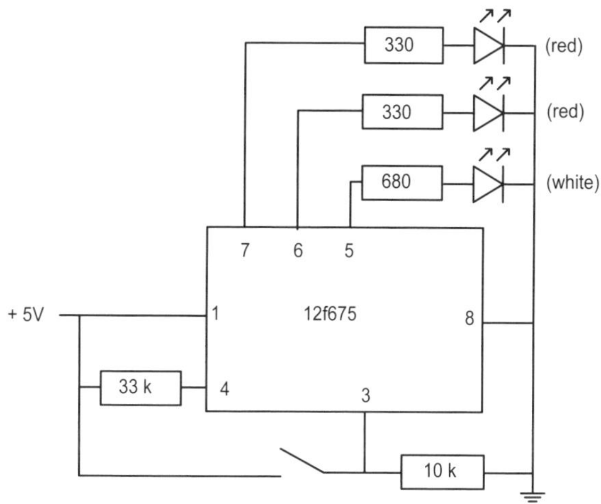

Figure 188. AKI with 12F675.

There are so few pins that even the pins used by the programmer are used for the red LEDs. During programming with the Wips628 programmer they can remain connected; they will just flash, but it has no impact on the programming.

There is still one pin available, so you could connect this to a bell if you want. The bell should ring the entire time that the red LEDs are flashing. The picture shows that this project is very small and could easily be hidden in a guardhouse or under a bush.

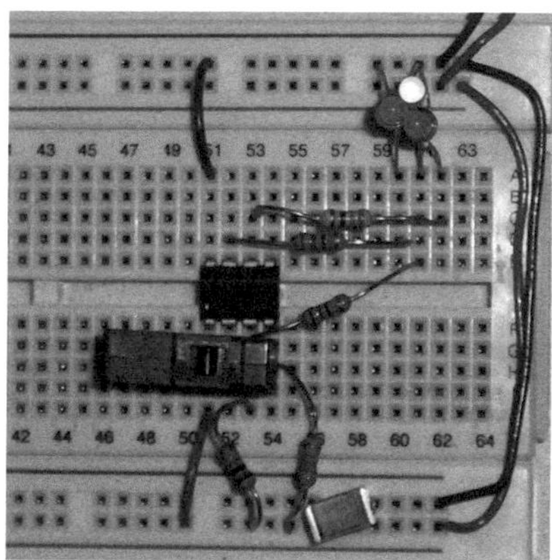

Figure 189. AKI with 12F675.

13.1.5 RGB fader

A small program to make your own Object d'Art: an RGB (Red Green Blue) fader. Three different colored LEDs alternately fade in and out, turning an old box or a camera film canister into a special lamp.

A fading LED is quite easy to make using the PWM - pulse width modulation - module. We need three PWM modules, however, and even the big 16F877 doesn't have that many onboard. So we will make our own PWM modules in the smallest PIC™ in this book: the 12F675.

In section 7.2 PWM is discussed in detail. In this project we will make the module as simple as possible by not concerning us with the exact frequency; we will simply make it "as high as possible". Instead we will focus on the duty cycle, which is the ratio of "on" signal to "off" signal.

In order to do this we will make a pin high and start a counter at the same time. By defining the counter as a byte it will rollover to 0 again after 256 increments. This will be our period.

At a certain count we make the pin low and then when the counter resets to zero we make the pin high again. That is the duty cycle. If we make the pin low when the counter is zero the duty cycle is 0, because there is no "on" time. But if we do this when the counter is 100 then the duty cycle is $100/255 = 39\%$.

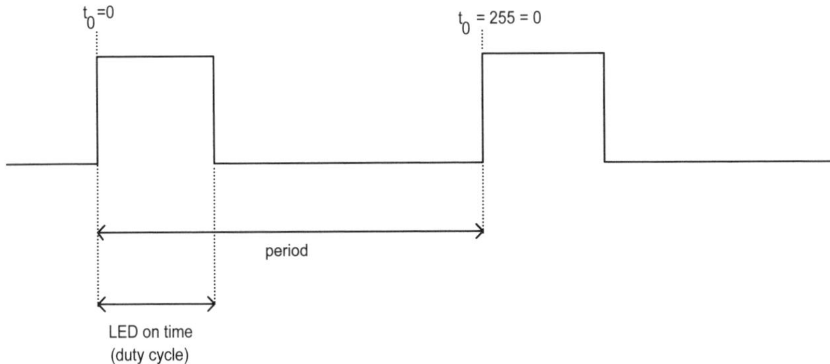

Figure 190. DIY PWM.

For the three LEDs it looks like this:

```
procedure fade_pwm is
    if t0 == 0 then
            blueled = 1
            redled = 1
            greenled = 1
    end if
    if t0 >= tblue then blueled = 0 end if
    if t0 >= tred then redled = 0 end if
    if t0 >= tgreen then greenled = 0 end if
    t0 = t0 + 1
end procedure
```

The variables *blueled, redled* and *greenled* refer to the pins that these LEDs are connected to. The variables *tblue, tred* and *tgreen* refer to the counter positions at which these LEDs need to be turned off again. In the final program we will turn this into a procedure (*fade_pwm*), because we will need this routine often.

In theory, an LED will fade in slowly when the duty cycle goes from 0 to 100%. In reality, that is not quite true, because an LED will be (at least visually) saturated at a much lower duty cycle, usually around 78% (for the blue LED it is even lower at around 20%). During the slow fade the PWM module needs to remain in action, so we can't use a simple delay statement. We will solve this as follows:

```
counter = counter + 1
if counter == 500 then
    tblue = tblue + 1
    counter = 0
end if
fade_pwm
```

In the loop a counter is running. At each pass the PWM module is executed. But in only 1 out of 500 calls the brightness of the LEDs is actually adjusted.

You will get the best visual result when one LED fades in while the other one fades out at the same time. In the following loop the duty cycle of the green LED decreases from 200 to 0 while the duty cycle of blue LED increases from 0 to 50:

```
           tgreen = 200
           tblue = 0
           while tgreen != 0 loop
              counter = counter + 1
              if counter == 800 then
                 tblue = tblue + 1
                 tgreen = tgreen - 4
                 counter = 0
              end if
              fade_pwm
           end loop
```

The difference between 50 and 200 is caused by the fact that the blue LED is saturated much sooner. This cycle will repeat until the green time is zero. By using three of these loops in a row all of the colors can be faded in pairs.

The complete program looks like this. Please note that you need the dongle described in section 2.2 in order to program this PIC™:

```
-- JAL 2.0.6
include 12F675_bert

-- define variables
var byte t0
var word counter
var byte tblue, tred, tgreen

-- define the pins
pin_a0_direction = output
pin_a1_direction = output
pin_a2_direction = output

var bit blueled is pin_a0
var bit greenled is pin_a1
var bit redled is pin_a2

procedure fade_pwm is
   -- set brightness using simple pwm
   if t0 == 0 then
      blueled = 1
      redled = 1
      greenled = 1
```

```
    end if
    if t0 >= tblue then blueled = 0 end if
    if t0 >= tred then redled = 0 end if
    if t0 >= tgreen then greenled = 0 end if
    t0 = t0 + 1
end procedure

forever loop

  tgreen  = 200
  tblue = 0
  while tgreen != 0 loop
    counter = counter + 1
    if counter == 800 then
      tblue = tblue + 1
      tgreen = tgreen - 4
      counter = 0
    end if
    fade_pwm
  end loop

  tblue  = 50
  tred = 0
  while tblue != 0 loop
    counter = counter + 1
    if counter == 800 then
      tblue = tblue - 1
      tred = tred + 4
      counter = 0
    end if
    fade_pwm
  end loop

  tgreen = 0
  tred = 200
  while tred != 0 loop
    counter = counter + 1
    if counter == 800 then
      tgreen = tgreen + 4
      tred = tred - 4
      counter = 0
    end if
```

```
        fade_pwm
        end loop

    end loop
```

The hardware consists of a 12F675 with three LEDs. The LEDs should be red, green and blue to get the desired effect.

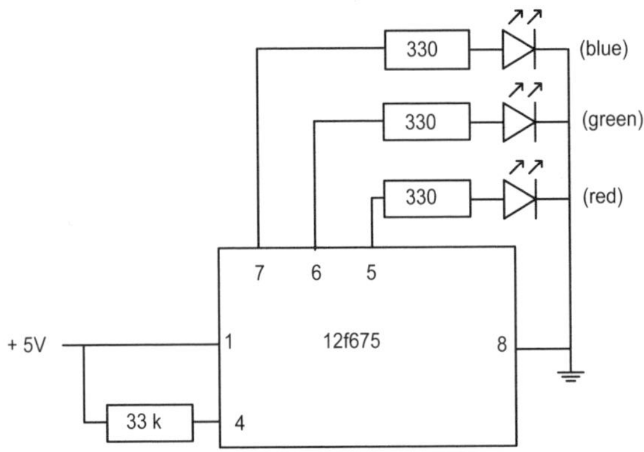

Figure 191. RGB fader.

The breadboard:

Figure 192. RGB fader.

You will get the most beautiful effect when you put the LEDs into something opaque, such as an empty camera film canister. It is not very easy to photograph this; Figure 193 is the best I could do.

Figure 193. The RGB fader.

What the PWM frequency turns out to be depends, of course, on the length of the program loop. More commands in the loop mean a lower frequency. According to the frequency meter software (from the download package) we obtained about 60 Hz.

Next steps

Although it is beautiful to watch, the amount of light is very small. It is, after all, just one LED per color.

An LED with a 330-ohm resistor uses about 15 mA, so you can connect only one of them to a pin. An alternative is to use three TC4427A driver chips[160]. At a capacity of 1.5 A each this will give you enough power to connect almost 100 LEDs per color; surely enough make a nice Object d'Art. Check out the website of artist James Clar.[161] With the knowledge you have gained in this book you can build almost all of his projects!

13.2 The 16F628

13.2.1 Introduction

This is an 18-pin PIC™ that is very popular, because it is pin-compatible with the old 16F84 that you will often see in articles, books, and projects on the Internet. The 16F628 is not completely software compatible, though, so it will take a little time to get old 16F84 software up and running.

---

[160] One for each color.
[161] The address of this strange website is http://www.jamesclar.com

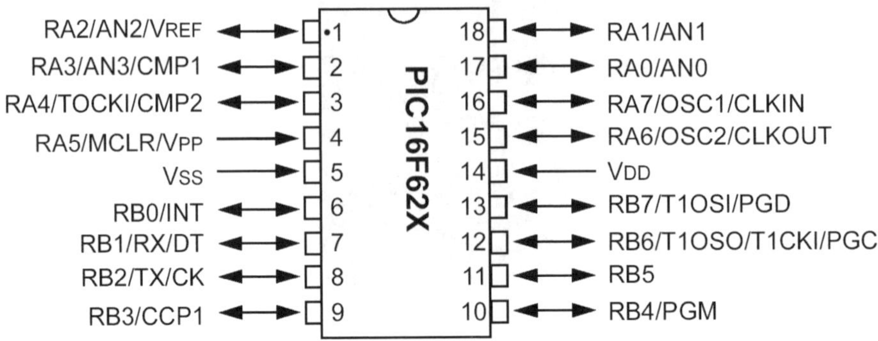

Figure 194. Pin layout of the 16F628.

Note the bizarre arrangement of the port A pins. The port starts at pin 17, rotates to pin 18, 1, 2, 3, 4, and then back to the other side to pins 15 and 16.

These are the properties of the PIC16F628:

Item	Specification
Program memory	2048 words (14 bit)
RAM	224 bytes
EEPROM	128 bytes
I/O pins	16
A/D pins	none
USART	yes (b1/b2)
Speed	5 mips
Cost	US$ 3 to 4
PWM	yes (b3)
I2C	no
Integrated oscillator	yes

It may be less impressive than the 16F877, but it still has plenty of possibilities for exciting projects.

These pins must always be connected:

Pin	Name	Description
4	MCLR/Vpp	Master clear pin and programmer voltage input. This pin requires a 33k resistor to +5 V.
5	V_{SS}	Power supply ground (0 V)
14	V_{DD}	Power supply +5 V
15	OSC1/CLKIN	Crystal[162]
16	OSC2/CLKOUT	Crystal

If you use the Wisp628 the wires need to be connected as follows:

Wire	Connects to
yellow	pin 4
blue	pin 13
green	pin 12
white	pin 10
red	+ 5 V
black	ground (0 V)

Interestingly enough the Wisp628 programmer also uses this PIC™ (hence the name). When a new version of the programmer software becomes available all you need to do is buy a 16F628, use your programmer to put the new version of the software in the PIC™, and then swap the chips (full details are in section 13.2.6). You could keep the old one (better safe than sorry) or use it in a new project.

---

[162] A crystal is not mandatory; the 16f628 can run without it, but slower (at 4 MHz). In this book a crystal is used in all projects and this has been set in the 16f628_bert library.

Figure 195. The 16F628[163] in the Wisp628 programmer.

13.2.2 16F628_bert library

The standard library for this PIC™ is 16F628_bert.[164] This library enables a lot of the functionality discussed earlier in this book (RS232, PWM, delays). At the same time the pins are set to a default configuration to enable you to build projects quickly. And the comparators are all switched off.

This is the default configuration for the 16F628_bert library:

16F628 pins	Function
pin_a6	Crystal
pin_a7	Crystal
pin_b1	RS232 hardware RX
pin_b2	RS232 hardware TX
pin_b3	Can be used for PWM
pin_b6	RS232 software RX
pin_b7	RS232 software TX
All others	Digital input/output

The default configuration enables you to use the pass-through feature of the Wisp628 programmer.

In section 14.2 the standard library functions of the 16F877 are described. This next table indicates which library functions are also applicable to the 16F628. An x in the 16F628 column indicates that you can use the exact same command as you do for the 16F877, just with the limitations of the smaller PIC™.

---

[163] The latest version uses a 16f628A.
[164] This library is part of the download package.

Functionality (using the standard libraries)	16F877	16F628
Serial communication - hardware	x	x
Serial communication - software	x	x
Pulse width modulation (PWM)	x	x
A/D conversion	x	
Program memory	x	
EEPROM	x	x
ASCII	x	x
Delay	x	x
Registers and variables	x	x
Random numbers	x	x

13.2.3 Demo program

As demonstration of the capabilities of the 16F628 and the 16F628_bert library a small demo program is discussed.

Technical background

This program contains the following functionality:

- RS232 communication
- Reading a digital signal
- Writing a digital signal

It will increment a counter in the main loop and send the value to the PC over a serial connection.

```
-- increment counter and send to PC
counter = counter + 1
serial_sw_write(counter)
```

The yellow LED on pin a1 flashes and the blue LED on pin a0 will be on as long as the switch on pin b5 is engaged.

```
-- flash yellow led
yellowled = ! yellowled

-- blue led on if switch is pressed
blueled = switch
```

The software

This is the completed program:

```
-- JAL 2.0.6
include 16F628_bert

-- define variables
var byte counter

-- define the pins
pin_a1_direction = output     -- yellow led
pin_a0_direction = output     -- blue led
pin_b5_direction = input      -- switch

var bit yellowled is pin_a1
var bit blueled is pin_a0
var bit switch is pin_b5

yellowled = low
blueled = low
forever loop

   -- increment counter and send to PC
   counter = counter + 1
   serial_sw_write(counter)

    -- wait a bit
   delay_100mS (1)

   -- flash yellow led[165]
   yellowled = ! yellowled
```

---

[165] Using *yellowled = ! yellowled* is elegant, but cannot be used in all circumstances; see section 4.2.

-- blue led on if switch is pressed
blueled = switch

end loop

The hardware

The schematic shows that a 20 MHz crystal is used, just like we do with the 16F877. This means RS232 communication at a high baudrate is be possible. The 16F628_bert library uses 1200 baud for software serial and 19k2 for hardware serial to facilitate moving programs from one microcontroller to another. Higher speeds are possible in case this is a requirement for your program.

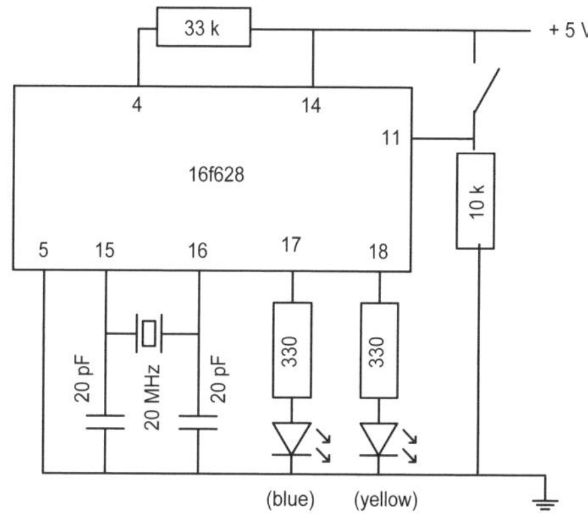

Figure 196. Demo project for the 16F628.

Which looks like Figure 197 on the breadboard. The blue and green wires are from the Wisp628, which is in pass-through mode for the RS232 connection to the PC.

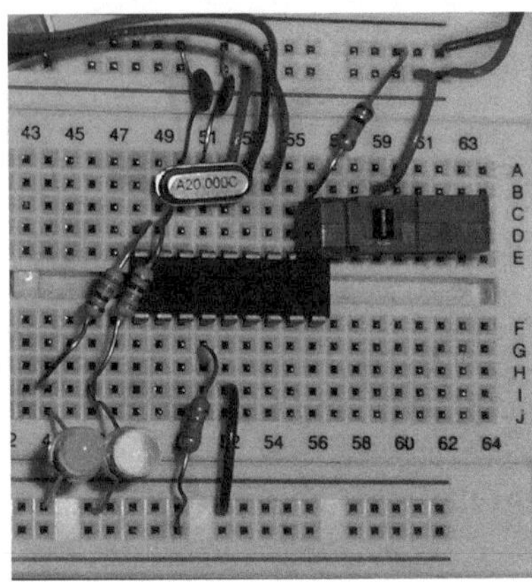

Figure 197. Demo project for the 16F628.

13.2.4 Electric candle

Here we have a small Christmas project using the 16F628.

Technical background

The electric candle is actually a light bulb that constantly changes in brightness, causing a candle-like flickering effect. We do this by connecting a small bulb to the PWM pin and adjusting the duty cycle abruptly at random times. The randomness is created with the *dice* command that generates a number from 1 to 6.

In the source code this command is used twice:

    if dice == 1 then

These are truly separate program sections. Each time the *dice* command is called it rolls again. So even if the first roll is a 1 there is a chance of only 1 in 6 that the next number is also a 1.

The software

If you feel the flickering is too much (or not enough) you can modify the program by playing with the *bright* variable, and the statement affecting when the PWM value is changed.

```
-- JAL 2.0.6
include 16F628_bert

-- define variables
var byte bright, time

pin_b3_direction = output      -- red led

-- enable pulse width modulation
PWM_init_frequency (true, true)

forever loop

   -- modify brightness based on dice
   if dice == 1 then
     for 5 loop
        bright = 150
        PWM_set_dutycycle (bright, 0)
        delay_1ms(15)
        bright = 200
        PWM_set_dutycycle (bright, 0)
        delay_1ms(15)
        bright = 150
        PWM_set_dutycycle (bright, 0)
        delay_1ms(15)
     end loop
   end if
   if dice == 1 then
     bright = 50
     PWM_set_dutycycle (bright, 0)
     delay_1ms(25)
   end if
   if dice < 3 then
     bright = 200
     PWM_set_dutycycle (bright, 0)
     delay_1ms(100)
   end if
   bright = 255
   PWM_set_dutycycle (bright, 0)
   delay_100ms(10)

end loop
```

The hardware

The 16F628 can deliver 25mA per pin, but this is not quite enough for the little light bulb that uses 30 mA. A 4-volt bulb has been selected here, because a transistor typically has a power drop of 0.7 volt, which effectively limits the light bulb to 4.3 volts. Using the technique discussed in section 12.7.1 a suitable transistor and base resistor can be determined.[166]

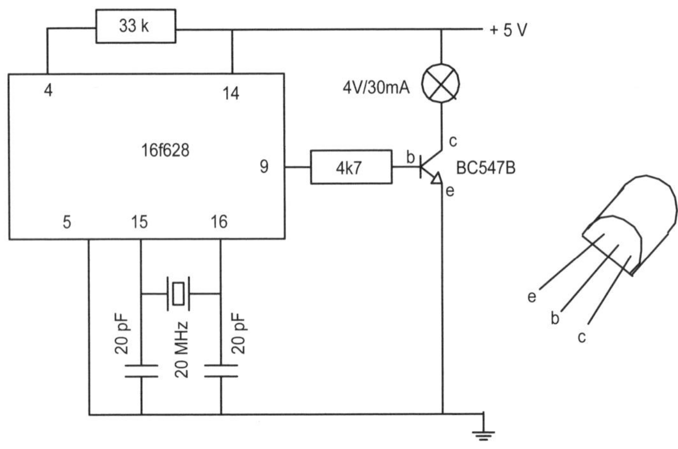

Figure 198Electric candle

The breadboard looks very cozy. A good idea would be to use a rolled up piece of paper as a surrogate candle and mount the bulb on top. The whole thing can be placed into a Christmas ornament. Be sure that neither the paper candle nor the electronics are subjected to water!

---

[166] The h_{FE} has to be at least 5 x (30/25) = 6 and the current at least 30 mA. According to the table in section 14. 5 the BC547 transistor would be a good choice. The resistance of the bulb is 4/0.03 = 133 ohms. The base resistor must therefore be 0.2 x 133 x 200 = 5320 ohms; the nearest commercial value is 4k7 (yellow-purple-red).

Figure 199. Electric candle.

13.2.5 Adjustable clock frequency

The 16F628 has the bizarre capability of having an infinitely adjustable clock frequency.[167] Of course, the frequency is not as accurate as with a crystal, and RS232 communication is hampered, but it is quite interesting nevertheless.

Technical background

These are the clock frequencies according to the datasheet:

RESISTANCE AND
FREQUENCY RELATIONSHIP

Resistance	Frequency
0	10.4 MHz
1K	10 MHz
10K	7.4 MHz
20K	5.3 MHz
47K	3 MHz
100K	1.6 MHz
220K	800 kHz
470K	300 kHz
1M	200 kHz

Figure 200. Resistance – clock frequency relationship.

---

[167] The A version of this PIC, the 16F628A, does not have this capability.

Apart from normal resistors, as assumed by the table, you can also use a variable resistor. For this project we will need to change the microcontroller configuration bits. So far this hasn't been discussed, because the standard libraries handle this for you. We will limit ourselves to the clock speed part of the configuration.

The 16F628_bert library assumes that you will be using a crystal, so that part needs to be changed. The following configuration settings are available with respect to speed:

Configuration	Description
XT	Crystal
LP	Low power crystal
INTRC_NOCLKOUT	Internal clock without clock signal on a7
INTRC_CLKOUT	Internal clock with clock signal on a7
HS	High speed crystal
EXTCLK	Connected to an external clock
ER_NOCLKOUT	External resistor without clock signal on a7
ER_CLKOUT	External resistor with clock signal on a7

The default setting of the 16F628_bert library is HS (High Speed crystal; in our case 20 MHz). This time, however, we use ER_NOCLKOUT.[168] This is the command for the compiler:

```
pragma target osc  ER_NOCLKOUT
```

For this particular setting the compiler uses the last command that it encounters. Which means we do not have to modify the 16F628_bert library.

The program will flash an LED using a delay statement. By changing the clock frequency the length of the delay statement is also changed. This is because the length of a delay statement is determined at the moment the program is compiled, based on the selected clock frequency. But in this case the clock frequency is changed after the program has

---

[168] When other parts of your project need to work with exactly the same clock frequency of the 16f628 you can generate a clock signal for these parts on pin a7. That signal will have the frequency of the instruction processing of the PIC (Fosc). For the 16F628, Fosc is equal to one fourth of the clock frequency. In this project an external signal is not selected; so you can use a7 as normal.

been compiled, so the compiler cannot correct for this. The effect of all this is a variable speed flashing LED.[169]

The software

This is the program:

```
-- JAL 2.0.6
include 16F628_bert

pragma target osc  ER_NOCLKOUT

pin_b5_direction = output  -- red led

forever loop

  pin_b5 = ! pin_b5
  delay_100ms(1)

end loop
```

Since the adjustable frequency may have an impact on programming it is best to use the following steps:

1. Build the schematic, but with a crystal.
2. Program the 16F628 (the program will not run).
3. Switch off the power.
4. Remove the crystal and connect the variable resistor.
5. Switch the power back on (the program now works).
6. Adjust the flashing speed by adjusting the clock frequency.

---

[169] Using *pin_b5 = !pin_b5* is elegant, but cannot be used in all circumstances; see section 4.2.

The hardware

It doesn't get any simpler than this:

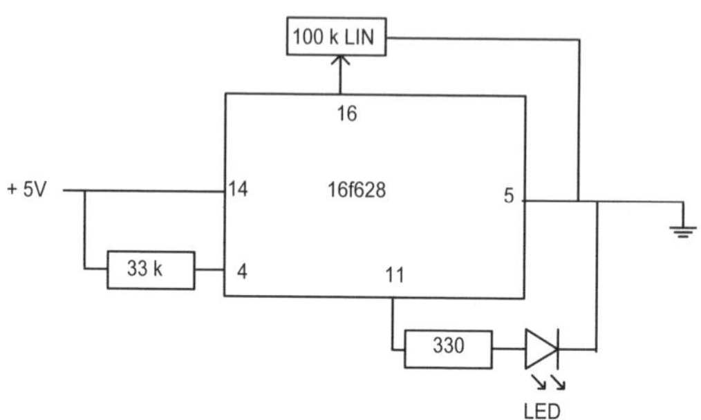

Figure 201. Infinitely adjustable clock frequency.

Note that one side of the variable resistor is not connected. This is because the variable resistor is used as a true variable resistor and not as a voltage divider, as in many of the other projects in this book.

According to the datasheet a 1M variable resistor may be used. The 100k variable resistor used in this project creates a nice operating range of 1.6 to 10.4 MHz.

This is what it looks like on the breadboard:

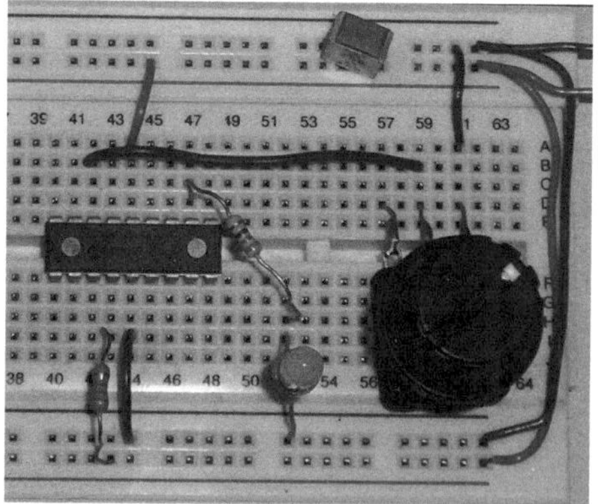

Figure 202. Adjustable clock frequency.

13.2.6 Upgrade using HEXview

The 16F628 is used in the Wisp628 programmer (and gave it part of it's name). This PIC^{TM} contains the intelligence of the programmer, such as how to program the different microcontrollers and the pass-through functionality. The software in the programmer is called "firmware".

Should new versions of the firmware become available you can use this section to upgrade the programmer yourself. Just be sure to check if the new version has the capabilities you need, as there are versions available that have no pass-through functionality and instead have the capability to program other PICs.[170] Whether you consider that an "upgrade', or perhaps a "downgrade', depends on your own requirements.

Follow these steps to upgrade the Wisp628:

1. Purchase a new 16F628.
2. Download the latest hex file for the programmer. Official versions can be found on www.voti.nl; alternate versions can be found in different places by searching for "Wisp628 firmware". You can even find projects where the 16F628 is exchanged for another PIC^{TM}. How useful this is remains to be seen, so you are perhaps better off by restricting yourself to the official versions.
3. Build the hardware for this PIC™ according to Figure 196, but without the switches and LEDs (you can leave them in if you find that more convenient, but they are not used).
4. Download the hex file into the new 16F628 using HEXview:
    - Select the COM port your programmer is connected to.
    - Do not change the speed, the default value of 19k2 is correct.
    - Enter the name of the new hex file including the path. Remember the backslash at the end of the path name.
    - Click on the "VIEW file" button to verify that you have indeed selected a hex file. The content is shown in the blue window.
    - Click on "GO file". A black window appears that displays the progress; wait until the window is closed again.

---

[170] If you purchased the Wisp628 using the link at http://www.boekinfo.tk then it contains firmware version 1.09 with pass-through functionality and support for at least the following types: 12F629, 12F675, 16F627(A), 16F628(A), 16F630, 16F648A, 16F676, 16F72, 16F73, 16F74, 16F76, 16F77, 16F818, 16F819, 16C84, 16F84(A), 16F870, 16F871, 16F872, 16F873(A), 16F874(A), 16F876(A), 16F877(A), 16F88, 18F1220, 18F1320, 18F2220, 18F242, 18F248, 18F252, 18F258, 18F4220, 18F4320, 18F442, 18F4439, 18F448, 18F452, 18F458. For all versions where the /MCLR pin can also be used as an input (such as the 12F675) you will need the dongle discussed in section 2.2.

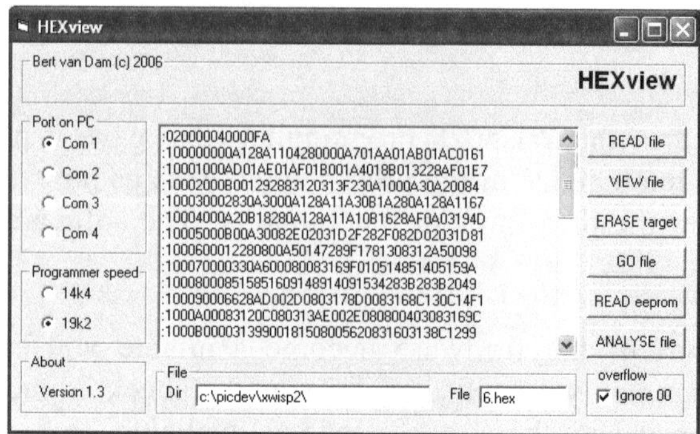

Figure 203. HEXview.

5. Disconnect the power from the programmer and unplug it.
6. Remove the 16F628 from the programmer and exchange it for the new one you just made. Keep the old 16F628 until you are absolutely convinced that the new version works perfectly.
7. If you want you can recycle the old 16F628 (personally, I would keep it as a backup).
   - Connect the 16F628 to the hardware of step 3.
   - Enter a name for the file (such as "old hex programmer") and enter a path. Remember the backslash at the end of the path.
   - Select the COM port your programmer is connected to.
   - Use the default speed setting of 19k2.
   - Click on "READ file" and wait for the black window to disappear.
   - Click on "VIEW file" to verify that the hex file has been created.
   - Save the hex file in a safe location in case you ever want to go back to the old version.
   - You can now use the 16F628 for other projects.

You can also use HEXview to look at data in the EEPROM of a PIC™. See section 10.3 for details.

13.3 The 16F876A

13.3.1 Introduction

The 16F876A is the little brother to the 16F877. This PIC™ has all the functionality of the 16F877, but in a smaller, 28-pin package. Missing are the D and E ports and one of the power pins for +5 V. In total, 12 pins less than the 16F877, but still a mighty impressive PIC™ for smaller projects.

Here are the properties of the 16F876A:

Item	Specification
Program memory	8192 words (14 bit)
RAM	368 bytes
EEPROM	256 byte
I/O pins	22
Analog inputs	6 (each 10 bit)
USART	yes (c6/c7)
Speed	5 mips
PWM	yes (c1/c2)
Cost	US$ 5 to 7
I2C	yes (c3/c4)

The packaging is, of course, smaller:

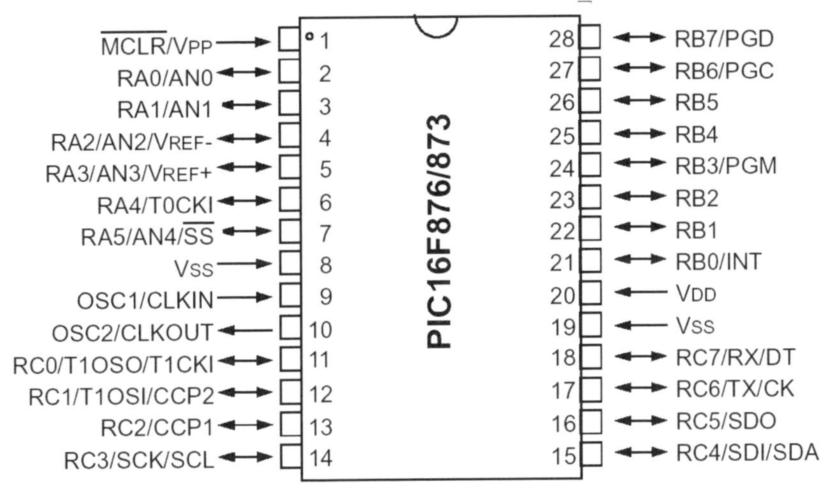

Figure 204. Pin configuration of the 16F876A.

These pins must always be connected:

Pin	Name	Description
1	MCLR/Vpp	Master clear pin and programmer voltage input. This pin requires a 33k resistor to +5 V.
8	V_{SS}	Power supply ground (0 V)[171]
9	OSC1/CLKIN	Crystal[172]
10	OSC2/CLKOUT	Crystal
19	V_{SS}	Power supply ground (0 V)
20	V_{DD}	Power supply +5 V

If you use the Wisp628 the wires need to be connected as follows:

Wire	Connects to
yellow	pin 1
blue	pin 28
green	pin 27
white	pin 24
red	+ 5 V
black	0 V

13.3.2 16F876A_bert library

The standard library for this PIC™ is 16F876A_bert[173]. You can read about the functionality of the 16F877 library in section 14.2, because all of these functions are also available for the 16F876A.

---

[171] All power supply connections MUST be used (pins 8, 19, 20).

[172] A crystal is not mandatory; the 16F876A can run without it, but slower (at 4 MHz). In this book a crystal is used in all projects and this has been set in the 16F876_bert library.

[173] This library is part of the download package

Since some functionality is loaded by default certain pins have been reserved. If you want to use these pins for something else you'll need to modify the standard library. This is the default configuration:

16F876A pins	Function
9 and 10	Crystal
12	PWM (2)
13	PWM (1)
17	RS232 hardware TX
18	RS232 hardware RX
27	RS232 software RX
28	RS232 software TX
2 to 5 plus 7	Analog input (adjustable)
All others	Digital input/output

The analog pins 2, 3, 4, 5, and 7 can be switched to digital using the command from the standard library (see section 14.2).

13.3.3 Demo program

As a demonstration of the capabilities of the 16F876A and the 16F876A_bert library a small demo program is discussed.

Technical background

This program contains the following functionality:

- A/D conversion
- RS232 communication
- Reading a digital signal
- Writing a digital signal

This program will read the position of the variable resistor on pin a0 and send it to the PC over a serial connection. The yellow LED will flash and the blue LED will switch on when the switch is engaged.

The software

```
-- jal 2.0.6
include 16F876a_bert

-- general variables
var byte resist
var bit led0 is pin_c2
var bit led1 is pin_c3
var bit switch is pin_c4

-- define the pins
pin_c2_direction = output
pin_c3_direction = output
pin_c4_direction = input

forever loop

   -- take a sample on AN2 (pin_a0)
   resist = ADC_read_low_res(0)

   -- and send over RS232 to the PC
   serial_sw_write(resist)

   -- flash the led if the switch is pressed
   if switch  then
      led0 = high
   else
      led0 = low
   end if

   -- wait a bit otherwise the led flashes a bit fast...
   delay_100ms(1)

   -- flash led[174]
   led1 = ! led1

end loop
```

---

[174] Using *led = ! led* is elegant but cannot be used in all circumstances; see section 4.2.

The hardware

The hardware is rather straightforward. Blue LEDs are pretty, but a bit expensive; if you didn't buy the hardware kit feel free to use an LED of a different color.

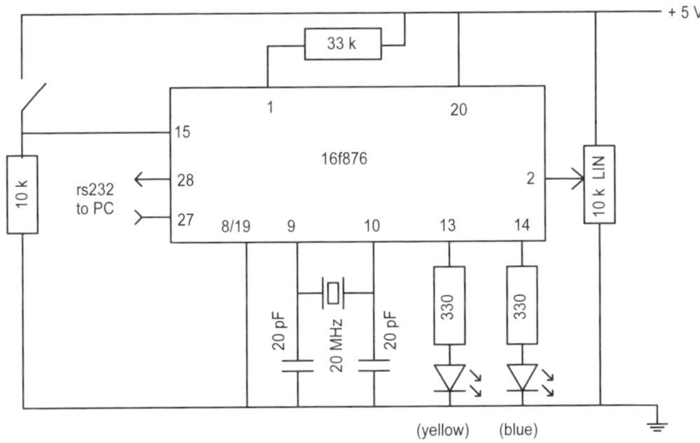

Figure 205. Demo program for the 16F876A.

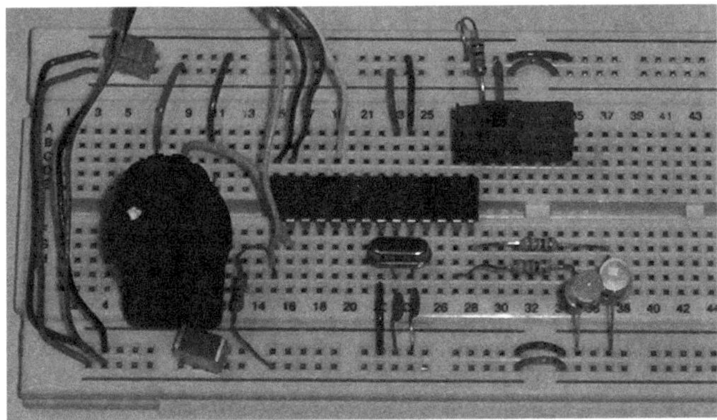

Figure 206. Demo program for the 16F876A.

13.3.4 VU meter

A VU meter which will show the volume of music in an LED bar.[175]

Technical background

A sound source is connected to the A/D converter of the PIC™. Depending on the measured voltage a number of LEDs is switched on. At which voltage this happens depends on the sound source. In this project a small transistor radio is used. Adjust the threshold values in the following (and similar) statements if needed:

> if resist > 10 then pin_b0 = 1 else pin_b0 = 0 end if

Be careful to never apply more than 5 V to any pin of a PIC! Start with the volume of the sound source off, and then slowly increase it until the LEDs flash.

The software

```
-- jal 2.0.6
include 16F876_bert

-- general variables
var byte resist

-- define the pins
pin_b0_direction = output
pin_b1_direction = output
pin_b2_direction = output
pin_b3_direction = output
pin_b4_direction = output
pin_b5_direction = output
pin_b6_direction = output
pin_b7_direction = output

forever loop

   -- sample sound
   resist = ADC_read_low_res(0)
```

---

[175] VU means volume unit. Technically, a VU meter measures the average voltage over a certain (short) period of time.

-- and display
if resist > 10 then pin_b0 = 1 else pin_b0 = 0 end if
if resist > 20 then pin_b1 = 1 else pin_b1 = 0 end if
if resist > 30 then pin_b2 = 1 else pin_b2 = 0 end if
if resist > 40 then pin_b3 = 1 else pin_b3 = 0 end if
if resist > 50 then pin_b4 = 1 else pin_b4 = 0 end if
if resist > 60 then pin_b5 = 1 else pin_b5 = 0 end if
if resist > 70 then pin_b6 = 1 else pin_b6 = 0 end if
if resist > 80 then pin_b7 = 1 else pin_b7 = 0 end if

end loop

During programming you don't need to remove the LEDs from pins b6 and b7. They will flash, but it doesn't affect the programming.

The hardware

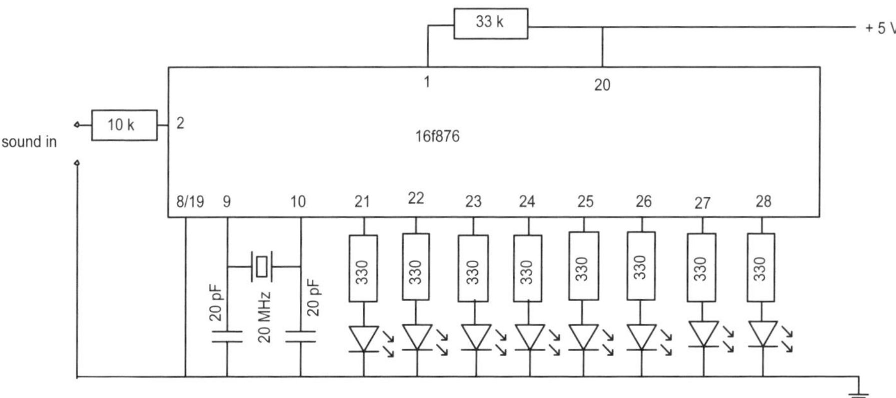

Figure 207. VU meter.

On the breadboard you can see the VU meter in action with a simple transistor radio. Keeping the radio this close to the crystal does not improve reception. Hidden under the connecting wires to the radio is the 33k resistor on pin 1.

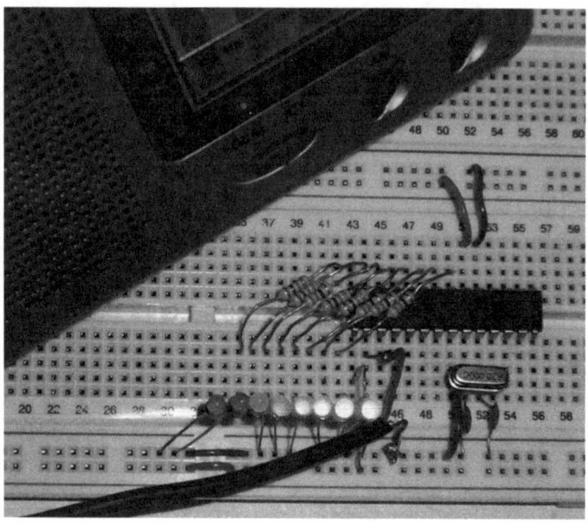

Figure 208. VU meter with transistor radio.

Optional

Although this is a simple VU meter you could use the techniques discussed in section 12.7 to replace the LEDs with large lamps and turn this an Object d'Art, especially if you use a microphone and amplifier instead of the radio (just remember to keep the input volume low). Now the light in the room will adjust to the sound level. With a lot of people in the room it will be brightly lit, but when everyone leaves it will get dark. Take a look at the website of artist James Clar[176]. With the knowledge you have gained in this book you can build almost all of his projects!

13.3.5 Infrared RS232

This is a very unusual but interesting project involving infrared RS232 communication between a 16F877 and a 16F876A.

Technical background

In section 11.1, two PIC™ microcontrollers were connected to each other using a wired RS232 connection. In this project we will do the same thing, but using infrared instead of wires!

We will use the Fairchild QRB134 that has already been discussed in sections 7.3 and 7.4, and obviously this time we need two. The disadvantage of this sensor is that it is

---

[176] The website address is http://www.jamesclar.com

meant for short-range applications.[177] This is because the infrared LED doesn't produce much light. A possible solution would be to connect a few together and use a transistor to switch them on and off.[178] Another solution is to remove the daylight filters. The sensors are mounted opposite each other in such a way that the LEDs and receivers (phototransistors) directly face each other, as shown in Figure 209.

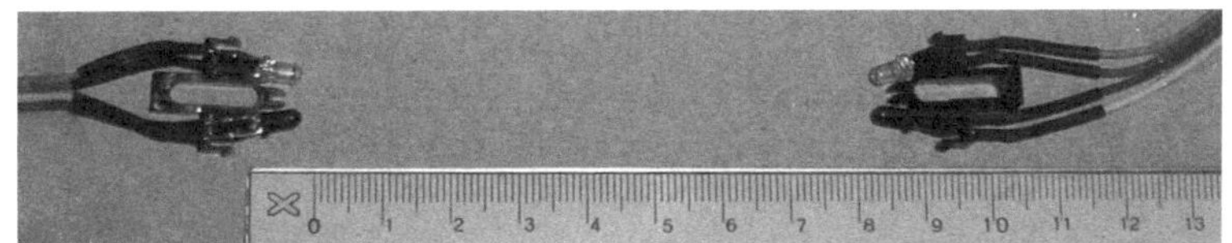

Figure 209. Facing each other with daylight filters removed.

The maximum distance you can reach this way is about 8 cm (3 in.) if you line the sensors up nicely. If you use the sensors with the daylight filters installed the maximum distance is about 5 mm (0.2 in.). In that case the sensors must face each other "crossed over', so that the LED of one sensor faces the phototransistor of the other, not as in Figure 209.[179]

The normal communication speed for the hardware serial port is set to 19k2 in the standard library, but that would be too fast for this infrared setup. We will reduce the speed to 1200 baud, which means we have to modify the libraries of the 16F877 and the 16F876A.

Follow these steps for modifying the libraries:

1. Copy the 16F877_bert.jal library from the library directory on the harddrive of your PC to the folder where you keep the files of this project.[180]
2. Start JALedit and open the library (using File – Open, etc.)
3. Search for the *const Serial_hw_baudrate = 19200* command and put a semicolon (;) in front of this line. The line will become gray, because now it is a comment line.
4. Save the file (using Ctrl-S)
5. Repeat steps 1 to 4 for the 16F876A_bert.jal library.

---

[177] According to the datasheet the optimum distance is 0.51 cm (0.2 inch).

[178] If you use a transistor you can reduce the resistor to the LED. This is now 220 ohms, because the PIC™ can deliver 25 mA max. According to the datasheet the infrared LED can handle 50 mA, which works out to a 100-ohm resistor. This will seriously improve the usable distance.

[179] In the picture you see that LED is facing LED and phototransistor is facing phototransistor. If you use the daylight filter the LEDs should face the phototransistors, because the signals cross due to the short range.

[180] If you installed the software package as instructed your library directory is c:\picdev\jal\libraries. The project directory is where you are storing your PIC™ program.

When JALedit looks for a library, it first looks in the directory where your JAL program is located. In this case it will find, and use, the modified libraries. If the library is not found in the JAL program directory JALedit will search for it in the library directory. The libraries that you keep with the JAL program are called "local copies".

If you make changes to libraries it is always a good idea to use local copies. This ensures that other programs can still use the original libraries. And if your modifications don't work out you can go back to the original version by simply deleting the local copy. So it is very helpful to use a different directory for each project.

The software

Since we commented out the speed of the hardware serial connection we must declare it in the main program:

```
const Serial_hw_baudrate = 1200
```

And since the library needs to use this value you'll need to place this statement before the library call.

```
-- jal 2.0.6
const Serial_hw_baudrate = 1200
include 16F877_bert

-- general variables
var byte data1, data2

forever loop

   -- fetch incoming data
   serial_sw_read(data1)

   -- relay to 16F876
   serial_hw_write(data1)

   -- get byte from serial PIC
   if Serial_hw_read( data2 ) then
      -- echo to PC
      Serial_sw_write(data2)
   end if

end loop
```

Aside from that the programs are basically copies of that in section 11.1, with the exception of using the 16F876A_bert library:

```
-- jal 2.0.6
const Serial_hw_baudrate = 1200
include 16F876A_bert

-- general variables
var byte data

forever loop

   -- get byte from serial PIC
   if Serial_hw_read( data ) then
      -- echo
      Serial_hw_write(data)
   end if

end loop
```

When both programs run you can use the pass-through function of the Wisp628 programmer to connect to the 16F877 using MICterm, or other terminal program. Everything you enter in the send box (the lower green window) is sent to the 16F877, then by infrared to the 16F876A, then by infrared back to the 16F877, and from there back to the PC through wires, where it is visible again in the receive window.

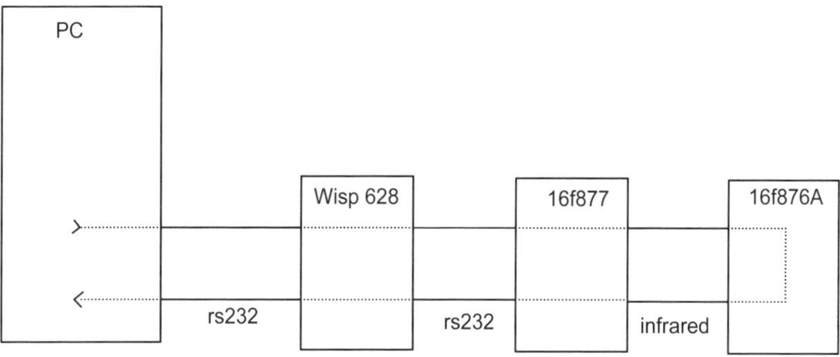

Figure 210. Data transfer.

The hardware

In the schematic you can see that both units are almost identical. To make things clearer the Fairchild QRB1134 is represented by its individual components. In reality, the LED and phototransistor are contained in the same case. The wire colors refer to that casing.

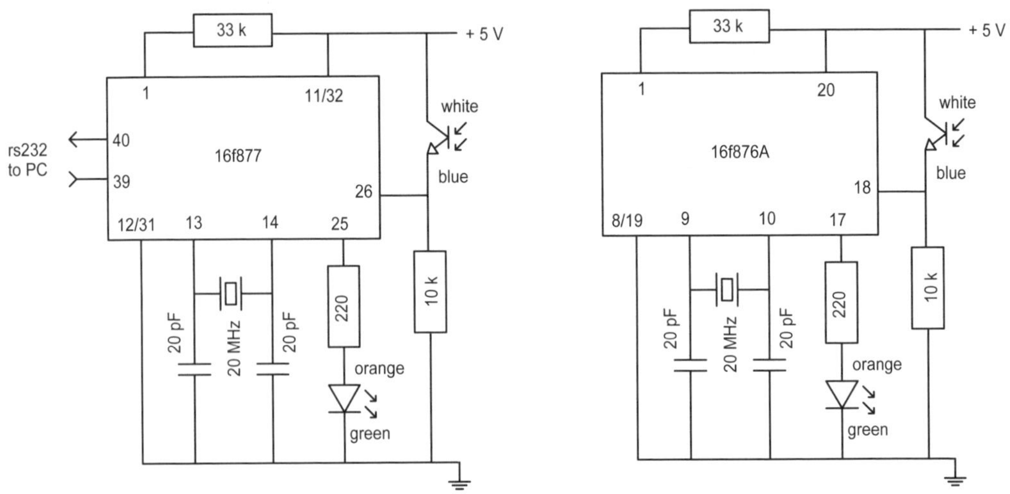

Figure 211. Infrared serial set up.

And this is what it looks like on the breadboard:

Figure 212. The 16F877 with infrared unit.

The green and blue wires at the top left corner belong to the Wisp628 programmer, and allow for communication to the PC through the pass-through connection. The sensor is soldered to a 4-pin plug, with the wires leaving the picture on the right side.

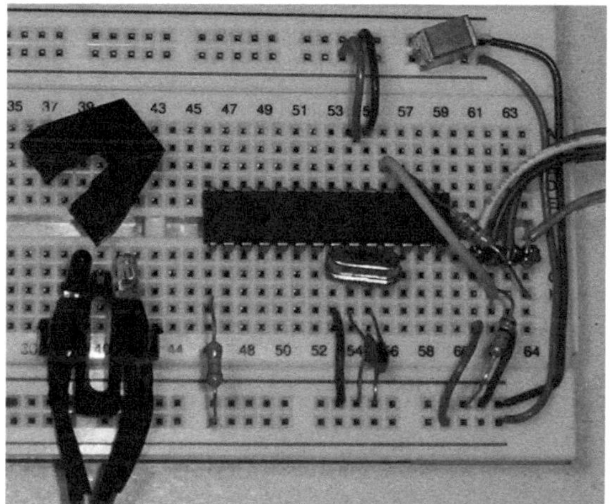

Figure 213. The 16F876A with separate daylight filter.

The daylight filter is on the left side of the picture, just to show it; it serves no function.

Figure 214 shows that horizontal alignment is very important. If you tilt the sensors just a little bit the signals will completely miss the receivers. When testing for the maximum possible distance it doesn't make any difference whether it is daylight or not.

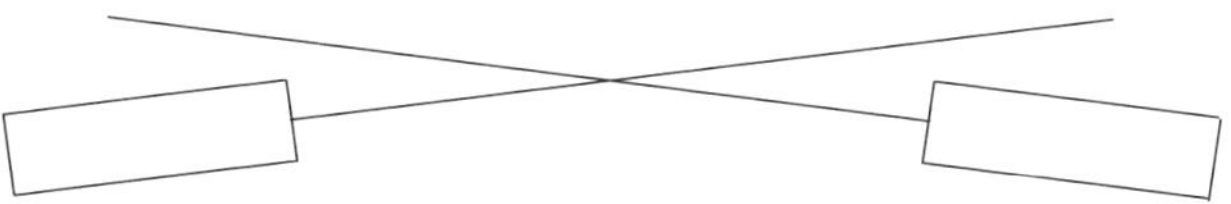

Figure 214. Importance of horizontal alignment.

Optional

You can use this project as a code lock. The 16F877 sends a signal and the 16F876A (built as a portable keychain device) will have to give a certain reply before the lock will open.

I created this project for a mobile robot that could exchange information with a base station, without physically connecting to it. It only needs to maneuver itself into the right location and initialize communications. In any case you need to make sure that horizontal alignment is in order.

13.4 Portability

Using JAL as the programming language, in combination with the 12F675_bert, 16F628_bert, 16F876A_bert, and 16F877_bert libraries makes programming a PIC™ a lot easier. If this book had used assembler there would have been only a fraction of the projects, and you would have learned quite a bit less.

There is yet another major advantage to JAL with these libraries: portability. Programs written for one PIC™ can be quite easily transferred to a different PIC™. Say, for example, you started programming for the 16F628, but your program got so big that you expect to run out of memory. With a few simple changes you can port your program to the big 16F877 and solve your memory problem. Or perhaps you started on the 16F877, but then realized that your program is very small and doesn't need all those inputs and outputs. Simply port your program to the smaller and cheaper 12F675.

Functionality (using the standard library)	16F877	16F876	16F628	12F675
Serial communication - hardware	X	X	X	
Serial communication - software	X	X	X	X
Pulse Width Modulation (PWM)	X	X	X	
A/D conversion	X	X		X
Program memory	X	X		
EEPROM	X	X	X	X
ASCII	X	X	X	X
Delay	X	X	X	X
Registers and variables	X	X	X	X
Random numbers	X	X	X	X
Analog-digital switchable pins	[181]	[182]		X

---

[181] It is possible with the 16F877 library, but you need to set the pin configuration as a group using *no_ADC = X*.

[182] It is possible with the 16F876A library, but you need to set the pin configuration as a group using *no_ADC = X*.

It is, of course, important to remember the different features of these PIC™ microcontrollers as shown in the previous table. There are physical limitations to consider as well. The 16F628, for instance, has only one PWM module, while the 16F877 has two.

The 12F675 has analog-to-digital conversion on 4 pins, while the 16F877 has it on 8. And the 16F628 doesn't have it at all.

Another thing to take into account is that the standard library settings may differ. Pin a0 of the 12F675 is used for software RS232, while the "same" pin on the 16F877 is used as an analog-to-digital converter.

The following table maps the limitations:

Function	12F675	16F628	16F876	16F877
Crystal		a6 and a7	9 and 10	13 and 14
PWM[183]		b3	c1 and c2	c1 and c2
RS232 hardware TX		b2	c6	c6
RS232 hardware RX		b1	c7	c7
RS232 software RX	a1	b6	b6	b6
RS232 software TX	a0	b7	b7	b7
Analog in (flexible)	a2 and a4[184]		a0, a1, a2, a3, and a5	a0, a1, a2, a3, a5, e0, e1, and e2
Digital input/output	other	others	others	others

An example

As an example of migrating programs we will compare two programs that read a voltage on pin a2, make it digital, and send it to the PC. One program can run on the big 16F877, the other on the tiny 12F675. The programs are listed next to each other on the next page.

Perhaps you think this is a bit corny, but it does show the power of JAL and the 12F675_bert and 16F877_bert libraries. The only difference between the programs is the library *include* on line 2.

---

[183] PWM can be switched on and off, but this is only important for porting PWM functionality.
[184] On the 12F675 A/D channel AN3 is on pin a4, but on the 16F877 it is pin a3. On the 16F877 pin a4 doesn't have an A/D module at all.

<table>
<tr><td>

```
-- jal 2.0.6
include 16F877_bert

-- general variables
var byte resist

-- define the pins
pin_a2_direction = input

forever loop

   -- take a sample on AN2 (pin_a2)
   resist = ADC_read_low_res(2)

   -- and send over RS232 to the PC
   serial_sw_write(resist)

   -- wait a bit
   delay_10ms(1)

end loop
```

</td><td>

```
-- jal 2.0.6
include 12F675_bert

-- general variables
var byte resist

-- define the pins
pin_a2_direction = input

forever loop

   -- take a sample on AN2 (pin_a2)
   resist = ADC_read_low_res(2)

   -- and send over RS232 to the PC
   serial_sw_write(resist)

   -- wait a bit
   delay_10ms(1)

end loop
```

</td></tr>
</table>

14 Appendix

This is the reference guide part of the book. It contains a few unique overviews not found anywhere else. For this reason the book will find its place next to your PC even after the projects have long been built.

14.1 JAL

14.1.1 General

JAL[185] (Just Another Language) is a free-format language for programming PIC microcontrollers. The commands can be spread out over the lines as you please. Tabs, spaces, and newlines are all considered whitespace. There is no delimiter between different commands. In theory you could put all commands on one long line. In practice, however, appropriate whitespace results in easier-to-read programs because any convention you choose is possible. JAL is the only advanced free language, and has a large and active international user base. It is configurable and extensible by use of libraries and can even be combined with assembler.

A typical JAL program will start with a call to a library that contains relevant details for the PIC™ for which the program is written.

```
include 16F877_bert
```

Then the variables will be declared:

```
var byte a
```

Next are the commands:

```
forever loop
   a = a + 1
end loop
```

---

[185] JAL was originally designed by Wouter van Ooijen as a free high-level language comparable to Pascal. After a few years JAL continued its life as an open-source program. In 2006, Stef Mientki initiated the development of a brand new JAL version: V2. Kyle York is the programmer of this new version, and an international user group (alphabetically: Bert van Dam, Sunish Issac, Dave Lagzdin, Javier Martinez, Stef Mientki, Wouter van Ooijen, Michael Reynolds, André Steenveld, Joep Suijs, Vasile Surducan, and Michael Watterson) took care of beta testing. In this book the latest version (at the time of writing) was used. The download page contains a link to the latest version available.

14 Appendix

It is a good practice to add comments to your program to indicate what it does and for which JAL version it is written. So a simple program might look like this:

```
-- JAL 2.0.4
include 16F877_bert

var byte a

-- demo program
forever loop
     a = a + 1
end loop
```

14.1.2 Syntax

Variables

Here the power of JAL is immediately clear. Both unsigned (positive) as well as signed (positive and negative) variables can be used, containing up to 32 bits.

bit	1 bit unsigned boolean value (0 of 1)
byte	8 bit unsigned value (0 t/m255).
sbyte	8 bit signed value (-128 t/m127).
word	16 bit unsigned value (0 t/m 65,535).
sword	16 bit signed value (-32,768 t/m 32,767).
dword	32 bit unsigned value (0 t/m 4,294,967,296).
sdword	32 bit signed value (-2,147,483,648 t/m 2,147,483,647).

You can even define variables with any bit length you want, such as:

```
var bit*2 demo
```

Variable *demo* is now 2 bits long (and can thus contain the values 0, 1, 2 or 3). When a value is assigned to *demo* it doesn't necessarily have to be two bits, but only the lowest two bits will be put into the variable (the others do not fit).[186] So the statement:

```
demo = 99
```

---

[186] The compiler will notice and give you a warning. If you did it intentionally, you can ignore the warning. If you use the settings in the download package you will not see the warnings, because they are switched off by default.

will result in a value of 3 for *demo*, because the number 99 in binary is 1100011, and the lowest two bits are set to 1, which equals 3 in decimal.

Besides decimal values you can use other number bases as well. In that case you need to add a prefix to the number. Possible bases are:

23	decimal
0x1F	hexadecimal
0q07	octal
0b01	binary

And of course you can use letters:

"Hello"	string

For readability purposes underscores can be added to numbers in any position you want. To the compiler the number 10_0 is identical to 100.
Binary value assignments almost always use underscores to make them easier to read:

a = 0b_1001_1110

Declaring variables must be done before they can be used. Here are a few possibilities to do this:

var byte a   *a* is declared as a byte

var byte a = 0x1F   *a* is declared as a byte and assigned a value at the same time

var byte a at 0x06   *a* is declared as a byte at memory location 0x06 [187]

---

[187] It is important to understand what you are doing when you force variables to a certain memory location. It can also be used as a convenient way to split variables. This example declares an array in exactly the same memory location as the word variable *demo*:
    var word demo
    var byte dem[2] at demo
Demo is a word (two bytes). Since the array *dem* is also two bytes long, and in the same memory location, this means that the first item in the array, *dem[0]*, is the low byte and the second item, *dem[1]*, is the high byte.

> var byte volatile a   *a* is declared as a byte and will not be optimized away by the compiler[188]
>
> var byte a is b   *a* is a synonym or alias for *b* (*b* must be declared first)

The final declaration can be used to give pins names that are easier to remember. Lets suppose that a red LED is connected to pin c1. If you use this command you can refer to pin c1 using the *redled* alias:

> var bit redled is pin_c1

For example, *redled = 1* would make pin c1 high and thus turn on the LED. This will make the program easier to read. But it is also easier if you want to migrate your program to another PIC. If this PIC™ doesn't have a pin c1 all you have to do is change the declaration to a pin that the PIC™ does have, such as:

> var bit redled is pin_a1

Mixing different variable types in a calculation is possible, but care should be taken that intermediate results will be stored in the variable type that the calculation started with. If you multiply a byte with a byte and put the result in a word, like this:

> var byte num1, num2
> var word num3
>
> num3 = num1 * num2

the result will never be larger than 255. This is because *num1* and *num2* are multiplied using bytes and the result is transferred into *num3*.

You can force the compiler to use a word for intermediate calculations by changing the multiplication to *num3 = word(num1) * word(num2)*.

---

[188] The compiler optimizes the program during compiling, and will remove all unused parts. References to a pin will also be removed since the compiler doesn't know that pins can change "from the outside". So, to the compiler the command seems useless. The *volatile* keyword is used to prevent this. The compiler will leave a *volatile* variable alone. The average user will almost never need the *volatile* keyword.

Constants

When you know in advance that a variable will be assigned a value once and will never change it is not a variable but a constant. This can be declared using *const*, like this:

    const byte demo = 5

The advantage of using constants is that a variable uses RAM memory and a constant doesn't (the compiler uses the value rather than the constant name). So it is a good idea to use constants whenever you can. In small programs such as in this book it is not really an advantage, because we are never even close to running out of memory.

Forever loop

This command ensures that a particular part of the program is executed forever. Many PIC™ programs use this command since it is a convenient way to make sure the program never stops.

    forever loop
        [commands]
    end loop

While loop

The *while* loop executes a series of commands as long as a certain condition is met.

This loop is executed as long as a is smaller than b:

    while a < b loop
            [commands]
    end loop

For loop

The *for* loop executes a series of commands a fixed number of times.

This loop is executed ten times:

    for 10 loop
            [commands]
    end loop

Normally the compiler will count "internally", but you can force it to use a certain variable to count the loops, with the *using* command. This is very convenient if you want to know inside your loop how many times it has already been executed. For example, when you want to determine the position in an array. Note that *counter* will count from 0 to 9 in this program:

```
for 10 using counter loop
        [ commands ]
        value = demo(counter)
end loop
```

Procedure

A procedure is a part of program that is needed more than once. Rather than typing it several times it is put aside and given a name. This particular part of the program is only executed when it is "called" by that name. Using procedures usually makes a program easier to read and maintain.

This is an example procedure *demo*

```
procedure demo is
        [ commands ]
    end procedure
```

You can call this procedure simply by using the name as a command. For the procedure shown above the call would be

```
demo
```

In procedures you can use variables just as in any other part of the program. Any variable declared outside the procedure is also valid inside a procedure. If you define a variable inside a procedure you can only use it inside that particular procedure. This is called a "local variable". For example:

```
procedure demo is
    var byte a
    [ commands ]
end procedure
```

In this example variable *a* is unknown outside the procedure.

If you want to give a value to a variable from outside the procedure you need to "pass" it to the procedure. The procedure would look like this:

```
procedure demo (byte in a)  is
     [ commands that use variable a ]
end procedure
```

and a call to this procedure would be like this:

```
demo (6)
```

In this same way you can pass variables out of the procedure, but then you need to declare them as "*byte out*" instead of "*byte in*" in the procedure name.

This is a good way to make new commands that you can add to JAL. If you have made new procedures, for example to control a certain component or function, you can put them in a separate file. This file is then called a library and you can use it by "including" it in your program using the *include* command.

The advantage is that your program becomes much easier to read, and the next time you need that particular component or function you can simply load your library, and off you go.

Function

A function is basically the same as a procedure. The main difference is that a function always returns a value. The returned value needs to be declared using the *return* statement.

In this function variable *a* is incremented by one:

```
function demo (byte in a) return byte is
     var byte b
     b = a + 1
     return b
end function
```

In the declaration of the function it is indicated that an input is expected (*byte in*) and that the answer the function will return is a byte (*return byte*). Inside the function the "*return b*" statement indicates that *b* will be the value that is returned.

14 Appendix

This is an example of a function call:

x = demo(4)

where x will get the value 5 (4 + 1).

Functions are often used to return a status rather than a number, such as *true* or *false*.

In-line assembler

You can use assembler inside your JAL programs. I don't think this will ever be really necessary, but perhaps you found a nice snippet on the Internet or want to use an example from the datasheet.

You can use individual assembler statements using the *asm* prefix, like this:

```
asm movlw 0xFF
```

If you need multiple statements it is easier to use an *assembler* block, like this:

```
assembler
    movlw 0xFF
    bsf 5
    movwf pr2
    bcf 5
end assembler
```
[189]

When your program is compiled the JAL compiler generates a HEX file for the PIC™, as well as an assembler file. You can use this to exchange programs with assembler users or to use Microchip tools.

All assembler commands ("mnemonics") that you find in the 16F877 datasheet can be used.

---

[189] Assigning value 0xFF to pr2 is quite complicated in assembler, because the program executes from bank 0 and pr2 is in bank 1. In JAL this is totally irrelevant (you don't even need to know what banks are); you can simply write pr2 = 0xFF.

Additionally, a few assembler macros that are often used on the Internet can be used too:

OPTION k	Copy literal k to the *OPTION* register [190]
TRIS {5,6,7}	Copy W to the TRIS {5,6,7} register
MOVFW f	Copy f to W (a synonym for MOVF f, W) [191]
SKPC	A synonym for BTFSS _status, _c
SKPNC	A synonym for BTFSC _status, _c
SKPZ	A synonym for BTFSS _status, _z
SKPNZ	A synonym for BTFSC _status, _z

If you use variables from the JAL program in your assembler block you cannot be sure where they are because JAL may store them in any available memory bank. This also means that at the moment the JAL program is interrupted for your assembler block, you have no clue where the bank pointers are pointing to. That means you don't have access to the registers, even though you do know where they are.

The solution is to ask the compiler to fix the bank pointers for you. You can do this by adding *bank* to every line in which you use JAL variables or registers.

```
procedure register_write( byte in Address, byte in Data ) is
    assembler
        bank  movf address,w  ; move address to working variable w
        movwf FSR             ; move address to file select register
        bcf irp               ; make irp zero so we use bank 0 and 1
                              ; (indirect register bank select), 0 = bank 0/1
        bank  movf data,w     ; move data to w
        movwf indf            ; move data to indirect file register as
                              ; referenced by fsr
    end assembler
end procedure
```

I wrote this fragment for the regedit [192] library and you see that the bank statement is used in all lines containing *address* and *data,* because the location of these JAL variables is

---

[190] The official explanation is *move*. However since the original version is retained it is in fact *copy*.

[191] W is the working register, f is the register file address. *MOVFW myvar* puts the value of *myvar* in W, *MOVLW myvar* puts the address of *myvar* in W.

unknown. The line referring to the registers FSR, IRP and INDF do not have the bank keyword, because they are accessible from all banks.

Task

Even though a PIC™ can only do one thing at a time you can still do multitasking, just like on a PC. The different tasks can be defined using the *task* command. Every time the program encounters a *suspend* command the current task is interrupted. The scheduler then checks to see which task has been waiting for the longest time and hands control over to that task. This system only works if the tasks are "honest" and use the *suspend* command regularly.

Just like in a procedure, tasks can have their own local variables.

```
task name1 (parameters) is
[ commands ]
    suspend
    [ commands ]
end task

task name2 (parameters) is
[ commands ]
    suspend
    [ commands ]
end task

start task1(parameter values)
start task2(parameter values)

forever loop
    suspend
end loop
```

Before a task can be run you need to start it using *start*. The task can be stopped using *end task*.

---

[192] This is a library to read and change registers while the program is running, see section 12.1. The latest version of the library (contained in the download package) is written in JAL, so the fragment is no longer used.

<u>IMPORTANT</u>: If you want to compile a program containing tasks you need to tell the compiler how many tasks there are. Note that the main program is also counted as a task. So the previous example should be compiled using *-task 3* on the command line.[193]

If then else

This command is used to make a choice between two possibilities. *If* one condition occurs *then* something is done, *else* something else is done.

In this example *b* gets the value of 2 when *a* is equal to 1. In all other cases *b* gets 3.

```
if a == 1 then
    b = 2
else
    b = 3
end if
```

This command can be nested, like in this example.

```
if a == 1 then
    b = 2
else if a == 2 then
    b = 3
    else
        b = 4
    end if
end if
```

Note that *else if* are two words.[194] The above program yields the following results:

if	then
a = 1	b = 2
a = 2	b = 3
a = something else	b = 4

---

[193] If you use JALedit you can enter this at *Compile - Environment Option - Additional Commandline Parameters*.

[194] The statement *elsif* is also legal, but it is not used very often.

Case

If you need to make multiple decisions based on the value of a single variable the *case* statement is a good alternative to a row of *if then else* statements. In the following example *b* is given a value based on the value of *a*. If *a* is 3 than *b* will be 4. If the value of *a* is not listed then *b* will get the value 6.

```
case a of
      1:  b = 20
      2:  b = 13
      3:  b = 4
      4:  b = 59
      otherwise b = 6
end case
```

Contrary to the *if then else* statement the *case* block can only have one statement per choice. So if you want to give *b* the value 13 and *aa* the value 188 when *a* is 2 then this is not possible. You will have to use a *procedure*, or the *block* statement.

Block

The *block* command can be used to group statements together. Variables defined inside a *block* can only be used in this *block*. A block is a program section and will be executed when it is encountered. In cannot be called form another location.

```
block
     [ commands ]
end block
```

This is particularly useful in combination with *case,* for example:

```
case a of
      1:  b = 20
      2:  block
                b = 13
                aa = 188
           end block
      3:  b = 4
      4:  b = 59
      otherwise b = 6
end case
```

Another reason to use *block* is when you want to use variables locally This may occur when you are mixing program parts together that use the same variable names for different purposes.

Array

Normally speaking a variable has only one value. With an array a variable can be given a whole range of variables. In the following example the *demo* array is assigned a row of five values.

        var byte demo[5] = {11,12,13,14,15}

To get a value out of the array the number between square brackets indicates the position that you want. Remember that computers start counting at 0, so the first position in the array is 0. In our example *demo[0]* contains the value 11.

This command selects the fourth number in the array (the value 14):

        a = demo[3]

Adding a value to an array (or modifying one) is done in a similar way. In this command the fourth position in the array is assigned the value in *a*:

        demo[3]= a

Your program can use the *count* statement to determine the length of an array. For example:

        a = count(demo)

Be careful with your array size, since an array has to fit within a single RAM memory bank (see section 10.2).

Long table

If you need more space that you can fit into an array you can use the long table. This is an array with just constants. That means you define it once, and afterward you cannot make changes to its content. This is because even though it is an array, it is not contained in RAM, but in program (flash) memory.

The long table can be very long indeed; in the 16F877 a whopping 8000 bytes! Of course the length can never be more than the available program memory. So in a small PIC, or with a large program, long tables must be shorter. You can check this by compiling the program with a long table with a length of 1. Based on the resulting program size the available length for the long table can then be calculated. See section 10.1 for more information on how to determine the size of a program.

If the long table doesn't fit the compiler will generate an error, and your program will not be downloaded into the 16F877.

The syntax of the long table is:

```
const byte demo[2049] = { 1, 2, 3, 4, 5, ...}
var word x
var byte y


y = demo[x]
```

where the above values are just for demonstration purposes.

Operators

JAL has a wide variety of operators. The most important ones are shown below:

Operator	Explanation
! !	Logical. Indicates whether a variable is zero or not. For example !!5 = 1, and !!0 = 0
!	Not, or Complement.. Flips 0 to 1 and 1 to 0 at the bit level. So !5 = 250 because !0b_0000_0101 = 0b_1111_1010
*	Multiply.
/	Divide without remainder. So 9/2 = 4
%	The remainder of the division So 9%2 = 1
+	Add.
−	Subtract.

Operator	Explanation
<<	Left shift. Move all bits to the left by one. Note that the newly created bit is set to 0. When a signed variable is shifted the sign is retained.
>>	Right shift. Same as left shift, but in the other direction.
<	Less than.
<=	Less than or equal to.
==	Equal to. Note that these are two equal signs in a row. Accidentally using only one is a very common mistake (feel free to view this as an understatement)
!=	Not equal to.
>=	Greater than or equal to.
>	Greater than.
&	AND comparison at the bit level. The truth table is:

$$1 \& 1 = 1$$
$$1 \& 0 = 0$$
$$0 \& 1 = 0$$
$$0 \& 0 = 0$$

|	OR comparison at the bit level. The truth table is:

$$1 \mid 1 = 1$$
$$1 \mid 0 = 1$$
$$0 \mid 1 = 1$$
$$0 \mid 0 = 0$$

^	XOR (eXclusive OR) comparison at the bit level. The truth table is:

$$1 \wedge 1 = 0$$
$$1 \wedge 0 = 1$$
$$0 \wedge 1 = 1$$
$$0 \wedge 0 = 0$$

14 Appendix

Pragma

Pragma is a command for the compiler. It is a very powerful but complex command. A detailed explanation would be out of scope for this book, particularly since you will never (or rarely) use most of the commands.

This table lists the most important *pragma*s:

pragma eedata	Stores data in the EEPROM of the PIC™. For example *pragma eedata "O","K"* will store the letters O and K.
pragma interrupt	This can only be used inside a procedure. The result is that the procedure is added to the interrupt chain, a series of procedures that is executed when an interrupt occurs. There is no limit to the number of procedures in the chain, but the execution order is not defined. Interrupt procedures may not be called from the program itself.

Comments

Lines containing comments are preceded by two dashes or a semicolon. You need to do this for each line, as there is no block comment statement.

```
; this is a comment
-- and this too
```

Comment lines are used to clarify what a program is for, or why things are done the way they are done. This is very handy for future reference, or when you want to share programs over the Internet.

It is good practice to indicate the JAL version on the very first line of your program. That eliminates a lot of questions!

Good comments are not about what a certain statement does (unless you are writing a book), because the reader may be expected to know this. They are about <u>why</u> you use the statement. If you make a library you should use comment lines to explain in detail what the library is for and how it should be used. Libraries without these comments are completely useless.

14.2 16F877_bert library

Libraries are used to keep the specific PIC™ settings, registers and variables easily accessible, and to add extra commands to JAL. Because everyone can write and publish libraries, not all of them work will together.

With the free download that comes with this book you will find a series of libraries[195] that have been combined into one big library for each microcontroller, such as the 16F877_bert library.[196] This library is very popular on the Internet, because it adds a wide range of extra commands to JAL. Besides, all compatibility problems have been fixed. The credit for the individual libraries within this pack goes to the individual writers.[197]

This combination library (the "standard library") adds commands to JAL that occur in many different parts of the book, such as analog to digital conversion, serial communication, reading and writing memory, and much much more. The most important ones are explained in this section.

Serial communication

These are the commands for the serial hardware port, which is a standard port of the 16F877:

usart_hw_serial	Set the right protocol: true = RS232, false = SPI (default is true).
serial_hw_baudrate	Set the baudrate (communication speed) for the RS232 connection. Hardware communication speed in the standard library is set to 19k2 by default, but other speeds such as 1200 or 115k baud are also possible.
serial_hw_read(data)	Receive serial data and store it in the variable *data*.

---

[195] Such as: 16F877_inc_all, pic_general, format, delay_any_mc, adc_hardware, pic_data_eeprom, pic_program_eeprom, pwm_hardware, serial_hardware, random, jascii, extradelay.
[196] The download package also contains standard libraries for the PICs discussed in Chapter 13: the 12F675, 16f628, and 16F876A.
[197] Stef Mientki, Wouter van Ooijen and Bert van Dam.

serial_hw_write(data)	Send the contents of the variable *data*.
serial_hw_data = data	The same as above, but called as a function.

Software serial communication is also possible, this means RS232 connections can be made with PIC™'s that have no USART. A very powerfull set of commands! This is the technique used when the Wisp628 programmer is in pass-through mode:

serial_sw_baudrate	Set the baudrate (communications speed) for the RS 232 connection. Software communication speed in the standard library is set to 1200 by default, but other speeds such as 19k2 or 115k baud are also possible.
serial_sw_invert	Invert the signal.
serial_sw_write_init	Prepare to send data from the PIC™ over the RS232 connection.
serial_sw_read_init	Prepare to receive data over the RS232 connection.
serial_sw_read(data)	Receive data and put it in the variable *data*.
serial_sw_write (data)	Send the contents of the variable *data*.

Contrary to hardware serial communication, software serial communication does not have a buffer. If a signal is received at the moment that the PIC™ is not actually waiting for it, it will be lost. More information on this subject can be found in section 14.4.

Pulse Width Modulation (PWM)

The PWM module of the PIC™ is used, so these commands can only be used for PIC™'s that have a PWM module.

const pwm_frequency = number	This sets the PWM frequency. You can only chose the frequencies listed in the datasheet and as you have seen in section 7.2 this has consequences for the available resolution.
const pwm1_dutycycle = number1 const pwm2_dutycycle = number2	If you use frequency modulation (FM) instead of PWM this is where you set the desired duty cycle.
PWM_init_frequency (boolean,boolean)	Initialize the PWM modules.
PWM_set_dutycycle (var,var)	Set the duty cycle. When using PWM this is the variable that controls the power output (if an electric motor is used this controls the speed)

For the 16F628, which only has one PWM module, you can use the same commands. This makes migration from one PIC™ to another simple. Values for the second PWM module will be ignored. To allow migration to dual PWM microcontrollers it is best to use the value 0 for the modules that don't exist.

PWM_init_frequency (boolean,0)	Initialize PWM module 1.
PWM_set_dutycycle (var,0)	Set the duty cycle on module 1. When using PWM this is the variable that controls the power to the user (if the user is an electric motor it controls the speed)

A/D conversion

ADC_init	Initialize the A/D converter.
no_ADC = X	Set the number of A/D channels you want to use (see the table).
ADC_on	Switch A/D on (for the selected channels).
ADC_off	Switch A/D off (all pins become digital).
ADC_read (ADC_chan)	Read the analog value on a channel into a word (channel is the AN number in the table).
ADC_read_bytes(ADC_chan, ADC_Hbyte, ADC_Lbyte)	Read the analog value on a channel into two separate bytes.
ADC_read_low_res (ADC_chan)	Read the analog value on a channel[37] into one byte, with low resolution (max value: 255).

Using the no_ADC command may be confusing due to the lack of logic. Consult the following table to see which pin is used for a specific channel.

pin	A0 AN0	A1 AN1	A2 AN2	A3 AN3	A5 AN4	E0 AN5	E1 AN6	E2 AN7
0 channels								
1 channel	a							
3 channels	a	a		a				
5 channels	a	a	a	a	a			
6 channels	a	a	a	a	a	a		
8 channels	a	a	a	a	a	a	a	a

Please note that pin a4 has no A/D converter and that a6, a7, and a8 do not exist (port A is only 6 bits wide). Channel AN0 is connected to pin a0. But, confusingly enough, AN4 is connected to pin a5, and AN7 is connected to pin e2. So take care when developing programs; mistakes are easily made.

Also note the strange configuration when three analog channels are selected. Against all expectations pin a2 is switched off and pin a3 is switched on.

Program memory

program_eeprom_read (address, data)	Read the program memory *address* and store the result in *data*. This command is safe; you could even write a program that reads itself.
data = program_eeprom(address)	A different way to achieve the same result.
program_eeprom_write(address, data)	Writes the value in *data* to program memory location *address*. You can accidentally overwrite your program with this command.[198]

EEPROM memory

data_eeprom_write(address,data)	Write the value in *data* to the *address* memory location in EEPROM.
data_eeprom_read(address,data)	Read the *address* memory location in EEPROM and put the contents into the *data* variable.
data=data_eeprom(address)	The same as above, but written as a function.
pragma EEDATA data1,data2, etc	Let the compiler store data in EEPROM. No need to mess with addresses, and you can fit a lot of data on a single line.

ASCII

Computers use numbers, not letters or other signs. So in order to use these letters and signs it is agreed upon that they are represented by certain numbers. Which letters and signs are represented by which numbers is recorded in the so-called ASCII[199] table. This agreement was made back when computers used 7-bit numbers; therefore only 127 signs were defined. Numbers above 127 can be used, but every manufacturer can make his own choices. These are often used for language dependent signs such as the euro sign

---

[198] Of course you can also overwrite your program on purpose, which would be a self modifying program.

[199] American Standard for Computer Information Interchange.

The control characters (the first 32 ASCII codes) are defined separately in JAL. This means instead of using character #10 for a line feed you can simply use *ascii_lf* (an example of this can be found in section 10.3). The defined control characters are:

```
const byte ASCII_NULL = 00
const byte ASCII_SOH  = 01
const byte ASCII_STX  = 02
const byte ASCII_ETX  = 03
const byte ASCII_EOT  = 04
const byte ASCII_ENQ  = 05
const byte ASCII_ACK  = 06
const byte ASCII_BEL  = 07
const byte ASCII_BS   = 08            Backspace
const byte ASCII_HT   = 09
const byte ASCII_LF   = 10            Line Feed
const byte ASCII_VT   = 11
const byte ASCII_FF   = 12            Form feed
const byte ASCII_CR   = 13            Carriage return
const byte ASCII_SO   = 14
const byte ASCII_SI   = 15
const byte ASCII_DLE  = 16
const byte ASCII_DC1  = 17
const byte ASCII_DC2  = 18
const byte ASCII_DC3  = 19
const byte ASCII_DC4  = 20
const byte ASCII_NAK  = 21
const byte ASCII_SYN  = 22
const byte ASCII_ETB  = 23
const byte ASCII_CAN  = 24
const byte ASCII_EM   = 25
const byte ASCII_SUB  = 26
const byte ASCII_ESC  = 27            Escape
const byte ASCII_FS   = 28
const byte ASCII_GS   = 29
const byte ASCII_RS   = 30
const byte ASCII_US   = 31
const byte ASCII_SP   = 32            Space
```

The other characters are not defined separately, but you can find them in the next table. If you want to send the letter A to the PC you can use the command serial_sw_write(65)

In your terminal package on the PC this is translated back to A (if you use MICterm select ASCII as display method).

JAL knows all of the ASCII codes, so you can also use this command:

serial_sw_write("A")

But note that this will still result in sending the number 65 to the PC. Here is the entire list of ASCII codes :

ASCII	Character	ASCII	Character	ASCII	Character
0	ctl@	43	+	86	V
1	ctlA	44	,	87	W
2	ctlB	45	-	88	X
3	ctlC	46	.	89	Y
4	ctlD	47	/	90	Z
5	ctlE	48	0	91	[
6	ctlF	49	1	92	\
7	ctlG	50	2	93	]
8	ctlH	51	3	94	^
9	ctlI	52	4	95	_
10	ctlJ	53	5	96	`
11	ctlK	54	6	97	a
12	ctlL	55	7	98	b
13	ctlM	56	8	99	c
14	ctlN	57	9	100	d
15	ctlO	58	:	101	e
16	ctlP	59	;	102	f
17	ctlQ	60	<	103	g
18	ctlR	61	=	104	h
19	ctlS	62	>	105	i
20	ctlT	63	?	106	j
21	ctlU	64	@	107	k
22	ctlV	65	A	108	l
23	ctlW	66	B	109	m

ASCII	Character	ASCII	Character	ASCII	Character
24	ctlX	67	C	110	n
25	ctlY	68	D	111	o
26	ctlZ	69	E	112	p
27	ctl[	70	F	113	q
28	ctl\	71	G	114	r
29	ctl]	72	H	115	s
30	ctl^	73	I	116	t
31	ctl_	74	J	117	u
32	Space	75	K	118	v
33	!	76	L	119	w
34	"	77	M	120	x
35	#	78	N	121	y
36	$	79	O	122	z
37	%	80	P	123	{
38	&	81	Q	124	|
39	'	82	R	125	}
40	(	83	S	126	~
41	)	84	T	127	DEL
42	*	85	U		

Delays

The following delays are available for your programs. The number indicates how often a particular delay is executed. *Delay_100ms(3)* means a delay of 3 x 100 ms = 300 ms.

```
delay_1us
delay_1usM (byte in N)
delay_2uS
delay_3uS
delay_4uS
delay_5uS
delay_6uS
delay_7uS
delay_8uS
delay_9uS
delay_10uS (byte in N)
delay_20us (byte in N)
```

delay_50us (byte in N)
delay_100us (byte in N)
delay_200us (byte in N)
delay_500us (byte in N)
delay_1ms (byte in N)
delay_2ms (byte in N)
delay_5ms (byte in N)
delay_10ms (byte in N)
delay_20ms (byte in N)
delay_50ms (byte in N)
delay_100ms (word in N)
delay_200ms (byte in N)
delay_500ms (byte in N)
delay_1s (byte in N)
delay_2s (byte in N)
delay_5s (byte in N)

Random numbers

number = random_word	Generate a random number in the range 0 to 65,535.
number = random_byte	Generate a random number in the range 0 to 255.
number = dice	Generate a random number in the range 1 to 6 (specifically meant for dice).

Registers and variables

The 16F877 contains several registers. Each of these registers is defined in the library. This means that any register you encounter in the datasheet can be directly addressed in your program.[200] The INTCON register, for example, can be set as follows:

    INTCON = 0b_1010_0000

---

[200] If you use JAL you'll think this is very normal. Just for fun take a look at the 16F877_inc_all.jal file. This is a list of memory locations and banks of all registers and variables. For the INTCON register this is 0x0B,0x8B,0x10B,0x18B in bank 0. For the GIE variable it is intcon : 7.

In many cases individual bits in a register have their own name. In the INTCON register they are GIE, PEIE, T0IE, INTE, RBIE, T0IF, INTF, and RBIF (see Figure 216). These individual variables are also defined and usable.

So instead of the command:

INTCON = 0b_1010_0000

You could write:

GIE = 1
T0IE = 1

The difference is that the first option explicitly sets all unused bits to 0, while the second option leaves the unused bits in whatever status they were before. The individual variables, therefore, are especially convenient when the entire register is set and you want to change just one bit.

INTCON REGISTER (ADDRESS 0Bh, 8Bh, 10Bh, 18Bh)

R/W-0	R/W-0	R/W-0	R/W-0	R/W-0	R/W-0	R/W-0	R/W-x
GIE	PEIE	T0IE	INTE	RBIE	T0IF	INTF	RBIF

bit 7   bit 0

bit 7   **GIE**: Global Interrupt Enable bit
1 = Enables all unmasked interrupts
0 = Disables all interrupts

bit 6   **PEIE**: Peripheral Interrupt Enable bit
1 = Enables all unmasked peripheral interrupts
0 = Disables all peripheral interrupts

bit 5   **T0IE**: TMR0 Overflow Interrupt Enable bit
1 = Enables the TMR0 interrupt
0 = Disables the TMR0 interrupt

bit 4   **INTE**: RB0/INT External Interrupt Enable bit
1 = Enables the RB0/INT external interrupt
0 = Disables the RB0/INT external interrupt

bit 3   **RBIE**: RB Port Change Interrupt Enable bit
1 = Enables the RB port change interrupt
0 = Disables the RB port change interrupt

bit 2   **T0IF**: TMR0 Overflow Interrupt Flag bit
1 = TMR0 register has overflowed (must be cleared in software)
0 = TMR0 register did not overflow

bit 1   **INTF**: RB0/INT External Interrupt Flag bit
1 = The RB0/INT external interrupt occurred (must be cleared in software)
0 = The RB0/INT external interrupt did not occur

bit 0   **RBIF**: RB Port Change Interrupt Flag bit
1 = At least one of the RB7:RB4 pins changed state; a mismatch condition will continue to set the bit. Reading PORTB will end the mismatch condition and allow the bit to be cleared (must be cleared in software).
0 = None of the RB7:RB4 pins have changed state

Figure 215. Variables in the INTCON register.

In section 12.1 you will find a very interesting technique to look at (and even modify) registers in a PIC^{TM} program while it is running!

14.3 Other libraries

In this section libraries are discussed that are part of the download package, and are used in this book. You can use these libraries in your own programs with the *include* command. You'll also need the *16F877_bert* standard library. If, for example, you want to use the *i2c_sw* library your program would start with the following lines:

```
include 16F877_bert
include i2c_sw
```

I2C databus

This is a software library, this means it can also be used with PIC^{TM}'s that don't have a I2C module. Commands in the i2c_sw library:

i2c_sw_write(chipaddress,addressH, addressL, value)	Write *value* to *addressH*, *addressL* of the EEPROM having an address of *chipaddress*.
i2c_sw_read(chipaddress,addressH, addressL, value)	Read the contents *(value)* of *addressH*, *addressL* of the EEPROM having an address of *chipaddress*.
i2c_sw_ackpoll(chipaddress)	Wait for an acknowledgement from the EEPROM having an address of *chipaddress*.

The pins on which this library will work are defined in the i2cp.jal file. If you want to use the library on other pins you will have to change this section:

```
var volatile bit i2c_clock_in   is pin_c3
var volatile bit i2c_clock_out  is pin_c3_direction
var volatile bit i2c_data_in    is pin_c4
var volatile bit i2c_data_out   is pin_c4_direction
```

14 Appendix

LCD display

Commands in the lcd_44780 library:

LCD_init	Initialize the LCD display for use (this command is automatically called when you load the library).
LCD_clear_line (line)	Clear line (note: the first line is number 0).
LCD_char_pos (character , position)	Print a character at the position indicated (note: the first position is 0).
LCD_char_line_pos (character, line, position)	Print a character on the position and line indicated.
LCD_num_pos (byte, position)	Print a number (0 to 255) at the position indicated.
LCD_num_line_pos (byte, line, position)	Print a number (0 to 255) at the position and line indicated.
LCD_num_pos_1dec (byte, position)	Print a number (0 to 255) at the position indicated with one decimal digit (so 255 will be printed as 25.5).
LCD_high_low_line_pos (hbyte, lbyte,line, position)	Print a number (0 to 65535) at the position and line indicated.
LCD_progress (byte, line)	Display a bar graph with length of *byte* (maximum 16).
LCD_shift_right	Move the entire display (both lines) to the right.
LCD_shift_left	Move the entire display (both lines) to the left.
LCD_cursor_pos = position	Place the cursor at the position indicated.

LCD_cursor = off	Switch the cursor off (or "on").
LCD_blink = on	Switch cursor blinking on (or "off").
LCD_display = off	Switch the entire display off (or "on").
LCD_custom(memory address)	Put a custom character in the LCD memory (use only addresses 0 to 7).
CharData[]	Array to define the custom character. Send to the LCD memory one character at a time.
LCD_clock_line_pos (byte, line, position)	Print a number (00 to 99) at the indicated position, uses a leading zero if less than 10.

The layout of the display used in this book is as follows:

Line	Position															
0	0	1	2	3	4	5	6	7	8	9	10	11	12	13	14	15
1	0	1	2	3	4	5	6	7	8	9	10	11	12	13	14	15

Note that both line and column numbers start at 0.

The *LCD_num_pos(byte,18)* command writes outside the visible area. This is not a problem, but you won't see any of it. If you make the position larger you eventually end up on the next line. For the display in this book this happens at position 40, but sometimes you need to go to 80 for it to happen.

View and edit registers

This library is meant for use with the REGedit (register editor) program for the PC.

See section 12.1 for more details on this interesting tool.

Commands in the regedit library:

procedure register_write(address, data)	Write the *data* byte to the register *address*.
procedure register_read(address, data)	Read the value of the register at *address* and put it into the *data* variable.
procedure register_debug	Communication procedure for REGedit, which uses a serial connection to observe and modify registers on the fly.

Connection of a 4 x 3 keypad

This library has been discussed in detail in section 4.4. It is meant for connecting a 7 pins 4 x 3 keypad (4 rows, 3 columns). Here are the commands:

procedure debounce (byte in pinnumber)	Eliminates bouncing, uses 3 pins of port c.
procedure read_keypad (byte out key)	Check to see which key is pressed and put its value into *key* (where # = 10 and * = 11).

14.4 Programmer pass-through

The recommended Wisp628 programmer has some unique properties. One of them is that it can be put in pass-through mode. When you do that, a direct link between the PC and the PIC™ is established, without the need for additional hardware.

Of course both sides, the PC as well as the PIC™, need to run software to handle the actual communications. On the PIC™ side the standard library handles this.

On the PC side you have three options:

- You use a special PIC™ communication program
- You write your own software
- You use a standard terminal program that you start with a batch file

14.4.1 MICterm communication program

MICterm is a communication package specially designed for use with PIC™ microcontrollers. Special features are:

1. Can automatically switch the Wisp628 programmer to pass-through mode.[201]
2. Shows data raw, in hex, or in ASCII.
3. Can show data in a graph, both real time and average. Time axis speed is adjustable.
4. Shows data on a scale for rapid "gut feeling" measurements.
5. Shows data in binary - ideal if you are debugging pin positions.
6. Separate send and receive windows with scrollback.
7. Optionally space the incoming data for easier reading.
8. Optionally send files to, or receive files from, the PIC™.
9. Optionally record all incoming data for future analyses (for example in third party software such as a spreadsheet).

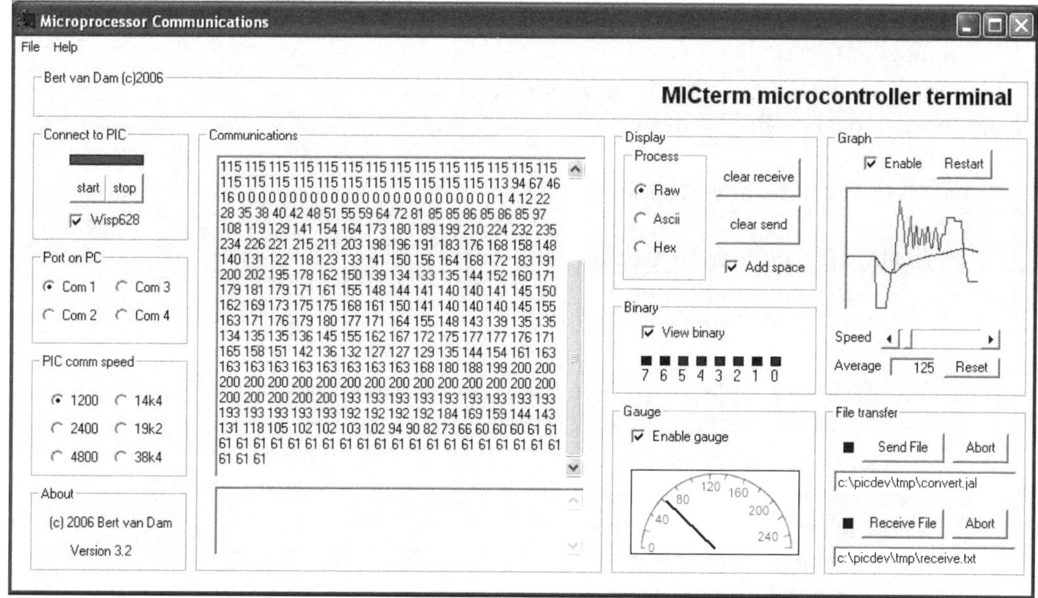

Figure 216. MICterm communication program.

This program is part of the free download package.

---

[201] If you do not use the Wisp628 un-check the checkmark at the *Wisp628* option.

14 Appendix

14.4.2 DIY software in Visual Basic

Writing your own software is the most fun, because you can fit it exactly to your own needs. Any programming language that can communicate with the COM port can be used. Microsoft often has special offers where simple versions of their development software can be downloaded for free.[202]

All PC programs in this book were written in Microsoft Visual Basic 5.0. A few snippets of these programs may be of interest to you.

Wisp628 programmer pass-through

To get the programmer into pass-through mode you need to take the following steps:

1. Send a break condition during 0.1 seconds to switch the programmer into attention mode.
2. Use the programmer speed and settings (19200,n,8,1) to issue the pass-through command (0000p).
3. Wait for the command to be processed (0.1 seconds).
4. Switch back to PIC™ speed.

In Visual Basic it can be handled like this:

```
Private Sub Command1_Click()
    'enable communications
    MSComm1.PortOpen = True

    'switch Wisp628 programmer to pass-through mode

    'Set the Break condition for 0.1 seconds to switch the
    'programmer to attention mode
    MSComm1.Break = True
    Duration! = Timer + 0.1
    Do Until Timer > Duration!
        Dummy = DoEvents()
    Loop
    MSComm1.Break = False
```

---

[202] This website also features free development software http://www.thefreecountry.com. Of course you can also simply buy software, new or used.

```
        'switch to programmer speed
        MSComm1.Settings = "19200,n,8,1"

        'send pass-through command
        MSComm1.Output = "0000p"

        'wait to make sure the command is processed by the programmer
        Duration! = Timer + 0.1
        Do Until Timer > Duration!
           Dummy = DoEvents()
        Loop

        'switch to microcontroller speed
        MSComm1.Settings = "1200,n,8,1"
     End Sub
```

You now have a direct link to the PIC™. Obviously the PIC™ needs to run a program that communicates too, using software serial.

Everywhere in this book the communication speed between the PIC™ and the PC is set to 1200 baud. It can be done a lot faster - 19k2 would be no problem at all. I also use other PIC™ microcontrollers, without a crystal (you have seen one with the 12F675 in section 13.1). These can have difficulty at higher speeds. So to allow maximum portability of the programs between the different microcontrollers I have set all standard libraries to 1200 baud.

You can experiment with higher speeds if you like; if you don't use the pass-through function but a direct RS232 link instead, I have been told that even 115k2 is possible!

Read incoming data

Give MSComm the following settings:

```
     MSComm1.CommPort = 1
     MSComm1.DTREnable = True
     MSComm1.EOFEnable = False
     MSComm1.InputLen = 1
     MSComm1.InputMode = comInputModeText
     MSComm1.NullDiscard = False
     MSComm1.ParityReplace = 0
     MSComm1.RThreshold = 1
     MSComm1.RTSEnable = False
```

```
MSComm1.SThreshold = 0
MSComm1.Settings = "1200,N,8,1"
MSComm1.ParityReplace = 0
```

To collect incoming data a special routine is used that is automatically called whenever something happens on the COM port. That "something" doesn't necessarily have to be new data, so first we check the buffer:

```
If MSComm1.InBufferCount Then
```

If there is something in the buffer we will read it character by character. The entire routine looks like this:

```
Private Sub MSComm1_OnComm()

    If MSComm1.InBufferCount Then

        datapresent = MSComm1.Input
        For Counter = 1 To Len(datapresent)

            'put all data one by one in variable reading
            reading = Mid$(datapresent, Counter, 1)

            'this is where the rest of your program goes

        Next Counter
    End If

End Sub
```

The incoming characters are one by one put into the *reading* variable, so that you can process them. This variable is a string and can contain all characters up to ASCII code 255, and includes control characters. If you want to print the received data you must remove the control characters and replace them with, for example, a star:

```
If Asc(reading) < 32 Then NewText = "*"
```

Optionally convert to the ASCII value:

```
NewText = Asc(reading)
```

Or to hex:

    NewText = Hex(Asc(reading))

Establishing communication

In most cases you will be communicating from the PC to the PIC™ using the pass-through function. This means that on the PIC™ you use <u>software</u> serial communication, because the programmer is never connected to the hardware serial pins.

Using software serial communication means that you don't have a buffer available. So data sent to the PIC™ at a moment when it isn't listening are lost. Note that the other way around, from the PIC™ to the PC, is no problem because the PC does have a buffer. This means you have to make sure that the PIC™ is ready and waiting before you send anything. There are three ways to arrange this.

1. You let the user start the communication by having him press a button connected to the PIC™ and then one on the PC keyboard. The PIC™ program makes sure that the *serial_sw_read(data)* command is executed, which means the program will wait for data. Note that the programmer pass-through must be enabled before the user presses the buttons.

2. The PIC™ initiates the communication by sending a signal to the PC, such as the letter "s". The PC does have a buffer and a communication interrupt so it won't miss any data (assuming the buffer doesn't overflow). As soon as the letter "s" is sent the *serial_sw_read(data)* command is executed.

3. You keep track of the communication timing. This is often used in combination with option one or two. If you are sending bulk data to the PIC™ and you know how long it takes to process you simply have the PC send the data at a slightly slower speed.

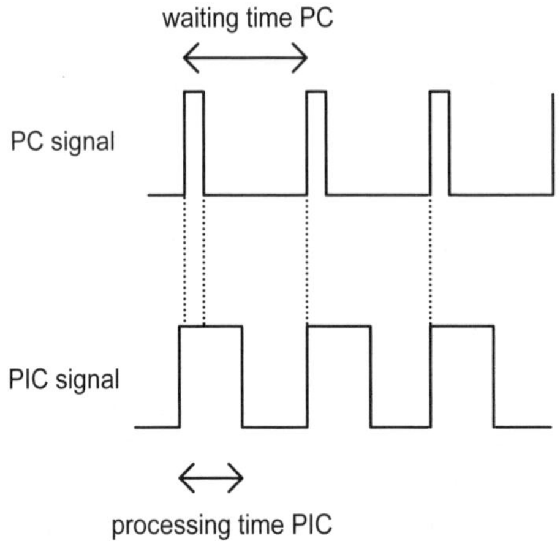

Figure 217. Communication with waiting loop.

A waiting loop in the PC takes care of the delay. Visual Basic handles it like this:

```
Duration! = Timer + 0.1
Do Until Timer > Duration!
    Dummy = DoEvents()
Loop
```

The delay in this case is 0.1 seconds. The *Dummy = DoEvents()* command is a multitasking command. It allows the PC to take care of other things during this loop, such as looking at the mouse position. Without this command the PC will ignore everything (including the mouse and keyboard) as long as the loop is executing.

14.4.3 Terminal program using a batch file

If you use a batch file to switch the Wisp628 to pass-though mode you can subsequently start any terminal program you like.

The batch file needs to consist of only two lines. The first switches the programmer to pass-through mode and the second starts the terminal program. Note that the communication speed is set in the batch file, so you need to match this in your terminal program.

An example of a batch file for Serialterm:

```
c:\picdev\xwisp2\xwisp2w pass 1200
serialterm com1 1200 ascii empty yes
```

Serialterm is a super simple terminal program with just a black window.[203]

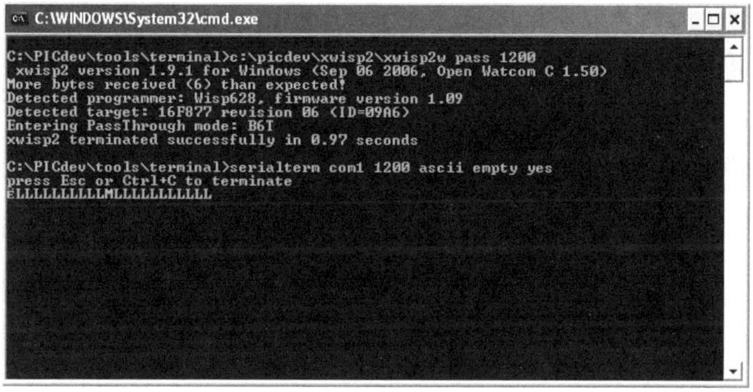

Figure 218. Serialterm started with a batch file.

Regardless of its size it has many possibilities, that can all be called from the command line, and thus used in a batch file. A snippet from the documentation:

```
Commandline Serial Terminal - Version 1.1 by A. Schmidt, Oct 2001
Lancaster University - http://www.comp.lancs.ac.uk/~albrecht/

serialterm port [speed] [DisplayMode] [Separator] [Echo][logfilename]
    port ::= com1 | com2 | com3 | com4 | com5 | com6
    speed::= 300 | 4800 | 9600 | 19200 | 38400 | 57600 | 115200 | 230400
    DisplayMode::= ascii | hex | decimal
    Separator::= empty | space | newline | tab
    Echo::= no | yes
    logfilename::= <anyname> (if not provided no log is written)

Usage examples:
    serialterm com1 115200 hex space no logfile.txt
    open the terminal on port com1 with 115200 bit/s, print hex code of
    incoming characters, seperate them by space, no local echo, save
    output to the file "logfile.txt"
```

---

[203] This program is part of the download package.

serialterm com2 19200 decimal tab yes
open the terminal on port com2 with 19200 bit/s, print decimal code
of incoming characters, seperate them by tabs, do local echo, no logfile

Also a very nice program to build into your own software!

14.5 Transistor data

NPN types:

Code	Type	Case style	I_C max.	V_{CE} max.	h_{FE} min.	P_{tot} max.	Category (typical use)	Possible substitute
BC107	NPN	TO18	100mA	45V	110	300mW	Audio, low power	BC182 BC547
BC108	NPN	TO18	100mA	20V	110	300mW	General purpose, low power	BC108C BC183 BC548
BC108C	NPN	TO18	100mA	20V	420	600mW	General purpose, low power	
BC109	NPN	TO18	200mA	20V	200	300mW	Audio (low noise), low power	BC184 BC549
BC182	NPN	TO92C	100mA	50V	100	350mW	General purpose, low power	BC107 BC182L
BC182L	NPN	TO92A	100mA	50V	100	350mW	General purpose, low power	BC107 BC182
BC547B	NPN	TO92C	100mA	45V	200	500mW	Audio, low power	BC107B
BC548B	NPN	TO92C	100mA	30V	220	500mW	General purpose, low power	BC108B
BC549B	NPN	TO92C	100mA	30V	240	625mW	Audio (low noise), low power	BC109

Code	Type	Case style	I_C max.	V_{CE} max.	h_{FE} min.	P_{tot} max.	Category (typical use)	Possible substitute
2N3053	NPN	TO39	700mA	40V	50	500mW	General purpose, medium power	BFY51
BFY51	NPN	TO39	1A	30V	40	800mW	General purpose, medium power	BC639
BC639	NPN	TO92A	1A	80V	40	800mW	General purpose, medium power	BFY51
TIP29A	NPN	TO220	1A	60V	40	30W	General purpose, high power	
TIP31A	NPN	TO220	3A	60V	10	40W	General purpose, high power	TIP31C TIP41A
TIP31C	NPN	TO220	3A	100V	10	40W	General purpose, high power	TIP31A TIP41A
TIP41A	NPN	TO220	6A	60V	15	65W	General purpose, high power	
2N3055	NPN	TO3	15A	60V	20	117W	General purpose, high power	

PNP types:

Code	Type	Case style	I_C max.	V_{CE} max.	h_{FE} min.	P_{tot} max.	Category (typical use)	Possible substitute
BC177	PNP	TO18	100mA	45V	125	300mW	Audio, low power	BC477
BC178	PNP	TO18	200mA	25V	120	600mW	General purpose, low power	BC478
BC179	PNP	TO18	200mA	20V	180	600mW	Audio (low noise), low power	
BC327	PNP	TO92B	500mA	45V	100	625mW	General purpose, switch and ampl.	BC807
BC477	PNP	TO18	150mA	80V	125	360mW	Audio, low power	BC177
BC478	PNP	TO18	150mA	40V	125	360mW	General purpose, low power	BC178
TIP32A	PNP	TO220	3A	60V	25	40W	General purpose, high power	TIP32C
TIP32C	PNP	TO220	3A	100V	10	40W	General purpose, high power	TIP32A

Explanation of the columns:

Type
This shows the type of transistor, NPN or PNP. The polarities of the two types are different, so if you are looking for a substitute it must be the same type.

Case style
There is a diagram showing the leads for some of the most common case styles. Note that this is a bottom view, with the wires facing you.

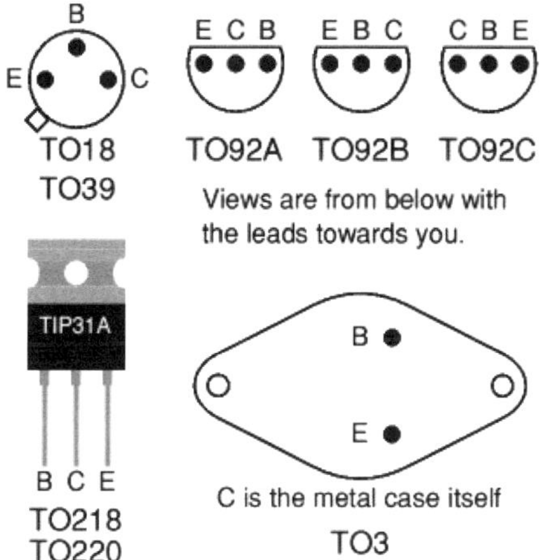

Figure 219. Leads for different case styles.

I_C *max.*
Maximum collector current.

V_{CE} *max.*
Maximum voltage across the collector-emitter junction.

h_{FE}
This is the current gain (specifically, the DC current gain). The guaranteed minimum value is given because the actual value varies from transistor to transistor - even for those of the same type!

P_{tot} *max.*
Maximum total power that the transistor can handle. Note that a heat sink will be required to achieve the maximum rating. This rating is important for transistors operating as an amplifier, where the power is roughly $I_C \times V_{CE}$. For transistors operating as switches the maximum collector current (I_C max.) is more important.

Category
This shows the typical use for the transistor.

Possible substitutes
These are transistors with similar electrical properties, which will be suitable substitutes in most circuits. However, they may have a different case style so you will need to take care when placing them on the circuit board

14.6 Contents of the download package

The download package is a zipped file of approximately 10 Mb (unzipped it is about 22 Mb so you do need room for this). You can unzip the file using the pkunzip program. Follow the instructions on the download website:

http://www.boekinfo.tk

Download the file to the root directory of drive c. Unzip the file while maintaining the directory structure on drive c:\. That way you know for sure that everything will work because the preset configuration files of the different programs expect to be in the c:\picdev\... directory.

Now run the setup.exe program in the c:\picdev\vb50\setup directory. It doesn't make much difference which directory you choose to install it; perhaps it is best to accept the suggested location. The point is that the different DLL and OCX files are installed that the Visual Basic programs in this book require.

You should have this directory structure on your PC:

```
<DIR>        JAL
       <DIR>        Compiler
       <DIR>        Libraries
       <DIR>        Tools
       <DIR>        JALedit
<DIR>        Projects
       <DIR>        Progress
       <DIR>        Completed
<DIR>        xwisp2
<DIR>        tmp
<DIR>        VB50
       <DIR>        Setup
       <DIR>        CHARmaker
       <DIR>        HEXview
       <DIR>        PEconverter
       <DIR>        REGedit
       <DIR>        SKYwriter
       <DIR>        WAVconvert
       <DIR>        MICterm
```

<DIR>   **tools**
<DIR>	Resistors
<DIR>	Capacitors
<DIR>	Frequency
<DIR>	Oscilloscope
<DIR>	Datasheets
<DIR>	Freewheel
<DIR>	Terminal
<DIR>	Tinyboot

The main files and programs in this structure are:

<DIR>   **JAL**

C:\PICDEV\JAL\Compiler	This is the directory of the JAL compiler with its support files.
jalv2.exe	This is the JAL compiler. It is called from JALedit, so normally you don't need to do anything with this file. If you want to work from the command line this would be the place to do it.
jalopts.txt	These are the compiler switches, for reference only.

<DIR>   **Projects**

C:\PICDEV\Projects\progress	This is the "working" directory, which contains projects in progress. It is convenient to use a separate directory for this, which could also contain modified local copies of libraries and Visual Basic source code. In this way the original files remain intact.

C:\PICDEV\Projects\completed	Completed projects. All of the programs in the book are in this directory, arranged by section number. If you want to modify projects it is perhaps best to copy them to the working directory so that the originals remain intact. For project 9.6 the directory also contains the sound files to try BTc yourself plus a recording of BTc8 with a PIC™.

<DIR>   **xwisp2**

C:\PICDEV\xwisp2	This directory contains the program that transfers the compiled source (the hex code) to the programmer.
xwisp2w.exe	This is the transfer program itself.
Readme	An overview of the commands you can use in combination with xwisp2. You only need this if you are not using JALedit.

<DIR>   **VB50**

C:\PICDEV\VB50	In this directory you will find all Visual Basic programs used in this book, mostly arranged by section.
CHARmaker	Program to design your own characters for use with an LCD display.
HEXview	Program to read programs from a PIC™ or to look into EEPROM.
PEconverter	Program to convert text to *pragma eeprom* or *array* commands.
REGedit	A program to observe and modify registers in a PIC™ while it is running. Equipped with all registers discussed in the book, and easily expandable.
SKYwriter	Program to convert text and pictures into port code for use with the "pictures in light" technique.

WAVconvert	Program to convert WAV files to other formats such as BTc encoding.
MICterm	Terminal program with functionality specially developed for use with PIC™ microcontrollers.
Setup	Program to install all dll and ocx files required by the other Visual Basic programs in this directory.

<DIR>   Tools

C:\PICDEV\tools	A collection of useful programs that are used and discussed throughout the book. All programs are written by third parties and collected for your convenience.
resistors	The colour_code.exe program for decoding resistor color codes. Also includes a .gif for those who prefer to do it manually.
capacitors	A similar program for capacitors: capcoder.exe
dis-assembler	A program to go from hex code back to assembler.
frequency	The Counter.exe program is used to measure the frequency of pulses. It uses your soundcard, so you'll need the special connections as described in section 2.2 Take care to keep the voltage low so that you don't damage your soundcard.
oscilloscope	The Winscope.exe program is a simple software oscilloscope. It uses your soundcard, so you'll need the special connections as described in section 2.2. Take care to keep the voltage low so that you don't damage your soundcard.

datasheets	By request from a few manufacturers, datasheets are no longer included in order to ensure that you always use the latest versions. Check out the website http:/www.boekinfo.tk for download addresses.
Freewheel	A resident program to use the scroll wheel of your mouse in Visual Basic 5 (and other software).
tinyboot	The bootloader as discussed in section 12.9, complete with all support files.
terminal	The serialterm.exe terminal program for connection between the PIC™ and PC.

<DIR>   Libraries

C:\PICDEV\JAL\Libraries	In this directory you will find an extensive collection of libraries. Most of them are discussed in the book, but others are not. Feel free to browse and experiment!
16F877_bert.jal	The standard library for the 16F877. This is the most important library. .
16F876A_bert.jal	The standard library for the 16F876A.
16F628_bert.jal	The standard library for the 16F628.
12F675_bert.jal	The standard library for the 12F675.
adc_hardware, compiler_constants, i2c_sw, random, pwm_hardware, serial_software, pic_program_eeprom, regedit, random, etc.	These libraries are a valuable addition to JAL, providing extra commands and extensions.

<DIR>   JALedit

C:\PICDEV\JAL\JALedit	In this directory you will find JALedit and its supporting files.

JALedit.exe

This is JALedit. It is perhaps a good idea to make a link to your desktop, because this is the program you will be using most. Of course you can also use another editor, but this one is specially designed for use with JAL and has convenient features, such as one-click compiling and downloading.

14.7 Hex files

Using HEXview you can retrieve programs from a PIC™ and store them as a file. In addition, data from EEPROM can be viewed (see sections 10.3 and 13.2).

Unfortunately the data is in hex. HEXview is capable of decoding the EEPROM, but not the program itself. In this chapter you will find a short description of the structure of the hex files.

EEPROM

Evaluating an EEPROM file can be useful for debugging, as you've seen in section 10.3. If you take a look at the file for this section, without decoding in HEXview, it would look like this:

```
:104200004C004500440020006F006E0020000D00AF
:104210000A004C004500440020006F006600660064
:044220000D000A0083
:00000001FF
```

It looks worse than it is. This is the structure:

Data record structure									
:	10	4200	00	4C	00	45	00	etc	AF
				L		E			
start record	10 bytes (so 16 decimal)	fist memory location	type record (00 = data)						checksum

The first data line says *LED on* followed by a space and a carriage return (the table above only shows the very first part, LE). Every character is followed by 00. The file format for this hex file is INHX16. Which means that the combination low byte – high byte is stored. The high byte is not in use (EEPROM is only 8 bits wide) so it is always 00. HEXview will ignore all 00 bytes when you click on *ANALYSE file* unless you uncheck *Ignore 00*.

The second and third lines are structurally identical to the first, but the fourth line is different. That is because it is the termination record.

Termination record				
:	00	0000	01	FF
start record	always 00 because it contains no data	also always 00 because it contains	type record (01 = termination)	checksum

Of course HEXview does all of this work for you automatically.

Program

You will probably never in your life need to look at a program in hex, let alone analyze it.

Just for fun, the Pic-Disasm program can be used to convert hex back to assembler. Unfortunately it is not possible to convert this back to JAL. The program is part of the download package.[204]

---

[204] The latest version can be obtained here: http://www.hagi-online.org/picmicro/picdisasm.html

```
PIC-Disasm v1.4
File  Edit  View  Info    File:  C:\PICdev\Projecten\lopend\test8.hex

     processor 16F877
     #include <P16F877.INC>
     __config 0x3F32

     Org 0x2100
     DE  0x4C, 0x45, 0x44, 0x20, 0x6F, 0x6E, 0x20, 0x0D
     DE  0x0A, 0x4C, 0x45, 0x44, 0x20, 0x66, 0x66
     DE  0x0D, 0x0A

LRAM_0x21 equ 0x21
LRAM_0x22 equ 0x22
LRAM_0x23 equ 0x23
LRAM_0x24 equ 0x24
LRAM_0x25 equ 0x25
LRAM_0x26 equ 0x26
LRAM_0x27 equ 0x27
LRAM_0x2A equ 0x2A
LRAM_0x2B equ 0x2B
LRAM_0x2C equ 0x2C
LRAM_0x2D equ 0x2D
LRAM_0x2E equ 0x2E
LRAM_0x2F equ 0x2F
LRAM_0x30 equ 0x30

     Org 0x0000

     BCF  PCLATH,4
     BCF  PCLATH,3
     GOTO LADR_0x0004
     NOP
LADR_0x0004
```

Figure 220. Dis assembly using DisAsm.

14.8 Tips and tricks

This is a small selection of handy tips and tricks.

1. Wait for a pin change

Suppose you want to wait until a switch is no longer engaged.

        while switch loop end loop

2. Combine bits to make a byte

When you want to combine a number of bits to a byte you can do that by declaring them at a certain location of that byte. Lets assume you have a byte called *Demo* and you want a bit variable called *dPC0* to be at the first bit of this byte, you can use this statement:

        var volatile bit dPC0 at Demo : 0

In this way you could declare the entire byte in bits:

```
-- clear the variable
var byte Demo

-- show which bit goes where
var volatile bit dPC0 at Demo : 0
var volatile bit dPC1 at Demo : 1
var volatile bit dPC2 at Demo : 2
var volatile bit dPC3 at Demo:  3
var volatile bit dPC4 at Demo : 4
var volatile bit dPC5 at Demo : 5
var volatile bit dPC6 at Demo : 6
var volatile bit dPC7 at Demo:  7
```

Now if you set one of the bit variables to 1, like this:

```
dPC5 = 1
```

Then *Demo* has gotten the value 0b_0010_0000 or 32 (assuming the other bits were still 0). Of course this also works the other way around; if you give *Demo* the value 4 *dPC2* will be 1.

3. Take a byte apart to bits

You can remove bits from a byte one by one. Declare a bit variable, such as *codec*, as the leftmost bit of a byte, such as *value*, like this:

```
var byte value
var bit codec at value : 7
```

Now shift the byte left by one position 8 times to make *codec* get all of the bits of *value* one by one, starting at the high bit.

```
for 8 loop
  led = codec
  value = value << 1
end loop
```

4. Input or output pin on the fly

In the beginning of your program you need to declare whether a pin will be an input or an output. But that doesn't mean it has to stay that way. While the program is running (on the fly, so to speak), you can easily change the direction of a pin. For example, when you are communicating over a single wire:

```
if pin_a5 then
        -- signal from the other pic
        -- wait until it's low again
        while pin_a5 loop end loop
        -- switch to output and make high
        pin_a5_direction = output
        pin_a5 = true
        -- wait 10 seconds and make low again
        delay_1s(10)
        pin_a5 = false
        -- make the pin input again
        -- and wait for the next instruction
        pin_a5_direction = input
    end if
```

5. Scroll wheel in Visual Basic

If you use Visual Basic 5 I am sure you have noticed that the scroll wheel on your mouse doesn't work. In the download package you will find a small program called Freewheel written by Jim Berry that fixes the problem for you.

6. Pin that doesn't go high

Pin RA4 is a so-called open collector pin. This means it cannot be made high. The best thing to do is use a pull-up resistor (a 10k resistor to +5 V). That way the pin is always high, unless you make it low. If you need more power you can reduce the resistor value a bit.

The 12F675 doesn't have this problem, because it doesn't have an RA4 pin. It does have an MCLR pin, which cannot be used as an input.